L DES EIS MEERES

AMERICA

Kunegau
Neschin
Tuguten
Kygichtan
Leglelachtoch
Hohe Klippe

Tschunegrün
Chibamech
Topak
Pyktepata
Kugagtin
Chikichter
Agunich
Chigygtagruen
Chigriptin
Negnegnorsch
Nutemek
Uwelen
Ischich
Tschitolkemi
rSKOI NOS
Nuchan
Agulich
Nuenein
Igtilium
Nemylamin
Tugulin
Puchan
Gun
Inf. Imaglin
Inigrin
Tschiein
I. Iga...in
I. Ukien
Kigygmin
GWOSDEFS LAND
Festung
Nuny...un
Ankerplatz der Engländer in Jahr 1778.
Iepchagyrgurt
Chalybgyk
Putera...gmin
SPIZE
Fl. Cheuuverun
Lugren
Agnikin
Chikin
Chinkun
Kagägei
Paitamut
Paktagmyin
Atsch
Agasemag
...gawa
Nugmat
Tschekevui
Nat...chin
N...uginin
Ukipen
Norton Sound
nach Cap. Cook

HATKISCHEN MEERES

Pugun
ukuli

Agibanich
Chalamachmit
Kuragmit
Gieen
Putigmit
Ungutschamat
Nohraligtschmalik
Putumak
Tschagnamit
Nutitschan

Chailchotschoch
Tschugruckhumi
Antichirag
Memtachagran
Amutach
Ochrutulach
Hytchalimy
Annalim
Tschigrilit
Tschivach
Kitoch
Iglumit
Tschinik
Annure
Kuntgach
Kuimin

19 Horpu

18 Urup

Hafen

lichsten   Kurilischen Insuln

Alaska History, No. 23

Ethnohistory in the Arctic

The Bering Strait Eskimo

By Dorothy Jean Ray

Edited by R.A. Pierce

THE LIMESTONE PRESS
P.O. Box 1604
Kingston, Ontario, Canada K7L 5C8
1983

International Standard Book Number 0-919642-98-5

Printed and bound in Canada by: Brown & Martin Ltd.
Kingston, Ontario

PREFACE

Ethnohistory reflects no esoteric doctrine, but instead the commonsense view that whatever can help solve a problem should be used, and that several disciplines may take the researcher farther than only one. Approached with the combined resources of the historian, ethnographer, physical and cultural anthropologist, archeologist, biologist, philologist and folklorist, the silent centuries before written records in Alaska have begun to yield information unobtainable with older, more limited techniques.

Dorothy Jean Ray has thus combined in her research the study of Russian and American sources, accounts written by explorers, travelers, teachers and missionaries, and observations made during her own extensive field work. She has published a number of specialized studies on the history of the Bering Strait area, culminating in THE ESKIMOS OF BERING STRAIT, 1650-1898 (University of Washington Press, Seattle, 1975), and on the historical development of Eskimo art, in the companion volumes, ESKIMO ART: TRADITION AND INNOVATION IN NORTH ALASKA, and ALEUT AND ESKIMO ART: TRADITION AND INNOVATION IN SOUTH ALASKA (University of Washington Press, 1977 and 1981).

By its nature a summing up, THE ESKIMOS OF BERING STRAIT could not include valuable details found in the articles which preceded it. Since these articles are scattered through a number of publications, it has seemed worthwhile to bring some of them together in one volume, along with previously unpublished material.

In the first four articles in this volume the author describes early contacts with Europeans. An account of the Vasil'ev-Shishmarev expedition of 1819-1822, which made an important study of the region, is followed by translations of the Russian naval historian V. N. Berkh's remarks about the expedition, and the lengthy account of K. K. Hillsen,

who took part in it. On the basis of this and other
material the author then discusses the crucial date of the
introduction of firearms. This is followed by several
articles of more local significance: one on the historical-
ly known native settlement of Kauwerak involves the
question of whether Russians may have settled in Alaska
long before Bering. Others follow on the Russian settlement
of St. Michael, another on two historic signal posts which
the author found in a museum and identified, and one on the
rise and decline of the early twentieth century Omilak
silver mine, the region's most important mining center.
Finally, there are three major articles fundamental to the
history of northwestern Alaska: on settlement and subsistence patterns before the dislocations of modern times, on
native land tenure and polity, and a detailed study of
native place names.

These materials, as well as several articles and
translations published here for the first time, will shed
light on the movements of ethnic groups, on early Chukchi-
Eskimo contacts, on the first Russian penetration of the
region, and other questions. They help to reconstruct a
history once thought irretrievably lost, and to record
cultural information otherwise doomed to vanish.

Thanks is extended to ARTS AND CULTURE OF THE NORTH,
ARCTIC ANTHROPOLOGY, THE ALASKA JOURNAL, THE JOURNAL OF THE
WEST, and NAMES, in which some of the articles first
appeared, for permission to republish. Ross Hough of the
Cartography Laboratory of the Department of Geography,
Queen's University, made several of the maps. Linda Freeman
did the typing.

Richard A. Pierce
Queen's University
Kingston, Canada

CONTENTS

ILLUSTRATIONS

MAPS

THE VASIL'EV-SHISHMAREV EXPEDITION

TO THE ARCTIC, 1819-1822

One of the least known maritime expeditions in the
history of Alaska was a Russian one that spent the summers
of 1820 and 1821 exploring the Chukchi and Bering seas
between Alaska and Siberia. Two sloops, the Otkrytie
(Discovery), commanded by Mikhail N. Vasil'ev, and the
Blagonamerennyi (Good Intent), under command of Gleb S.
Shishmarev, left Kronstadt in 1819 and returned safely in
1822.

The standard references for Alaska's history have
either omitted the expedition or confined their remarks to
a few words. Neither C. L. Andrews in The Story of Alaska
or C. C. Hulley in Alaska 1741-1953 mentions it, and W. H.
Dall in Alaska and Its Resources and H. H. Bancroft in
History of Alaska, 1730-1885 wrote next to nothing about it.

Dall, in his chronological section, said: "1819.
The exploring vessels Discovery, Good Intent, Western, and
Peace, fitted out at St. Petersburg for a voyage of dis-
covery, under Wasilieff, Shishmareff, Bellingshausen, and
Lazereff...

"1820....The expedition under Wasilieff arrived in
the North Pacific. The Discovery went to Petropavlovsk;
the Good Intent visited the Aleutian Islands, afterwards
passing through Bering Strait as far as Icy Cape, and,
returning, described the island of Nunivak...." (1870:
331, 332).

Bancroft said even less, and almost all of it was
wrong, even the Russian name of the Blagonamerennyi:
"From Petropavlovsk the [Russian-American] company sent the
sloop Dobroie Namerenie (Good Intent) to explore the Arctic
coast. This craft sailed in 1818, but was delayed at the
mouth of the Anadir River, and did not return till three
years later. No report of the expedition is extant, but
the voyage was continued at least as far as East Cape."
(1886: 525-26).

There are three entries for the expedition in James
Wickersham's Bibliography of Alaskan Literature, 1724-1924:
numbers 6287, 6291, and 6292 (Wickersham 1927: 329).
Number 6287 is a three-part account of the activities of
the Blagonamerennyi, published 30 years after the voyage by
Karl K. Hillsen (or Gillsen) who was a midshipman on that

sloop. Number 6291 refers to two progress reports of only
a few sentences written in 1820, and number 6292 is a
summary in German of Hillsen's article, published in
Archiv für Wissenschaftliche Kunde von Russland for 1851.

However, the earliest summary of this expedition,
published in 1823 by Vasilii N. Berkh in volume 2 of his
Chronological History of all Voyages to the Arctic, has
never been listed in any English bibliography. I came
upon it by chance in 1968 in the Smithsonian Libraries
among the then-uncatalogued collection of W. H. Dall's
books (and apparently the source for his few words on the
subject). Volume 1 of this chronological history was in
the Library of Congress, but volume 2 was missing.

Berkh (1781-1834) was a well-known Russian historian
who had gone to England to learn English after serving
with the Baltic fleet as a midshipman, but was also fluent
in other languages. He had sailed on the round-the-world
voyage of the Neva in 1803-1804, and had spent some time
in the Russian American colonies. Of special importance
to Alaskan history are his two chronological compilations
--the one from which the Vasil'ev-Shishmarev account is
taken, and The Chronological History of the Aleutian
Islands, which was translated into English in 1938 as a
WPA project, and published in 1974 by The Limestone Press.

By leafing through all of the issues of the journal
Zapiski Gidrograficheskago Departamenta in the Library of
Congress I found two more articles about this expedition:
G. Ivashintsov's summary of the voyages in 1849, and G.
S. Shishmarev's article about the Chukchi people in 1852.

Not until 1950 was Aleksei P. Lazarev's journal,
which had languished in Russian archives for 130 years,
published in the Soviet Union. Lazarev, who was a
lieutenant on the Blagonamerennyi and a member of a famous
seafaring family of the nobility, had tried unsuccessfully
to get his journal published shortly after his return home.
The journal is now in the Central State Naval Archives of
the USSR, and the published edition of 1950 includes not
only this journal, but all of the expedition's papers
concerning the Arctic explorations as well as a long
introduction about prior northern discoveries and
explanatory footnotes by A. Solov'ev.

(The translation of Berkh's complete account and the
sections devoted to the Arctic in Hillsen's journal are
given in the next two chapters.)

From the resume of publications about the expedition
it can be seen that a number of accounts were "extant"
before Bancroft's history was published in 1886. Moreover, the entire expedition of four vessels that left
Kronstadt in 1819 reached not only "at least as far as
East Cape [at Bering Strait]," but went as far north as
Icy Cape and as far south as Antarctica.

The ambitious plans of this expedition called for the
simultaneous exploration of the Arctic and the Antarctic.
The head of the First, or Antarctic, Division was F. F.
Bellingshausen, skipper of the Vostok (East; not the
Western as Dall said), and Mikhail P. Lazarev, brother of
Aleksei, commanded the Mirnyi (Peaceful, not Peace). The
two ships in the Second, or Arctic, Division were the
Otkrytie (Discovery) and the Blagonamerennyi. Mikhail N.
Vasil'ev was in charge of the Second Division.

It is not known who initiated the plans for this
expedition, which was sent out under the auspices of the
Imperial government (not the Russian-American Company as
Bancroft said), but the famous mariners, G. A. Sarychev
and I. F. Krusenstern, were busily engaged in developing
the project in 1818. Sarychev had begun his American
Arctic career in 1791 as a lieutenant on the Slava Rossii
[Glory of Russia] under Joseph Billings, and had attained
the rank of admiral in 1816 when Kotzebue bestowed his
name on what is now Sarichef Island off the coast of
Seward Peninsula. Krusenstern, also an admiral, had made
the first Russian round-the-world trip to the Russian-
American colonies in 1803 in the Neva. Kotzebue commemorated his name also on Cape Krusenstern at Kotzebue Sound.

During the early stages of the planning, it was proposed that Vice-admiral V. M. Golovnin, who had made round-
the-world voyages on the Diana in 1807-1809 and on the
Kamchatka in 1817-1819, should command the Antarctic
Division with Bellingshausen as alternate, and that
Kotzebue should command the Second, or Arctic, Division,
but the government chose Bellingshausen and Vasil'ev for
the respective posts (Lazarev 1950: 21-22).

The objective of the Vasil'ev-Shishmarev expedition
was to find a northwest passage, which had been of great
concern to the Russians for many years. It was the main
purpose of Kotzebue's expedition of 1815-1818 in the
Rurik. Because the sloops did not find the passage during
1820 and 1821, the expedition was considered a failure;
yet, Kotzebue's voyage had not been looked upon as a
complete success either since he had likewise failed to find
a way to the Atlantic. He had, however, made several new
discoveries, and had finally proved to everyone's satis-
faction that Asia and America were definitely separated,
a controversy that was still debated by geographers at
that time. Furthermore, he had seen the potential danger
to the Russian-American Company by the advance of English
traders across the North American continent, and urged
the Russians to extend their trading posts north of the
Aleutian Islands.

Although Russian fur hunters had thoroughly exploited
the Aleutian Islands beginning shortly after the official
discovery of Alaska by Vitus Bering and Aleksei Chirikov in
1741, the land north of the islands was not at all well
known by 1820. Most of the information about northern

Alaska during the eighteenth century--fragmentary at best
--had come through the Chukchi and Eskimos of Siberia and
islanders of the Bering Strait. Later, organized expeditions obtained first-hand information, but data were still
sketchy. In 1732 Michael Gvozdev and Ivan Fedorov discovered Alaska in the vicinity of Wales on Seward Peninsula, but their report contained only very generalized
information. In 1778 Captain James Cook, who made the
first chart of the coast of western Alaska, sailed along
Alaskan shores as far north as Icy Cape, which he named,
but he recorded relatively few details. In 1779 a brief
report accompanied a map of Seward Peninsula, which the
cossack sotnik ("leader of a hundred") Ivan Kobelev made
when he visited Little Diomede Island. Kobelev's unusual
map contained 69 settlements, 61 with names, many of which
are still recognizable today.[1] In 1791 the voyage of
Joseph Billings to Cape Rodney resulted in accounts
written by Ivan Kobelev, Carl Heinrich Merck, Martin Sauer,
and Sarychev, which combined, provide the first ethnography of any Eskimo group living north of the Aleutians,
in the vicinity of the present town of Nome (Chernenko
1958: 131-35; Jacobi 1937; Sauer 1802: 242-48; and
Sarychev 1806, part 2: 44-46). There were no other voyages
until Kotzebue's expedition in 1816, which was supposed to
have filled in the geographical gaps while searching for
the northwest passage, but he missed seeing Grantley
Harbor, Port Clarence, and the Kuskokwim, Yukon, Kobuk,
and Noatak rivers.

The Russian-American Company, which had received a
20-year monopoly from the Russian government in 1799 for
the exploitation of natural resources and the exploration
of Russian America, had begun to look northward from its
headquarters in Sitka only in 1818 when it sent out Petr
Korsakovskii to explore the Nushagak River and to
investigate rumors of Russians supposedly living on the
"Kheuveren River". They established a post on the Nushagak,
but learned that there were no Europeans living north of
there (Berkh 1823b: 15; Tikhmenev 1939, part 1: 300-2)[2].

In 1821 the Russian-American Company sent two brigs,
the Golovnin and the Baranov, under commands of V. S.
Khromchenko and Adolf K. Etolin for further exploration
to the North. Khromchenko had been a shipmate of Shishmarev's on the Rurik as a midshipman, and in 1821 both were
again on the northern seas, each in command of his own
vessel. In all, four Russian brigs and sloops and a small
boat sailed the Alaskan waters that year in the continuing
Russian search for trade and geographical knowledge. One
of the sidelights of the activities of the various
voyages during 1821 was the dispute over the discovery of
Nunivak Island. On July 11, 1821, Vasil'ev first saw the
island, which he named "Discovery Island" after his sloop,
and Etolin, of Khromchenko's expedition, saw it on August
12. In 1861, P. A. Tikhmenev said that Khromchenko had
been its discoverer, but it is clear from Berkh's account,
published in 1823, that the honor fell to Vasil'ev (Berkh

1823b: 47, 57; Tikhmenev, 1939, part 1: 331).

The Blagonamerennyi and Otkrytie sailed together from
Kronstadt until they reached the south Pacific. After
parting, Shishmarev arrived at Unalaska on May 30, 1820,
and procured four umiaks and six Aleuts from the Russian-
American Company, but was unable to get an interpreter
acquainted with the northern language. On the 19th of
June he sailed north to Saint Lawrence Island, and on the
30th proceeded to Kotzebue Sound. For more than a week
the Blagonamerennyi encountered almost constant fog, and
the entrance to the sound was blocked by ice. Finally, on
the evening of July 9 they were able to get near Cape
Espenberg. On the 10th the ice suddenly moved out of the
sound and they sailed east, anchoring halfway into the
sound, and on the 11th, went to Chamisso Island. On July
14, 20 officers and crewmen left in a sailing tender and a
skin boat for the "ice cliffs" that Kotzebue had seen in
1816 (near Elephant Point, a name given by Frederick W.
Beechey). Shishmarev, who had accompanied Kotzebue in 1816,
thought that the coast was uninhabited, but to their
surprise they saw a large settlement of a hundred or more
conical tents and opposite each, an overturned umiak.
About 150 persons met them armed from head to foot with
bows and arrows, spears, and "even long rifles", according
to Hillsen (Lazarev did not mention the guns, nor subsequent shooting episodes). After spending some time ashore
with this tribe of 300 persons, which called itself Tatui
(a word probably related to tutu, or caribou) the men left
hurriedly after Lazarev shot a blank cartridge too close
to an Eskimo man's face. On their departure they were
shot at with arrows and then guns.

On July 16 Vasil'ev and the Otkrytie arrived at
Kotzebue Sound from Petropavlovsk. On June 27 near Saint
Lawrence Island he had met an American brig, the Pedler,
which was trading for furs with the Chukchi. On July 16
the Pedler arrived in Kotzebue Sound and Captain William
J. Pigot went aboard the Otkrytie. On July 18, the
Otkrytie and the Blagonamerennyi sailed together past Cape
Krusenstern to a little north of Icy Cape where they were
turned back by ice. On August 2 they surveyed 90 miles
around a cape that Vasil'ev named Golovnin in honor of
the famous navigator, V. N. Golovnin, but Beechey later
changed it to Point Hope. Vasil'ev continued toward the
American shore, and Shishmarev surveyed Saint Lawrence
Island before leaving the Arctic for California and Hawaii.
Vasil'ev left a pre-cut boat in Sitka to be assembled
under the direction of Lieutenant Ivan Ignat'ev the
following year.

Having spent the winter in balmy climates, the
Blagonamerennyi and the Otkrytie returned to Sitka in the
spring of 1821. On May 30 with the newly-built boat in
tow of the Otkrytie they sailed to Unalaska. The
Blagonamerennyi then went to the Siberian coast and the
Otkrytie towed the boat to Cape Newenham where Vasil'ev

placed Lieutenant Aleksandr Avinov in charge, directing
him to explore the coast as far north as Cape Darby, and
to meet him by July 20 at Stuart Island. If he had not
completed the survey, he was to remain until August 20,
and if he failed to meet him, he was to go to Unalaska or
to Petropavlovsk. They did not meet again on the American
coast. Avinov left Goodnews Bay on July 13 for the northward, but the water was too shallow, the winds too strong,
and the boat too clumsy to continue; and coupled with
crowded conditions on board and the danger of scurvy, he
hurried on to Petropavlovsk.

On July 11, Vasil'ev had discovered Nunivak Island,
and from there went to Cape Darby. Not finding Avinov, he
sailed north to Cape Lisburne, across the ocean to Asia,
back to Lisburne, and south through Bering Strait where
he met Shishmarev near the Diomede islands on August 11.

Shishmarev's explorations in 1821 were almost entirely
confined to the coast of Asia and around Saint Lawrence
Island, although on his way northward along the American
coast on July 4 he discovered, but did not name, Cape
Romansof [Rumiantsev], which was sighted and named 38
days later by Etolin.

After leaving Cape Romanzof, he touched at only one
other place on the American coast, at about latitude 67°
34' N (near Cape Mulgrave) to get wood and water. On
September 21 he ended his Arctic voyage at Petropavlovsk.

After meeting Shishmarev at the Diomedes, Vasiliev
sailed to Cape Darby, and again not finding Avinov, sailed
to Stuart Island where he sent Lieutenant Roman Boil
ashore for information. The inhabitants (who lived on the
site of present-day Stebbins) said they had seen no
foreign ships, but told him about a large river called the
"Kuiukhtpak" (the Yukon) located south of the cape. On
September 8 Vasil'ev returned to Petropavlovsk via Saint
Lawrence Island, and in 1822 both ships sailed back to
Kronstadt via the Hawaiian Islands.

Many of the so-called round-the-world expeditions to
Alaska sponsored by both the Russian-American Company and
the Imperial government stopped at Hawaii and California
for provisions and recreation, and the Blagonamerennyi and
the Otkrytie were no exceptions. Although Hillsen wrote
vivid and detailed descriptions of his stay in California
and Hawaii, as well as the journey through the south
Pacific, they are not included in the excerpts printed
herein because this volume is devoted to northern topics.

Hillsen's descriptions of the southern paradises
make them appear to be glorious compensations for the
"misery and deprivations" of the North, but the fact was
that all three areas--Alaska, California, and Hawaii--
were inextricably entwined in Pacific trade and international
politics of the early nineteenth century. This can be

seen from examining the exploration and trade in the three
areas in this period, often involving the same persons,
which will help place the Arctic expedition of Shishmarev
and Vasil'ev in perspective.

Spain had claimed the north Pacific Ocean until the
early nineteenth century, when the English, the Americans,
and the Russians began chipping away at her crumbling
authority. Captain Cook discovered the Hawaiian Islands in
January 1778, before he had explored the coast of Alaska,
and he named them the Sandwich Islands in honor of Lord
Sandwich. After charting the coasts of Cook Inlet, Bristol
Bay, and the Arctic Ocean as far north as Icy Cape, Cook
returned to the Sandwich Islands where he was killed at
Kealakekua Bay on the island of Hawaii on February 14, 1779.
Most of the islands then plunged into civil wars. From
these Kamehameha emerged by 1791 as ruler of Hawaii, and by
1810, of most of the other islands.

Soon after discovery, the Hawaiian Islands became
favorite ports of call for traders sailing between the
Northwest Coast and Canton. In 1785 the first of these,
Captain James Hanna, stopped at the Hawaiian Islands en route
to Canton. Two more English ships arrived the next year,
and in 1789, Captain Robert Gray, in the Columbia Rediviva,
of the United States, after his discovery of the Columbia
River. After only ten years' time, the New England traders
had a virtual monopoly of the American Northwest Coast-
Hawaii-China trade route, and "the majority of the vessels
which could be found in Hawaiian ports flew the flag of the
United States".(3)   Earlier, however, the English had given
formal notice that the islands were under their dominion.
Captain George Vancouver, in his three visits there--in
1792, 1793, and 1794--was convinced that Great Britain should
protect the islands, and finally in 1794 claimed them for
England. However, actual sovereignty was never established,
and even when the Hawaiian rulers, fearing Russian encroachment, asked for protection, England made no move to show
that it acknowledged its responsibility (Bradley 1968: 9-13).
Nevertheless, as late as 1820, from Hillsen's observations,
British influence was visible in the naval officers'
uniforms that the hefty Hawaiian rulers wore, straining at
the buttons, their greatcoats donned without trousers or
underwear, and their shoes worn without stockings.

From Alaska, the Russians tried to establish themselves
in both California and Hawaii, their aspirations seeming to
threaten for a short time the American dominance over trade
in the mid-Pacific. In 1804 the Neva and the Nadezhda
under Krusenstern and Lisianskii stopped in Hawaii during
their round-the-world voyages; in 1807 the Russian-American
Company vessel Nikolai sailed from California to Hawaii
under Pavel Slobodchikov (Pierce 1965: 2); and in 1808,
Aleksandr Baranov, governor of the American colonies, sent
the Neva to Hawaii under L. A. Hagemeister. Then, in
October 1815, an adventurous German physician, Georg Anton
Schäffer, was recruited by Baranov to go to Kauai to

regain the cargo of the Russian-American Company's ship
Bering, the former Atahualpa, which had been wrecked there
and the cargo of furs seized by the local king, Kaumualii.
This fascinating chapter in Hawaiian-Russian relations has
been summarized from original documents by R. A. Pierce,
and in a less complete treatment, by Klaus Mehnert.
Schäffer, masquerading as a scientist, was given land on
Oahu, and seeing opportunities for trade, raised the Russian
flag and began building a fort at Honolulu. Kamehameha I
therefore ordered him to leave the islands. However,
Schäffer went to Kauai where King Kaumualii, chafing under
the oppression of Kamehameha, saw in Schäffer a chance to
recover his lost power. As Pierce says, "All in one
glorious day," Kaumualii agreed to trade exclusively with
the Russian-American Company (especially for sandalwood),
to permit workshops to be built, to supply food for ships
and men for erecting buildings; and to give back the Bering's
cargo (Ibid.: 11).[4] But Schäffer's triumph was short-lived.
The Russian-American Company had hoped to establish a
settlement in the islands, but his methods were not to its
liking. Kotzebue, on his visit there in 1816, withheld
needed support. The foreign traders and residents on the
islands, concerned about their privileges, urged Kamehameha
to oust the interloper. Therefore, in 1817 the Hawaiians
were able to banish Schäffer and his compatriots.

Less than three years after Schäffer's departure, the
Otkrytie and the Blagonamerennyi stopped at the Hawaiian
Islands both on their way to and from Alaska, but it is
plain from Hillsen's account that no resentment remained
over Schäffer's schemes because the Russians were given
warm hospitality. Perhaps the medical aid that the ships'
physicians provided was partly responsible. According to
Hiram Bingham, one of the first missionaries in the Hawaiian
Islands, these Russians conducted themselves admirably, and
left a good impression. Bingham had arrived on the islands
with Asa Thurston and several other assistants sent out by
the American Board of Commissioners for Foreign Missions
only a year before. Kamehameha I, with his liberal leanings,
had paved the way for Christianity, and everyone was cordial
to Bingham and his colleagues. One of the Winships, who
owned several trading vessels, placed his house at their
disposal and Captain Pigot, who sailed to Kotzebue Sound
later that summer, invited them to tea their first evening
ashore (Bingham 1847: 95).

Bingham responded warmly to the conduct of the
Russians during their two visits in 1821 (going north and
returning), and said, "The same day [in April 1821] we
received a very polite call from Commodore Michael
Vascilieff, of the Imperial Russian Navy, his aged chaplain
of the Greek Church, with a long white beard hanging down
upon his bosom, and thirteen of the officers of the
Exploring Squadron, all in their appropriate uniforms.
They showed the mission repeated kindnesses, which were
very grateful" (Ibid: 132).

Bingham also described the generosity of the Russians
in curing the queen for the second time on their return
trip to the islands in December 1821. At this time, said
Bingham, "Commodore Vascilieff...in his visit to the
islands, this year, besides allowing the aid of his
physicians in her illness, treated the rulers and the
missionaries very courteously, gaining their high esteem,
and aided their cause. He read a letter to the king from
Governor Reicord [Petr I. Rikord] of Kamtschatka,
favorable to the independence of the islands, proposing to
acknowledge the Hawaiian flag. He assured the chiefs he
should report to the Emperor Alexander the happy arrival
and favorable reception of the mission established there,
and the good system of instruction which the missionaries
had commenced among the people." Vasil'ev had taken a
collection of "seven gold ducats and eighty-six Spanish
dollars", which he had presented to Bingham's mission on
December 19, 1821 (Ibid: 150).

No native kings had paved the way for foreigners in
Mexico, which the Spaniards had steadfastly occupied since
August 1521. San Francisco Bay, however, was not explored
until 1769, less than a decade before Captain Cook discovered the Hawaiian Islands and charted the coast of
western Alaska. In 1769, Sergeant Jose Francisco de
Ortega, under command of Gaspar de Portola, first explored
the peninsula on which San Francisco now stands. Before
that, California was known mainly from the expeditions of
Juan Rodríguez Cabrillo during 1542-1543; of Sir Francis
Drake, who bestowed the name New Albion on the coast in
1579; of Francisco de Gali in 1584; of Pedro de Unamuno in
1857; of Sebastian Rodríquez Cermenho in 1595; and of
Sebastian Vizcaino in 1602-1603 (Bancroft 1884: chapters 3,
4 and 13). The mission and the presidio of San Francisco
were established in 1776-1777, and the Santa Clara mission
shortly thereafter. In 1792, Vancouver was the first non-
Spanish navigator to visit San Francisco Bay during the
course of his voyage to Hawaii and Nootka Sound on the
Northwest Coast.

American ships were comparatively slow in getting to
the California coast, but once they began, they reaped a
rich harvest from the seals and sea otters in the coastal
waters. After Captain Gray returned to the United States
from the Northwest Coast and Hawaii in 1790, Yankee
interest in the fur trade increased considerably, and in
1791 there may have been as many as seven American vessels
trading on the Northwest Coast. As in Hawaii, their
energies had effectively reduced the British traders to
only one vessel by 1801, while their own numbers had increased to 15, backed principally by Boston owners
(Bradley 1968: 17, 18). Seals and sea otters, however,
began to get scarce in the North, and shortly after the
turn of the century, American ships began to sail to
California for hunting and trading. A few American ships
had already been on the coast for one reason or another.
In 1796, the Boston ship Otter was the first American vessel

to anchor in a California port, Monterey. In 1798 and
1799 two American merchant vessels had sailed along the
coast, and in 1800 Charles Winship in the Betsy had stopped
at San Diego for wood and water (Bancroft, 1884: 539,
545-46).

The first vessel known to poach for sea otters in
California waters was the O'Cain, whose skipper, Joseph
O'Cain, had traded for many years on the Northwest Coast.
In September 1803, O'Cain and one of the ship's owners,
Jonathan Winship, Jr., persuaded Baranov to provide kayaks
and Aleut hunters to take otters from the coast of
California on shares. This first poaching expedition
netted 1,100 skins in 1804, but O'Cain is suspected of
selling hundreds more to the California missions before
returning north to settle accounts with Baranov (Bancroft
1885: 25-26).[5]

The Winship brothers had been trading for a number of
years along the Northwest Coast when, with the Albatross
(which was also a seal-poaching vessel), they attempted to
establish a trading post 45 miles up the Columbia River
in 1810, the first attempt since John Meares, to use
Hawaiians as colonists, but the project was soon abandoned.
(Bancroft 1885: 93; Howay 1932: 70). The Albatross arrived
at Sitka in August 1811, sailed to the Hawaiian Islands
"so loaded with furs that some water-casks had to be
broken up and the hemp cables carried on deck", went back to
California to pick up some more furs, and then returned to
Hawaii where the Winships and Captain William Heath Davis
took on a load of sandalwood. After selling it at a
profit, they persuaded Kamehameha I to grant them a
monopoly in the trade for a period of ten years, and
finding sandalwood more profitable than Northwest Coast
furs, they abandoned their American trading in 1811.

In the same year, 1810-11, three other American ships
were poaching on the California coast: the O'Cain, the
Isabella, and the Mercury. Some of the vessels employed
Aleut hunters, but the Mercury and the Isabella reinforced
their hunters on the Farallon Islands with a contingent of
Hawaiians. Several ships were operating under Russian
contracts (Bancroft 1885: 92-96; Bradley 1968: 29-30).

Meanwhile, certain Russian officials had for some time
urged occupation of the coast north of Spanish California
while those territories remained unclaimed by any European
power. In 1812, Fort Ross was established about fifty miles
north of San Francisco, intended as a base for sea otter
hunting, to provide a basis for claims to the coast, and to
furnish a source of food for the Alaskan colonies.

Spain regarded Ross as an encroachment on territories
rightfully hers, but was not in a position to resist, and
relations between the two countries remained friendly.
Early in 1814 the Spanish king issued orders that strict

neutrality was to be observed toward England and the United
States during the War of 1812, and no encouragement was to
be given to either country's ships, but when Kotzebue
arrived in San Francisco Bay in October 1816 under the
Russian flag, he was treated cordially upon orders from
both Mexico and Spain. While Kotzebue was there, Governor
Pablo Vicente de Sola came to visit him, and saw to it that
Kotzebue was provided with a large supply of fresh food for
his return to the Arctic. At that time, Kotzebue and Ivan
Kuskov, manager of Ross, held a meeting in San Francisco
(Bancroft 1885: 279-80). Kotzebue, in his much too brief
account about California, concluded, as did Hillsen, that
it was an extraordinarily fertile country, which could be
made productive and profitable if it were not for the lack
of enterprise of the Spanish and mestizo colonists.

Little ethnographic information about the early
Indians of the San Francisco area has been preserved, but
by the early nineteenth century their contact with the
Spanish had proven disastrous. The mortality rate was high
among the Indians who had been gathered into the missions,
and as Hillsen infers, the Indians, especially those who
tried to run away from the missions, were treated harshly.
In 1817 the mission San Rafael was founded north of San
Francisco Bay. The move was made mainly because the death
rate at the San Francisco mission had reached alarming
proportions, and the missionaries hoped to halt the decline
of the Indians by moving them away, but the Russians inferred,
correctly, that the mission was intended as a barrier to
further expansion from Ross.

Despite lack of Spanish enthusiasm earlier for foreign
vessels, especially English and American, by 1822, 20 such
vessels, including six whalers taking on supplies, called
at California ports (Ibid.: 473-74). Some were trading
en route from Hawaii to the Northwest Coast, and some brought
goods for Ross. John Jacob Astor owned several of these
ships, including the brig _Pedler_, under command of William
J. Pigot, which met the _Blagonamerennyi_ in Kotzebue Sound
in 1820. This meeting with the _Blagonamerennyi_ and with the
Otkrytie near Saint Lawrence Island was only an episode for
either party, but it is of importance in the history of
northern trade because it leads us to the identity of the
ship or persons responsible for trading the first guns to
the Eskimos of northern Alaska, an incident of considerable
mystery until the translation of Hillsen's journal and
investigation of other sources. This episode is discussed
in "Early Maritime Trade with the Eskimo of Bering Strait
and the Introduction of Firearms" (Ray 1975a).

The _Otkrytie_ and the _Blagonamerennyi_ visited California
at the end of an old regime, and arrived in Hawaii at the
beginning of a new one. Only a year after their visit--
1822--Mexico became independent of Spain. Relations with
the new regime remained cordial, but the Russians were
already aware that Ross was neither an economic nor a
political asset. Nevertheless, they held onto it until 1841,

when they sold their livestock and equipment to John Sutter. Mexico ceded California to the United States by the Treaty of Guadalupe Hidalgo in 1848, and the territory was given statehood in 1850.

In 1867, 26 years after the sale of Ross, Russia sold Russian America to the United States. In 1913, after a long struggle for self-government and efforts to participate in affairs of the United States, Alaska became a territory, and in 1959 was given statehood.

The first American missionaries and whalers had arrived in the Hawaiian Islands only a year before Hillsen's visit. Honolulu became the principal Pacific whaling port until San Francisco took over in the 1880's with its new fleet of steam whaling vessels. In 1893, royal sovereignty ended when Queen Liliuokalani was deposed. The United States annexed Hawaii in 1898; it became a territory in 1900, and a state in 1959. The three corners of the Pacific triangle that had once figured in Russia's dreams of trade and empire had become an American reality.

Notes

1. Identification of Kobelev's settlements relative to those remembered by today's Eskimos is discussed in "Eskimo Place-Names in Bering Strait and Vicinity" (Ray 1971).

2. The Russian village, or fort, Kheuveren, was actually an Eskimo village called Kauwerak, located on the Kuzitrin River, Seward Peninsula. (See Ray 1975b: 26-28, 37, 172; and 1976).

3. Information about Hawaii for the years 1778-1789 has been summarized from Harold W. Bradley, The American Frontier in Hawaii: the Pioneers, 1789-1843 (1968: 9-13).

4. Schäffer was the original spelling of the usual Scheffer or Sheffer. Information about the Russian colonizing is from Bradley 1968: 49-51; Mehnert 1939; but especially Pierce 1965.

5. According to Howay, this "notorious poaching vessel" began another long voyage in 1809 and ended in 1815, poaching on the coast of California, trading with Baranov in Alaska, collecting sandalwood in Hawaii, and trading in China (Howay 1932: 84; Howay 1933: 126).

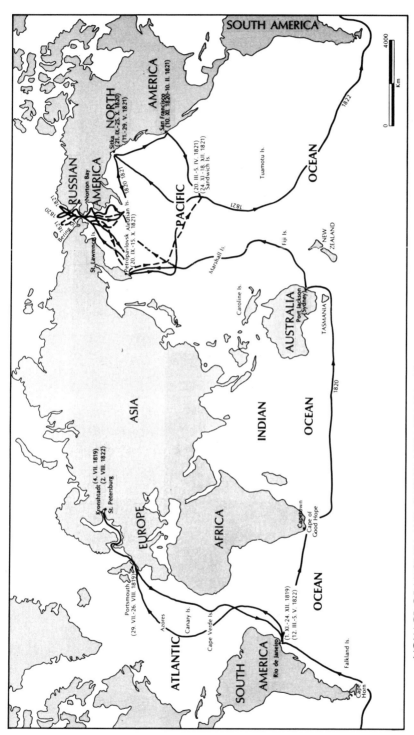

VOYAGE OF VASIL'EV AND SHISHMAREV ON THE "OTKRYTIE" AND "BLAGONAMERENNYI" (1819–1822)

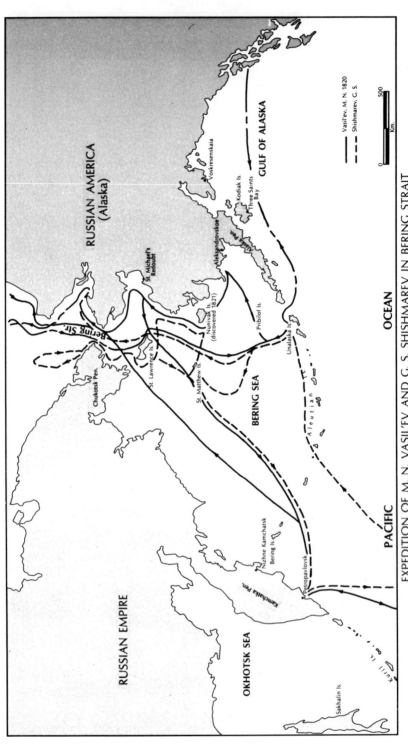

EXPEDITION OF M. N. VASIL'EV AND G. S. SHISHMAREV IN BERING STRAIT

RUSSIAN AMERICA
(Alaska)

RUSSIAN EMPIRE

OKHOTSK SEA

BERING SEA

GULF OF ALASKA

PACIFIC   OCEAN

St. Michael's
Redoubt

Bering Str.

Chukotsk Pen.

St. Lawrence Is.

St. Matthew Is.

Nunivak Is.
(discovered 1821)

Pribilof Is.

Unalaska Is.

Aleutian Is.

Aleksandrovskoe

Kenai Pen.

Kodiak Is.
Three Saints
Bay

Voskresenskaia

Nizhne Kamchatsk
Bering Is.

Petropavlovsk

Kamchatka Pen.

Kuril Is.

Sakhalin Is.

Vasil'ev, M. N. 1820
Shishmarev, G. S.

0   500
          Km.

II

CAPTAIN-LIEUTENANTS VASIL'EV AND SHISHMAREV, 1819

BY VASILII N. BERKH

The famous reign of the Emperor Alexander I, so glorious in the annals of Russia because of its political benefit to all of Europe, will also remain memorable for its geographical discoveries.(1)

Although Russia had a fleet from the beginning of the eighteenth century, her ships cruising the Baltic, the North, and the Mediterranean seas, they did not go beyond the Arctic Circle. The Pillars of Hercules [at the Strait of Gibraltar] were the limits of their voyages. In 1803 they went beyond this point and made their first trip around the world. But because this work is to include only voyages made to the northern arctic regions, I shall therefore omit mention of various [other] voyages undertaken by the Russians during the period of sixteen years and direct my attention to the year 1819.

In that year a highest sovereign edict was made concerning the equipping of two expeditions. The first one, under the command of the well-known Mr. Captain-Commander Faddei Faddeevich Bellingsgauzen, was instructed to sail to the Antarctic Circle, and the second under command of Captain-Lieutenant M. N. Vasil'ev was to survey the northern shores of America and to look for a passage to the Atlantic Ocean.

On June 4 [according to Alexei Lazarev it was on July 4],(2) Captain Vasil'ev put to sea with two naval sloops, Otkrytie [Discovery] and Blagonamerennyi [Good Intent]. Their personnel consisted of the following persons:

Chief of the division and commander of the sloop Otkrytie, Captain-Lieut. Mikhail Nikolaevich Vasil'ev.

Commander of the sloop, Blagonamerennyi, Captain-Lieut. Gleb Semenovich Shishmarev.

Lieutenants:

[Aleksandr](3) Avinov [on the Otkrytie]

[Pavel Zelenoi] Zelenyi [Otkrytie]

---

* Translated by Rhea Josephson, edited by Dorothy Jean Ray.

[Ivan] Ignat'ev [Blagonamerennyi]

[Aleksei] Lazarev [Blagonamerennyi]

[Roman] Boil [Otkrytie]

[Ivan] Stogov [listed as a midshipman on the
                Otkrytie]

Midshipmen:

[Nikolai] Shishmarev [Blagonamerennyi]

[Roman] Hall [Otkrytie]

Prince Pahava [not listed in the Lazarev volume, 1950]

[Karl Karlovich Hillesem, or Gillesem] Gelinsgem
                [Blagonamerennyi. This is K. K. Hillsen].

Pilots:

[Mikhail] Rydalev [Otkrytie]

[Vladimir] Petrov [Blagonamerennyi]

Astronomer:

[Pavel] Tarkhanov

Naturalist:

[Fedor] Shtein

The voyages of 1820

    Captain Vasil'ev arrived safely at Kamchatka with the
sloop entrusted to him. He sent Capt. Lieut. Shishmarev to
Unalashka [Unalaska] Island to take on interpreters,
instructing him to sail from there to the shores of America
to the sound described by Lieutenant Kotzebue in 1816.

    On June 27, 1820, Captain Vasil'ev left the harbor of
Petropavlovsk and made his way toward Bering Strait. Near
Saint Lawrence Island he sighted an American brig [the
Pedler] and on questioning it, learned that it had come
here from the Sandwich Islands [Hawaiian Islands] to buy
furs from the Chukchi. On June [July] 16, Captain Vasil'ev
arrived at Kotzebue Sound where he found Capt. Lieut.
Shishmarev, who had been at anchor near Chamisso Island for
five days.

    Captain-Lieutenant Shishmarev reported to Captain
Vasil'ev that on June [July?] 3d he had arrived at Unalashka
Island and received a report from the manager of the local
office that he had no interpreters who knew the language of
the North Americans, and therefore, requesting from him four
baidaras [umiaks or skin boats] and six Aleuts, he left that
island on the 19th. Going around Saint Lawrence Island

toward the NE he saw ice, and found Kotzebue Sound completely covered with it. This circumstance prompted him to sail for an inspection of Ratmanov Island [Big Diomede].* Although he passed the point where it should have been visible in clear weather he did not see any sign of land. Returning again to Kotzebue Sound, he found no more ice there.

On July 18, C[aptain] V[asil'ev] put out to sea with both sloops, and decided to sail northward along the American shore for a most exact survey. Frequent fogs, an overcast horizon, and ice in various directions did not permit Captain Vasil'ev to carry out this project. On the 29th at latitude 71° 06', longitude 166° 08' west of Greenwich, they approached the ice and saw that the entire area as far as the eye could see was covered. "It was possible to sail westward along the ice," says Captain Vasil'ev in his report, "but as we were 35 miles above Icy Cape and about four degrees farther west in longitude, it was desirable for me to examine Icy Cape and I turned around at a depth of 24 sazhens [168 feet]."

New obstacles prevented Captain Vasil'ev from carrying out this intention, and therefore he cruised southward on July 31, "About 8 o'clock in the morning," he continued, "we saw Cape Lisburne and ice against the shore from the ENE to the NNE. The thermometer rose 2 1/2° [Reaumur].[5] I cannot say whether the ice seen by us northward from Lisburne on the shore was stationary." This observation of Captain Vasil'ev is very correct; the great [James] Cook said, says [Sir John] Barrow: "But C. Cook observes, he did not suppose any part of this ice to be fixed; on the contrary, he considered the whole as a movable mass";[6] that is, Captain Cook said that in his opinion all of the ice he saw was not stationary; on the contrary, he considered all of it to be shifting.

All of the above-mentioned circumstances probably prompted Captain Vasil'ev to leave the arctic regions. He said, "On this day August 9 came out of the Arctic Ocean where I was for 26 days. We explored the shore rather well from Cape Lisburne to Cape Krusenstern, but could not see Cape Mulgrave because of the haze. The American shore has no bays whatsoever. We did not see any rivers flowing into the sea. In some places we saw water beyond low-lying banks." This remark leads to the conclusion that the whole coast of America from Icy Cape to Cape Newenham consists of islands. The Honorable Davis concluded back in the year 1587 that the northern shores of America were formed of islands.**

Here are the interesting remarks of Captain Vasil'ev about the northern shores of America: "The current of the

* See the first part of this history, pp.

** See this history, volume 1, p. 25.[7]

sea was observed from NE to SW at about a half knot per
hour, but near the shore it was swifter and changed
direction. The declination of the compass was at its
greatest, 35° 45' at latitude [?][8] but at Cape Lisburne,
35°." Remarkably, Captain Cook, being at Cape Lisburne
42 years before Captain Vasiliev (1778), had almost the
same declination of the compass. At latitude 69° 57',
longitude 193" 41' he found its declination 35° 32' east.

"At latitude 71° the declination of the magnetic needle
was found to be 78° 30'. The Reaumur thermometer rose to
about 11 1/2° and fell to 2 1/2° below freezing, but mostly
it was 5° to 6° [43° to 45° Fahrenheit]. Near shore the
depth of the ocean was sometimes found to be between five
and seven sazhens [35 and 49 feet]. We did not find the
depth of the sea to be more than 30 sazhens 80 miles west
of the shores of America. The land was completely bare.
Here and there in the valleys moss was seen, but standing
timber was nowhere to be found. On the shores was seen a
quantity of driftwood; the trees were very large poplars and
fir [spruce] with roots." This remark about the forest
and shallow depth near the ocean shores serves as indisputable
evidence that there must be deep harbors and rivers flowing
from the interior of the continent at various places on the
continental shores of America between latitudes 70° and 65°
by means of which the mentioned driftwood is carried out to
the seacoast. The above-mentioned sea current from NE to
SW also serves as new and very strong evidence in corroborating this conclusion.

"Above latitude 68° 30' we did not see any inhabitants.
From afar their drying racks look like masts with yards."
Captain Vasil'ev concludes, "We had no intercourse with the
inhabitants because of the inconvenience at shore anchorages,
bad weather at times, and not having interpreters."

From Cape Prince of Wales, Captain Vasil'ev went to
East Cape, and passing the Gvozdev Islands [Diomede Islands],
set his course for Saint Lawrence Bay [Gulf of Anadyr],
which was closed by ice. "This ice," he says, "must have
been carried by the NE wind from the Arctic Sea. But one
has to take into consideration that Saint Lawrence Bay is
still not free of ice." According to new information about
the polar regions, and considering the remarks of various
travelers, one must conclude that Arctic waters begin to be
free of ice in the middle of August. The voyage of Captain
Parry serves as strong evidence to that. Among the journals
of Captain Shmalev, at one time the commander of Ishiga
[Gizhiga], are found the answers of a Chukotski [Chukchi]
chief to questions asked him.

"The chief said when the Bering Strait becomes free of
ice, a multitude of whales, walruses, and seals go north and
remain there until October and then return south. Therefore,
it must be assumed that it is possible to sail in Bering
Strait during the whole of September."[9]

Coming into sight of Saint Lawrence Island, Captain Vasil'ev instructed Capt. Lieut. Shishmarev to finish surveying it, and he sailed toward the American shore. The gradual decrease in the depth of the sea from the eastern end of Saint Lawrence Island was the reason that Captain Vasil'ev turned west and sailed toward the islands of [Saint] Paul and [Saint] George. Determining their geographic position, he continued his way to Unalashka and arrived there on August 19.

"Being in the Arctic Sea," says Captain Vasil'ev, "I saw the necessity for a small sailing vessel, which could keep quite close to shore. On the sloop Blagonamerennyi there were parts of a disassembled boat in the hold." Therefore, Captain Vasil'ev set his course from Unalashka to Novo-arkhangelsk port [Novo Arkhangelsk, or Sitka] where there were more facilities than elsewhere to assemble that boat. He arrived there on September 15, and entrusting Lieutenant Ignat'ev with the assembling of the boat, sailed from there on October 25.

Having spent the winter season in southern regions, Captain Vasil'ev arrived in Sitka at the port of Novo-Arkhangelsk on May 13, 1821. Finding that the boat was completely ready, he took on a reserve of water and wood, and receiving interpreters from the Chief Manager of the American district, Fleet Capt. Lieut. Matvei Ivanovich Murav'ev, he put out to sea with all three vessels on May 30.

Because the newly-assembled boat could not keep up with the sloops, Captain Vasil'ev took it in tow and continued on to the Aleutian chain. Upon approaching Unalashka, Captain Vasil'ev entered the harbor in order to repair some damages.

Here Captain Vasil'ev formed a new plan for the pending voyage in Arctic waters. He instructed Capt. Lieut. Shishmarev, upon putting out to sea, to proceed toward the north-eastern shores of Asia and to look for a passage into the northern sea. If he failed in that he was instructed to survey the shore of Chukotski land [the Chukchi Peninsula]. Captain Vasil'ev retained the boat, intending to survey the shore of America between Bristol Bay and Norton Sound. After that, he planned to go to the Arctic Sea along the northwest coast of America and look for a passage into the Atlantic Ocean.

Vasil'ev's voyage, 1821

On June 27th, Captain Vasil'ev put to sea. The sloop Blagonamerennyi made its way to the shores of Asia, and the Otkrytie and the boat sailed toward [Saint] Paul and [Saint] George islands. Again verifying their geographic position, they sailed toward Cape Newenham and cast anchor on the southern side.

Here Captain Vasil'ev appointed Lieut. Avinov commander

of the boat, and gave him as assistant Midshipman Hall,
son of the Honorable Vice-Admiral Roman Romanovich Hall,
who had sailed these seas under the command of Captain
Billings in 1790 and 1791. Captain Vasil'ev instructed
Lieut. Avinov to survey the coast of America lying between
Capes Newenham and Darby. He told him to join the sloop
Otkrytie on July 20 at Stuart Island, but if Lieut. Avinov
had not succeeded in finishing the survey of the shore
by that time, he was permitted to remain there [at Stuart
Island] until August 15, and if he did not meet Captain
Vasil'ev in Norton Sound then, to winter on Unalashka
Island or at the harbor of Petropavlovsk.

On July 6 the boat went on its way, and Captain
Vasil'ev, at the same time going to Cape Stephens, discovered on the 11th a coast not indicated on the maps.
Coming to a depth of eight sazhens he cast anchor and
going ashore with the interpreters was informed that they
were standing off an island called Nunivok [Nunivak Island]
--located not far from the mainland coast of America--
which is inhabited, and that until now its inhabitants had
had no contact whatsoever with Europeans. The latitude of
his anchorage was 59° 54', longitude, 193° 17' east of
Greenwich. Captain Vasil'ev named this island after his
sloop, the Otkrytie.

On June [July] 12, Captain Vasil'ev weighed anchor and
directed his course to Norton Sound. Arriving at Cape
Darby on the 19th he remained at anchor for 24 hours, and
since Lieut. Avinov had not arrived with the boat, Captain
Vasil'ev sailed north. At latitudes 68° 01' and 68° 21'
Captain Vasil'ev sighted two prominent capes, which
Captains Cook and Clerke had not seen.

On July 31, the sloop Otkrytie neared Cape Lisburne,
from which, as was observed from the crosstree, the coast
turned northward, but Captain Vasil'ev says, "The fog, the
variable winds and calm prevented coming closer; we saw
only heights at some places. On the morning of August 2nd
we encountered several pieces of ice upon which were lying
many walruses. We took a course toward Icy Cape, the wind
springing from the south. Although the ice was getting
thicker, it was still possible to go northward.

"On August 3rd," continues Captain Vasil'ev, "we were,
by observation, at latitude 70° 40', longitude 161° 27'
west of Greenwich. The depth of the sea increased from 13
to 21 sazhens. We had passed Icy Cape judging by the
latitude which we were in. The ice was seen continuously
from N to W; from N to E less frequently. Toward Z
(south?) there was no ice."

Captain Vasil'ev bore up toward Icy Cape wishing to
inspect and identify it, and saw it on August 4 at latitude
70° 23'. A very strong wind continued until the 9th. The
sloop was surrounded by ice several times, and as Captain
Vasil'ev says, "The sloop was pressing toward the ice; we

lowered boards, doors, and such small masts as we had;
laid them round the entire side so that the ice would not
damage the sheathing. The crew were used as much as
possible to hold back the ice to soften the blows.
However, some were so strong that they broke three-inch
thick planks."

On August 9, Captain Vasil'ev sighted Cape Lisburne
and the coast of Asia. On this date, he says, "We came
out of the Arctic Ocean."

On August 13 Captain Vasil'ev arrived at Cape Darby,
and learning that Lieut. Avinov had not been there, went
toward Stuart Island. Casting anchor, he sent Lieut. Boil
ashore in an armed longboat. Returning on the 16th, this
officer reported, "The inhabitants who had come to this
island from Cape Stephens stated that they had never seen
foreigners, and that no vessel had ever visited them. To
the south of Cape Stephens," they continued, "flows into
the sea a large river, Kuiukht-pak [Yukon], from which
shoals extend far out."

"Not finding the boat," says Captain Vasil'ev, "we
weighed anchor and taking course W went to a depth of
seven and eight sazhens. Having rounded the shoals we
bore up to the eastern side of Saint Lawrence Island and
passed on the north side of [Saint] Matthew Island and
among the Commander, Bering, and Attu islands. On
September 8 we arrived at the port of Petropavlovsk where
we found the sailing boat."

Avinov's voyage, 1821

Lieutenant Avinov reported to Captain Vasil'ev that on
July 6 he had sailed from Bristol Bay toward Cape Newenham.
A strong wind and heavy seas forced him to head for
Hagenmeister [Hagemeister] Bay. Coming out of it on the
19th he surveyed the shore from Cape Newenham northward.
On the 11th he arrived at Goodnews Bay, where he collected
reliable information from local inhabitants that along the
whole American coast northward so far as it was known to them
lived one nation. The report by those who were in these
places with the land expedition in the years 1818 and 1819
undertaken by the [Russian-] American company in Kadiak
[Kodiak], that to the north of the Kuskokvim [Kuskokwim]
River on the mainland coast lived some European people
proved to be incorrect.(10)

On July 13 Lieut. Avinov came from Goodnews Bay, and
going northward found shallow banks in many places, which
in his opinion were dry at low water. In Goodnews Bay he
noticed an approximate 13-foot tidal rise of water.

Captain Vasil'ev says, "Lieuten. Avinov found sailing
near the banks dangerous since the boat drew four feet
(loaded), and with crosswinds and light seas could not
hold in the wind. The bottom was unsuited for anchoring

in the open sea. In addition, the crew started to show
signs of scurvy from continuous wet weather and crowding."
For these reasons he decided to sail to Kamchatka and
arrived at the port of Petropavlovsk August 19.

Shishmarev's voyage, 1821

On June [July] 27th Captain-Lieutenant Shishmarev
directed his way from Unalashka Island to Transfiguration
Island, which was discovered in 1766 by Lieut. Sind, and
not finding it, concluded, "If Transfiguration Island
exists at all, it is not near that place where it is
indicated on the maps."(11)

On July 4, the sloop Blagonamerennyi was at latitude
62° 32', and longitude 193° 11' east of Greenwich. From
it they sighted a high shore extending from S by E to SE
at an approximate distance of 70 miles, but according to
the map of Mr. Khromchenko, it appears that Captain Lieut.
Shishmarev was only 45 miles from it.

Captain-Lieutenant Shishmarev, comparing it with all
known maps, saw that this shore was located at a distance
of 245 versts [162 miles?] from the mainland shore of
America, and therefore acknowledged it very rightly as a
new discovery. Wishing to survey this new and unknown
land, he sailed toward it but after 15 miles he found the
depth to be five sazhens, and for that reason dared
not sail farther. Below we shall have occasion to talk
about this new shore again.

From this place Captain-Lieutenant Shishmarev went to
Saint Lawrence Island, and surveying the northern part of
it collected much curious information about the inhabitants.
On July 11 the sloop Blagonamerennyi entered Saint Lawrence
Bay and Captain-Lieutenant Shishmarev compiled a very
interesting description concerning the manners, customs,
and character of the Chukchi people.(12) It is noteworthy
that he saw there two rifles, which they had received
from an American brig [apparently the Pedler] that had
come there because the Russians trading with them in Izhiga
and Nizhne-Kovymsk [Lower Kolyma] may not sell them firearms.

Captain-Lieutenant Shishmarev sailed near the Asiatic
shores until July 21, and met ice everywhere, and for the
most part, bad weather. On that day he dropped anchor near
the American shore at latitude 67° 34' in order to take
on a supply of wood and water. This coast was low and
covered with grass, and a lake was visible not far away.
One could see a great deal of driftwood, and in some
places at a considerable distance from the sea some trees
lay [piled] rising 40 feet above sea level. Here they
gathered wild onions, dock, wormwood, and saw many different
varieties of flowers and grasses. They noticed sandpipers
here as well as the birds inhabiting the polar regions.
The ocean proved to be 20 miles southward in 24 hours.

On July 22 Capt.-Lieut. Shishmarev again got under sail and sailed toward the coast of Asia where the ice surrounding the sloop did not permit him to come near it. Capt.-Lieut. Shishmarev says, "Turning in all directions we could not find free passage any place and were liberated [from the ice] only by making our way through solid ice and receiving three blows from large ice floes without any damage, however, to the sloop."

After this unsuccessful trip Mr. Shishmarev directed his way to the north and reached latitude 70° 11' where he saw very high solid ice and encountered fresh north winds. On August 1 Mr. Shishmarev was at latitude 70° 13' where he again encountered ice and rather thick snow that covered all the sails, rigging, and deck. "On the 4th, we saw Cape Serdtse Kamen." Mr. Shishmarev says, "The shore from this cape has a general direction SE and a chain of low mountains. Toward the sea several cliff-like capes about 500 feet high stand out. Between these capes the shore is low and forms small inlets, but timber is nowhere to be seen, not even a little green grass is to be seen. What a contrast to the shores of America. In many places we saw large settlements, but could not approach them because of the ice."

Ice, headwinds, and stormy weather prompted Mr. Shishmarev to abandon further attempts, and to sail to Mechegmenskaia Bay [Mechegmen Bay] where he hoped to fortify his crew with fresh provisions. The Chukchi here received the Russians very amicably and the chief delivered ten live deer [tame reindeer] to the sloop. Captain Shishmarev collected here, too, rather interesting information, discovering at the same time that among the Mechegmen Chukchi lived four more nations talking various languages different from the Chukchi dialect.

On August 15 Mr. Shishmarev left Mechegmenskaia Bay and went to Saint Lawrence Island. Having surveyed its northern shore and having established communications with the inhabitants who, in his opinion are much poorer than the Chukchi, Mr. Shishmarev went his way to Saint Matthew Island, which was discovered in 1766 by Lieut. Sind. Determining the geographical location of this island and both [?] located near it, Mr. Shishmarev decided to end his voyage in Arctic regions, and went toward the harbor of Saint Peter and Paul [Petropavlovsk] where he arrived safely on September 21.

Both sloops departed in the middle of October on the return trip and arrived safely in Kronshtadt [in 1822] after nine months.

Notes

1. This account is the first chapter (pp. 1-20) of volume 2 of Berkh's <u>Chronological History of all Voyages to the Arctic</u>. It was translated by Rhea Josephson and Dorothy Jean Ray, and edited by Dorothy Jean Ray. A copy of the translation is in the Dartmouth College Libraries.
In this account headings have been added for clarity, but Berkh's abbreviations of names have been retained.

2. All dates are Russian old style, which according to the Gregorian calendar would be 12 days later.

3. Information in brackets is from Lazarev 1950; 83-87 and 99. The editors of the Lazarev volume give the complete ships' rosters. There was a total of 74 persons on the <u>Otkrytie</u>. On the <u>Blagonamerennyi</u> there were 83; a captain-lieutenant, two lieutenants, two midshipmen, a doctor, a pilot, a chaplain, and 75 seamen.

4. Kotzebue thought that he had discovered a fourth Diomede Island; therefore, he gave the name "Ratmanov" to Big Diomede, which had already been discovered and named Saint Diomede by Bering in 1728. Ratmanov had been one of Kotzebue's shipmates when they sailed with Krusenstern (Kotzebue, vol. 1: 198).

5. To obtain Fahrenheit temperature from Reaumur, multiply by 9/4 and add 32.

6. This quotation is in English in Berkh's account.

7. John Davis made three voyages, in 1585, 1586, and 1587 to Greenland and Labrador. For many years it was thought that Alaska was a large island, an idea influenced especially by Ivan (Johann) Sindt, who submitted a map after his voyage to Bering Strait in 1766 showing many fictitious islands, including one called Preobrazhennyi, mentioned by both Berkh and Hillsen.

8. The latitude was omitted.

9. The Bering Strait is sometimes free of ice for almost five months, depending on weather conditions. The ice usually moves out sometime in June and returns by October.

10. This refers to the search for the elusive "Russian fort or settlement, Kheuveren, which was actually an Eskimo village, Kauwerak, sought by Korsakovskii in 1818. This is discussed by Ray in <u>The Eskimos of Bering Strait, 1650-1898</u> (1975b) and in "The Kheuveren Legend" (1976).

11. See note 7.

12. <u>Zapiski Gidrograficheskago Departamenta</u>, 1852.

III

A VOYAGE OF THE SLOOP 'BLAGONAMERENNYI' TO EXPLORE
THE ASIATIC AND AMERICAN COASTS OF BERING STRAIT,
1819 TO 1822*

At the beginning of Hillsen's three-part article, the editor of Otechestvennye Zapiski wrote the following note:

This voyage, so far not described by anyone either in whole or in part although completed 27 years ago, contains so much that is curious both in its goals and results that its description will always arouse the most intense interest; more so because there was none completely similar thereafter.

The expedition, the exploits of which are described in this article, consisted of the two sloops Otkrytie and Blagonamerennyi under command of Captain-Lieutenant (subsequently Vice-Admiral and General-Commissioner of the Fleet), Mikhail Nikolaevich Vasil'ev, and had the purpose of exploring the shores of America as far northward as possible from the Aliaska Peninsula, and the coasts of Asia only from East Cape. The expedition reached the latitudes practicable in the two summers in the Arctic Ocean, overcoming almost insurmountable obstacles, and resolved the question concerning the feasibility of penetrating from this side [Asia?] as far north as the point reached by its vessels.

The author, Mr. Hillsen, chose as the beginning of his narrative the time of sailing from Port Jackson [Sydney, Australia] because places hitherto visited by him such as Brazil, Cape of Good Hope, and New South Wales are already well known.

[Pages 213 to 220 in volume 66 describe the journey from Australia to the Aleutian Islands. The Arctic portion of the journal encompasses pages 220-38 in volume 66 and pages 1-6 in volume 67. The rest of the article, pages 7 to 24 and pages 215-36 in volume 67 describe conditions in California and the Hawaiian Islands.][1]

---

* Translated by Rhea Josephson, edited by Dorothy Jean Ray.

Hillsen's narrative:

[After a severe storm in the north Pacific Ocean]
About noon of the 21st [of May, 1820], the wind gradually
began to abate, and toward evening died down completely.
Immense heavy swells continued to rock the sloop,
preventing our undertaking urgent repairs, which we could
begin only in the evening of the next day. Setting new
topmasts and rigging a brand-new suit of sails, we directed
our course toward a chain of small islets with a steady SW
wind. The customary passage from the [Pacific] Ocean into
the Kamchatka Sea [the Bering Sea] for ships sailing to
Unalashka is Umnak Pass, in the middle of which is a
tremendous rock resembling a ship under sail [Ship Rock]
for which it was so named. Because of this and the narrowness of the strait in which the current is very strong, we
directed our course toward the pass near Amchitka Island.
The captain also intended to examine John the Theologian
Island [Bogoslof Island], which lay more to the west, and
which had surfaced at the end of the last century.

At dawn of the 27th we saw the whole northern horizon
bordered by a chain of high, wild islands, and Amchitka,
directly in front of us. We approached this island toward
noon, and safely sailed through the pass and entered the
Kamchatka Sea about three o'clock. Amchitka Island is
lower than all the rest of the islands of the Fox Chain
[Aleutian Islands]. Its length from E to W is about
1 1/2 miles and its width from N to S is about 3/4 of a mile.
[Amchitka Island is 35 miles long and about three miles
wide.] It consists of bare red rock on which not the
slightest vegetation is seen. On its low banks lay thousands
of sea lions and sea otters, which, on our approach, plunged
into the water, roaring and bellowing, crowding each other.
Toward the northwest at a distance of six miles from
Amchitka, Semisopochnoi Island came into view, presenting
a sight unique in the world, it received its name from
seven conical volcanoes--of almost equal height--called
sopki in those regions. Three of these volcanoes smoke
constantly, and according to the Aleuts on Unalashka,
recently had strong eruptions.

The constant SW winds left us as we entered the
Kamchatka Sea, and instead, variable weak ones blew more
from the SE and E, which slowed down our sailing considerably, and we were able to approach John the Theologian
Island only on June 1. This island appeared from the water
and rose to its present height of about 250 feet above the
surface of the ocean during a violent earthquake and
eruption of the Umnak and Unalashkan volcanoes in 1797
[Baker (1906: 142) said that the eruption was on May 18,
1796]. Since it had not been closely explored by anyone
as yet and the weather was calm and clear, the captain
ordered us to lower the tender for a trip there by our
naturalist. Command of the tender was entrusted to
Lieutenant [Aleksei P.] Lazarev, assisted by the junior
pilot, [Mikhail] Vedeneev. Stocking up with provisions and

water for seven days in case of fog or other unforeseen
events that would prevent his rejoining the sloop and
therefore having to go directly to Unalashka, a distance
of 40 miles from John the Theologian Island, and taking a
map of the Kamchatka Sea, a compass, a chronometer, a
sextant, and the log, they left at six o'clock in the
morning.

They neared the island about nine o'clock and rounding
its eastern end disappeared behind it. At ten o'clock the
previously quiet SE changed to a NE, bringing a thick fog.
The situation of our tender became very unpleasant. We,
on our part used all possible means to lead it out of this
predicament; we came closer to the island, lay to, and
started to beat the drums, to ring the bells, and to fire
the cannons every ten minutes to indicate our position to
him. But as these means are very inexact near high shores,
the echo reverberating from them heard from various sides,
the captain decided to continue lying to until the fog
cleared and then take appropriate measures. About three
o'clock the fog began to lift and we saw our tender coming
directly toward us. In one hour it joined us.

Lieutenant Lazarev reported that before the fog they
came so close to the island that they could have landed on
the long low sandspit extending almost a mile into the sea
from the eastern end if they had not been prevented by an
infinite number of sea lions settled down on it. It is
very dangerous to approach these sea monsters when they
are on land. The sea lion attacks people when they impede
his way to the water and is able, with his terrible jaws
filled with pointed round teeth, to snap off a hand with
one bite, as   happened a few years before to an
Unalashka toion [chief]. Seeing the impossibility of
landing on the spit, Mr. Lazarev went along the shore to find
another suitable place, but everywhere the banks rose per-
pendicularly above the water and the surf did not permit
approaching them. Under these circumstances they were
obliged to be satisfied with what they could observe from
the tender. The island is about three miles in circumference and forms a steep mountain of clayey and rocky soil,
covered in places with thick layers of congealed lava. On
top a crater is constantly spewing a black column of smoke.
Here, nature does not provide anything from the plant
kingdom but moss. The Unalashkan and Umnak Aleuts often
come here to hunt sea lions whose meat and fat they use for
food, the guts for kamleikas [waterproof coats], whiskers
for decoration of their wooden hats, bones for arrows and
for fuel instead of wood, and finally, the skin to cover
their baidaras.

Noticing the approaching fog Mr. Lazarev abandoned
his fruitless attempts to land on the island and started
back to the sloop which soon disappeared from view, but
following the known course he could distinguish the
direction clearly from the noise of the shots, and aiming
toward it safely reached the sloop, as we have seen.

Continuing light variable winds brought us only on
the third to the entrance of Captains Bay on Unalashka,
which we did not dare enter, however, because there is no
ground for anchorage until Amaknak Island, and the high
shores of Unalashka block out the light breezes from the NE
all around through the S to the NW. The captain ordered
us to shoot the cannons and in about three hours we saw
three large baidaras coming toward us from the harbor.
Joining our rowboats, they took the sloop in tow and
toward evening pulled it into the harbor at the northern
end of Amaknak Island. Here we anchored until the next
morning when, with a good NE wind, we made the remaining
seven miles to the settlement, Illiuliuk [now the village
of Unalashka] from which we dropped anchor a half mile away,
and on the same day undertook necessary repairs. We hardly
had time to cast anchor when the company manager of the
island came to see us. The other six Russian promyshlenniki, [2] and the Aleutian toions, all knew our captain
[Gleb S. Shishmarev] who had been here twice on the brig
"Riurik" with Captain Kotzebue.

I consider it superfluous to describe the island and
the manners and customs of its inhabitants because it
would only be a repetition of what has been said by many
travelers who were there before and after us. Having
finished checking the movements of the chronometers and
repairing the rigging we weighed anchor about noon on the
15th with a light SE wind, but coming to the end of Amaknak
Island from which a long sandy spit extends into the harbor
the wind began to abate, and finally, with the sunset, died
down completely so that we were forced to drop anchor again.
Toward midnight the wind started to blow from the NE,
gradually getting stronger so that about three o'clock it
turned into a storm. In the open sea it blew NE, but here,
bursting through the mountain passes, it assailed us from
all sides and suddenly sometimes from several sides with
such fury that the sloop started to drift. The situation
was not only very unpleasant but dangerous. We were no
farther than 300 sazhens from the spit and the sandy ground
held anchor badly, weakened even more by the constant
movement of the sloop from one side to the other. We let
out the cable to about 50 sazhens but the drifting
continued; then we cast the other anchor, letting out 100
sazhens from the first on a 50-sazhen cable. Then the
sloop stopped. The sandspit abaft the stern was very close
and if the anchors had not held we would inevitably have
run aground and though we need not have feared a shipwreck
we would not have avoided severe damage.

Meanwhile the gusts increased, the cables stretched
like strings, and the sloop moved again. We immediately
lowered the longboat, placed it on the third sheet anchor,
and towed it 100 sazhens. Taking up the slack of the cable
by means of the capstan we drew it evenly with the two
others and then the sloop stopped completely. For greater
safety we lowered the topmast and braced the yards. Being
no farther than 50 sazhens from the sandspit, we remained

in this position the whole evening of the 18th. At that time it started to quiet down, and having raised two anchors we remained in position with one until morning, and on the morning of the 19th, weighed it too, and sailed from the harbor. While we were anchored in this dangerous place we entertained ourselves by watching an unusually large number of foxes that came to the sandspit toward evening to catch sea urchins [?], which they like to eat. Among them we noticed a few dark brown ones. It would have been very easy to shoot them with rifles from the sloop, but in the first place, the skins at this time of year molt, and are not good for anything, and secondly, every animal on the islands and in the sea is the property of the company.

Our stay in Unalashka was notable for many weddings and christenings. For almost twelve years it had not had a priest and from this it is possible to see how much ours had to do.

Leaving the harbor with a light SE breeze we set our course toward Saint George Island [which had been] very exactly determined by Admiral [G. A.] Sarychev, in order to confirm once more the movement of our chronometers. The captain also planned, weather permitting, to go to the island in order to trade sea lions, sea otters, and murres from the Aleuts who were settled there by the company in order to supply the crew with at least some fresh food, a very important commodity in these latitudes where more than elsewhere people are subject to scurvy, its development furthered by salted murres, a sea bird that resembles a duck in size and body [but] with the difference of a sharp, not flat, beak. Its back and wings are black and the abdomen white. Its feathers and down are so thick that shot does not penetrate them. They constitute the main part of the trade of the Aleuts who are settled on [Saint] George Island. They are caught with nets stretched opposite their nests in rocky cliffs facing the sea. The eggs and the meat are used for food. It is very tasty when roasted without the skin; with it, it retains a very unpleasant fishy flavor.

At dawn of the 20th we saw the tall bare cliffs of the island and soon approached it, but because the wind was rather strong we could not carry out our intention of going ashore, and only checking our chronometers with the longitude of the island we continued our trip and held for Saint Lawrence Island in order to survey it as far as possible.

We slowly moved ahead with light changeable breezes. The weather was clear, which is a rarity in this area. Its inhabitants, the whales, played on the surface and we saw them by the several thousands. They jumped out of the water, and falling with the whole body cause an agitation on the surface resembling the wake created by a paddle steamer. They imparted an unbearable stench to the air, spurting whole clouds of water spray from their nostrils. The local whale has a sharp snout, and is much smaller than the sperm whale.

Saint Lawrence Island

On the 23rd we had the misfortune of losing our cook
from a stroke. Hoping to reach Saint Lawrence Island the
next day the captain ordered us not to throw the body into
the sea, wishing to bury it on shore. When the fog lifted
at five o'clock in the morning we saw a shore to the NNE
at a distance of 15 miles. It was Saint Lawrence Island
presenting itself to our eyes in all of the majesty of its
wild and infertile nature. Rather high interior mountains
were covered with snow almost to the foot even at this
time of year. Extending from the southern side of the
island to the shore, their slopes presented a dismal view,
infertile, wild, and not covered by the least vegetation.
When the sun rose a few degrees from the horizon on its
oblique heavenly journey a thick fog rose with it, con-
cealing this view from our eyes. We had despaired of the
possibility of giving our dead one a small place of rest
in its bosom from earthly burdens, but about ten o'clock
the fog started to lift, and forming thick black clouds,
covered the whole heavenly dome. Meanwhile, we approached
the southern cape and when we rounded it we saw in the
depth of the open bay a large number of yurts [dwellings],
ten or twelve of which were situated closely side by side
at somewhat of a distance along the shore. The latter
were the summer abodes of the island's inhabitants and
consisted of conically-shaped tents covered with walrus
skins. The other ones were earthen huts similar to those
at Unalashka except that they were more spacious inside.

Nearing the shore at a distance of a half mile we
lowered two skiffs. On one we loaded the body of the dead
cook and a cross on which was carved the name of the sailor
and the sloop, and the year, month, and date of his funeral.
The captain and two of our officers went out on the deck.
We and the sailors on both skiffs were armed. The sloop
lay to and we set forth. Approaching the shore we saw that
the islanders with their children and wives were retreating
to the nearby mountains and only about ten old men remained
on shore. They were unarmed and were holding dried fish
and walrus tusks in their hands. We landed on a sandy beach
directly opposite them and they received us amicably with
their customary greeting; this is, spitting in the palm of
their hand, they smeared us on the face. To avoid this
greeting would mean offending them; therefore, we endured
this disagreeable and repulsive anointing with stoic indifference. Becoming somewhat acquainted with them we
carried out the body of the deceased man and started to dig
a grave about 200 sazhens from shore, but this work
progressed very slowly because the ground was frozen solid
about one arshin [28 inches] below the surface. With the
help of a crowbar, we finally excavated about six feet,
lowered the body sewn into a hammock for the lack of a
coffin, buried it, and set up the cross. The savages
looked at us with amazement during all that time and
apparently only understood what it was all about when the
Agalagmiut[3] interpreters explained through sign language

that this was a dead man who would come out and haunt them
if they did not leave him and the cross in peace. Of
course we had no right to protect the peace of our dead
one by such means, but we certainly could not abolish all
the superstitions they had concerning this matter in our
short stay.

Having performed this duty we began to barter with the
inhabitants. We proposed various small things to them, but
they did not take them very willingly, not even the axes
and cast iron pots. These things were of less value to
them than ordinary leaves of tobacco. Knowing its name,
they were constantly shouting tabago, tabago, and for a
leaf of it gave away all they had: walrus tusks, their
arms consisting of spears and bows and arrows, sleds, and
even their deerskin parkas. They do not smoke or snuff
tobacco, but simply eat it. Chewing it up they do not
spit it out, but swallow it.

In the meantime, observing our peaceful conduct all of
those who had gone to the mountains returned to their yurts.
Wishing to see the inside of their dwellings, we told the
chief who immediately led us to his winter abode; that is,
into the earthen hut. Inside, it was about two square
sazhens in area, and the entrance was through the only
opening at the very top, which served as door, smoke hole,
and window. One half of this yurt was lined with polar bear
skins; the other was behind a curtain hung from the ceiling,
or better to say, from the dome of the hut to the floor.
The whole family generally sleeps behind this curtain,
undressing to nakedness, and in winter spends all its time
here. From the stifling air and the constantly burning
walrus fat the heat was so great that we could not stay in
that place for even a minute. The suffocating heat and stench
surpassed all credence.

The inhabitants of the island are short, their face is
wide, flat, and of a dirty yellow color as though smoked,
with protruding cheek bones, heavy lips, wide nose and
narrow eyes. Their clothing consists of a parka of deerskin
with a hood, and trousers and boots of sealskin.[4] The
women are much whiter and more handsome than the men and
are dressed in the same way, but their parkas are longer than
the men's. The only domesticated animals are dogs of the
Kamchatka breed: that is, large, shaggy ones with sharp
snouts, erect sharp ears, which are used for traveling in
winter just as in Kamchatka. They do not have deer [tame
reindeer] on the island and barter their skins from
neighboring Chukchi for walrus teeth [tusks] and yukola,
or dried fish.

Having spent about three hours on shore we left,
accompanied by the shouts of the inhabitants. Withdrawing
a few sazhens away they began to throw rocks at us but not
a single one fell on our skiff. Knowing how skillfully
they throw them hitting seagulls in flight we concluded that
this must be by no means a hostile custom, but one for

leave-taking, and continued our trip paying no attention
to it. On arriving at the sloop we lifted the skiffs and
weighed anchor, setting a course to the NE in order to
round the eastern cape of the island to sail toward Bering
Strait. On the next day, the 25th, we approached this cape
and saw the impossibility of going N because all the
visible expanse of sea was covered with closely connected
ice floes, which formed an endless ice field on the edge of
which were settled hundreds of thousands of walruses.
Some swam around the ice and often approached the sloop.
We tried to shoot them with muskets and rifles, but without
success. The bullets bounced off their thick skin from the
closest distance. Their cry, like the bellowing of an
enraged bull, is deafening. Some plunged from the ice into
the water; others, with the help of their long tusks,
climbed back out again onto the ice with difficulty,
throwing themselves with frenzy upon those who lay on the
ice and were either thrown back into the water or succeeded
in driving off their enemies.

Bering Strait

     Seeing the impossibility of penetrating to Bering
Strait from this side of the island, the captain ordered
us to turn and go along the southern shore of the island
to its western cape. Having a favorable wind we started
to measure the island by means of angles. Continuing this
activity toward the southern cape we were compelled to
abandon this work because of descending fog and continued
our trip to the above-mentioned cape. We doubled it and
slowly moved ahead turning N. The fog lifted on June 30
at eight in the morning and we saw in front of us the
Gvozdev Islands [Diomede islands] in Bering Strait. In
an hour East Cape [now called Cape Dezhnev] and Cape Prince
of Wales appeared. At three o'clock we went through the
strait and entering the Arctic Ocean set our course for
Kotzebue Sound. Having a favorable wind we approached the
entrance to this sound at ten o'clock on July 1, but found
it blocked with ice. Having no way of entering it the
captain ordered us to turn again to explore Bering Strait
and to verify the existence of the island seen and named
Ratmanov Island by Captain [Otto von] Kotzebue.

     Approaching the Gvozdev Islands near which should
have been situated Ratmanov Island we determined, in
completely clear weather, that this island did not exist
and Kotzebue was probably deceived by an ordinary
phenomenon here, an optical effect of light rays on clouds
that are on the horizon. This was thought to be the case
at that time by our captain who was with him on the brig
Riurik. Having corrected this error we tacked to the
sound under least sail, accompanied by almost constant fog
and often encountering large thick blocks of ice. [The
fog] lifted toward the evening of the ninth and we again
saw the entrance to the sound, still covered with ice. The
wind was very light and in order not to be carried by the
current we dropped anchor at a depth of 12 sazhens. Near

midnight such thick ice started pressing against us that
we were forced to cast off and go under sail. We spent the
rest of the night in frequent tackings and shifting of our
course to avoid being hit by an ice floe. Toward morning
of the tenth the sea cleared and we saw the entrance free.
Not wasting time we entered the harbor, but having a very
light breeze could only get to the middle where we dropped
anchor toward evening.

Kotzebue Sound

Kotzebue Sound extends for 75 miles from Cape Krusenstern to its northeastern end, and its greatest width is
20. Its depth is from five to eight sazhens. The northern
shore is high and hilly and the southern, sloping and low.
Fifty-six miles from the entrance, at the place where the
bay begins to narrow is an islet--in the very middle--
called Chamisso Island by Captain Kotzebue after the
naturalist and astronomer who was with him. From this
island the bay widens again and appears to be a round
lagoon, the eastern shores of which look blue in the distance.

We scarcely had time to drop anchor when we saw
visitors in three large baidaras. They stepped fearlessly
on deck and traded marten and otter skins for axes, cast
iron pots, knives, and needles, but immediately went back
without having traded even one tenth of their cargo. They
took almost no tobacco and wanted only big knives, guns,
powder, and lead, but as it was forbidden to sell them
these articles they stopped trading and returned to shore.(5)

On the 11th a light W wind starting blowing. We
weighed anchor and went farther into the sound. Wishing to
take refuge from the outer surf, we passed Chamisso Island
and went behind its high banks and dropped anchor a half
mile from the island. Its rocky shores rise steeply to a
hundred or more feet. The surface is very evenly covered
with black earth on which grows short dry grass, moss, and
many cloudberries, the only fruit that we saw in these
regions. In its coastal cliffs nest an innumerable quantity
of murres and puffins. The first bird has already been
described by me. The body of the second is quite like it
but has a flat, long beak, which is red and yellow, its
shape resembling the beak of a parrot; therefore, it is also
called a sea parrot. Its meat is as tasty as that of the
murre and we knocked down a few hundred of both kinds in a
day. The Aleuts from Unalashka who left in the morning in
their three baidaras returned toward evening with a full
load. They shot them with five-pronged spears.

The Otkrytie still was not there. The weather was
overcast so we could not engage in astronomical observations and were extremely bored from this inactivity. For
amusement the captain proposed that we visit the northeastern part of the bay; namely, the place where he saw
whole mountains of ice on the shore in 1816. Everyone
gratefully accepted this proposal. We immediately began

to prepare for a two or three day absence. We armed the
longboat, put four falconets on it, took provisions for
three days, and two Aleuts with us on one baidara. On the
morning of July 14 at seven o'clock 20 persons started
out on the journey. The wind blew rather briskly from the
W and by noon we saw the mountains. The captain had told
us that these shores were completely uninhabited.(6) We
were surprised therefore to see a large settlement consisting of a hundred or more conically-shaped skin tents
on a long sandspit extending from the high shores for about
a mile and a half inside the bay (the only place it was
possible to land because of shoal water). Opposite each
[tent] on the beach lay a baidara turned upside down. As
soon as the inhabitants noticed us 150 persons gathered on
the shore armed from head to foot with spears, bows, and
a few even with long rifles. Observing that, the captain
ordered us to remove the sails and lay to in order to
decide whether to go ashore or to return. Seeing that,
the savages started to wave various furs and to shout
"toki, toki," which meant to trade as we found out later.

We decided to go ashore and to repel any attack by
loading the falconets, guns, and pistols, and by preparing
side arms. Upon completing that we lifted the grapnel,
and using oars approached the very end of the above-
mentioned bar, two or three cables' lengths away from the
settlement. The principal reason for this action was the
high tide, since we could not hope either to maneuver or
to row out against the wind and currents and therefore we
wanted to wait on shore for the low tide, especially since
everyone was very hungry and longed to eat warm sour
cabbage soup for which we had the necessary ingredients.
So we neared the shore, but not so close that we could get
directly off the boat. In the meantime, the savages
following our route also approached the end of the sandspit
and sat down in a semicircle from one side of the shore to
the other, putting all their weapons on the ground behind
them. Lieutenant Lazarev who was wearing high hunting
boots forded from the boat, but we crossed in the baidar.
When the lieutenant stepped ashore a chief rose from the
circle and greeted him with a long speech of which our
Aleuts and Kodiak Islanders understood nothing. Then,
exactly the same way as on Saint Lawrence Island he spat on
the palms of his hands, leading them through the air, but
not touching them to his face. The Indians [Eskimos]
seemingly rejoiced at our arrival and constantly shouted
in chorus, "toki! toki!" The trading started at once.
They did not at all want tobacco and knickknacks highly
valued by other peoples, but asked only for knives,
hatchets, needles, scissors, cast-iron kettles, and
especially gunpowder and lead. But seeing that they could
not obtain [the latter] they stopped asking and were
satisfied with the above articles for which they gave their
weapons, clothing, and marten, otter, bear, and fox furs;
but generally, they priced them very high.

Meanwhile, our sailors put up tents, made a fire, and

started to cook dinner and we, in company of the chief to
whom we explained our intentions through sign language,
went toward the ice mountains where it was necessary to
walk the length of the sandspit past the settlement. It
consisted of a hundred and one conical skin tents of a
rather neat finish but we were unable to see inside because
the chief blocked such an attempt by putting himself, with
a long unsheathed knife that he pulled out from under the
back of his parka and over his head, between us and the
yurts. We did not insist further, and stepping away to the
edge of the beach continued our trip, which pleased him
very much. Having come to within about 20 sazhens of the
mountains, the chief, with an apprehensive look, wanted to
detain us from further walking, but seeing our determination
he remained on the spot and let us continue by ourselves.

These mountains begin where the sandspit ends. They
stand back from the shore about three or more sazhens.
This expanse consists of sandy oozy ground resulting from
the melting ice forming continual small streams. The
exterior side of the ice cliffs rises vertically 20 or
more feet and when the sun's rays reflect from this wall as
from a polished surface, one must avert one's eyes so
blinding is the glare. [7] The flat top of this ice mass
slopes gradually toward the interior of the land and is
covered with a layer of earth about two feet thick as tested
with the bore. This layer is overgrown with moss and other
northern bog plants. The continual rotting of these grasses
creates a pungent swampy odor. Having satisfied our
curiosity we hurried back to the tents accompanied again
by the chief and by women who joined us at this time and
whom we had not seen at first.

This tribe calls itself Tatui and to the question,
"Where did they come from?" they pointed to the southeast
[Buckland River]. There were about 300 persons of both
sexes. [8] They are tall, well built, with pleasant faces,
and they could have been called a very good looking
people if their features had not reflected some kind of
savage ferocity. Both men and women wear their hair
braided in two braids down the sides. The former adorn
themselves with cufflinks [labrets] of walrus bone put
through openings pierced at both sides of the mouth. The
latter paint their eyes at the top and the bottom, joining
these circles with a line across the nose and chin of a
dark blue color. The rich ones wear crowns and necklaces
of large blue glass beads. Men and women dress according
to their wealth in marten or deer [caribou or domesticated
reindeer] parkas and seal trousers and boots. [9]

After dinner we began to prepare for our journey.
Although the wind still blew rather strongly from the W
we hoped to maneuver with the ebb tide, and especially
hastened to leave because we noticed that the Indians,
entirely unarmed before with the exception of their long
knives behind their shoulders, and not having received the
powder and lead they desired, started to gather completely

armed in crowds and to provoke our people. We pushed off, putting everything into the longboat, and rowing to the deep, set sail and began to tack. But this did not last long. Toward evening the wind began to grow stronger and developed such heavy seas that every wave got into the longboat. It started to get dark, but knowing the direction [to the sloop], we held our course, preferring to get drenched rather than to return to shore where unfriendly action from the Indians undoubtedly awaited us. Suddenly there came a terrible squall and broke both masts. To row out against the wind and the surf was impossible. We knew no other place to go ashore and could not search in the dark. There remained no other way for us but to return to shore. Our situation was critical because our firearms were wet. First it was necessary to put them back into proper order. After doing so we anchored, using the grapnel, and having finished this job went ashore again.

Seeing that, the Indians dashed shouting to the landing place, seemingly wanting to prevent us from landing. We paid no attention to them, and only waved our handkerchiefs, shouting "toki! toki!" They quieted down and let us come ashore and pitch our tents. Then the captain ordered us to present the rest of the trade goods to the chief and the principal warriors who were easily distinguishable because of the respect paid to them by the rest of the crowd. We asked them to withdraw to their settlement and to leave us alone. All was in vain. They thronged near the tents shouting "toki! toki!" and even started to pilfer various things from the sailors, a cover from a large copper kettle, and a long kitchen knife among other things.

We probably would not have been able to get rid of them the whole night, and God knows how it would have ended if Mr. [Vladimir] Petrov, our senior pilot, had not thought of taking advantage of their superstitions to get rid of them. He took the boat hook from the longboat and drew a deep line in the sand from one bank of the sandspit to the other, mumbling something in a low voice and spitting from time to time in the direction of our tents near which the Indians stood. [10] As soon as they saw this maneuver they hastily dashed across the line and ran toward the settlement. Only then, putting guards with loaded muskets and one falconet on the line, were we able to give ourselves a much-needed rest, without undressing, however, despite the fact that we all were soaked through. The night was very cold and we waited impatiently for morning, especially when we saw that the wind started to abate after midnight. Finally, despite the wetness and the cold, and exhausted by the exertions and anxieties of the day we fell asleep toward morning.

But our rest was not long. At dawn the shouts of the guards woke us up, informing us that armed savages were breaking across the line. With all possible speed, we

immediately removed everything to the longboat while those
not busy with that task tried to hold them back in a
friendly manner. We found the last things that we did not
need and used them for trade, but this had unfortunate
consequences. One of our sailors, giving an Indian his
folding knife for four or five marten furs, wanted to cut
off the counted ones from the other unpurchased skins, but
was so careless that he severely cut the finger of the
Indian holding the furs. The savage glared at him,
retreated a step and pulled out his long knife with which
he would surely have killed the sailor had not another
sailor, Ivan Salnikov, who had unusual physical strength,
caught sight of this. He threw him to the ground with one
blow of his fist to his head, tore away his knife, and
started to hit him with it so hard that the other one jumped
up and began to run toward the settlement, howling.

Almost at the same time, one of our officers [Lazarev]
had a similar experience with another savage. He had a
Turkish pistol which went off very easily after it was
cocked. Loading it with powder and wanting to get a bullet,
he put it on a stone beside him. The Indian took it in
his hands and began to play with the trigger. Seeing this,
the officer took the pistol away from him, and imitated the
sound of a shot with his voice wishing to explain to him that
playing with the pistol was dangerous. The savage, interpreting this pantomime otherwise, immediately pulled out his
knife and struck him with it but hit only the cartridge bag
buckled round his belt. To stop him from repeating the
blow, the officer fired a blank cartridge into his face and
inflicted a severe wound on his cheek because of the nearness.
Screaming, the Indian took to his heels toward the settlement, and after him all the rest when they saw blood
flowing.[11]

It was then impossible to tarry longer because we
supposed that they surely would all return soon to avenge
their comrades. We jumped into the longboat and pushed off
although the water was still rising. We had succeeded
rowing out not far from shore when all the Indians appeared
on it and shot a whole cloud of arrows at us, which,
however, caused no harm whatsoever because we protected
ourselves with walrus skins traded from the Saint Lawrence
Islanders. We did not respond and only tried to get away
from their shots. But when they started to shoot guns and
the bullets began piercing the skins, the captain ordered
us to fire a falconet ball over their heads. They quieted
down for an instant hearing the whistle of the ball, but
soon raising a horrible cry, shot arrows and bullets at us
again and dashed toward their baidaras, pushing them into
the water to pursue us. The captain then ordered us to
aim the falconet at the largest one. The cannon fired and
the ball ripped out the entire side of the baidara,
wounding one man. They then abandoned further attempts to
attack us and retreated to their abodes. We also left
them in peace and with the changed current arrived safely
on the sloop after three hours.[12]

The Otkrytie was still not there but we started
immediately to get ready for the further journey: hoisted
the longboat and filled empty barrels with water from a
spring on Chamisso Island.

On July 16 at 7 o'clock in the morning we saw our
sloop going toward the island. It stopped in the outer
part of the bay. We immediately weighed anchor, and crossing
the strait dropped it again beside it. At four o'clock in
the afternoon an American brig [the Pedler] entered the bay
and dropped anchor not far from us. Its captain by the
name of Piget [William J. Pigot] boarded the Otkrytie. He
announced that he had come here from the Sandwich Islands
to trade furs with the local inhabitants. We advised him
to go to the smaller part of the sound as close as possible
to the northeastern shores but not to go on land, and to
permit the Indians on the brig only after taking all precautions because these people were crafty and unreliable. As
proof, we related our adventures with them and advised him
of the principal article that they requested. After nine
months we met him again on Vagu Island [Oahu] and learned
that he had had a profitable trade following our advice.(13)

Sailing northward from Kotzebue Sound

On July 17 we weighed anchor and on the 18th, passing
Cape Krusenstern, we set out toward the north. About noon
a thick fog hid the Otkrytie and the shore from us. Then
we started to give each other fog signals every quarter of
an hour. The fog lifted toward evening and we again saw
the Otkrytie and the shore. The latter was so close that
we saw a large settlement with the naked eye. Many
inhabitants came down to the shore and waved fox and other
furs at us. But not paying any attention to them, we
continued our trip on course. The clear weather did not
remain long. After midnight the fog thickened again and
persisted uninterruptedly until the 22nd. At first we
constantly heard shots from the Otkrytie but later we did
not receive answers to ours. The fog separated us. On
this day it cleared and we saw again the dismal shores of
America in these latitudes, but our comrade was not there.
Meanwhile, we had reached latitude 69°. We often encountered solid fields of thick ice. Attempting to keep as
far north as possible, we picked our way into every clearing
between them, and reaching that latitude encountered solid
ice covering the whole horizon to the north. We turned back
hoping to find the Otkrytie. Until the 25th we had daily
fogs around midday but clear sky in the morning and evening.
We could see nothing except the long and unchanging spit
extending along the shore for a few miles between Capes
Lisburne and Mulgrave, and on it a small settlement of
Americans. At all times we had a strong current from the NE.

On the 28th we reached Cape Mulgrave, the place of our
separation from the Otkrytie, which was not to be seen. We
turned back again, and here a terrible storm from the SW
overtook us, which continued until the 31st.(14) During

all this time a thick wet snow fell so that the crew could
not shovel it off the deck. It started to abate that day
and turned to the NE. The snow stopped and was replaced by
freezing of seven or more degrees. All the rigging was
iced and moved with great difficulty in the blocks. The
sails were completely stiff so that in unreefing the men
had blood coming from under their fingernails. This
situation cruelly exhausted us and our crew as there is
nothing more unbearable than freezing under sail, especially
shortly after damp and inclement weather. On deck it was
cold, and below it was suffocating from stuffy damp, fire-
place-warmed air. During the night of August 1 the wind
shifted to the SW and with it a thick wet snow started
falling again. Toward morning we saw the Otkrytie directly
in front of us keeping under least sail. We were extremely
overjoyed by this event because we had got bored cruising
aimlessly in one spot and could hope now to get instructions
for further activity. The weather cleared completely around
noon and the wind died down. At that time we were at
latitude 68° 34'. We had noticed a strong current from the
NE during our first time in this latitude, but now during a
calm there was no doubt whatsoever. Being near stationary
ice fields and shores we clearly saw how we were being
carried toward the SW with reference to these objects. To
keep our position we had no other course but to drop anchor.
We dropped it at a depth of 18 sazhens. In order to measure
the strength of the current we lowered a log and it proved
to be almost two knots. Captain Vasiliev requested through
the telegraph [semaphore] that our captain come to him, and
some of our officers, taking advantage of the good weather
went out to hunt walrus on the ice. But this was very
unsuccessful. There are very few [walrus] in these latitudes
and those are so fearful that they would not let us approach
within shooting distance. Toward evening our captain returned from the Otkrytie, after which we weighed anchor,
taking a direction S along the American shore with a weak NW.

Turning southward

In Kronshtadt our sloop had been loaded with pre-cut
parts of a seagoing shallow draft single-masted vessel or
boat, indispensable for exploration and survey of the shores
of America from Cape Prince of Wales to the Aliaksa [Alaska]
Peninsula. The intention was to assemble and build it in
Kamchatka or in Sitka so that it would be ready for navigation in 1821. Having only eight ship's carpenters it was
necessary to begin building in good time so that it would
be ready on schedule. Due to the condition of the ice,
extending to an infinite distance northward, as we mentioned
before, we could not hope to penetrate farther to the pole
without wasting a lot of time. We took our present direction
to the south.

Although from here we did not have such frequent and
thick fog as before, it henceforth was supplanted by snow-
storms from the N and the NW from which we suffered
cruelly, especially when they were accompanied by freezing.

Moreover, scurvy began to appear among the sailors from
wetness, cold, rare calm, and sailing near shores and ice
where we were often forced to fight storms. This sickness,
once it gets the upper hand on such a vessel, is most
terrifying. Its symptoms are so varied that sometimes one
does not realize that it is scurvy. It is even more
dangerous when immediate aid is not given, and is always
fatal. No matter how well our crew was equipped with coats
and underclothing, constant bad weather and the impossibility of drying out thoroughly what was soaked through
produced the seeds of this illness. Besides, the salted
food with which the crew had to be satisfied for almost
five months contributed to its development. We had taken
from England fresh meat prepared in tin cans--to this we
owed the fact that there was no further increase in the
sickness and that it did not carry off any of us during that
summer. We tried in all ways to protect the crew. They had
exercise, one of the best measures against scurvy. To keep
up their strength we gave the men tea in the morning; a
glass of madeira or port wine after dinner; punch in the
evening in cold and damp weather; and in addition, brewed
spruce beer, or beer from spruce buds. But all these means
really could not protect us for long if we had remained
in these regions, and that is why we were most elated when
we learned of our new course.

At six in the morning of August 2 when the fog lifted
and the snow stopped, having fallen the whole night in
large flakes, we neared the shore, and coming as close to it
as possible, took a course along it and started surveying.
The weather was clear, the wind N, rather brisk and with
its help we succeeded in surveying 90 miles that day. Within
the surveyed range was also the already-mentioned long sandspit, the end of which Captain Vasil'ev called Cape Golovin
[Golovnin][15] after the name of our famous traveler who
had the misfortune to be imprisoned by the Japanese. Toward
evening the wind began to increase and we had to delay our
plan to continue surveying the next day, and moved away from
shore. Coming to an open place we sailed close-hauled and
stood under least sail. During the night the wind increased
to such an extent that we were forced to reef all topsails.
It continued until the evening of the 3rd, then slackened,
but the fog and gloomy weather began again so that we could
not continue our survey. Therefore, following the track of
the Otkrytie, we bore away to Cape Oriental, or East Cape,
of Asia. We did not sail long with a favorable wind. It
shifted to the SW and almost turned into a storm, delaying
us, and we reached the cape only on the ninth. It appeared
to us at dawn that day in all the majesty of its wild
nature. High rocks rise vertically and the ocean waves
breaking against them produced a thundering noise heard 20
or more miles on the wind. Here and there in the [valleys]
and on the slopes we noticed the summer yurts of the coastal
Chukchi [Eskimos] settled there to catch seals, fish, and
sea birds nesting in the rocky gorges.

We rounded East Cape the same day and set our course

toward Saint Lawrence Bay lying almost on the same parallel
of the island by the same name. The intention of our
captains was to enter it to buy deer [tame reindeer] from
the Chukchi to supply the crew with fresh food necessary
to prevent scurvy, especially as we probably could not
obtain anything of this kind going from here to Unalashka
or to Sitka, and would have to wait until our arrival in
California, where we intended to go from [Sitka]. We
reached the entrance of the bay at about nine o'clock but
finding it clogged with ice could not enter. Hoping that
during the night the ice would be carried out with the
current we lay to until morning but we were deceived; the
ice remained as before and we were obliged to go on because
of lack of time.

A course taken to the west end of Saint Lawrence Island
brought us within sight of this island on the 11th. That
day Captain Vasiliev ordered our captain by telegraph to
continue surveying the island and to join him later at
Unalashka. The sloop Otkrytie departed to explore the
American shore between Norton Sound and Bristol Bay. Heading
in that direction it soon disappeared from our sight.
Because it was too late that day to start surveying, we
tacked and withdrew farther from the shore for the night
where we hove to under least sail.

The night was very dark. We lay close hauled on a port
tack having only the reefed topsails, foresails, staysails,
and mizzens. According to our calculations we were more to
the north, almost opposite the middle of the strait between
the island and the continent of Asia; therefore, a tack to
starboard was proposed only at midnight. At about 11 o'clock
the boatswain on watch came from the forecastle to report
that the sound of breakers was heard from leeward. The
lieutenant on duty, knowing that we were more than 30 miles
from both shores at eight o'clock and having no more than
three knots speed--in three hours we had made only nine
miles--did not want to believe this, but finally the breakers
were also heard on the quarterdeck. Through the darkness of
the night we saw a dark high mass with luminous stripes,
that is, snow lying in the ravines. We immediately came
about on the opposite tack and thereby escaped this danger.
While tacking we cast the lead right near the shore but did
not reach bottom at 200 sazhens [1400 feet].[16] It is
obvious from this how great the danger was to which we were
exposed because if the sloop under such shortened sail had
not tacked, it would have been impossible to rely on the
anchor and we could not have avoided crashing on the rocks.
One may ask why were we so close to the island? Our calculations were correct, but we were carried by the current
flowing from Bering Strait. I have already mentioned the
current that exists in the Arctic Ocean constantly flowing
from the NE. From where did this mass of water constantly
flowing from one direction come? We could only think that
the shore of America does not extend to the pole or farther,
but has a broad passage through which the waters of the
Arctic and Atlantic oceans flow into the Pacific. Thus, one

has only to find this passage. We did not doubt that it
exists, but it was not fated for us to achieve this feat
as we met an insurmountable obstacle in the solid ice as
will be seen from the continuing description of this voyage.

The next day with a favorable wind from the NNW we
began to survey the northern shore of the island from its
western cape. Toward noon we got to the middle, projecting
at a blunt angle into the sea, and were in the curve of
the shore extending between it and East Cape. This was
about three o'clock in the afternoon and an already rather
brisk wind started to increase. Fearing that we would be
pushed against the shore the captain ordered us to proceed
close-hauled, but the high seas threw us off and the
drifting was so strong with reefed topsails that the
impossibility of maneuvering was obvious. It was necessary
to add canvas or we were done for. We put on topsails to
relieve the strain on the shrouds, left the topsails reefed
in two rows, put on the topgallant sails, and put up the
fore- and mainsails. With such wind this amount of sail
produced the desired effect, the sloop started moving, and
with its design and the high seas, almost incredible: we
were going five knots. The topmasts bent like small twigs
and we feared that they might break despite our precautions.
The sloop lay complete on its beam ends. In this manner we
spent two and a half hours between fear and hope. Finally,
we reached a point from which it was possible to change
course, port the helm, brace the yards, clew up the mainsail;
and the sloop, as if sensing its dangerous position, inclined
leeward, escaping the point of danger and flew southeast.
Hiding from the heavy seas behind East Cape we removed the
topgallant sails, clewed up the foresails, and directed our
course to Saint Matthew Island, without any hope of carrying
out our orders without a big loss of time.

We saw the island on August 14 at six o'clock in the
morning. Its forerunners were an infinite multitude of
sea birds such as puffins, murres, seagulls, and grebes.
About noon we neared the island and determined its
latitude, 60° 13' 48" N and longitude, 187° 45' 48" E of
Greenwich. It consists of high bare rocks in which
millions of the mentioned birds nest. A separate little
islet is located near the northern end, and at the southern,
an immense rock resembling a saddle and named Pennikl
[Pinnacle] by Captain Clerke. This large island is about
60 miles long, but completely sterile and uninhabited.
The existence of multitudes of sea lions, seals, and sea
otters on its low shore prompted Mr. [Aleksandr] Baranov,
former manager of the colonies of the [Russian-] American
Company, to settle a few score Aleuts there for hunting
these animals, but after three years he was compelled to
abandon this undertaking and to transport the rest of the
people back to Unalashka and Umnak from where they had
been taken. I say "the rest" because the greater part of
them perished from the cruel frosts existing on the high,
unprotected island, and from scurvy. Furthermore, in
autumn, the ice brought a terrible scourge for the people

and animals living in this land--polar bears, by whom
several persons also perished every winter.

At Unalashka

From here we went to Unalashka and on the 17th saw
Saint Paul Island, which belongs to the Pribilof Islands,
as does Saint George Island, and is separated from it by a
channel 60 miles wide [actually, only 40 miles wide].

On the 22nd we saw Makushin Volcano with its constantly
smoking summit. By 10 o'clock, having a rather strong NW
breeze, we approached the harbor where we caught up with
three single-hatch Aleut baidaras [really "baidarkas," or
kayaks] returning with a full load of codfish they had
caught. They said that the Otkrytie had been in Unalashka
for three days. Toward noon we entered the harbor and
dropped anchor near the Otkrytie, accompanied by the
baidaras. Entering the harbor the sloop had a speed of
seven and a half knots and the baidaras outdistanced it.
From this it is evident how fast and light these skin
boats are.

The day after our arrival we started the most
necessary repairs to the rigging. Preparing to sail on a
most stormy and very unjustly called Pacific Ocean,
especially around the equinox, we tightened the lower [and?]
mast shrouds, and put on the auxiliary shrouds as an aid.

The manager, [Ivan Vasilievich] Kriukov, told us that
there was a hot spring at the foot of a high mountain on
the northeast side, almost at the entrance to the harbor.
Our naturalist, desiring to investigate its character,
was dispatched there in a cutter on the 25th in the company
of officers not otherwise busy with tasks and with the son
of Kriukov. We were told that it shoots up out of the
ground an arshin [28 inches] or more and that it is as
thick as the arm of a man. But what did we find? Miserable
remains of a spring that had formerly existed, scarcely
visible under the ashes that covered the whole island
during the eruption of the Umnak volcano in 1819. This
eruption was accompanied by a severe earthquake which was
felt on all the islands of the Aleutian chain and finished
with the sinking of the coastal lowland on Umnak Island,
an expanse seven versts in circumference.

There were several rather strong earthquakes
accompanied by a subterraneous rumbling during our stay on
Unalashka.

The impossibility of obtaining in this place fresh
meat and vegetables so necessary for restoring and main-
taining the health of the crew prompted us to rush the
repairs and the taking on of water, especially since we
could get nothing until California, according to all
reports, and had to expect difficult and exhausting voyages,
first to Sitka and afterward to the port of San Francisco,

to which our common longings rushed as to the promised
land. Somehow, the meat was substituted with excellent
fresh fish, and vegetables with wild garlic, or ramson,
but this did not have the desired effect, and the crew,
although improved, still ailed. We were given a kind of
salmon of excellent quality, but we caught cod ourselves
in the following manner. On a seven-foot pole we attached
about 15 fish hooks also baited with cod. In the middle
of the pole we fastened a stone instead of a weight and
lowered it to the bottom of the harbor. In about two
hours, pulling up the pole, we found a codfish on every
hook. The catch was so abundant that fish were cooked
daily for the crew, and in addition, eight barrels were
salted.

During our stay in Unalashka a dead whale, thrown up
on Amaknak Island, had been killed by an Umnak Aleut as
determined by the spear on which every whale hunter cuts
his mark, still sticking under its left fin. He was
immediately notified of it and arrived the next day in
company of many baidaras [kayaks?] for the dividing because
half of every animal used at that place (except for the
skin, which is always the property of the company) also
belongs [to the company]. The Aleuts use the meat of
whale, sea lion, seal, and sea otter for food, especially
the first. They also eat the fat, using it as a condiment,
but mostly to burn in their yurts instead of candles and
wood.

No matter how expert the Aleuts are in sailing baidaras
and in throwing spears, whale hunting is done by only a
small number of them because it requires special agility
and skill. From accounts they kill them in the following
manner. On a clear sunny day when the whales sun themselves
and play on the surface of the water, the whale hunter puts
out to the open sea in his small baidara. Sighting a whale
he approaches it exclusively from the left side to about
50 paces or to the distance from which he can throw a
spear, designated by his mark, as already mentioned. It is
one and one-half arshins long [42 inches]. In one end is
inserted a [piece] of walrus ivory, a foot long, with a
serrated and pointed flint instead of iron; the other end
is feathered. It is thrown from a small board one third as
long as the spear.

Approaching closely he follows all the movements of
the whale. Always keeping it on his right side he waits
until its left fin comes out of the water. Then he throws
the spear with his usual marksmanship and plunges it into
the heart of the animal. Receiving the blow, the whale
generally leaps out of the water in a frenzy and striking
its tail on the surface plunges to the bottom. This is the
most dangerous moment for the hunter. The baidarkas
[kayaks] of the Aleuts are extremely unsteady and if the
hunter does not succeed in rowing out of the way
immediately after the blow the sudden waves will swamp
him, or a blow with the tail will smash a clumsy one.

Generally, the Aleut is satisfied with his booty if he kills one whale, although he might have killed a few more that are found on the surface on a warm sunny day.

Sea lions and sea otters are also killed with arrows, but only in their rookeries. These arrows are much longer and thicker than those for whales and are used like spears. They do not go alone for this pursuit, but all adult Aleuts together. Coming to the place where these animals are lying, they all step out suddenly onto shore and with clubs try to stun them and straightaway plunge their spears into their open jaws. The sivuch, or sea lion is an awkwardly large animal resembling a seal but is a more dirty yellow color with short hair. On shore it is very dangerous to approach directly from the front, as already mentioned, because having unusual strength in its fins and spine it can suddenly move forward ten or more paces and grab with its awful jaws. Realizing that, the Aleuts usually attempt to approach it suddenly and from the side in order to stun it with a blow on the forehead with a thick heavy club, as said.

In June and July terrible fights arise among the males who often bite each other to death while the females remain quiet spectators. Each male has 20 or more females. Another member of this group, not as abundantly supplied, endeavors to attack, and that starts the described fights. The vanquished either remains on the spot or runs back into the water and goes in search of a weaker opponent. The conqueror remains complete master of his group of females. He drives them into the sea or on the shore as it suits him, and they willingly obey him.

For hunting the precious sea otter, erroneously called beaver by us, only the rare Aleut sets out--as in the whale hunt--not because it is fraught with huge dangers, but because it requires special training and skill, first to search for, and second, to kill it. These animals, strongly pursued, left these regions for farther south and now appear in great numbers in California. Those remaining are so cautious and apprehensive that they let one approach only when lying on their backs, sleeping on the surface of the sea. The small spears that strike them are of a different construction--but of the same size and appearance--as those used for whales. When they penetrate the body, their bony end separates from the shaft, to the middle of which is attached a bladder and from which extends a line braided from seal sinews or sea lion guts to the front part of the arrow. The animal receiving the wound sinks into the depths. The shaft, separating and floating on the surface, shows the place where the otter is fighting death. The Aleuts wait quietly until it rises to the surface and then if there is more than one baidara, they join them together and skin [the sea otter] right then, throwing the meat back into the sea. If there is only one Aleut he tows the animal to the nearest shore where he performs this operation.

The skill and daring of the Aleuts in sailing their baidarkas are almost unbelievable. They venture in them not only from island to island but sail to Kadiak [Kodiak Island] and even to Sitka keeping as much as possible near shore, but if they are overtaken in an open place by a sudden storm they join five, six, or more baidaras together with their oars, which they thrust through loops of thong, made for this purpose, on the decks.

Having finished the repairs and having taken on fresh water we weighed anchor on the 29th, but because of the ensuing calm could proceed no farther, and dropped anchor again near the end of Amaknak Island. Only on the 30th with a slight SE breeze could we leave the harbor, taking a course through the pass between Unimak and Ugamak islands. On the 31st we passed through it and entered the Pacific Ocean. In the pass, the surf, influenced by the struggle of the wind and the current called "suloi," was so great that it inundated the sloop. From here we had frequent strong winds and fog, which on September 6 separated us from the Otkrytie. On the tenth we saw the conically-shaped mountain, Edgecumbe, lying on the north shore of the entrance to Norfolk Sound [Sitka Sound] in the depths of which lies the fortress Novo-Arkhangelsk, the main administrative seat of the [Russian-] American company in the colonies. The next day we approached it but could not enter because the wind shifted to the SSE and we had to maneuver until the 21st [September], holding in the offing for three days in sight of the quiet port. The Otkrytie entered on the same day, having approached the sound more from the south on the fifteenth.

At Sitka

Norfolk Sound, discovered and surveyed by Captain Vancouver,[17] is located on Sitka Island [Baranof Island], one of the innumerable islands constituting the archipelago near the northwestern shores of America. At the end of this sound, which is formed by a large harbor and islands, is located Mount Edgecumbe. Norfolk Sound extends 14 miles from the entrance to a chain of small islands overgrown with tall spruce forest. Beyond it is the real harbor or port of Novo-Arkhangelsk. Until these islands [are reached] there is no anchoring ground in the bay, but a multitude of underwater and partly protruding rocks called Vitse-Kari [among which is one now called Viesokoi Rock--DR] are very dangerous because the current is generally driven toward them during a calm. Because of this it is impossible to enter unless there is a completely favorable wind.

There are three channels usable for the passage of vessels among the chain of islands forming the harbor. The others are clogged with underwater rocks, so to say, and there is no way to navigate over them. The pilot sent to meet us guided the sloop through Lighthouse Channel [Western Channel] and toward evening we dropped anchor at

an island with the same name, so-called because of the
lighthouse built on it [now called Signal Island]. The
Otkrytie, which had arrived before us, was anchored near
the fort where we, too, crossed the next day and stopped
near an empty company blockship where we had to unload
because parts of the boat had been stored at the very
bottom of the hold.

Although the harbor is completely protected from the
sea swells and has excellent anchoring ground, it is very
turbulent during the fall. The wind agitates it despite
the fact that it is surrounded by tall   mountains
partially covered with a dense spruce forest. Blowing from
the southwest, [the wind] is deflected from the mountains,
becomes northern and northeastern, and sometimes breaks
out suddenly with double strength through the numerous
passes and forces a vessel standing at anchor to toss from
side to side. Under these circumstances it was impossible
to unload completely without danger while remaining
rigged, and we began to unload and then to discharge
[cargo] the same day. This work proceeded extremely slowly
because of unceasing rains so that we were unable to reach
parts of the boat before the beginning of October. All
these parts were made of oak, and many of them that lay
under water barrels in the hold without touching air had
rotted or warped. They had to be replaced with new ones,
but because of the lack of oak here we decided to replace
them with spruce. For this reason we detailed an officer
with 20 sailors for woodchopping in the eastern harbor
where the forests extend to the beach. Cutting suitable
timber from such a great number of most excellent spruce
trees was very easy to accomplish, and in two days we
succeeded in preparing not only the trees needed for the
boat, but for reserve--two topmasts to replace broken ones
and about 30 sazhens of firewood. Although the Koloshi
[Tlingits] (as the native inhabitants of Sitka Island call
themselves) were at peace with the company, their cunning
forced us to take all necessary precautions. Because of
this, everyone was armed with rifles, muskets, and pikes.
They put guards at the working place in the forest and
hurried up the work as much as possible. Cutting the trees,
they only cut off their tops and branches, and lowering
them into the water joined them into rafts and then towed
them to the fort where they began to shape them according
to designated use.

Since the building of the boat required constant
watchful supervision by an experienced officer, instructions
were given to [Ivan N.] Ignat'ev, the senior lieutenant
of the sloop Blagonamerennyi to move ashore and attempt to
finish the work by the end of March 1821. To him were
detailed an experienced ship's carpenter with the rank of
warrant officer, one sergeant, four carpenters, one blacksmith, and one caulker.

Having set up the ways, we laid the keel of the boat
on the 16th and sang a Te Deum.

After that we began loading again. It was necessary
to load rocks to replace the reduced cargo, which had
consisted of the boat parts. For this we had to detail all
of our longboats and one from the port to the same beach
where we had cut timber, the only place where it was
possible to find rocks--and with great toil at that. We
were barely able to gather about 3,000 puds [54 short tons].
All these tasks detained us until the 25th. That day became
a holiday for all of us [because] we left this region with
the most unbearable climate we had [ever] visited. We
went to California, or better, to New Albion where an
abundance of everything awaited us, as well as a rest from
labor carried on for eight months.

While we were stationed in Sitka there came in an
American brig under command of Captain Mik [Meek?] for
repairs; a [Russian-American] company schooner the
Baranov, under command of Lieutenant de Livron from
Okhotsk; and a large three-masted vessel, the Borodino,
under command of Captain [Z. I.] Panafidin from Europe.
This vessel belonging to the [Russian-] American Company
came with various European and Chinese merchandise for the
colony and was supposed to take a cargo of furs from
Sitka. On its way it had called at Manila where cholera
broke out during its stay. Captain Panafidin, losing
several of his men and even his medical officer, hired
another one there and hastened to leave port in the hope
that a change of air would end the sickness, but it only got
worse and by the time he arrived in Sitka he had lost more
than 30 men. Here he had five more sick sailors, four of
whom got well, but one died, and with that the sickness
stopped. But upon our arrival at Kronshtadt we learned that
cholera began again after he had left Sitka. Thank God,
the epidemic did not develop ashore or among our crews.

A few days before our arrival at Novo-Arkhangelsk the
new chief manager of the American colonies, Fleet Captain
of the Second Rank [Matvei I.] Murav'ev, arrived there in
company of Midshipman Khramchenko [Vasilii S. Khromchenko]
in capacity of captain of the port, Secretary Gribanov,
and Physician Volkov. Thus, there gathered a rather large
company of officers endeavoring to compensate by an
exchange of conversation from the boredom from the eternally
bad weather and the distance from any educated society.
All of us except those who were on duty were always together either on the ships or at the commander's, who
occupied the biggest house in the whole fort. For variety,
we presented little plays, gave masquerades, balls, and
made excursions to the surrounding shores of the harbor
and to the hot springs. In this manner time passed rather
pleasantly. But despite all that, as has already been
mentioned, we were very glad when we left Sitka.

During our six-weeks stay we did not have one single
clear day. There was an almost constant drizzle.
According to the old timers such weather continues almost

the whole year except for two winter months, but even then
it also becomes damp with west winds. Freezing below eight
degrees is rare so the harbor almost never freezes and
navigation continues the year round.

Founded in 1804,[18] the fort Novo-Arkhangelsk is
situated on the shore at the foot of high mountains
surrounding the whole harbor and is located directly opposite
the middle passage into the harbor. It consists of two
parts, the upper and the lower. The upper fort lies on an
emormous flat rock about 60 or more feet high [Baranof Hill]
called a kekur in those regions.[19] It is surrounded by a
continuous fence of thick planks about nine feet high with
gun embrasures cut into it here and there. It is protected
by two hexagonal towers into which cannons are set in two
tiers. On one of these towers is raised the flag of the
[Russian-] American Company.

In the upper fort are located the two-storey house of
the commander of the colonies and the principal storehouses. The lower part of the fort joins the upper one on
three sides and consists of a similar plank timber fence
protected by several towers. Within its walls are barracks, a
wharf, various workshops, and the hospital placed on an
elevated blockship on the shore. Behind the fortress on
the shore is a settlement consisting of a church, a wind-
mill, and 12 residential houses occupied by employees of
the company. Quarters were also allocated in this settlement to our Lieutenant Ignat'ev. All these buildings are
wooden and were mostly in decaying condition at that time.
If the procurement of iron, copper, and rigging had not
been accompanied with such difficulties and expense it
would have been possible to build the largest ships here
because there is an inexhaustible abundance of the best
building lumber. Because of that, the Company seldom built
new ships at that time, and the dockyard was more adapted
for repairing those already existing.

There were about 300 residents then in Novo-Arkhangelsk,
the majority consisting of Aleuts who had been transported
there from the Fox Islands [the Aleutians][20] and Kadiak
Island. The rest were Russian traders employed in the work
of the dockyards and serving as sailors on the Company's
vessels. The Aleuts, however, caught fish and went in their
baidaras into the straits of the archipelago to catch
beavers [i.e., sea otters]. Their toions [chiefs] came to
our sloop every Sunday to wish the captain a good holiday
and to receive a glass of rum and a few leaves of tobacco.

At that time the condition of the colony with reference
to stores of provisions was very good. The grain storehouses were full but despite that they allowed only one pud
of wheat flour per person from the stores and the management
sent the office manager, Mr. [Kirill T.] Khlebnikov, on a
large ship [the Il'men] to California for the purchase of
new provisions. Such precaution was necessary in colonies
not producing their own grain, because if the California

monks suddenly decided not to sell wheat, or if the ship
sent out would encounter a misfortune, then the residents
would have to feed themselves with just yukola [dried fish]
and [fresh] fish, quite inadequate for so many people. At
this time these measures proved advantageous. Mr.
Khlebnikov, who was expected back in the middle of September,
did not return, and came back only at the end of January of
the following year. He had suffered a shipwreck near
Bodiaga [Bodega], the place where our California colony the
"Ross settlement" was situated. All the people were saved,
but the ship, the cargo, and the time were lost. With the
greatest dispatch he began building a new ship and in a
short time--from August to December--succeeded, loaded the
ship in Port San Francisco with wheat and salt beef
and, as stated, arrived in Sitka in January. To ward off
hunger in such cases, it should have been possible to engage
in cattle breeding, but it was hindered on the one hand by
lack of pasture land and hayfields, and on the other by the
Koloshi, who suddenly broke the concluded peace and had no
mercy for the people, not to mention the cattle belonging
to the settlers.

These people, by nature most brutal and crafty, lead
a nomadic life, coming in spring and summer to the seashores
to catch herring and other fish and withdrawing in winter
to the interior of the land. When we arrived at Sitka only
two tribes remained near the fort. Their leaders or toions
by the names of Katlian and Saginak[21] often visited us,
each in a separate boat hollowed out of a huge tree, which
carried ten or more people. Coming on deck they immediately
began to dance and to sing, then sat down in a circle and
waited to be served with a glass of rum and a few leaves of
tobacco. Having eaten and drunk they returned to shore,
each chief to his own settlement, one on one side of the fort,
and the other on the other side. Katlian's settlement,
which we visited now and then, was located on the seashore
a few hundred sazhens from the hospital blockship and consisted of five yurts. They were built of a few poles stuck
into the ground and tied together at the height of a man with
crossbeams against which were leaned three or four such
poles that served for the support of spruce bark that
covered the walls and the roof. The shape of these yurts was
quadrangular, about two sazhens square in size. The side of
each facing the sea was completely open.

The Koloshi are for the most part more than medium
height, wide-shouldered, and very well built. Their facial
features are more good looking than ugly, but have some
kind of brutish expression making them very unpleasant.
The chiefs that we saw wore men's shirts of cloth or
ticking, and across their shoulders a mantle of animal
skins or blankets of their own manufacture from the wool
of argali, or wild sheep, with yellow and black embroidery
on the edges. Otherwise the rest of the body was naked.
Their hair is black, long, and stiff like horsehair.
During wars or festivals they wear hats cut very artfully
of wood, depicting the heads of various animals and birds

such as bears, foxes, and eagles. During dances they do
not wear these hats but sprinkle their hair with eagle down.

The faces of the women are not so repulsive, and some
could even be called pleasant if they would not disfigure
them with a most hideous ornament. They insert into the
lower lip a small board one and one-half inches long and
one inch wide, and the bigger this board, which they call
"kaluga," the better the decoration. For this reason the
mouth is always open, and they cannot retain the flow of
saliva. It is so repugnant that it is impossible to look
at them with indifference. Besides this, they paint their
forehead, nose, and chin with red and black paint. The
clothing of the wives of the chiefs is exactly the same as
of the chiefs themselves, but the common folk of both sexes
wear only the above-described blankets. Their slaves
called "kalga"[22] walk around altogether naked and wear
only a strip around the body covering the lower part of
the stomach down to the knees. These slaves or "kalga" are
bought from neighboring islanders or become slaves from
being war prisoners. Their existence is the most miserable
in the world. They are very poorly kept and are treated
not like human beings, but like cattle, and finally, in the
event of war or change of domicile, are offered as a
sacrifice to the gods. The whole creed of the Koloshi consists of offering sacrifices to some kind of evil spirit
that does not even have a name. The ceremony of the
sacrificial offering takes place without any preparations
or formalities. When one of these events is pending, a
victim is selected, generally from the "kalgas" of the chief
and who remains ignorant of his fate up to the moment of the
sacrificial offering. Then he is surreptitiously attacked,
knocked off his feet with a club, and struck with a wide
double-bladed dagger, the handle of which is in the middle.
The body is left to be eaten by birds and animals in the
same place where it was deprived of life.

In summer they live on fish and in winter, prepared
yukola, bear meat, goat, and deer, which inhabit the
forests.

The dances of the Koloshi consist of twisting the
body and stamping the feet accompanied by unharmonious wild
howls which they call singing.

In the channels of the archipelago are found sea
otters, now seldom encountered, sea lions, and seals. The
waters abound with fish. In spring before June the
herring run takes place here, and later, red fish [salmon?].
Turbot [halibut] are caught almost the whole year. In
the woods live small black bears, foxes, wolves, and
martens whose furs the company trade with the Koloshi.
Wild sheep live in the mountains, enormous eagles nest on
the heights, and in summer, humming birds fly in the valleys.
The Koloshi catch all the animals with snares or shoot them
with rifles, which they receive from American ships
entering the strait to trade. For its own protection, our

company sells them neither powder nor lead and has received
permission from the government to establish military
cruises for both the suppression of this trade and for
protection of the monopoly of the company, which alone has
the right to trade with the natives.

This is the condition in which the colonies of the
[Russian-] American Company was found at the end of the
year 1820, but since then they have improved immeasurably
due to the constant efforts of Baron [Ferdinand] Vrangel
[Wrangell] who was the commander here after Mr. Murav'ev.

We lifted anchor on October 25 and went through
Lighthouse Channel into the sea. The Otkrytie, which stood
directly opposite the middle passage, wanted to pass
through it, but the wind rose and it had to abandon this
intention and follow the same course we took. Because of
this, having come out into the sea, we hove to to wait for it.
Toward evening it, too, entered the ocean and we filled
the sails, directing our course southward.

Notes

1.   The Hillsen account was translated by Rhea
Josephson and Dorothy Jean Ray, and edited by Ray. The
translation of the complete journal is in the Dartmouth
College Libraries. I have added headings and have broken
up the original long paragraphs for easier reading. I wish
to thank Verne F. Ray for help in clarifying the correct
English usage of nautical terms.

2.   Promyshlenniki in Russian denotes men of trade or
industry. In Alaska, its popular meaning became fur hunters.

3.   The Agalagmiut, or Aglegmiut, were Eskimos from the
Alaska Peninsula. For a brief discussion of these Eskimos
see Oswalt 1967: 4-5.

4.   Parka is not an Eskimo word, but was a Russian
adaptation of a Kamchadal term for the coat-like fur garment
known in most Eskimo dialects as atigi.

5.   Aleksei Lazarev describes a trading episode near
Cape Espenberg, but not this one [Lazarev 1950: 199).

6.   Some of Hillsen's observations in the Kotzebue
Sound area are quoted in the article, "Early Maritime Trade
with the Eskimo of Bering Strait and the Introduction of
Firearms," but are retained herein so that the continuity
will not be broken.

7.   These were not icebergs, but frozen earth with
pockets of ice.

8. Lazarev said that there was a total of 200 persons (1950: 204, 209). Since both authors made errors of fact and spellings, it cannot be ascertained who was correct.

9. Lazarev said that the men wore their hair like some Catholic monks, in a little crown, and the women arranged theirs on the temples in small pigtails. They changed clothes several times a day, he said, either because they wanted to show off their riches, or because of changes in the weather (Ibid: 204, 205).

10. Lazarev infers that Petrov drew a line around the officers' tent (Ibid.: 207).

11. Lazarev's account is quite different. He said that after he had explained about the pistol, the Eskimo misunderstood, and in a minute flew into a rage. He hit him in the left side with his spear, tearing the clothing and leaving the point in his skin. The Eskimo grabbed a knife from behind his back, but Lazarev merely kept quiet and waved his hand to show that he was not afraid of threats. Just then Salnikov and another man came into the tent, and the Eskimo, seeing them, put back his knife "with the greatest coolness," pulled out the spear, and quietly left the tent. Lazarev said that he did not tell the sailors what had happened, fearful that they would avenge their officer (Ibid.: 209).

12. Lazarev says nothing at all about this episode or about the Eskimos having guns.

13. Lazarev said that they met the Pedler in Sitka on September 26 where it had gone to sell cargo to the Russian-American Company (Ibid.: 233), but Hillsen does not mention it.

14. In the meantime, Vasil'ev and the Otkrytie sailed to 71° 06' N latitude on the 29th. See Berkh's account.

15. Beechey named this same cape Point Hope, its present name.

16. The Bering Strait is a shallow body of water, and is nowhere deeper than 700 feet. The figure given in Hillsen's article is probably a misprint.

17. This information is not correct. Sitka Sound was "discovered" in 1775 by Don Juan de la Bodega y Quadra and Francisco Antonion Maurelle. In 1787, George Dixon named it after the Duke of Norfolk, which was later adopted by Vancouver (Orth 1967: 881).

18. Aleksandr Baranov established a fort called Novo-Arkhangel'sk six miles from the present town of Sitka in 1799. In 1802, it was attacked and destroyed by

Tlingits, but in 1804, after the Russians had defeated
an Indian force at the site of Sitka, the fort was
re-established at that location.

   19. Andrews 1922: 22, 60.

   20. At that time, the entire Aleutian Chain was often
called the Fox Islands. Lazarev said that a thousand men
had been brought from Kodiak for hunting, and that there
were 200 Russians (1950: 243).

   21. Lazarev spells Katlian, "Kotlilian," (Ibid.: 232).

   22. Aurel Krause said that the Russians called the
slaves "kalgi" (1956: 105), but this is not a Russian word.

IV

EARLY MARITIME TRADE WITH THE ESKIMO OF
BERING STRAIT AND THE INTRODUCTION OF FIREARMS[*]

Firearms are generally thought to have been introduced to the Eskimos of northwestern Alaska at mid 19th century by American whalers or traders. However, information in the accounts of two officers of the Vasil'ev-Shishmarev expedition to the American Arctic between 1819 and 1822 reveals that guns were sold in both the Siberian and the American Arctic as early as 1819, and were in use at Kotzebue Sound in 1820.

The information recorded in the journals of Lieutenant Aleksei P. Lazarev and Midshipman Karl K. Hillsen, both of the sloop Blagonamerennyi, is discussed here within the context of early 19th century trade in the Pacific Ocean, especially John Jacob Astor's Hawaiian trade and his attempts to extend his operations to the Arctic. The identity of the initial source of the firearms is thus derived from this analysis.

Observations concerning the use of firearms in 1820 at Kotzebue Sound and various related ethnographic facts are quoted verbatim from Hillsen's journal, which contains the first published account about the Buckland River Eskimos.

Firearms and ammunition apparently were first obtained by the Eskimo of Bering Strait in 1819, when an American captain named Gray[1] visited the Arctic supposedly "to verify the discoveries made in the north by Kotzebue," but actually to trade with the Eskimos; and again, in 1820 when officers of the Vasiliev-Shishmarev expedition reported that an American brig was trading at Bering Strait.

The explanation for Gray's voyage was given by Lieutenant Aleksei P. Lazarev, who said that Count Nikolai P. Rumiantsev, who had financed Otto von Kotzebue's expedition, had also sponsored Gray's journey (Lazarev 1950: 214). The statements for the trading of 1820 were made by both Lazarev and Midshipman Karl K. Hillsen, Lazarev's shipmate, in their respective journals. Hillsen also presented substantial evidence that the Eskimos of

* from Arctic Anthropology, 1975, Vol. 12, No. 1, pp. 1-8.

56

the Buckland River already possessed firearms in 1820 and
were anxious to trade for more. Moreover, after the
Russians refused to provide these people with ammunition,
and an altercation developed from an accident that resulted
in injury to an Eskimo, the Eskimos responded at first
with arrows, then with gunfire: "But," said Hillsen,
"when they started to shoot guns and the bullets began
piercing the skins [of walrus used as shields] the captain
ordered us to fire a falconet ball over their heads. They
quieted down for an instant hearing the whistle of the
ball, but soon raising a horrible cry shot arrows and
bullets at us again..." (Hillsen, 1849, Part 1: 231).

      The only vessel that could have supplied the Eskimos
with these guns was Captain Gray's. The demonstration of
this fact demands a detailed survey of the movements of
vessels trading with the Eskimos at this period as well
as those in the North Pacific at an earlier time leading
up to the Arctic trade. All of these contacts were
significant in the exposure of the Eskimos to the outside
world and the various degrees of acculturation that
followed. The history of acquisition of firearms by
peoples culturally dependent upon less effective weapons,
such as bow and arrow or spear, has generally been one of
economic revolution. In 1819-1820, so far as we can
ascertain, this was not the case with the Buckland River
Eskimo. It is indeed surprising that the Buckland people
had enough ammunition, a year after obtaining it, to attack
the Russians as they did. Either they had received a
large supply from Gray or they had hoarded it, perhaps in
the hands of chiefs for intertribal warfare or for
encounters such as this. In any event, they apparently
bought more from the American brig in 1820, not being able
to get it from the Russians, but none for about 30 years
after that. We do not know how much ammunition or how many
guns were obtained in 1820, but in economic terms, the
acculturative impact was probably minimal, although the
gunfire exchange with men of the outside world (the first
on record in northern Alaska) could have been nothing less
than a traumatic intercultural event.

      These intervening years have been erroneously assumed,
by historians and anthropologists, to have preceded the
first acquisition of firearms. It is Hillsen's journal
that definitely establishes the contrary. In his doctoral
dissertation, Don Charles Foote wrote that Lazarev had
said that Americans were trading firearms in August 1820,
as indeed he had, for Lazarev said an American brig had
come "to trade with the inhabitants fur for leather, sables,
rifles, gunpowder, and so on" (Foote 1965: 56; Lazarev
1950: 214). But in an article about American whalemen,
Foote rejected this statement and concluded that firearms
did not reach them until about 1848: "As early as 1820
Russian explorers accused Americans of introducing firearms,
powder and shot to the Eskimos around Kotzebue Sound.
But there is no evidence to support this claim. Rather,
it would seem that firearms did not reach Northwestern

Arctic Alaska until about 1848" (1964: 17).

Hillsen's journal, published as a three part article in Otechestvennye Zapiski in 1849, has never before been used in English for the history of western Alaska, nor, with the exception of Foote's dissertation, has Lazarev's, which was issued only in 1950. Foote's interpretation might have been considerably different had he been acquainted with Hillsen's journal. No other narratives of the Vasil'ev-Shishmarev expedition have been published, and the only other article of any length accruing from the three year journey was one about the Chukchi people by Captain-Lieutenant Gleb S. Shishmarev (1853). There are unresolved contradictions in the writings of Lazarev and Hillsen on the subject of firearms, and for that reason, and because Hillsen's journal is in a comparatively rare publication, the following pages will offer numerous verbatim quotations.(2)

Two sloops, the Otkrytie (Discovery) and the Blagonamerennyi (Good Intent), left Kronstadt in 1819 to spend two summers exploring the waters of the Siberian and Alaskan Arctic, especially to find a passage between the Atlantic and Pacific oceans. Hillsen and Lazarev were officers aboard the Blagonamerennyi, commanded by Shishmarev who had been to the Arctic with Kotzebue in 1816. The Otkrytie was commanded by Captain-Lieutenant Mikhail N. Vasil'ev, leader of the expedition.(3)

This expedition was looked upon by the government as a failure because no passage was found to the Atlantic and, contrary to the usual custom, no account of the expedition's activities was printed upon completion of the journey. However, Vasilii N. Berkh published a substantial resume of the expedition in his Chronological History of All Voyages to the Arctic only a year after their return home (1823, Part 2: 1-20). Despite the official snub by the Russians until the publication of Lazarev's journal in 1950, and its almost total neglect as a part of Alaskan history, the expedition not only recorded ethnographic information (and met Eskimos from the Buckland River for the first time), but discovered Nunivak Island and Cape Romanzof; learned definitely about a large river called the "Kuiukhtpak" (or Yukon); completed a survey of St. Lawrence Island begun by Kotzebue; sailed farther north than Captain James Cook had in 1778; and discovered Point Hope, which Shishmarev named Golovnin, and surveyed 90 miles in its vicinity.(4)

The Otkrytie and the Blagonamerennyi parted in the south Pacific to meet at Kotzebue Sound. Shishmarev, in the Blagonamerennyi, arrived at Unalaska on May 30 (Old Style calendar; June 10, New Style, or present day Gregorian calendar). On June 19th, he sailed north to St. Lawrence Island, and on June 30th proceeded to Kotzebue Sound. His entry to the sound was blocked by ice, but suddenly it moved out and he anchored near Chamisso

Island on July 11. The Otkrytie had not yet arrived, and since the men were bored by waiting, Shishmarev proposed a visit to the place where Kotzebue had seen "mountains of ice" in 1816 (later named Elephant Point by Frederick W. Beechey). On July 14 at 7 o'clock, 20 persons set out in a longboat and a skin boat for the shore. Shishmarev had told them that the shores were completely uninhabited, but only five hours after leaving the sloop, Hillsen said,

> We were surprised to see a large settlement con-
> sisting of a hundred or more conically-shaped
> skin tents on a long sandspit extending from
> the high shores for about a mile and a half
> inside the bay...Opposite each on the beach lay
> a baidara turned upside down. As soon as the
> inhabitants noticed us 150 persons gathered,
> armed from head to foot with spears, bows, and a
> few even with long rifles. Observing that, the
> captain ordered us to remove the sails and lay
> to in order to decide whether to go ashore or to
> return. Seeing that, the savages started to wave
> various furs and to shout "toki, toki" which
> meant to trade as we later found out.

The Russians went ashore and found the Eskimos eager to trade. They asked for goods like knives and hatchets, and especially "gunpowder and lead," which the Russians would not provide. Meanwhile the sailors had set up camp, and while they prepared dinner the officers, accompanied by the Eskimo chief, went toward the "ice mountains," passing a settlement of 101 conical skin tents on the way.[5]

After satisfying their curiosity about the ice cliffs, the Russians returned to the tents "accompanied again by the chief, and by women who joined us at this time and whom we had not seen at first." This tribe calls itself Tatui [probably a reference to tutu, or caribou] and to the question 'From where did they come?' they pointed to the southeast [direction of the Buckland River]. There were about 300 persons of both sexes.[6]

Having finished their supper of sour cabbage soup, the Russians prepared to return to the sloop. Although the wind was unfavorable, they hastened to leave because the Eskimos had become obstreperous, not having obtained the ammunition they desired. The Russians set out for the sloop, but had to return to shore because of heavy seas. The Eskimos apparently did not want them to land, but Shishmarev, wishing to appease them, ordered the remainder of the trade goods to be given to the chief. Then, all of the Eskimos began crowding around hoping to trade, and some even started to pilfer.

Mr. Petrov, the senior pilot, "taking advantage of their superstitions," was able to get rid of them by drawing a line in the sand and mumbling and spitting in the direction of the Russian tents. The Eskimos then

retreated, leaving the Russians to a brief rest, but at
dawn they began to cross the line. The Russians
immediately made preparations to leave, and haste became
especially imperative when two Eskimos were injured in
separate altercations.

They had not rowed far from shore, however, when
the Eskimos began to shoot at them with arrows, which the
Russians ignored. "But," said Hillsen, "when they started
to shoot guns and the bullets began piercing the skins,
the captain ordered us to fire a falconet ball over their
heads." The Eskimos responded with more arrows and
bullets, and began to get into their skin boats, whereupon
Shishmarev ordered another firing of the falconet. The
ball ripped out the entire side of a skin boat, injuring
one man, and the Eskimos then retreated.

At 7 o'clock on July 16 the Otkrytie arrived from
Petropavlosk and at 4 o'clock "an American brig entered
the bay and dropped anchor nor far from us. Its captain
by the name of Piget [Pigot] boarded the Otkrytie.(7)
He announced that he had come here from the Sandwich
[Hawaiian] Islands to trade furs with the local inhabitants.
We advised him to go to the smaller part of the sound as
close as possible to the northeastern shores but not to
go on land, and to permit the Indians on the brig only
after taking all precautions because these people were
crafty and angry. As proof we related our adventures with
them," said Hillsen, "and advised him of the principal
article [i.e., firearms] that they required. After nine
months we met him again on Vagu Island [Oahu] and learned
that he had a profitable trade following our advice"
[emphasis supplied].

This brig was the Pedler (identified by Lazarev
1950: 214), the same Pedler that had evacuated some of
the colonists from John Jacob Astor's Astoria on the
Columbia River in 1814, after it was taken over by the
North West Company. The knowledge of who owned this
vessel will eventually lead us to the probable source of
firearms traded to the Eskimos before 1820.

In order to track down this initial trade in firearms
we must briefly review earlier non-Russian activities in
the Alaskan Arctic and possible trading enterprises,
especially among the Americans. It is quite certain that
none of the explorers to northwestern Alaska prior to 1819
had sold guns to the Eskimos: Cook in 1778, Cossack Ivan
Kobelev to Little Diomede Island in 1779, the Billings
expedition to Cape Rodney in 1791 (and Kobelev's second
trip to Little Diomede Island, and then to King Island as
part of the Billings expedition) or Kotzebue in 1816.

The Russian-American Company, based far to the south,
had not yet sent trading ships to the Bering Strait. They
furthermore did not sell firearms to natives. The
Hudson's Bay Company posts were at that time too far to

the east for trade in such large and valuable commodities.
This leaves only the likelihood of guns coming from Russian
traders in Siberia through the Chukchi traders at posts like
the Anyui market on the Kolyma River, or from non-Russian
trading vessels. Since the trading of guns was prohibited
by the Russians in Siberia, this leaves only the trading
ships, which were American-owned, as we shall see.

Don Foote has come to the conclusion that muskets
seen at St. Lawrence Bay, Siberia, by Lazarev in 1821
could have come from Nizhne-Kolymsk as well as from the
Americans: July 1821, "The Russians observed two natives
at St. Lawrence Bay, Siberia, with muskets of British
manufacture. The Russians admitted the firearms might
have originated at the Kolyma Fair just as well as from
Captain Meek [of the Pedler]" (Foote 1965: 162). However,
this statement was incorrectly translated because Lazarev
actually said that the firearms could not have come from
the Kolyma: "One of them had, we saw, two muskets of
English manufacture, probably received from Americans who
had been here in the Bering Strait in 1820, since it is
not permitted to sell firearms to savages at Kolyma"
(U odnogo my videli dva mushketona angliiskoi raboty,
veroiatno, poluchennye ot amerikantsev, byvshikh zdes v
Beringovom prolive y 1820 godu, ibo na Kolyme ne pozvoleno
prodavat dikim ognestrelnoe oruzhie) (Lazarev 1950: 303).

That American traders were at Bering Strait by 1819
is not surprising, since their energies were a source of
admiration even to Lazarev, who observed that they seized
the opportunity to trade as soon as they had heard about
some new discovery (Lazarev 1950: 214). Trading by
Americans in the Pacific Ocean began shortly after Captain
Robert Gray called at the Hawaiian Islands following his
discovery of the Columbia River in 1789. Within ten
years after his return to the east coast of the United
States, New England traders had a virtual monopoly of the
Northwest Coast-Hawaiian Islands-Chinese fur trade. By
1791 there may have been as many as seven American vessels
trading on the Northwest Coast of America, and American
energies effectively reduced the British traders to only
one vessel by 1801, while their own numbers had increased
to 15 (Bradley 1968: 17, 18). By the early 1800s, some
American-owned vessels were taking goods to Ross, the
Russian-American Company's settlement established in 1812
on the California coast in present Sonoma County. Several
of these ships were owned by Astor who also had entertained
hopes of acquiring a trading foothold in Kamchatka and
the Arctic through efforts of his Kamchatkan agent, Peter
Dobell, and others who went north on his ships.

Of six American vessels that we know could have
been in Arctic waters between 1815 and 1820, half were
owned by Astor: The Forester, the Pedler and the Sylph
(the others were the Brutus, the Isabella and the San
Martin) (Golder 1917; Howay 1973). Americans, however,

had been on the coast of Kamchatka even before 1815
because the Russian-American Company manager, Alexander
A. Baranov, had agreed to at least seven contracts with
American captains for sea otter hunting and for trading
between 1808 and 1812, and at least two of them had disposed of the skins of Kamchatka or Okhotsk (Bancroft 1886:
479-81).

William J. Pigot (skipper of the Pedler in 1820)
was captain of the Forester when it was sent out in 1813
under English colors from the east coast of the United
States with supplies for Astoria. In 1814 both the
Pedler and the Forester were at Sitka, the Pedler
apparently then sailing to the Hawaiian Islands under
contract with Baranov to get provisions for Ross. After
delivering part of the supplies, the Pedler was held by
the Spanish at San Luis Obispo between August and October
1814 for illegal trading on the California coast, and by
the Russians from July 29, 1815 to sometime in October
for selling ammunition to the Indians at Sitka. The
Pedler then sailed to New York for trade goods and,
eventually, on to Oahu under command of John Meek. After
arriving there in May, 1820 she continued her voyage
under Pigot's command (Bancroft 1885: 271-72; Howay 1933:
127; Porter 1930: 504, 1931, Vol. 2: 644). From Oahu the
Pedler went to Sitka where 2620 sealskins were purchased
and then sailed to Kotzebue Sound (Howay 1934: 20),[8]
whence her meeting with the Russian sloops.

Before Pigot's departure from Kamchatka for Hawaii
in 1818, he had proposed a ten-year agreement with the
Russian government for whaling in the waters of eastern
Siberia under a trading group name of "Pigot, Davis,
Ebbets, Meek, and others." Dobell also offered a scheme
to P. I. Rikord, governor of Kamchatka, to supply goods
for the employees there, and to provide Chinese goods to
Kronstadt. However, both proposals were turned down and
the government, apprehensive of American enterprise, told
both Pigot and Dobell that they were no longer to live
in Okhotsk and Kamchatka (Tikhmenev 1939/40, Vol. 1: 234-41;
Howay 1932: 70; Golder 1917: 140).

Pigot, however, prevailed upon Count Rumiantsev to
send one Captain Gray to the North. According to Lazarev
(1950: 214-16), Vasiliev learned from Rikord in 1820 that
Rumiantsev did not realize that the American proposal to
explore and to check Kotzebue's men actually meant
Russian sponsorship for a voyage to investigate fur trading
possibilities north of the Bering Strait. Gray said that
he explored the entire shore from Shishmaref Inlet to
Kotzebue Sound, measuring the depth, and that the map was
very inaccurate. He also told Rikord that in 1820 there
would be further exploration by him or some other craft,
and Shishmarev was curious as to the Pedler's business.
Said Lazarev:

Curiousity forced Shishmarev to go to the

American brig, inviting me along, to look at
the map composed by Gray, more so because he
himself [Shishmarev] had been a participant in
the placing of the shore and sound on Kotzebue's
map. Upon arriving on the brig we saw that the
mentioned map was nothing else but a roughly
copied one from Kotzebue's map, on a very thin
transparent paper, and it was obvious that
Messrs. Americans still had no time to transpose
it onto good paper. On it were made a few minor
changes with reference to the capes and mountains,
but instead of the strait at the mouth of Good
Hope [the Goodhope River] is shown a lake.

Showing us this map the Americans tried with
all their might to assure us of its correctness,
confirming Gray's story that he allegedly did
measure all the places near the shore with a
pole, and though he went along the shore, he did
not see the strait.

Captain Rikord had given Gray an interpreter in 1819,
who was, in 1820, a sailor on the Otkrytie. The interpreter told them that the Americans had stopped near
Shishmaref Inlet in the longboat, but did not think they
went all the way into Kotzebue Sound. Lazarev concluded
that Gray would not have gone on the longboat the entire
distance "without any useful purpose" when he could have
gone in his ship, and that the purpose of the Americans
was not a voyage of discovery, but to trade with the
inhabitants without interference from the Vasil'ev-
Shishmarev expedition since they had sailed under
Rumiantsev's auspices and, by inference, the Russian
government.

Gray's vessel in 1819 was possibly the Sylph, the
Astor-owned brig in which Dobell left Kamchatka in 1819.
According to F. W. Howay, this brig, commanded by "Dubell,"
arrived in the Hawaiian Islands in late 1819 or early
1820 after "'laying up some time at the northward'"
(Howay 1933: 147). The "northward" at that time was
usually interpreted as the Northwest Coast, but Howay
thought that the Sylph had been on the northern Asiatic
coast, which apparently was the case, Dobell probably
taking over command from Gray after his voyage across the
Bering Strait in late 1819.

Despite Hillsen's convincing encounters with the
Eskimos and their guns, we have to reckon with the fact
that Lazarev mentioned none of them; Lazarev's account of
the episode in which Hillsen said he shot a blank
cartridge in a man's face differs considerably from
Hillsen's.[9] According to Lazarev, the Eskimo apparently
misunderstood his explanation about the pistol, and
immediately flying into a rage, struck him in the left side
with a spear. The spear point tore his clothes and picked
his skin. The Eskimo then pulled a knife from his back,
but Lazarev said that he kept cool and waved his hand to

show that he was unafraid of threats. Just then Salnikov
and another man entered the tent and the Eskimo, upon
seeing them, put his knife back "with the greatest
coolness," pulled the spear out of Lazarev's clothes and
quietly left the tent. Lazarev said that he did not tell
the sailors what had transpired, fearful they would try
to avenge their officer (Lazarev 1950: 209).

One of Lazarev's most mystifying statements is that
the Russians wanted to instill fear into the Eskimos by
shooting a gull on the wing with a rifle. This produced
the fear they expected, Lazarev writing as if the Eskimos
had never seen a gun before (1950: 205-7).[10]

Why would Hillsen mention repeatedly, in various
contexts, a subject about which Lazarev said nothing?
Perhaps Lazarev deliberately omitted these episodes for
official reasons, because, according to the Russian editor
of his account, he wanted to get his journal published
very badly, and to admit that firearms had been inadvisably
used by the Russians, or that firearms were already in
use by northern natives, might have reflected unfavorably
on Russian activities. As it turned out, publication of
the journal was blocked by red tape involving the printing
of government instructions and maps especially when
Vasil'ev did not have time to check and authorize Lazarev's
use of official data.

We should not overlook the fact that Hillsen's
journal was published 27 years after his visit to the
Arctic; yet his account accords with Lazarev's in most
other respects. Very possibly the reason he could mention
all of the episodes concerning gunfire was because it was
27 years after the journey, and he was not subject to
official embarrassment. There appear to be too many such
episodes for Hillsen to have invented them, since he was
apparently copying from his notes. Omission of this kind
of subject matter instead of fictional elaboration would
have been more logical for Hillsen, especially if he were
still in Russian service at the time his article was
published. It is of interest, however, that he did not
mention either the "lieutenant" or the "captain" by name
when discussing guns and their consequences.

Contradictions seemed to be the order of the day
at that time. For instance, the American Gray said he had
investigated Kotzebue Sound, but his interpreter thought
that they had not gone into the Sound. Perhaps they had
not sailed that far in the longboat, testing the depth,
but nothing was said about Gray's ship not having gone
there for trading. Then, there is the unexplained fact
of why "Messrs. Americans" of 1820 had not had time to
transpose corrections to Kotzebue's map onto good paper
when Gray was supposed to have made the map for Rumiantsev
the year before. It would have been very foolish of Gray
to have presented him with such a map, and apparently he
did not, because it was on board the Pedler. But why?

From 1820, no trading of firearms (or of any goods
for that matter, except by an occasional Russian-American
Company vessel after St. Michael was established in
1833) appears to have been undertaken at Bering Strait
and northward until the influx of whalers and traders in
the 1850s. This was partly because Americans were banned
from Siberian ports by the ukase of 1821, and partly
because the traders did not find the far north particularly
lucrative. Furthermore, business under such marginal
circumstances represented considerable capital, and Astor,
the sponsor of the early Arctic enterprises, left the
Hawaiian trade in 1828, when he sold his last brig
Tamaahmaah to the Hawaiian king. Dobell confined his
sporadic trading to Siberia (Dobell 1831) and Pigot moved
with his part-Hawaiian family and several other traders
to the then-uninhabited Fanning Island after his return
from Kotzebue Sound in 1820 (Bingham 1847: 112, 118).

The acquisition of these firearms apparently had no
lasting effect on life in the north. Only seven years
later, Beechey engaged in a fight with Eskimos (presumably
from the Buckland River or vicinity) who fought with bows
and arrows. The Eskimos exhibited considerable defensive
strategy, but Beechey thought they were entirely
unacquainted with firearms because they wore armor made
only of eider duck skins and caribou hide (Beechey 1831,
Vol. 2: 556-57). From 1827 until the search for Sir John
Franklin between 1848 and 1854, which coincided with the
huge numbers of whalers and traders to the Bering Strait
area, we have no documented information about the people
of the Buckland-Kotzebue Sound region, and so we do not
know whether hunting, especially that of caribou, for
which guns were mostly used later on, had changed. Only
during mid-century were firearms sold in large enough
quantities to cause any appreciable decline in game
resources, or to alter the Eskimo material inventory.

The relationship of two events that occurred at
roughly the same time--the acquisition of firearms and
the beginning of the only known "migration" in early
historic times by the same people--is a tantalizing one,
but apparently no more than a coincidence, because it has
been demonstrated that the movement of Inupiak-speakers to
the Yupik area of Norton Sound was a result of trade
(Ray 1964b: 63-64). Yet the cultural characteristics of
these people later called Malemiut--their boldness, energy
and aggressiveness, which contributed to their success as
traders--were all displayed to the Russians of 1820.

Notes

1. Not the Gray of Columbia River fame. Don Charles
Foote calls Gray "Nicky Gray" (1965: 54), but I have been
unable to find a record of Gray's first name even in
Foote's references. He may have been misled by a footnote
in M. I. Belov's history, which reads "Nekii Gray," or
"A certain Gray" (Belov 1956: 453).

2. Both Hillsen's and Lazarev's journals are in
the form of narratives prepared for publication, not as
daily logs. A. I. Solov'ev, editor of Lazarev's journal,
does not identify Hillsen other than saying he was a
midshipman on the Blagonamerennyi. My attempts to ascertain
his whereabouts in 1849 and the circumstances of
publication have proved fruitless. Hillsen is spelled
Gillesem and Gilsen in Lazarev's 1950 publication, but
Gill'sen, with a soft sign after the second "l", in his
own account.
   The complete text of Hillsen's journal was translated
by Rhea Josephson and Dorothy Jean Ray and is deposited
in the Dartmouth College Libraries. My translations of
Lazarev's journal and Belov's material were checked by
Ludmila Kuvshinoff and Martha N. Trofimenko.

3. In 1819 four ships left Kronstadt, two of them to
explore the Antarctic and two to explore the Arctic. The
head of the First, or Antarctic, Division was Captain (of
the second rank) Faddei F. Bellingshausen, also skipper
of the Vostok (East). The other vessel of this division,
the Mirnyi (Peaceful), was commanded by Captain-Lieutenant
Mikhail P. Lazarev, Aleksei's brother.

4. Vasil'ev's first sighting of Nunivak Island was
disputed by V. S. Khromchenko and A. K. Etolin who, also
in 1821, were sent north by the Russian-American Company
in the brigs Golovnin and Baranov. During that summer,
four large Russian vessels and a small boat explored the
western coast of Alaska. Vasil'ev first saw Nunivak
Island on July 6, 1821 and named it "Discovery Island"
after his sloop, and Etolin, of Khromchenko's expedition,
saw it on August 12. In 1860, P. A. Tikhmenev said that
Khromchenko had been its discoverer, but it is clear from
Vasilii Berkh's account, published only two years after it
was discovered, that the honor fell to Vasil'ev (Tikhmenev
1939/40, Part 1: 331; Berkh 1823, Part 2: 47, 57).
   In 1816 Kotzebue had recognized the existence of
the Yukon when he said that between Bristol Bay and Norton
Sound "A considerable stream from the interior of America
is said to empty itself here, and to form sandbanks on the
coast) (1821, Vol. 3: 263-64).
   Cape Golovnin was later named Point Hope by F. W.
Beechey in 1826.

5. The information about the Buckland River people, which was quoted verbatim in the original Arctic Anthropology article, has been paraphrased here since the original quotations can be found in context in Hillsen's account.

6. Lazarev said there were 200 persons (1950: 204, 209). This figure may not have included children.

7. Lazarev said that the owner of the brig was Pigot, and the captain, John Meek (1950: 214). Howay said that Pigot took over from John Meek at the Hawaiian Islands for this voyage (1934: 20). Porter said that Pigot was the agent, but that the Pedler left for the voyage in the summer of 1820 "with Meek and Pigot in charge" (1931, Vol. 2: 654).

8. Howay 1934: 20. Porter, who accumulated a vast amount of information about the Pedler, does not mention its 1820 voyage to the Arctic.

9. Solov'ev, the Russian editor to Lazarev's journal, does not mention these discrepancies; in fact, he mentions few of the discrepancies that appear here and there in the two journals.

10. It is most interesting that Kotzebue, four years earlier, had reported a similar experience in the Cape Espenberg area. He shot a snipe to see "what impression a shot would make on them...The sound occasioned the greatest fright..." (1821, Vol. 1: 229).

V

THE KHEUVEREN LEGEND*

In July 1880, Captain C. L. Hooper of the U.S. Revenue Marine steamer Thomas Corwin, seized from the Leo 50 gallons of contraband alcohol that was being sold to the Alaskan Eskimos as "Bay-rum," "Jamaica ginger," "Painkiller," and "Florida water." Captain Hooper's interpreter told the Eskimos at Cape Blossom in Kotzebue Sound about the incident, and by September when the Corwin returned to Saint Michael, 150 miles to the south, the story had already preceded her. Captain Hooper said, however, that the affair had become "so exaggerated and overdrawn as to be quite unrecognizable, as it accused us of sinking vessels and shooting down their crews as they attempted to escape over the ice."(1)

This simple tale is a well-substantiated example of how a folk tale can develop from fact and quickly change to fantasy in its travels across tribal boundaries and dialect changes. In parallel fashion, the "Kheuveren legend," as it has become known in writings about the North, is even more amazing in its growth of many parts over a much longer period of time.

The Kheuveren legend is the story of a Russian fort that was supposedly built in 1648 on the Alaskan side of the Bering Strait by survivors of a boat that had drifted from Siberia. In the late 1700's, Russians in Siberia believed it still existed as a full-fledged fortification, and that its inhabitants had maintained their Russian culture, religion and heavy beards throughout that entire time.

This folk tale developed in Siberia and northern Alaska, a vast area that was largely unknown and unmapped until the early 19th century. The date 1648 was 80 years before Vitus Bering sailed through the Bering Strait, and 93 years before he discovered Alaska hundreds of miles to the southeast. It was 130 years before James Cook made the first chart of the coast of western Alaska, and 170 years before the Russians, who had settled the Aleutians and southern Alaska after 1741, finally began expanding to the North.

The Cossacks had arrived on the Kolyma River on the northern shore of Siberia in 1644, and by 1700 knew that a

* The Alaska Journal, Summer 1976, pp. 146-53.

land with many trees, animals, fish and people existed many hundreds of miles to the east beyond a body of water. But the earliest knowledge about it received from the Siberian Chukchi, as well as from Alaskan Eskimos who were sometimes held prisoners in Siberia, often had a fictional and mythical air about it.

The first substantial information about the Bering Strait area was recorded between 1763 and 1765 by Nikolai Daurkin, a Chukchi who had been trained as a cossack. Daurkin had been captured as a child in the Chukchi campaigns of the 1730's, and was reared by Major Dmitrii Pavlutskii and his wife. In the 1760's, he was sent back to his homeland to scout among his people for trading and exploring information. Being a Chukchi he was able to get new facts about both Siberia and Alaska while traveling with his kinsmen on the Chukchi Peninsula and nearby islands where he met Eskimos from the mainland of Alaska.

His maps of the western Alaskan coast are the first to be drawn from "field research" despite their secondhand nature, and the one of 1765--with which we are concerned-- has a coastline extending roughly from Point Hope to Norton Sound. Though greatly distorted, as well it might be under the circumstances, there are four islands in the strait, including Fairway Rock and King Island. Daurkin also reported four Alaskan place-names 13 years before Captain Cook sailed along the coast: "Tikegan," or Point Hope; "Okibian," or King Island; "Kyng-Myn," or Wales; and "Kheuveren."[2]

It is with this map that the Kheuveren legend actually began.

Daurkin's "Kheuveren" was not a Russian fort, however, but an actual Eskimo village named Kauwerak, which is evident when the names are analyzed linguistically. With only two changes in orthography, Kheuveren becomes "Kheuwerek": first the substitution of a "w" for the "v" sound, and second, the Eskimo ending "k" for the Chukchi ending "n," which was invariably used in Siberian reports. The "v" sound was often used by persons not from the Kauwerak area, and has been retained in a present spelling, "Kaviruk," a river that is only a few miles from the old site of Kauwerak located on the Kuzitrin River.[3]

Daurkin's map has two unique features; a drawing of a building on the banks of a "Kheuveren River," and a notation describing the circumstances of the founding of this place. The building in Daurkin's drawing is a typical Eskimo dwelling, surrounded by what appears to be a fence made of oval posts. Men in typical Eskimo clothing stand on both the ground and a strangely shaped structure that looks like an elevated platform, or watchtower. The note says that "the fort near the Kheuveren River has been constructed; the structure is a wooden one; and they have an elder [or chief] called by the name Inakh Lun [Inakhlun] who is not tall, and is not only fat but also is strong; who [the people] came from their far lands not many years ago; according to my inquiry is said that he arrived in 1761 and built the fort."(4)

Daurkin was thus describing and illustrating an Alaskan Eskimo settlement on the Kheuveren River, and it would have remained Eskimo in the annals of history--and we would have no Kheuveren legend--had it not been for two occurrences about the same time. One was the repeated copying of Daurkin's map and its accompanying illustration by various Russian officials in eastern Siberia, with the result that the building and the people became Russified. The other was the publication of Gerhard Müller's history of Siberia in 1758 with information about the Semen Dezhnev expedition of 1648.

Müller, who was historian for Bering's expeditions, had found information about Dezhnev's expedition in the archives of Yakutsk only some 20 years before, or in 1736.(5) In 1655 Dezhnev had dictated some protests against Mikhail Staduchin's claim that he, and not Dezhnev, had discovered the Anadyr River and its rich deposits of walrus tusks. From these documents Müller learned that Dezhnev had set out from Nizhne-Kolymsk--800 miles from the Bering Strait--with seven boats, five of which foundered soon after. Dezhnev's boat was wrecked somewhere below the mouth of the Anadyr, which Dezhnev said he discovered after wandering around, lost, for 10 weeks. The seventh boat apparently was also cast up somewhere in southern Siberia.

Although Dezhnev did live at Anadyrsk, some persons have doubted that he had ever navigated the strait, but had arrived there by land. Consequently, writers of Siberian history have found themselves in opposite camps, and numerous papers and books have been written to prove that Dezhnev did or did not sail through the strait. He is an important personage in Russian history, and in 1898, on the 250th anniversary of his voyage, East Cape, the Siberian promontory closest to America, was renamed Cape Dezhnev.(6)

It is impossible to ascertain, more than 200 years after the beginning of this legend, whether Müller's information' about the Dezhnev expedition or the drawings were more responsible for transforming an Eskimo village into a Russian fort. The drawings were certainly visually tantalizing when caftans, pants, boots, and tri-cornered hats replaced Eskimo clothes, and a trim squared-up edifice supplanted the original building that probably represented an Eskimo ceremonial house.(7)

But most important for the fate of this folk tale was the supposition that the seventh Dezhnev boat had drifted to the American coast. Since information about any pre-contact Russian forts was recorded for the first time only in 1779, the most likely candidate for making a presumed connection of this boat with a rumored Russian fort was

Ivan Kobelev, a cossack sotnik ("leader of a hundred"), who made a trip by umiak to Little Diomede Island that year. In the report of his trip he said that the Anadyr Russians also thought that such a colony existed on the mainland of America, but they were probably the same Russians who had copied the map and changed the drawing.

Kobelev was born in Anadyrsk in 1739 (in the same decade that Daurkin was captured as a boy) and served as the first official cossack interpreter of the Chukchi language. He lived to be over 100 years old. Kobelev and Daurkin were acquainted, and from what we know, theirs was an uneasy relationship, with an intense rivalry.

Kobelev learned some strange facts about the mainland people on his first visit to Little Diomede in 1779. There, he said, was a village called "Kyngovei" (actually, Kingigan, the Eskimo name for Wales), which was situated on "Chevren" (Kauwerak) Creek where "they still retain their Russian speech, pray from books, write, worship before holy images, and are distinguished by their large and heavy beards from the other Americans." When Kobelev asked the Diomede people to take him there, they refused, but the chief promised to deliver a letter.

Kobelev also reported that Ekhilka, an inhabitant of a Chukchi village, "Kangun Tsvunmin," had gone to the American mainland five times for war and trade, and had become friendly with a man from "Ukipan" (a man from King Island) who gave him a board "3 spans long [about 24 inches] and 5 verchoks [i.e., 5 vershoks or 8.75 inches] wide" carved with red characters on one side and with black ones on the other. It supposedly had come from the Russian fort. Furthermore, it was said that the Russians needed iron, and had asked that a letter be delivered to Anadyrsk. (Bear in mind that this post was established by Dezhnev after 1648.) Kobelev was also told how the people prayed together in a large dwelling, made the sign of the cross, and "set up little boards out of doors with written characters, before which they hold common prayer."[8]

Kobelev's obsession with finding the Russian fort kept the fire of the legend burning. In June 1791, as a member of the Joseph Billings expedition, his dreams of reaching the "Kheuveren River" were almost realized when he crossed the Bering Strait from Siberia in a flotilla of 17 Chukchi umiaks. Kobelev's report mentions only 10 umiaks, but 7 others also made the trip under Daurkin's leadership. Never had the rivalry of these two men been more obvious than during this American expedition. Kobelev never once mentioned Daurkin's name in his report, and Daurkin erased and polished over Kobelev's name in a message that he had cut into a piece of walrus tusk, apparently intended for Captain Billings.[9]

En route to the mainland Kobelev revisited Big and Little Diomede Islands, and on June 11, arrived at

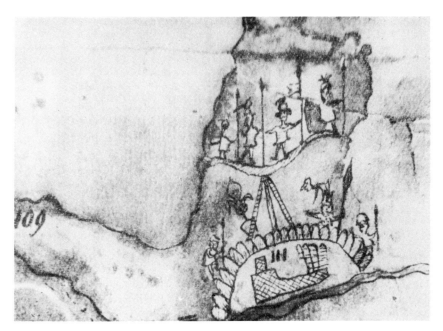

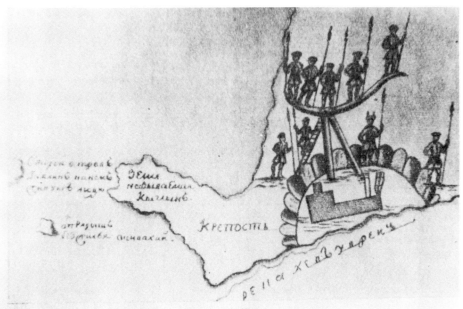

N. Daurkin's map of 1765, showing the alleged fort on the
river Kheuveren (above). The human figures, though crude,
are obviously natives, but after the map had been recopied
several times, as by A. Dakudin (below), several years
later, they looked like contemporary European soldiers.

"Kigigmen" (Kingigan, or Wales). Kobelev reported that the
village had 50 dwellings, but no one was home at the time
of his brief visit. (The inhabitants probably hid when
they saw a fleet of 17 skin boats coming from the west,
bearing their old enemies, the Chukchi.) The flotilla
proceeded southward on the same day to search for the
Kheuveren fort, but when they reached the entrance to what
Kobelev called "Kheverin Bay" (Port Clarence) they were
stopped by ice. The next day Kobelev persuaded the Chukchi
to take him to "Ukiben [King Island]."

The King Islanders met them wearing "kuiaks," or
Chukchi armor. They were in battle readiness with bows
and arrows drawn, and spears at hand. Kobelev asked them why
they were met in such a manner, and the islanders explained
that it was their "custom." Once ashore, Kobelev's party
was treated cordially by the 170 inhabitants and, through an
interpreter, was invited to walk freely through the settlement. They engaged in a lively trade, the Russians and
Chukchi bartering spears, knives, hatchets, "palmas" (long
knives with a wide, one-sided blade attached to a long
handle), iron pots, and beads for furs.

On this island, Kobelev met 10 Eskimos from the
Kheuveren River--that is, from the village of Kauwerak--who
had come the year before in three skin boats for trade, [10]
but he was unable to learn anything about the settlement
(i.e., the "fort") because the interpreters would translate
nothing except the fact that the people had heard his name
from the Diomeders after his visit of 1779. The interpreters finally left him so they would not have to translate.

Kobelev and the Kauwerak people then communicated by
sign language, and it was through this inexact technique
that Kobelev's belief in a Russian fort on the American
mainland was reinforced. (Pantomime was apparently his mode
of communication also on Little Diomede in 1779.) He
reported that when he spoke Russian, the people pointed to
their tongues, and then toward their homeland. They even
"crossed" themselves surreptitiously when they waved toward
their land. They invited him there by pulling on his
clothing and pointing to the east, and stroked both Kobelev's
and their faces and chests to show "a big and lasting
friendship."

The Kobelev-Daurkin party returned to Siberia shortly
thereafter, but on July 28, Billings in the Glory of Russia
(Slava Rossii) sailed to the American mainland from Siberia.
Billings, who had been one of Captain Cook's assistants,
was employed by Russia's Catherine II to explore Russian
America. In 1790, Billings had explored Prince William
Sound, and in the early summer of 1791 began his investigations of Cook Inlet, but he suddenly curtailed his work
and left for Siberia. Learning that both Kobelev and
Daurkin had gone to America in the vicinity of where they
suspected the Russian fort to be, he sailed across the
strait and anchored near Sledge Island and Cape Rodney.

During the four days at anchor, members of the expedition pursued the quest for the fort, but concluded that it did not exist. Lieutenant Gavriil Sarychev said there was only a settlement "built largely of driftwood," and Martin Sauer, the secretary, wrote, "Not withstanding all my endeavours, I could not find any body that knew aught of this matter, or had ever heard of any such place existing."

Sauer himself indirectly attributed the myth of a Russian fort to Kobelev when he said, "Kobeleff supposes them to be the remains of the shipwrecked companions of Deshneff, a Russian adventurer who left the river Lena [the Kolyma] with seven vessels in 1648."[11]

Despite their failure to find the Russian fort, the men of the expedition made many observations about the people camped near Cape Rodney, and from the combined writings of Sarychev, Sauer, and Karl Merck, the expedition's naturalist, we have the first substantial ethnographic notes about any Alaskan Eskimo group north of the Aleutian Islands.

The Russians began their northward explorations from southern Alaska in 1818 when a man named Korsakovskii was commissioned to explore both the Nushagak and the Kheuveren rivers, although the maps drawn by Sauer and Sarychev clearly showed the Kheuveren flowing into the Bering Strait more than 500 miles north of the Nushagak. Korsakovskii was unable to get **farther** north than the Kuskokwim River.

In 1821, a third expedition made inquiries about the supposed fort. Aleksandr Avinov, of an Arctic expedition headed by Mikhail N. Vasiliev, asked about its existence when they were in the vicinity of Cape Newenham and Good-news Bay, but without results. Vasilii Berkh, in his history, "Chronological History of all Voyages to the Arctic," published in St. Petersburg in 1823, said that Avinov "collected reliable information from local inhabitants that northward along the whole American shore, so far as is known to them, lived one nation [i.e., native Americans]. The report by those who were in these places with the land expedition of 1818 and 1819 [Korsakovskii] undertaken by the American Company in Kadiak that some European people lived on the mainland coast north of the Kuskokvin [sic] River proved to be incorrect."[12]

Finally, in 1861, Petr Tikhmenev, reviewing the activities of the Russian-American Company and Korsakovskii's inquiries, said that information "received about the white men from the natives was so conflicting that it was decided to repeat the search. Investigation made in the following years proved that the supposition that there are descendants of the cossacks in America is groundless."[13]

Yet, in 1944, the legend reappeared more vigorously

than ever as "a lost colony of Novgorod" in a reputable
journal. The colony, this time, was supposedly situated
on Kenai Peninsula, 400 miles south of Seward Peninsula
because a site of 31 "well-preserved European houses"
reportedly was found during a "United States government
survey" in 1937. Such a European village is unknown today,
but on the basis of an unconfirmed archaeological site and
on a letter from a Russian priest, Father Herman, in 1794,
the author decided that the houses were "nothing else than
those of the long lost colony founded by the subjects of
Ivan the Terrible [i.e., Dezhnev's men]."(14) This is
pure fiction.

In 1948, A. V. Efimov, a Soviet historical geographer,
concluded from the unsupported evidence contained in this
article that "it can be considered as proven that a Russian
settlement appeared in Alaska about 300 years ago in the
seventeenth century," and that "Alaska had not only one
but several, and possibly numerous, Russian settlements"
similar to this, dating back long before documented
Russian discoveries.(15) This, of course, was merely
speculative, and is not corroborated by archaeological
evidence.

From tracing the steps in its development, it is evident
that the "Kheuveren legend" became a part of Alaskan history
mainly through the persistence of early explorers trying
to verify rumors that had developed from incomplete or
misinterpreted information originating in a remote area.
That the Russian fort grew out of an Eskimo village is
conclusive, but what else can be derived from the maps and
reports?

A few facts in these 200-year-old reports are apparently
contemporary historical events, which are still retold in
folk tales that I have recorded in the Kauwerak area.
Daurkin's drawing, which is the first known illustration of
war or raid in the Bering Strait area, corresponds in
several respects to elements of "The Last Siberian Invasion,"
a folk tale that is always related as a victory for the
Alaskans. The "battle" of this story took place near
Kauwerak, and the "fortress" in Daurkin's drawing seems to
illustrate defensive measures taken by the Eskimos. Both
John E. Kakaruk and William Oquilluk, of Kauwerak parentage,
said that skins from umiaks were used to barricade the rear
of the village against attacks. Young men with spears went
outside the barricade, and the old men and women stayed
within. The "fence posts" in Daurkin's drawing, therefore,
might represent umiak skins.

Other elements are similar. Because of the flat
perspective, the towerlike structure may not be a watchtower, but may represent pathways, ditches, or bulwarks on
the ground beyond the fence. The four men on the curved
surface might be an advance guard of defenders at the rear
of the village, which was located on a downstream bend of
the river where invaders could leave their boats and sneak

into the back. The uneven terrain, which is still visible
behind the old house mounds, might have been old ditches
dug as defenses, although Henry B. Collins, the archaeologist
who made a reconnaissance examination of the old site long
after it was abandoned, thought they were probably natural
phenomena resulting from ground ice.(16)

Another Kauwerak folk tale, however, attempts to
explain these irregularities in the ground, and in doing so,
reaffirms Daurkin's story that the "fort" on the "Kheuveren
River" had been established as a planned Eskimo community
during historical times. According to William Oquilluk, the
settlement was founded by a legendary person named Tudlik
(a popular Kauwerak name, "Inakhlun's" name apparently
having been forgotten) who "invited people [after a time of
famine] from the upper end of Tuksuk clean up to Noxapaga
to make a village" near a sand bar on the Kuzitrin. The
place was flat, but the leader "told the people to gather
up ground from different places in order to make a village,
and they dug in the back, this ground from here, there,
and...further in order to build up the houses. The front
houses are facing to the river, and the back of the houses
faces to the west. So, in the middle of this town on the
river side they built a great big dance hall they call kazgi
from all that driftwood [as Sarychev had reported] they bring
from the coast in order to build the houses...of Kauwerak."

The Siberian wars ended during Tudlik's (or Inakhlun's)
time, when only "two men of the whole army of Siberia" were
left alive after a raid so they could return to Siberia with
the message that they had better not attack Kauwerak
again, or everyone would be killed.

Other portions of the early reports can be interpreted
from Eskimo culture itself. The "large dwelling" in which
the Russians supposedly gathered to pray was surely the
Eskimos' ceremonial house. The religious images and other
ceremonial objects, which Kobelev learned about through
pantomime, and the board with red and black characters, were
undoubtedly Eskimo objects. At Kauwerak itself during the
winter caribou hunting season, a shaman, in the presence
of hunters, consulted divination boards with masklike
carvings every morning out of doors to forecast their
hunting luck. This was a gathering that could very well
resemble a religious observance. The Kauwerak people also
used boards with marks to denote the passing of the months
according to the moon, and made many sculptured and engraved
objects of wood and ivory, the incisions filled with red
and black colors.

Tikhmenev's conclusions supposedly buried this myth
forever, but in the event it should show further signs of
regeneration, it should be remembered that the Eskimos have
no folk tales or traditions of the existence of a Russian
fort, nor is there such an archaeological site. Furthermore,
two questions should be kept in mind: By what genetic magic

had the Cossacks of 1779 been able to maintain a purely
Russian physical identity after seven generations of
Eskimo mothers dating from 1648? And through what clair-
voyance did these great-great-great-great-grandchildren
(all Eskimos by then) know about a trading post at Anadyrsk,
which had not yet been built at the time of the alleged
shipwreck 130 years before?

Notes

1. Hooper 1881, pages 21, 61.

2. Masterson and Brower 1948, page 27 (footnote);
Fedorova 1964, page 97.
This is not the first time, however, that four islands
had been placed in the strait. The same four islands
(Big Diomede, Little Diomede, King Island and Fairway Rock)
were shown on a map made by Mikhail Gvozdev after he and
Ivan Fedorov had sailed from Kamchatka to Cape Prince of
Wales to discover Alaska for the first time in 1732.

3. Soviet historians and geographers, who have been
interested in this supposed Russian installation, have not
identified the Kheuveren site as Kauwerak village, but have
usually placed the "fort"--in lieu of firsthand research
on Seward Peninsula--either on the Koyuk or the Yukon
rivers. M. B. Chernenko located the fort on the Kuzitrin
River, but apparently did not know of Kauwerak's existence
(Chernenko 1957).
Svetlana G. Fedorova had concluded that the Kheuveren
was the Koyuk River, partly on the supposition that the
"Kheuveren" was unforested, and partly on a mistake made
by Peter Simon Pallas the historian who redrew Ivan
Kobelev's map of 1779 for his history. Being unfamiliar
with Seward Peninsula, Dr. Fedorova did not know that
there are many stands of willow, alder, and large cotton-
woods on the upper Kuzitrin and nearby streams such as the
Pilgrim River. Kobelev had located 69 settlements, 61 of
them with names, between Kotzebue Sound and the vicinity
of Koyuk from information that he received on Little
Diomede Island in 1779, but Pallas divided them into two
groups: one located north of Norton Sound on a coastline
"nach Cap. Cook," and the other far to the south on the
coast of the Yukon and Kuskokwim deltas. All of the
settlements, however, belong to Seward Peninsula, as
Kobelev had drawn them, because I recorded the majority
of them in the same sequence as Kobelev's. Kobelev's
"Kheuveren" had flowed into an unnamed body of water in
the position of the yet undiscovered Port Clarence, but
Pallas had substituted Norton Sound for it instead. (See
D. J. Ray, "Eskimo Place-Names in Bering Strait and
Vicinity," for a complete discussion of this map.)

4.   Fedorova 1964, page 98 (footnote).

5.   In Gerhard Müller 1758, three volumes. This collection was published serially in Russian the same year in Volumes one and two of Ezhemiesiachnyia sochineniia i izvestiia o uchenykh, and was translated into English in 1761.

6.   Fisher 1973, page 9. This article is the latest and most comprehensive one about Dezhnev in the English language. (Since this was written, Dr. Fisher has written an even more detailed study of this topic in The Voyage of Semen Dezhnev in 1648 (1981).)

7.   Fedorova illustrates and discusses changes in the drawings in her article, 1964, pages 97-101. Daurkin's original drawing and one of the copies are illustrated here.

8.   Information about Daurkin's map is from Masterson and Brower 1948, and from Fedorova 1964. Information about Kobelev's 1779 journal is from Masterson and Brower 1948, and Chernenko 1957, and Fedorova 1964.

9.   Fedorova illustrates Daurkin's message on ivory in her article, 1964, page 106.

10.   In her discussion of why she equated the Kheuveren River with the Koyuk, Svetlana Fedorova said that people from the Kuzitrin River would not likely stay a year on King Island because they lived so close, but that the Koyuk people, who lived farther away, would. The opposite is true, however. The Kauwerak people from the Kuzitrin River and the King Islanders had trading and hunting partnerships, and were in constant communication. The King Islanders had little, or no, contact with the Koyuk people.

11.   Sarychev 1806-1807; Sauer 1802.

12.   Berkh 1823b.

13.   Tikhmenev 1939-40, Part 1, page 302.

14.   Farrelly 1944, page 34.

15.   Efimov 1948, page 152.

16.   Personal communication, 1963.

"Redoubt St. Michael (Norton Sound)", and "Inhabitants of Norton Sound". Sketches by I. G. Voznesenskii, 1843.

VI

SAINT MICHAEL IN THE NINETEENTH CENTURY

(NOTE: This essay was an introduction for Dr. H. M.
W. Edmonds' ethnography of the Eskimos living in the
vicinity of Saint Michael, published in the <u>Anthropological
Papers</u> of the University of Alaska, Vol. 13, No. 2, 1966.
Edmonds went to Alaska in the autumn of 1889 as a member
of J. Henry Turner's party, which was surveying the
Alaska-Canada boundary in the vicinity of the Porcupine
River. He made subsequent trips in 1898 and 1901. His
report, based mainly on observations at St. Michael and
its neighboring village, Stebbins, is valuable for its
contributions on medical and health problems faced by the
Eskimos of the area, and his account of Eskimo ceremonial
practices. The introductory essay reproduced here is also
an informative survey of the history of St. Michael.--Ed.)

The Eskimos of St. Michael and vicinity were numerically and ethnically an important segment of the great
western Eskimo world where many aspects of Eskimo culture
reached their highest development. They lived in an environ-
ment of abundant natural resources, and in a more hospitable
climate than their relatives in polar regions of the far
north. They resided in permanent villages during the winter,
and moved to fishing camps in the summer. Though the
villages and camps were usually located on flat tundra,
the surrounding country was rolling, and mountains and small
spruce forests were not far inland.

Like all Eskimos of Alaska they made fur clothing,
umiaks, kayaks, dog sleds, wooden dishes, and typical
Eskimo tools like the bow drill, adz, and ulu; built semi-
subterranean houses and kazgis (ceremonial houses) of
driftwood and sod; hunted fowl, seals, beluga (white whale)
and bearded seal; fished both summer and winter; and
celebrated various festivals based generally on the western
Eskimo religion.

Differences, however, resulted from local variations in
natural resources and cultural development. No Eskimos of
this area hunted the large bowhead or right whale of

northern Alaska, and only those near Sledge and Besboro islands of northern Norton Sound caught walrus. Their mainstays were seals and fish. They probably had more caribou meat either through trade or hunting than most northern Eskimo groups.

They built larger houses, kazgis, and storehouses than their kinsmen to the north. The large piles of driftwood on the beaches made this possible. Their art reflected the abundance of wood and the scarcity of ivory, and it was here and in areas to the south that the making of masks, and the painting of wooden dishes and boxes developed to a height unknown elsewhere during the nineteenth century.

All western Eskimos had developed a complex system of ceremonials integrated with various aspects of art and religion. The two most important ceremonials in the St. Michael area were the bladder festival, honoring the seals, their staff of life, and the feast of the dead, honoring the human dead and their living namesakes. The messenger feast, a predominantly northern trading festival originally celebrated between inland and coastal villages, also received considerable attention.

All clothing, weapons, tools, and transportation had an unmistakable western Eskimo look, but with local variations of design and construction. For example, in comparison with northern Eskimos, umiaks were generally smaller (they did not have to withstand the long journeys in the open sea to islands of the Bering Strait and Siberia); ceremonial dishes and spoons were painted with more intricate designs; the hunting visor was used more often; and greater use was made of fishskins in clothing and bags. In these examples they were more like the Eskimos between the Kuskokwim and the Yukon than those to the north.

The language spoken was Unaluk, a dialect of Yupik, the language prevailing south of Norton Sound. The entire area from Pastolik, near the Apoon branch of the Yukon, to Golovnin Bay was inhabited at one time by the Unalit, or Unaluk speakers.[1] However, by mid-nineteenth century, pockets of northern Inupiak speech (mainly the Kobuk River Malemiut and Kauwerak dialects) had been established here and there along the coast between St. Michael and Golovnin Bay within Unalit villages or at abandoned sites.

The Eskimos discussed by Edmonds were coastal Eskimos; he did not include the Yukon River Eskimos who lived as far upstream as Paimiut, about 200 river miles from the ocean. However, the people of the seacoast were sometimes visited by upstream people, particularly during the height of the fur trade. The most important aboriginal coastal villages related to St. Michael in speech, customs, and kinship were Kikiktauk (sometimes called Kiktaguk or Klikitarik on maps), Unalakleet, and Egavik to the north, and Stebbins (Atuik), Pikmiktalik,

Pastolik, and Chaniliak to the south, all within a fifty mile radius of St. Michael. (Some of these villages are not as important now as they were then.)

Thus, it can be seen that the area in which the Unalit moved freely and without apprehension was rather large. Along with the inhabitants of Kikiktauk and Unalakleet, the people of St. Michael hunted caribou as far north as the Shaktoolik River, 70 miles northeast of St. Michael (Zagoskin 1847: 78), and regularly hunted beluga in the shallow waters of Pastol Bay, fifty miles south, and caribou in the mainland hills. In the nineteenth century the northern Unalit occasionally took walrus at Besboro Island near Unalakleet with permission of its inhabitants.[2]

The Klondike gold strike of 1896, almost 2000 miles up the Yukon, made St. Michael a lively port. But no sooner had St. Michael begun to glow as a metropolis, when gold was found on Anvil Creek near Cape Nome, and the new town of Nome, 130 miles across Norton Sound from St. Michael, became, and remained, the center of commercial activities and population for northwest Alaska. Slowly St. Michael faded to a little village on the tundra, almost forgotten by the shipping companies, the airlines, and the tourists.

But St. Michael once had been a powerfully magical name in the history of both Russian America and American Alaska. In the 1830s, sixty years before gold seekers came to the Nome beaches, huge loads of pelts streamed down the Yukon into newly established St. Michael for trade with the Russian-American Company. And for fifty years before that, Bering Strait Eskimos had scoured the same country for furs to be taken to the international market at Kotzebue Sound. There they were transferred to Eskimo and Chukchi middlemen going to Siberia and the Anyui trade fair, which the Russians had established in 1789 expressly for the tobacco-fur trade (Ray 1964b: 86-87).

The Russian-American Company's attention was turned periodically to this rich intercontinental commerce, which they viewed with envy and greed. Consequently, a search for a strategic trading post location was an important part of their early explorations. In 1822 two ships, the Baranov and the Golovnin, set out from Sitka (then called Novo-Arkhangelsk or New Archangel) for a two-year journey to the Bering Sea. They sailed as far north as Golovnin Bay, which they named, but they ignored the coastline between Bristol Bay and Stuart Island, where shoal water compels ships to keep far from shore. Before 1822, three expeditions--Cook in 1778, Billings in 1791, and Kotzebue in 1816--had sailed past this stretch of coast, but only Cook commented on seeing land there.[3]

When the Kuskokwim River was explored for the first time by a land expedition in 1829-1830, I. F. Vasiliev, the leader, met Eskimos from Norton Sound who convinced

him that their territory was suitable for a trading post.
Thereupon, Etolin was sent to explore Norton Sound, the
Bering Strait, and St. Lawrence Island during the summer of
1830. He agreed with Vasiliev that Norton Sound was
ideally situated for a post, and plans materialized when
Lieutenant Michael D. Tebenkov explored the area further in
1833 and decided to build a small fort on an island--
really a peninsula--separated from the mainland by only
fifty feet of water. Tebenkov called his fort, which had
been brought in prefabricated form from Sitka, Mikhailovski
Redoubt, or Fort St. Michael, after his name saint. The
island was also called St. Michael. For many years English-
speaking persons used the name, St. Michaels or St. Michael's,
but by the end of the nineteenth century, most maps and
writings were printing today's accepted usage, St. Michael.

The fort, built that same year on the only harbor within
fifty miles of the Yukon (Kuikpak as it was then called after
its Eskimo name) was surrounded by palisades. However, the
Eskimos of the nearby village, Tachek, were friendly and
peaceable, and assured Tebenkov that they would trade with
the Russians, which was good news to an agent of a company
eager to put the Bering Strait trade out of joint.

By the time of St. Michael's establishment, the
inhabitants of the area already were familiar with a variety
of European goods brought from Siberia by northern Eskimo
traders.[4] Thus, they were alert to trading potentialities
when St. Michael was built, and fell easily into trading
relationships that continued throughout both Russian and
American occupation.

The Yukon, from which a great part of their furs were
to come, was explored from St. Michael for the first time
by Andrei Glazunov's expedition in 1834. He traveled via
a widely used route to the large village of Kikiktauk, ten
miles east of St. Michael, and then by portage to the Anvik
River, a tributary of the Yukon. Once on the Yukon,
however, the expedition was unable to proceed as planned,
and returned to headquarters. During the following two
years, however, a large area as far away as the Kuskokwim
was successfully explored (Bancroft 1886: 546-52;
Tikhmenev 1861, part I: 283-86; Zagoskin 1847: 63).

The Russians found two native villages on St. Michael
Island in 1833. Tachek (meaning bay) less than a half
mile from the post, an area that forms a part of the town
today, and Atuik (Zagoskin's "Atchvik") near Cape Stephens.
This village is now known as Stebbins, apparently after the
Russian pronunciation of Stephens (Baker 1906: 598).[5]
When Zagoskin visited the area in 1843-1844 the population
of Tachek was 19 and Atuik, 45 (Zagoskin 1847: 75). The
fort, though small with only a commandant and twenty-three
men in 1833, was a good-sized village according to Eskimo
standards. The villages of Tachek and Atuik were in year-
round communication, and both had strong, but less frequent

relationships with Pastolik to the south and Unalakleet to the north.

According to Zagoskin, two large aboriginal trading centers, Pastolik and Tachek, had been located between Norton Sound and the Yukon. This trade had been engaged in long before the founding of the Anyui market in Siberia by men of the same groups who particpated in the later fur trade: Sledge and King islanders, and people from Cape Prince of Wales and Kotzebue Sound. Aboriginal trade items were mainly domesticated reindeer skins from Siberia for wolverine furs and wooden dishes from America. The Anyui market intensified and accelerated already established trading relationship that took place at specified coastal points as far north as Point Barrow.

The intrusive northern Inupiak--the Malemiut and Seward Peninsula Eskimos--did not settle in Unalit territory until after the beginning of the fur trade, and not in any significant numbers until the middle of the nineteenth century. In 1842, more than half a century after the founding of the Anyui fair, Zagoskin wrote that the Malemiut were constantly on the move in their capacity as traders between Bering Strait or Kotzebue Sound and St. Michael, and had no permanent residence in the South. He reported no northern Eskimos living in St. Michael, and only Unalit, survivors of the smallpox epidemic of 1838, in Unalakleet. He stated, however, that King and Sledge islanders were known to go as far south as Pastolik by boat to trade (1847: 66, 76, 108, 138).

The establishment of St. Michael was decisive in deter- mining the permanent residency of northern peoples in Unalit territory, although the independent traders at first gave only half-hearted attention to the St. Michael trade, preferring to deal as usual with the Chukchi. By mid- nineteenth century, however, many more had drifted south to Norton Sound where the supply of goods was larger and more dependable.

It doubtless was difficult at first for the northern peoples to enter foreign territory. An Eskimo did not ordinarily enter strange country without the safety of a guide or a relative, even at the end of the nineteenth century, but apparently foreign wares gave special protection to traders in hazardous positions. Every man and woman in Alaska yearned for a puff of tobacco, and when the organized market of Anyui began providing tobacco with regularity, the safety of its bearers was paramount.

By 1865, however, both Malemiut and Kauwerak people (from east of Teller) had settled semi-permanently in the South, sometimes only as one-family villages. At that time, Unalakleet (Ungalaklik) was composed of three ethnic groups--Malemiut, Kauwerak, and Unalit. Dall wrote that a small Kauwerak contingent, headed by a man named Kamokin, was attached to Unalakleet: "To the north [of the fort] are two assemblages of houses occupied by Innuit of the Kaviak [Kauwerak], Mahlemut, and Unaleet tribes during part of the year, the latter being the only permanent residents" (1870: 24). Another observer said that the Kauwerak and Malemiut contingents were large (Whymper 1869: 159). A few northern Eskimos later settled in St. Michael and Pastolik, but Unalakleet with its satellite villages was better located for hunting caribou and trading with the Indians via the Unalakleet-Nulato portage than those farther south. The inhabitants of Unalakleet and other villages of Norton Sound are a mixture of these people today.

St. Michael had grown considerably by the time Lieutenant L. Zagoskin, of the Russian Navy, arrived in 1842, nine years after its establishment. It had six buildings enclosed within a stockade with two lookout towers and six three-foot cannons at opposite corners. Outside the fence were a blacksmith shop and a small chapel (1847: 67-68).

Shortly after his arrival, Zagoskin went to Unalakleet, where in 1837 the Russian-American Company had established a way station. The native village of Ungalaklik at that time was situated about a half mile from the mouth of the river on the left bank. It was strategically located for summer fishing in the river, winter fishing and sealing on the ocean ice, and hunting of caribou in the nearby hills. Berries, greens, and driftwood were abundant.

In 1842, however, Zagoskin found that the native village had been moved to the right bank, about a quarter mile from the Company's two buildings after the smallpox epidemic of 1838 (1847: 66). Zagoskin decided to make Unalakleet a full-fledged trading post with four additional men (ibid.: 65). He also harbored a desire to supplant St. Michael with Unalakleet, whose pure, fresh water, sandy soil for gardens, and abundant fish and animals far surpassed St. Michael's resources. St. Michael's two advantages--nearness to the Yukon and position for defense --became less important with discovery of the aboriginal trade portage from the Yukon to Unalakleet and the friendliness of the Eskimos.

St. Michael, however, remained as the main post, and Unalakleet's little palisaded huddle of buildings, its satellite. Unalakleet's Russian population, moreover, was always small, and unlike the capital at Sitka, few, if any, Russian women lived there, or in other trading posts of the Yukon or Norton Sound. Some of the company's employees married Eskimos, preserving a few Russian names for the future. However, Eskimo immigrants from the North made Unalakleet an important and large native village, overtaking St. Michael in population. It has kept the lead ever since except for the fleetingly busy days of the gold rush when thousands of people poured through the port of St. Michael.

Few outside events disturbed the dull but harsh existence of St. Michael Redoubt until the gold rush. In 1836 St. Michael supposedly was attacked by Sledge Islanders in ten umiaks (i.e., "Ten baidara from the island of Asiag [Ayak]"). Zagoskin reported that the Ayakmiut, disgruntled by the Russian's fur trade, attacked several men gathering wood at Cape Stephens, twelve miles from St. Michael. One Russian was killed and seven wounded, but the rest were saved by a workman named Kurepanov, who stole an umiak and pushed the rest out to sea (Tikhmenev 1861 part I: 287-88; Zagoskin 1847: 68-69). Though the Eskimos might have initiated a fight, it is more likely that they were defending themselves against a provocation. Seward Peninsula Eskimos rarely fought, particularly when 140 miles from home, and the umiaks undoubtedly represented traders from other places besides Sledge Island, which, at the most never had more than fifty men, women, and children at one time. At the end of his narrative, Zagoskin said: "The Asiagmut never dared show themselves again [at the time of his writing, 1842-1844] on the south coast of Norton Sound" (ibid.: 69).

The first real influx of foreigners other than Russians--the Yankee whalers--had little effect on St. Michael and vicinity. The whaling ships, which first sailed through Bering Strait in 1848, rarely stopped at St. Michael or appeared within sight of the coast because the seas were not whaling waters, and representatives of an alien power were too near.

However, almost simultaneous with the coming of the whalers to the Arctic was the search for Sir John Franklin, which affected the Eskimos of that area to a much greater degree. When no further word of Franklin's expedition (last seen in July 1845 near Baffin Island) had been received by 1848, two ships, the Herald under command of Captain Henry Kellett, and the Plover, with Commander T. E. L. Moore, were sent to Bering Strait. Northern Alaska was thoroughly searched during seven years (1848-1854) by eight government-sponsored vessels and a private yacht. The Eskimos came into greater contact with Europeans than ever before, and the resulting observations by members of the search party are an invaluable addition to the history of the Eskimo (see Bourchier; Collinson; Great Britain Sessional Papers; Hobson; Kellett; Simpson; Trollope).

A ship sailing on the high seas would not by itself have been of importance to the Eskimos, but all of the search ships stopped frequently at St. Michael for news about Franklin, and two of them, the Plover and the Rattlesnake, spent several winters frozen in the ice of Kotzebue Sound, Point Barrow, and Port Clarence, where they were visited constantly by Eskimos. The sailors learned that news from one part of Eskimo country to another, no matter how insignificant, was well known within a short time over an area of several hundred miles. The

native guides employed to aid in the searches usually knew
their territory well, and trips from Port Clarence to St.
Michael or from St. Michael to Nulato were common
occurrences.

Both Kellett and Moore offered rewards to Eskimos for
information about Franklin, but this ultimately led to a
flood of fabrications and exaggerations. However, they
tracked down every rumor, and when it was learned that
white men had been seen in the interior, the search party
used every means to ascertain whether or not these were
Franklin's men. After the Plover froze in the ice of
Kotzebue Sound, the crew hoped to hire guides to take them
to distant villages and tribes for information, but the
Eskimos misunderstood the reasons for the ship's presence
at first, and assumed it was a trader. Therefore, instead
of accepting guiding jobs, as offered, the Eskimos brought
huge loads of caribou meat, fish, and furs to the ship for
barter. Finally, however, Lieutenant Bedford Pim hired a
man to guide him overland to St. Michael for further news
of the rumored white men (Great Britain Sessional Papers
1856, Vol. 41: 2124). Pim made a successful trip to St.
Michael and back to the ship, but could learn nothing
about the men's identity.

That summer (1850), Berthold Seemann of the Herald
said that the Russians "could not be persuaded by Mr. Pim
...that the Plover was [not] trading; these suppositions
were...set aside by our visit...It is possible that the
Plover may have interfered with their trade,--the natives
finding they could obtain from her all they wanted for
fish and venison, articles much more easily obtained than
furs, and disposed of without going so great a journey"
(1853: 183).

By autumn, 1850, the men of the Plover, which was to
stay in Port Clarence that winter, determined to get to the
bottom of the rumors once and for all by traveling into the
interior. Therefore, Lieutenant J. J. Barnard and two
companions were taken by ship to St. Michael where they
learned conclusively that the men were not Franklin's but
instead, five English traders living on the upper Yukon.
We now know that they were Hudson's Bay traders, who, in
establishing Fort Yukon in 1847, had caused the decrease
in the Russians' fur trade.

St. Michael's pace quickened with the arrival of
members of the Western Union Telegraph Expedition in 1865.
The vigorous young men made St. Michael one of their headquarters, and explored the country in all directions for the
proposed telegraph line. They wrote journals and books of
their daily activities, and their composite descriptions
and narratives provide us with the most complete picture
of that area since Zagoskin's Pedestrian Journeys (in
Russian) of twenty years before. Books by Richard Bush,
W. H. Dall, and Frederick Whymper sold in both Europe and

America, and for English-speaking readers who longed for far away places, St. Michael became synonymous with the exotic land of Russian America.

Headquarters at St. Michael and subheadquarters at Unalakleet were provided by the Russian-American Company, whose posts had grown little in size since the Franklin search. According to Whymper, the English artist of the expedition, the St. Michael fort was painted yellow with red roofs, "which gave it a rather gay appearance" (1869: 153).

The Americans at St. Michael had a rare opportunity to observe the isolated, stringent life of a Russian outpost, and its relationship to the surrounding Eskimos. The workmen for the Russian-American Company were a hetero- geneous lot--Russians, Finns, Yakuts, Aleuts, and Eskimo half-bloods. Of the Russians, Dall wrote that all but the two company agents (at St. Michael and Unalakleet) were ex-convicts or outcasts from their homeland, and the consensus of the sprightly young expedition members was that they were one of the laziest bunches of men they had ever seen (Dall 1870: 11; Whymper 1869: 154).

Unalakleet in 1866 was still St. Michael's nearest outpost with a contingent of five Russians and a native helper (Adams diary, December 12 entry; James 1942: 201). Dall reported that on October 3, 1867, there was only one Russian workman (named Ostrofskoi), but two native men, and a half-blood woman (1870: 131). Unalakleet's principal purpose at that time was for summertime trade in oil, ivory, and furs, but even this little village had its foreign competitors. Along with the whaling ships to the Arctic at mid-century had come numerous independent traders, and Henry M. Bannister mentions a Honolulu brigantine, Victoria, whose "captain (Fish) is a great trader with the Eskimos and we had often heard of his vessel at Unalakleet" (James 1942: 242).

The telegraph men commented frequently on the Eskimos' constant, and often lengthy travels, particularly to the annual Russian supply ships. Fred M. Smith, in his diary for June 18, 1866, wrote: "Three Magamiuts from Cape Romanzoff [Eskimos near Hooper Bay] arrived here. The head chief and two of his men. Every two years all the head chiefs of Indian [including Eskimo] tribes in Russian America come here to meet the ships and receive presents from the Company. The chief brought with him 40 white fox skins, a few brown or yellow & 2 slate colored fox skins quite a rare fox. Steppy [Sergei Stepanoff, the commandant] had the old man in to take tea with him."

Not only did Indians and Eskimos come to St. Michael from the middle and lower yukon, and Eskimos from Kotzebue Sound, the Kobuk River, Bering Strait, and Cape Romanzof, but all the way from Kolmakofsky Redoubt on the Kuskokwim (ibid.: July 4, 1866).

Many names of individual Eskimos from St. Michael, Unalakleet, and the Yukon appear in the writings of the telegraph men. A few Malemiut and Seward Peninsula Eskimos had switched allegiance from the Bering Strait trade to St. Michael by that time, and had settled permanently in the Norton Sound area. Some traveled the year-round for the St. Michael fur trade, in winter with sturdy sleds and dogs, and in summer with umiaks that were carried on the sleds.

During the Franklin search a few Eskimos had found the guiding business to be lucrative after all, and in 1865 placed themselves out for hire as guides, packers, post-hole diggers, line-stringers, hunters, and cooks, but as the young telegraph men observed sadly, worked only according to some inner direction. Several men, however, were in constant attendance on the expedition: Attzik, chief of Erathluikmiut (now the ghost mining town of Council on Seward Peninsula); "old" Alluiyanuk, a Malemiut leader from the Kobuk, and whose many descendants now live in the Unalakleet-Yukon area; Arkhannok, Ark-na-py-ak, and Myunuk, also Malemiut; Kamokin and Kupola from Kauwerak; and Itaktak (Dall 1870: 125, 129, 135, 162; and passim in other sources). Many other helpers were given unidentifying English nicknames.

The men of the expedition were convinced that the Eskimos preferred them to the Russians, and tried to treat them kindly. Their buoyant behavior, as reflected in their books and journals, doubtless contrasted to that of the Russian workmen, of whom even Stepanoff said,'"You can expect nothing good of this rabble: they left Russia because they were not wanted there'" (Dall 1870: 12). It is not surprising, then, to find that the Eskimos were making efforts to speak English where heretofore Eskimo and Russian had prevailed. George R. Adams wrote that Lunchy, the "Boss cook," an Eskimo at one of the line camps, "is very high-toned and talks a heap of English to his [native] assistants who do not understand a word he says" (Diary 1867: February 5).

When Russian America became Alaska in 1867, the Eskimos had no cause to worry that their source of trade goods would disappear, for the Americans turned out to be as eager for trade as the Russians. In 1868, the Alaska Commercial Company was organized by a group of men who had bought some of the Russian-American Company's goods at Sitka in 1867, and who had made enormous profits hunting fur seals on the Pribilof Islands (Andrews 1938: 273-74n; Hulley 1953: 207). The Alaska Commercial Company was the only trading company in the St. Michael and Yukon area for many years through competition in the traditional American manner was occasionally attempted without success until the 1890s.

By the 1870s, the search for minerals had begun almost everywhere in the North, and an interest in many other

aspects of the country--biology, ethnology, geography--was
reflected in exploring expeditions and individual pursuits.
The latter 1870s and early 1880s were busy times for
collectors of biological and ethnological objects from one
end of Alaska to the other, and St. Michael played host to
all who came north. Whalers, traders, and explorers had
traded for Eskimo handiwork for many years, but a concentrated operation was not undertaken until Edward W. Nelson
of the U. S. Signal Corps, and J. A. Jacobsen, representing
the Royal Museum of Berlin, came on the scene. Alaska
Commercial Company agents gave both men unlimited cooperation
despite having to fill their own museum in San Francisco.
Eskimos made or saved objects especially for Nelson during
the four years (1877-1881) that he traveled to various
villages. This cooperation netted him thousands of art
objects, tools, utensils, and pieces of wearing apparel,
which are now in the U. S. National Museum (Nelson 1899; an
excellent summary of Nelson's activities is found in Lantis
1954).

Jacobsen had the misfortune to come the year after
Nelson left the country with his booty, but he managed to
garner a fine collection of objects, nevertheless
(Disselhoff 1935, 1936; Jacobsen 1884). Both Jacobsen and
Nelson became acquainted with the sub-agents of the Alaska
Commercial Company who covered the entire area between the
Kuskokwim River and Kotzebue Sound. These men were Eskimos
and each had a special territory for his trade, taking his
goods, mainly furs, periodically to the St. Michael
headquarters.(6) Occasionally an Eskimo trader brought
liquor to the Yukon and St. Michael from ships at Kotzebue
Sound, a development that revenue cutters tried unceasingly
to discourage.

Bering Strait commerce with the Chukchi continued,
though merely as a token trade for adventure more than gain,
and for luxuries such as spotted tame reindeer skins rather
than staple products. The real necessities of Eskimo life
--iron kettles, knives, calico, tobacco, hardtack, matches--
were now got almost entirely from roving Eskimo agents of
the Alaska Commercial Company, whalers, or independent
traders of the sea.

After 1880, explorations on the Yukon and its port
of St. Michael became common, and revenue service was
begun on the high seas. The U. S. Revenue Marine
Steamers, Bear, Corwin, Nunivak, and Rush, patrolled the
waters with a two-fold purpose: to help whalers in
trouble, and to keep contraband goods, particularly breech-
loading rifles and liquor from falling into Eskimo and
Indian hands. Beginning with the first Arctic cruise of
the Corwin in 1880, the steamer on active northern duty
stopped at St. Michael several times each summer. During
the Corwin's second cruise in 1881, E. W. Nelson was taken
aboard to make ethnological observations in the North.

St. Michael was headquarters for hiring interpreters
for the cutters and other ships. Interpreters were not
difficult to find, although they often spoke only the
southern Eskimo language, which was useless in northern
Alaska and Siberia. Myunik (the same Myunuk of telegraph
days) was unique in that he spoke both Unaluk and several
Inupiak dialects. He joined the Corwin to serve as
interpreter for revenue marine explorations of the Kobuk
River where Inupiak was spoken. Myunik was discharged
from his duties in September, 1885, with "Government trade
goods and money" (Healy 1887: 13 and plate, page 6).

The year 1885 was a busy one in St. Michael. Lieutenant
George Stoney of the U. S. Navy was on his way north also
to explore the Kobuk River, and at St. Michael he reported:
"I shipped, as ordinary seaman, the [Eskimo] interpreter
Aloka and "Riley' (Ounalook), whom I had employed on my
previous expedition, and 'Bill' (Oukutkoon). The families
of these two last were taken along to keep their husbands
contented, and to sew, wash, dry fish and assist in
various ways. Each family had one child. 'Bill's' wife was
Annutkan, and his child, Alluke; they were known to us as
'Mrs. Bill' and "little Sophie.' 'Riley's' wife, Shopshuuck,
and his child, Toggarack, were called 'Mrs. Riley' and
'little Riley.' Riley and Bill were paid the equivalent of
$15 per month in trade articles that in reality cost the
Govt. but $4. The wives and children were fed and
occasionally given small presents" (Stoney 1900: 16).

By 1890 and 1891 when Edmonds arrived for the first
time in St. Michael, the Eskimos had seen many changes.
Trading posts, exploring parties, and prospectors were no
longer unusual, but the land was still a straggling
frontier with no public buildings, no mail service, no
law enforcement, and with few schools. In 1892, the
governor reported that the closest commissioner, "when
there is one," was "at Unalaska...fully 900 miles away
(Knapp 1893: 22).

Though changes prior to 1890 had been many, Edmonds'
first look at St. Michael and the Yukon was of the pre-gold
rush calm: St. Michael, an easy-going trading center for
the Eskimos, and a leisurely host to explorers and
scientists of the North made possible by courtesy of the
Alaska Commercial Company. His second look at St. Michael
in 1898 was entirely different. The air of industry had
changed to frenzy, and the leisurely host had been
supplanted by huge, impersonal hotels for the estimated
20,000 persons who passed through within a few months' time.
New storehouses and wharves lined the waterfront. Ships
not only sailed in and out, but were built on the ways,
and hundreds of men and women rushed from ocean steamers
for transfer to river steamers and the Klondike, where
millions of dollars worth of gold already had been found.

The gold rushes to the Klondike, Nome, and Kotzebue

Sound in a space of three years at the end of the nineteenth
century were the greatest single factor in the rate of
culture change in western Alaska from the Yukon to Kotzebue
Sound. Almost overnight the thousands of persons that came
to the western beaches in a year's time spread out everywhere to the surrounding country to bring irreversible
changes to basic Eskimo settlement and subsistence patterns,
and cultural values. Many Eskimos from the Norton and
Kotzebue sounds area went to Nome to enjoy the new bonanza
vicariously by pursuing old interests of trade with a new
perspective: the carving of ivory and wooden objects to
sell to gold seekers and tourists. They remained, and
Nome grew to be a city.

The Eskimos of St. Michael and vicinity found themselves in almost the same position, but many left when the
white people went home. A number went to the culturally-
related Unalakleet, which had become a thriving garden and
educational spot through efforts of Swedish Covenant
missionaries, while others went toward the Yukon.

Because of the sudden changes that befell the Eskimos
during the gold rushes, it is not out of place to repeat
eye-witness accounts of this huge mass of people, 30,000 in
one year alone at Nome, or more than the total native
population of the whole of Alaska. St. Michael, at the
portal of the easiest, though most roundabout, route to
the Klondike, had its first glimpse of the future during
the summer of 1897 when its vast, sprawling calm was
rippled by news that gold had been found in Canada the
winter before. Nine boats went upstream that season as
ordinary river boats, but two of them, the North American
Transportation and Trading Company's Portus B. Weare, and
the Alaska Commercial Company's Alice, came down with
loads of gold that were to send more people through St.
Michael than it had seen in its entire history. The boxes,
bags, and jars full of gold were transferred to the
companies' respective ocean-going ships, the N. A. T. and
T's Portland, and the Alaska Commercial Company's Excelsior.
These loads of gold in '97 made St. Michael bustle as it
never had before. Ships unloaded passengers, machinery,
lumber, knocked-down steamers, and the all-important
"outfits," or collections of food, tents, and clothing indispensable to the prospective millionaires. The feverish
rush of the Klondike stretched almost unabated 1700 miles
down the Yukon, and for two months ocean steamers came
and went. Then, suddenly the ships left for the winter,
and St. Michael was brimming over with men waiting to
steam up the river to the Klondike.

Sheldon Jackson, who had spent almost every summer
since 1890 aboard the Bear, wrote W. T. Harris,
Commissioner of Education in 1897: "I am still detained
at this place waiting upon the movements of the 'Bear.'
Since reaching here, August 24, several expeditions of miners
have arrived on steamers and sailing vessels from Puget

Sound, Seattle, and San Francisco. They bring with them
lumber and mechanics expecting at this point to build small
river steamers and barges in which to proceed up the Yukon
to the mines. There are eight or ten of these vessels now
in the harbor and thirteen more are expected from the south.

"The season is now closed for getting up the river
this year, the most the miners now here can do will be to
get perhaps a hundred miles up the river to timber, then
go into winter quarters erecting log huts for shelter.
Those that come up later will be compelled to winter at
this place. As all these people were pledged to be taken
to the mines this fall you can imagine that there is not
only much disappointment but almost much irritation and
anger that is liable at any moment to break out into open
violence.

"Among the hundreds now camped upon the beach in tents
are all classes from the best to the lowest; professional
men of ability and standing, gamblers and desperate roughs,
the wealthy and the poor, and the presence of the 'Bear'
is the only restraint on lawlessness. We are hourly
expecting the arrival of another cutter, and when she
comes the 'Bear' will at once set sail for the Reindeer
Station, Siberia and St. Lawrence Island" (1897: 357-58).

During the winter of 1897-98, transportation companies
sprang into life like spring flowers along a snow bank, and
a motley of mechanical wonders was built for the Yukon, with
freight and men going upstream, and gold coming down. The
historian, C. L. Andrews, wrote that before the season of
1898 had closed, 32 transportation companies with 60
steamboats, eight tugs and towboats, and 20 barges were
plying the Yukon (1938: 191-92).

By 1898 the richest ground had been staked and the
rush to the Klondike was almost over, but the hundreds
going upstream, lured by heady advertising and headier
newspaper headlines, were not to be deterred by other
hundreds going down. St. Michael had its hands full with
this double tide of humanity, which was often ill-tempered
and unruly. Finally, with the establishment of a military
reservation and the building of barracks for soldiers, and
with the appointment of a commissioner, deputy marshal, and
deputy collector, St. Michael took on the semblance of
order, and the look of a city.

The discovery of gold near Cape Nome in 1898 both
softened and compounded St. Michael's troubles. As soon
as news reached the disappointed Klondikers of the strike,
they rushed pell-mell through St. Michael for Nome, high
hopes tempering their frustrations. Half of St. Michael
packed up, too, and left. The Cape Nome strike, however,
like that of the Klondike, sent thousands of men to claims
that were already staked and to a rainbow that ended in a
return ticket home.

Stranded prospectors wound up in St. Michael for several summers after the Klondike boom, but the summer of 1898 before the Nome rush (and when Edmonds was in the area) was one of the worst. Disgruntled Klondikers rubbed shoulders with sick and downhearted Kobuk River stampeders who had been swayed by false advertising of transportation companies of a fabulous discovery near Kotzebue Sound.

The sudden activity at St. Michael and on the Yukon also brought the U. S. Geological Survey and the U. S. Coast and Geodetic Survey into the area, and members of the 1898 parties observed an Eskimo way of life that had developed through internal as well as outside changes over a long period of time. After that summer, however, Eskimo culture changed rapidly north of the Yukon, and the first year of the twentieth century was a step into a new era.

Notes

1. Alternative spellings of Unaluk in anthropological literature is Unaaliq. I am using Unaluk to conform with the usual spelling of the name Unalit, for the people.

2. Perhaps this permission to hunt was forced a bit because a folk tale relates that the mainland people were so jealous of the good hunting and rich life of Besboro's inhabitants that they once killed everyone on the island by pouring hot oil down the ceiling hole of the community house (informant data). Informants, however, do not agree on whether Besboro Island had a permanent population or was used seasonally.

3. Since the publication of this manuscript, I found Russian sources containing information about the Vasiliev-Shishmarev expedition, and the Khromchenko-Avinov expedition, both of which sailed along the coast between Bristol Bay and Stuart Island in 1821. Therefore, there were six expeditions that had sailed along this coast before 1822, and three of them saw land. In 1821 Vasiliev discovered Nunivak Island, and Shishmarev and Etolin independently discovered Cape Romanzof (Ray 1975b: 69-71).

4. Before the Eskimos had ever seen a Russian, the traders had distributed pots, knives, spears, iron, and tobacco as far south as the Kuskokwim (Zagoskin 1847: 76, 107).

5. A brochure issued by the North American Transportation and Trading Company about 1900 used Stephan's for Stebbins: "The native women of Stephan's and Kilkikarck [Kikiktauk, east of St. Michael] were called in to make fur clothing for the members of [De Long's] expedition....One of Alexy's [an Eskimo guide] relatives at Stephan's had a silver medal afterwards awarded him by Congress for his conduct on the expedition" (n.d.: 43).

6. Among the traders were Kingaseak (from Irathluik near present-day Council); Saxo (from Sledge Island, and whose real Eskimo name, I have been told was Anakusuk); Kaleak ("Isaac," from Ukvignaguk on Norton Bay, and after whom Isaacs Point was named) (Jacobsen 1884: 231-34, 240-41, 271); and Tal-ya-luk (Nelson 1899: 304). The names Saxo and Tal-ya-luk are preserved today in the Unalakleet-St. Michael area as Soxie and Deliluk (Ray 1964b: 87).

St. Michael Eskimos posing near their houses and drying racks, 1902-I

VII

TWO HISTORICAL SIGNAL POSTS:

EARLY COMMUNICATION IN THE ALASKAN ARCTIC*

In 1973 while taking photographs of Eskimo-made artifacts in the Thomas H. Burke Memorial Washington State Museum in Seattle I saw, in a dark corner of the work area, a tall weathered post, 88 inches high, incised in Cyrillic characters, "RAK, Ekspedi[tsia] dlia 1838." This discovery, translated as "Russian-American Company Expedition of 1838," was most exciting because it had unexpectedly brought a tangible and realistic dimension to a little-known expedition, the first arctic expedition to originate in Russian America, all others having been sent out from Europe or Asia.

But there was more to come, for when I showed an interest in the post, James Nason, curator of anthropology, brought me another, shorter one (62 inches high), carved on one side with "HBMS Blossom, September 1826," and on the other, "HBMS Herald, September 1848"--lettering that commemorated two important events in Alaska history, Frederick William Beechey's expedition to northern Alaska in 1826 and 1827, and the search for Sir John Franklin, who was seen last in Baffin Bay in 1845.

These posts had apparently spent many years in anonymous repose, for there was no immediate information as to where they were originally erected or how they had come to the museum. But when I saw other names and dates like "Joe Jury 1898" cut into the posts, my memory stirred, and I faintly recalled having read about such poles, probably in books about the gold rush, because 1898 was the year that gold was discovered on Anvil Creek near the present town of Nome.

I subsequently found what I was looking for in Joseph Grinnell's Gold-Hunting in Alaska, the published diary of a 21-year-old prospector who later became an eminent orni-thologist. Along with twelve hundred men and women, Grinnell had been lured to Kotzebue Sound in the summer of 1898 by a false claim of a fabulous gold strike. A number of people, including Grinnell, spent a long winter in cabins on the banks of the Kobuk River, which suited him just fine because he had ample opportunity to collect birds, his principal interest even at that time, and

* Unpublished.

probably the main reason for his youthful adventure to the Alaskan wilds. When the summer of 1899 finally arrived, Grinnell and his high-spirited companions sailed their boat, the Penelope, to Nome to check out Anvil Creek, and on the way stopped at Chamisso Island, a small island off the tip of Choris Peninsula. There, Grinnell saw "records carved on logs in a fair state of preservation of the visit of 'H.B.M.S. Blossom, 1825,' 'H.B.M.S. Herald, 1848,' and some Russian vessel 1837 [he meant 1838] (Grinnell 1901: 85).

These were, of course, the same poles that I had seen in the museum, but I did not learn how they had arrived in Seattle until a search of the museum files turned up three documents that partially cleared the mystery. The first document is an accession sheet dated 9 November 1909, in which F. S. Hall, curator of the then Washington State Museum, and Thomas T. Kane, president of the university, acknowledged receipt of "One Old Monument Russian-American dated 1838; One Old Monument H.M.S. Blossom, dated 1825; One Old Monument, dated 1849 [all] wooden" from J. C. McBride, commissioner of the Alaska-Yukon-Pacific Exposition, Alaskan Exhibit. At the top left is written $200.

The three posts (the third one with the date 1849 cannot be found) were on display in the museum when C. L. Andrews, the Alaskan historian, caught inaccuracies on the exhibit card. He wrote to Mr. Hall on 21 March 1916 (his letter is the second document): "I take the liberty of calling your attention to a card on one of the monuments brought from the Kotzebue Sound, Alaska and placed in the museum. The card states that it was probably placed by Kolmakof or K-----[probably "Khramchemko"; see below]. I did not get the name.

"This is not correct as I read Alaskan history. Kolmakof...did not go farther north [than the Kuskokwim River]. The date 1838...indicates to me that it was the expedition of Kashavarof [sic] and this was the only Russian expedition into that part at any time at all near to that date."

Spurred by Andrews' letter, Hall wrote to Jack Underwood, a newspaperman, in care of the Times of Seattle where Underwood had once worked. In this letter, dated 24 March 1916 (the third document), he wrote: "We have in the Museum three old wooden monuments, one having a date 1838, another the date 1825, and another 1849, upon them. These monuments came from Alaska and were turned over to the Museum at the close of the A. Y. P. Exposition. I understand that you were responsible for securing them for the Alaska Exhibit, and as our information regarding them has not been as complete as I would like, I am wondering if you will give me what information you possess regarding their history. My attention has been called, by C. L. Andrews, to the fact that the information on one of them

Signal posts on Chamisso Island, indicating visits of
(left and center) H.B.M.S. Blossom, 1825, and H.B.M.S.
Herald, 1848, and (right) of the Russian-American Company
vessel Polyphem, 1838.

is not correct, and I am enclosing a copy of his letter. I would be greatly obliged if you would furnish us with this information as we are anxious to have the labels on our specimens as complete as possible."

Underwood apparently did not respond, thus ending the museum's quest for information. However, three years before, in 1913, Underwood had published a book, Alaska, an Empire in the Making, and since these posts had been left by aspiring empire makers, I thought that he might have mentioned them. And, so he did, but the information is so inaccurate and garbled that it is just as well that he did not respond to Hall's letter.

Underwood, an Australian adventurer and newspaperman, went to Alaska for the first time in 1897 where he was a prospector, mail carrier, special deputy United States marshal, and journalist. In 1902 he founded the Council City News in the gold-rush town of Council, about sixty miles northeast of Nome, but he left Alaska in 1904 for the east coast where he worked as a newspaperman. When he heard that Dodd, Mead and Company was looking for a person to write a history of Alaska, he applied, and got the assignment. He took the three posts from Chamisso Island in 1909 while gathering more material for this book (Castle 1912: 12; Ross 1913: 6; Grinnell did not mention the third post in his diary).

Underwood's sloppy account of the posts is a good example of how not to write history: "That the sound [Kotzebue Sound] was visited by some other Russian explorer a few years later [after its discovery by Otto von Kotzebue in 1816] and of which there is no record, is evidenced in the fact that a large post, used as a monument, upon which was carved in Russian the date, May, 1826, and which had the Russian letter 'K' at the head of it, was found by the writer in 1909 on an island opposite where the city of Keewalik now stands. Together with the monuments placed there by Captain F. W. Beechy [sic], of H. M. S. Blossom, and the monuments of Captain [Commander] Thomas E. L. Moore, Commander of H. M. S. Plover; and of Captain Henry Kellett, commander of H. M. S. Herald in 1849, this crude record of Russia's unknown explorer was removed to Seattle and became the property of the University of Washington" (Underwood 1913: 374-75).

What he should have written was that the Beechey expedition, not a Russian one, had lettered the pole "September [not May], 1826," and that the Herald inscription of 1848--not 1849--was on the opposite side. The Russian post did not have just a "k" at the top, but "RAK" (Russian-American Company). And there was indeed a record of this 1838 expedition in several Russian publications prior to 1909. Later on in his book he decided that Russia's "unknown explorer" (Kashevarov) was "Khramchemko," that is, Vasilii S. Khromchenko, who explored the coast of Alaska in 1821 and 1822. But Khromchenko did not go farther north

than Golovnin Bay. The third post was undoubtedly
inscribed in 1849 by Moore of the Plover, also a Franklin
search ship, which spent the winter of 1849-1850 frozen
in Kotzebue Sound.

Chamisso Island was a favorite rendezvous and watering
place for almost all Alaskan expeditions after Kotzebue,
who himself had been the first to erect a marker on the
island, according to Beechey. In the account of his own
expedition of 1826-1827, he said that one of his seamen
had found "a piece of board upon Chamisso Island, upon
which was written, in Russian characters, 'Rurick, July
28th, 1816,' and underneath it, 'Blaganome erinoy
[Blagonamerennyi, or Good Intent], 1820.' The former was of
course cut by Kotzebue when he visited the islands; and
the latter, I suppose, by Captain Von Basilief Schismareff,
his lieutenant [in 1816], who paid this island a second
visit in 1820" (Beechey, 1831, vol. 1: 286).

Even Beechey's writing needs a bit of explanation.
The date of 28 July 1816 is puzzling because Kotzebue was
near Saint Lawrence Island on that date, and did not come
to Chamisso Island until 3 August. The date 1820 refers
to a Russian expedition, which consisted of two vessels,
Blagonamerennyi or Good Intent, commanded by Gleb S.
Shishmarev, who had been with Kotzebue in 1816, and
Otkrytie, or Discovery, under command of Mikhail N.
Vasiliev. Beechey's inaccurate rendition of
Shishmarev's name was a combination of the surnames
Vasiliev and Shishmaref, which with the addition of "Von,"
made them Germans like Kotzebue, though indeed they were
Russian.

In the days before the telegraph and the airplane,
signal posts or letters painted on prominent cliffs were
the principal means of communication between expedition
ships. Beechey's expedition in 1826 and 1827 made ample
use of a variety of signalling devices to inform John
Franklin of his whereabouts. Beechey's expedition was
part of a three-way exploration of the Alaskan and Canadian
Arctic by Great Britain to acquire greater knowledge of the
country and to gain an advantage over Russia in territorial
expansion and trade. Franklin (who was later knighted)
planned to go overland through Canada to meet Beechey at
Kotzebue Sound, and William Edward Parry hoped to sail
through the Northwest Passage from the Atlantic Ocean.
Beechey's rendezvous with Franklin in 1826 was set for
20 May at Chamisso Island, but Franklin was not there when
he arrived on the 25th.

"By my instructions," Beechey wrote, "I was desired to
await the arrival of Captain Franklin at this anchorage;
but in a memoir drawn up by that officer and myself, to
which my attention was directed by the Admiralty, it was
arranged that the ship should proceed to the northward,
and survey the coast, keeping the barge [sailing tender
to the ship] in shore to look out for the land [Franklin's]

party, and to erect posts as signals of her having been there, and to leave directions where to find the ship." (This was in July, and the post in the museum is incised September.)

Beechey wanted to leave a small party on Chamisso, but did not do so because he was fearful of hostile Eskimos. However, "a tight barrel of flour was buried upon Puffin Rock [now called Puffin Island, two miles northwest], which appeared to be the most unfrequented spot in the vicinity, and directions for finding it were deposited in a bottle at Chamisso Island, together with such other information as he might require, and the place where it was deposited was pointed out by writing upon the cliffs with white paint" (Ibid.: 255-56).

Beechey wrote that signal posts were erected at Cape Thompson, Refuge Inlet (Walakpa Bay), Cape Franklin, and near Wainwright, but the messages on those posts were painted, not carved out as on these. Beechey returned to Kotzebue Sound in September and explored for miles around. On 12 October, he buried another barrel of flour on Chamisso Island (the Puffin Island barrel had been broken into by Eskimos), along with a large tin case of beads, and a letter. "Ample directions for finding these were both cut and painted on the rock; and to call attention of the party to the spot, which they might otherwise pass, seeing the ship had departed, her name was painted in very large letters on the cliffs of Puffin Island...Beneath it were written directions for finding the cask of flour, and also a piece of driftwood which was deposited in a hole in the cliff" (Ibid.: 336). It is possible that the Beechey post was this "piece of driftwood," but more likely it was another log because of the date and character of the inscription.

Franklin did not get anywhere near Alaska, but the tragedy of his third expedition to the Canadian Arctic almost twenty years later led to the most ambitious search ever mounted in Alaskan waters during the days of sailing ships. Although Franklin did not go through the Northwest Passage to Alaska (remains of his ships were found at King William Island, Canada in 1858) a total of nine vessels searched for him north of Bering Strait between 1848 and 1854. In 1848, the first year of the search, the Herald under command of Henry Kellett, and the Plover, under command of T. E. L. Moore, planned to meet at Chimisso Island to prepare winter quarters for the Plover, but the Plover, having proved to be a slow sailor, spent the winter of 1848-1849 on the Siberian side of Bering Strait. Not knowing the whereabouts of the Plover, Kellett remained at Chamisso Island until October 1848 when the weather turned very bad, and then left to spend the winter in Mazatlan, Mexico (Ray 1975b: 141-42). Presumably, the Herald's inscription on the opposite side of the Blossom post was made during this wait.

In 1849, the Plover and the Herald arrived at Chamisso
Island within one day of each other and both sailed north.
As during Beechey's voyage, the seamen erected innumerable
posts, painted numerous marks, and buried bottles for
communication. Explicit directions were given in official
orders. An example of such an order was written in 1849
by Commander Moore to Lieutenant Pullen, who was ordered
to sail in two decked boats from the Plover at Wainwright
Inlet as far east as the Mackenzie River. At Point
Separation, he was to find "land-marks of wood or stone
[left by Franklin on his third expedition], painted either
in white or red, or with black stripes; and also pieces
of rock similarly marked, and bottles buried on the
circumference of a circle drawn with a 10-feet radius from
the point of a broad arrow painted on the signal posts....
When you visit Point Separation, you will bury a bottle,
enclosing a note, therein stating the date of your arrival
...marking the place as distinctly as you possibly can
....[As you return to the ship, leave] marks in the most
conspicuous parts of the coast, with buried information of
the 'Plover's' position...In conclusion, I have to point
out to you Icy Cape, Point Hope, and Cape Lisburne, as
places of rendezvous where you will meet me, or find buried
information of my position; but you may be quite sure of
finding me at Chamisso Island" (Kellett 1850: 11).

In 1849 it was decided that the Plover would remain
frozen in the ice near Chamisso Island, and a house be
built on Choris Peninsula. The third post that was
brought to Seattle with the date 1849 undoubtedly was
erected by the crew of the Plover, for Moore wrote Kellett
on 26 September 1849 that when the ice broke up in the
spring of 1850 he would sail north, and if Kellett, in
the Herald, which was going to winter in the balmy climates
of the south, had arrived at the island before Moore had
returned, "you will find information of my position, &c.,
buried ten feet magnetic north of the post on Chamisso
Island, and in the house on Choris Peninsula" (Ibid.: 34).

In 1838, a large part of the Polyphem expedition was
undertaken in native skin boats brought from Sitka. On
5 July near Cape Lisburne, the ship discharged five three-
hatched kayaks and an umiak under the leadership of
Aleksandr Kashevarov to explore the coastline as far east
as Dease Inlet. Between that time and 26 August, the
Polyphem sailed here and there while awaiting the return
of the native boats. They apparently had agreed to meet
at Chamisso Island, because the skin boats arrived at Cape
Krusenstern at the northern edge of Kotzebue Sound,
where Kashevarov learned from Eskimos that the ship was at
the island. The Polyphem was not there by the time they
arrived on 29 August, but nevertheless, Kashevarov "found
an indication that the Polyphem had been there" (VanStone,
ed., 1977: 10, 64). The "indication" was probably the
Russian-American Company post now in the museum. On
5 September, the Polyphem arrived, and they left the Arctic
for home.

It is remarkable that the three signal posts erected between 1826 and 1849 had withstood the ravages of time, weather, and man until they were uprooted in 1909. They had weathered a bit; a few other names, dates, and initials had been added; and a "copper coin," which Beechey nailed "upon a post on the summit of the island" in 1826 had been stolen before he returned in 1827 (Beechey 1831, II: 534).[1] But the two hundred dollars paid for the posts bought more than three pieces of wood; it bought the adventures, hopes, tragedies, and dreams that go into making an empire.

Note

1. On the "Blossom" side of the English pole, at bottom right, is faintly carved, "Wieland, S. F. Cal. USA, 7/98," and on the right side is a "K," and under it, "1907." On the "Herald" side, the word, "Hi," is incised under the date. On the face of the Russian pole, "GA" is carved in English characters on the left, and the name and date, "Joe Jury 1898" are carved under 1838. Under Jury's name are some faint and hard-to-read Russian characters, over which the name and date, "E. D. Johnson, 1898," are incised in English letters. Below that are the initials, "J C" and "MC." On the lower round portion of the post are the initials, "J V C," and what appears to be "1908." There are no markings on the back of the Russian post, because of decay.

VIII

THE OMILAK SILVER MINE[*]

The first mine in northern Alaska had been in operation almost 20 years before the famous "Nome gold strike" was made on Anvil Creek, but unlike the Nome gold placers, which started many a man on the road to wealth, the Omilak mine was a silver lode whose shafts and tunnels ended mainly in failure. Yet the Omilak deserves a place in the history of Alaska mining both because of the perseverance that characterized the repeated attempts to make it a going concern and because it got its start almost as early as the famed Treadwell Mine in South-eastern Alaska.

When I first went to the Seward Peninsula in 1945 I became interested in the Omilak mine, but could find no one who knew about its discovery and early history. Printed sources gave little information, much of which later proved wrong. But in the course of gathering materials for an ethnohistory of the Bering Strait Eskimos I found newspaper stories about the origin of the mine in scrapbooks kept by both William H. Dall and Sheldon Jackson.[1] The actual discovery is somewhat befogged in the initial enthusiastic reports, but apparently in the summer of 1880 a schooner captain first drew public attention to silver and lead prospects on Omilak Mountain about 37 airline miles north of the Eskimo village of Cheenik, now called Golovin.

In 1892 the mine was recognized for the first time on the U.S. Coast and Geodetic Survey's Hydrographic Map No. 66 with the phrase, "Lead mines," but the name Omilak did not appear in Geological Survey reports until 1901 when W. C. Mendenhall incorrectly recorded it as "Omalik," with the vowels a and i reversed. In 1908, Alfred H. Brooks said that this word, Omalik, meant "high chief."[2] This is a commonly used meaning for umialik or "boat owner," but the name is really Omilak, pronounced with a diphthong a-ee. This means "it's heavy" and refers to the argentiferous galena found at the mine.

The first report of the discovery appeared in The San Francisco Chronicle on December 4, 1880, under the head-line, "A Silver Mountain. An Extraordinary Discovery in Alaska." According to this story, a whaling schooner had anchored in Golovnin Bay the previous summer and the

_____

[*] The Alaska Journal, Summer 1974, pages 142-48.

captain had been so liberal in trading sea biscuits to the local Eskimos that an appreciative chief invited him to get salmon on the upper Fish River, which flows into the bay.

While four of the crew fished for their supper, Captain William P. Gallagher and the chief climbed a mountain where they inspected rocks resembling "congealed iron." The rocks would "only bend," not break, although finally with one mighty whack of an ax, the captain managed to split off a piece. Later, in Oakland, California, this piece assayed $6,000 to the ton in silver. With this report of incredible riches ($130 to the ton was considered a very good assay value), a company was quickly organized and a schooner chartered to return to the site. The same captain and mate were to be hired on a share basis, and a crew paid for seven months. The newspaper article predicted that the discovery would be "only the beginning of vast discoveries which will soon be made in Alaska...to which thousands will rush."

Further news about the discovery appeared in the Chronicle on May 4, 1881, the day the schooner W. F. March sailed for Golovnin Bay. According to this story, Captain Gallagher had anchored his schooner in the bay the previous summer to procure fresh water.[3] Along with Mr. Ryan, the mate, and some sailors, he set out to get water from the Fish River. The Eskimos showed them some rocks and offered to guide them to the source. Captain Gallagher had to make quite a detour from his watering because Omilak Mountain is more than eight miles from the closest point on the Fish River, and the actual river mileage from that point on the Fish to their boat anchorage was probably no less than 120 miles.

At the site, Ryan dug a six-foot hole and found "an inexhaustible quantity of some kind of ore which cut as readily as lead or silver." These pieces were later given to a Captain Blaisdell in Oakland and he had the assays made. According to this story, they ranged from $2,000 to an astronomical $8,000 in silver to the ton.[4]

On May 4, 1881, all 10 stockholders of a newly formed mining company sailed for Golovnin Bay on the schooner W. F. March. The March was chartered from Joshua Y. Hendy, a San Francisco manufacturer of mining and other machinery and aboard her were Captain Gallagher, six seamen, provisions for five months, and the stockholders: Alphius Williams, president; R. B. Hard, James Hawley, C. McWorthy, J. C. McMullin, George C. King, D. S. Mackey, William S. Wells, John C. Green and C. O. Babb. They expected to "stake out their claims, work them, and on their return blossom into bonanza kings." All of these men were said to be "practical miners," but Williams was also a mining engineer; Hard was formerly in the livery stable and "collecting business" in Oakland, and Green was in the real estate business.(5)

The details of the first year of mining are told by Williams and Hard in an article they wrote for The Oakland Daily Evening Tribune soon after their return home in 1881: As soon as the March arrived at Golovnin Bay, on June 13, 1881, the men went to the mountain and, finding Gallagher's report to be true, "discovered" the mine, which they named the Galena. All of the bonanza kings worked hard at sinking a shaft until the end of July when King, Mackey and a man named Hoepfner who was mate on the March went to the Kuskokwim River to prospect for cinnabar. The March took them down and was to pick them up again on the voyage back to San Francisco.

In July, Green organized the Fish River Mining District. This was the first mining district in western Alaska and it included the entire Seward Peninsula. According to Alfred Brooks, the district was organized by the Alaska Gold and Silver Mining, Milling and Trading Company, which the Williams and Hard account called the Alaska Mining Company. On August 11 the schooner returned to Golovnin Bay from the Kuskokwim and began to load some ore which had been floated down the river in Eskimo skin boats. For several days they were beset by heavy winds and on August 15 the March was blown ashore on the rocks. She was a total wreck within 20 minutes but the men saved most of their clothing and a few supplies. The next day, Eskimos offered to take a letter all the way to St. Michael to inform the Alaska Commercial Company trader of their predicament. Babb, Green and Wells accompanied the Eskimos and after a journey of 17 days reached St. Michael. They sailed to San Francisco on the Alaska Commercial Company's Matthew Turner. Captain Gallagher, the other five partners, and the five seamen who were left at Fish River also went to St. Michael in Eskimo boats, arriving after a stormy trip of 21 days. On September 16 the Revenue Cutter Thomas H. Corwin arrived and took them aboard for San Francisco. No report has been found as to how the Kuskokwim party spent the winter, how they got home, or whether they ever did get home.

The account by Williams and Hard glowed with appreciation for both mining and living in the Fish River area, which they compared favorably to Maine. The mine was considered to be "very rich" and game and fish were abundant. The friendly Eskimos sold fish at bargain prices: a 10-pound salmon in exchange for two sea biscuits worth a quarter of a cent.

In another interview, Williams told a reporter that he was not sorry that the March had gone ashore, because they discovered that she had been coppered over to hide her worm-eaten condition. Had they sailed to San Francisco with the ore, the schooner might have proved to be their coffin.(6)

We learn of the 1882 silver miners from the writings
of Johan Adrian Jacobsen, a collector for the Royal
Ethnological Museum of Berlin. After spending some months
collecting in Southeastern Alaska, Jacobsen went to St.
Michael where he met the schooner Leo, which had carried
some Golovnin Bay miners north from San Francisco. The
Leo's main purpose that summer was to transport men to
Point Barrow for the International Polar Expedition, but
the miners and their cargo of ore were to be picked up
at the end of the summer to return to San Francisco. [7]

Jacobsen, who was travelling throughout the Bering
Strait area from July 1882 until the following spring,
gave no details of the actual mining operations, but his
path often crossed that of the superintendent, a "Mr.
Hartz," (R. B. Hard, one of the original stockholders).
"Hartz" spent part of the winter at "Singek" (Cheenik)
where he and his companions entertained Jacobsen in their
house. Hard also lent Jacobsen some dogs from his two
teams, which he used to transport supplies from St.
Michael and, presumably, for travel to the mine.

Jacobsen also mentioned that Mr. Hard's pleasures
during the winter included ice-skating on the smooth ice
of the bay and attending a feast for the dead at Ignituk,
a village about two miles northwest of Rocky Point, the
outer promontory of Golovnin Bay. Jacobsen, too,
attended the week-long festivities, and wrote a detailed
description of this important Eskimo ceremony.

When the Corwin arrived in Golovnin Bay early in the
summer of 1883, the surgeon gave medical assistance to a
miner who had broken his leg 29 days earlier. [8] That year
the company changed its name to the Omilak Gold and Silver
Mining Company and brought men and equipment north on
another chartered schooner, the Alaska. A stern-wheel
steamer and eight mules were reported to be aboard.

With considerable help from the Fish River Eskimos,
20 men worked all summer to mine only 55 tons of ore.
This, with 20 tons that Hard and his crew had mined during
the winter, was loaded on the Alaska, which sailed from
Golovnin Bay on October 21, 1883, with Captain Gallagher
and 15 other men aboard. They were never heard from again
and presumably went down in a gale between Saint Lawrence
and Saint Matthew Islands. Four lucky men remained behind
to take care of the mine during the winter.

When Captain Michael A. Healy of the Corwin sent
Lieutenant Hall ashore at Cheenik on June 9, 1884, he
learned that the miners had killed two Eskimos during the
winter, supposedly while defending their property from
theft. Through an interpreter, Hall learned that the other
Eskimos seemed to agree that the shooting had been
justified because the men were desperadoes. Healy did not
investigate further at the time and considered the incident
closed. [9]

A Revenue Marine vessel's principal duties were to curb the sale of contraband liquor and breech-loading rifles to natives and to render assistance to whalers and others in distress. In 1884, Captain Healy stretched his instruction to the limit when on June 9 he gave two bags of potatoes and four of flour to the miners to tide them over until mid-July when they expected to purchase provisions in St. Michael. The Corwin even transported the supplies to Golovnin Bay, but only a month later Healy found five of the miners at St. Michael "in a wholly destitute condition." He took them aboard because the Omilak Company was unable to either feed them or to provide means for getting them out of the country.

In his printed report for 1884, Captain Healy said: "I can not censure in too severe terms the employment of persons here without sufficient stores and with inadequate means of retreat," but at the same time he diplomatically reaffirmed his primary position to be "of service to citizens who have interests in the Arctic seas, and [believing in] the freedom with which they ask for the assistance of this vessel in matters of private importance, public interest and humanity...."(10)

D. S. Mackey, who had been the sole occupant at the mine during the winter, visited the Corwin early in the summer of 1885 and reported that he and the Eskimos were on friendly terms and that the mine was "very rich, with an inexhaustible quantity of ore." Shortly before the Corwin left on its cruise northward, the Bonanza, another vessel chartered by the company, arrived with a "more thoroughly organized company consisting of 15 miners and superintendent," from whom, said Healy, "better results are anticipated."(11)

But pessimistic notes about the mine had crept into Healy's reports. He noted that the shallowness of the Fish River and the enormous distance to the San Francisco market, with consequent high costs, could be detrimental to its development. He also began to have second thoughts about the tragedy of the winter of 1883-84 when he took exception to prophecies that the miners were to be attacked by Eskimos. On the contrary, Healy said, "the Indians [i.e., Eskimos] are generally well-behaved and peaceable....If there is any trouble it will be caused by the introduction of liquor among the Indians or the total disregard of their personal family rights, which, in all Indian territory, the whites seem to ignore."

On September 3, 1885, when the Corwin returned to Golovnin Bay from the Arctic, Healy sent two officers to the Bonanza, which was loading ore. They were satisfied that all was well at the mine, but reported that the miners were strangely reticent about the results of the summer's work.

In 1886 Captain Healy was in command of the Bear in

Alaskan waters and his logbook reveals that the Bonanza
was again at Golovnin Bay. Subsequent logbooks contain
no further references to the mine until 1891.

By 1886, the results of the mining operations must
have been disappointing. In 1885, 125 tons of ore were
shipped south on the Bonanza, but in 1886 only 30 tons
went out. In 1889 the shipment was a little more than
41 tons. The mine was completely closed down during 1890
following a report that there was no continuous vein of
ore. In all, the total production between 1880 and 1890
probably did not amount to more than 300 or 400 tons.(12)

But in 1891, the miners' hopes gleamed brightly
again when efforts were renewed "with increased capital
and new energy." John Green, through Army Captain A. M.
Brown, had induced a group of men from St. Louis,
Chicago, Denver and Pittsburgh to invest $250,000 in the
company. Development plans included a 45-mile tramway
from the mine to Golovnin Bay and two steamers to carry
the ore to San Francisco.(13)

On May 29, 1891, Green and Brown sailed north on
the chartered steamer South Coast, with J. H. Ferguson
who represented the new investors. Aboard were 55 men
and considerable equipment. Mining would no longer be
done on a shoestring, thanks to the new money. The outfit
was said to have included a stern-wheel steamer with a
capacity of 50 tons, a diamond drill, a dynamo to generate
electricity for lighting shafts and tunnels, 15 horses,
wagons, steam hoisting machinery, three 50-ton barges,
25,000 feet of lumber for buildings and provisions for 18
months. Some of this inventory, however, was apparently only
publicity because later reports said they had ascended the
Fish River in Eskimo umiaks rather than a sternwheeler;
that there were only four horses, and that they were so
short of coal that the Bear had to give them some at
Unalaska so the South Coast could continue to Golovnin Bay.

According to Captain Healy, Green's companions were
prospective purchasers who apparently had not yet sunk
all their money into the venture: "Mr Green's mine has
been on the market for sale for a number of years and
upon two occasions I have been consulted by capitalists
considering buying it. My proper representations to its
situation and worth may have stopped the sales."

In the 1891 season the miners again hired Fish River
Eskimos for camp and mining work and immediately plunged
into their labors. On one side of the mountain were two
shafts, 35 and 50 feet deep, and an incline 110 feet deep,
from which 40 tons of ore had been taken. On the other
side there was a 335-foot tunnel running parallel to the
ore formation rather than crosscutting it. They also
found some antimony. At the end of three months' work,
the miners took an inventory of supplies and came to the
disagreeable conclusion that they did not have a full

THE CAMP AT OMILAK.

A PARTY OF ESQUIMALT MINERS

Drawings from an article about the Omilak mine in
the San Francisco Chronicle, August 5, 1892.

allowance of food for six men for the winter. Ferguson
therefore decided to leave eight men at the mine, take
the rest back to San Francisco, and to send additional
supplies to those remaining behind.

The promised supplies never arrived. When the men
tired of a steady diet of beans and flour, they turned to
fish. When fish became monotonous, they tried seal oil,
which they liked. But yearning for something more
substantial they killed two horses, which by then were
almost skeletons. The other two horses froze to death.

Although the men were comfortable in the house at
the mine, they fretted all winter about being rescued and
had just decided to walk to Kodiak--of all places!--when
Captain Healy arrived in the Bear, having been alerted by
their associates in San Francisco that all might not be
well. On June 22, 1892, Healy sent a launch up the bay
to offer the miners passage home. Captain Brown, Frank L.
Johnson, George Juliam and William Carville accepted.
L. J. Dexter, H. G. Maud and Olaf Oleson (or Ohlsen)
elected to stay in the North. J. P. Peterson had been
killed by an explosion during the winter. "L. J. Dexter"
seems actually to have been John A. Dexter, of whom more
later.

By 1892, Captain Healy was looking quite differently
upon the two murders of 1883-84. The Eskimos had not been
desperadoes, as was first stated, but were killed while
defending their marital rights. In 1891, John Green had
asked Healy to stop frequently at Golovnin Bay to protect
the miners from the Eskimos, and when Healy refused--on
the grounds that there was no such danger--Green complained
to the Secretary of the Treasury under whom the Revenue
Marine Service operated. Healy, in defense of his decision
and in the light of what he considered to be false
statements by Green, said that Green wanted the Bear to
call at Golovnin Bay merely for his own personal convenience
and was using fear of the Eskimos only as an excuse.

Healy said that the employees of the mine suffered
far more at the hands of their employers than from the
Eskimos, of whom they had spoken highly. The plight of
one of the employees had recently come to his attention
when the man was taken aboard the Bear, "entirely destitute
and [having] to resort to the law to obtain his pay for
remaining at Mr. Green's mine."

Furthermore, said Healy, in 1883-84 the two Eskimos
had not been killed while intoxicated, as Green later said,
or because of breaking and entering, but because the miners
had "invaded the homes of the Indians and violated their
marital relations." When the Eskimos resisted, the miners
loaded rifles, selected two prominent men, and murdered
them in cold blood.

Healy continued: "[I have] found during all my

experience that where trouble comes between white men and
natives the white men are always in the wrong. If Mr.
Green's company and its employees will deal fairly with
the Indians, will not make stills and sell them the vile
productions...and will above all respect their marital
relations, there need be no more fear of trouble at
Golovin [sic] Bay than at St. Michael nearby."

Older Norton Sound Eskimos still have vague
recollections of this event from stories they heard in
childhood, mostly corroborating Healy's statement of 1892
that two brothers were killed by the miners in a fit of
sexual pique. Some added that the miners were drunk. In
1968, however, I heard a story with an entirely new twist,
which appears to have developed from the excitement
generated over the pending native land claims legislation.
In this version, two Eskimo brothers, one by the name of
Ayayuk, were killed while trying "to stop white people
mining, because 'this land belongs to Eskimos. You people
come from outside and steal our land.'"

It is very doubtful that land would have been an
issue in 1883, especially when all historical evidence
shows that the early Eskimos eagerly welcomed foreigners,
and particularly those with trade goods. So far as is
known, no word of criticism was ever leveled at the
Russian-American Company, which occupied considerable
acreage for trading posts at St. Michael, beginning in 1833,
and at Unalakleet, from 1840 or 1841. Nor did the
successor Alaska Commercial Company come in for such
criticism.

My informant told me that the two slain brothers had
also been dissatisfied with their wages: "The miners just
stole the work out of the Eskimos, who hauled skin boat
after skin boat of ore down the river--tons of it, and an
Eskimo getting only one 50-pound sack of flour, one pound
of tea and a little sugar for a whole summer's work."
The owner of the skin boat was paid double, sometimes with
the addition of a little gingham for pants and shirts.
This undoubtedly was true, for John Green himself corroborated the low pay when he admitted in 1893 that he had
to pay only a total of several hundred dollars' worth of
supplies every summer for the labor of 40 or 50 Eskimos.

Another "recollection" is exhibited in the Carrie M.
McLain Memorial Museum in Nome as a large printed text of
an interview with Joshua Akwinona. According to Akwinona,
his grandfather, Tacoma (or "Too-coe-ah") found "heavy
stuff" as he drove caribou between Telephone Creek and the
site of the subsequent mining operations. Tacoma's two
nephews took the ore to the captain of a "whaling ship,"
and mining began the following year.

"Later on," said Mr. Akwinona, "those two brothers
(my grandfather's nephews) found out that the 'heavy stuff'
was silver and lead, and that those things could be used

for rifle bullets. When they wanted to have an interest in the ores, the white people just killed them in front of their family."

Despite the unfavorable report about the mining prospects prior to 1890 and the logistics disaster of 1891-92, the mine was patented on February 3, 1894, under the name of Omilak Gold and Silver Mining Company. Two of the original directors, J. C. Green and A. F. Williams, were listed on the patent along with John Lowrie, A. Borgland, S. I. Marsten, D. S. Rouse and W. W. Whitman. (14)

A growing interest in other minerals in the Golovnin area probably prompted the patent, but an irony lies in the fact that this patented failure was to be indirectly responsible for the Nome gold rush of 1898-1900.

In 1891, silver mine employees John Dexter and George Julian, having wandered up the Niukluk River by mistake, successfully panned for gold at the mouth of what is now called Melsing Creek. Dexter, who turned down a "rescue" by the Bear in 1892, remained in the North and in September, 1892, returned to the prospected area and found even better showing on Kivik Creek.

Dexter established a trading post at Cheenik and in February 1895 outfitted a miner named George Johansen for a prospecting trip. Johansen was accompanied by two Eskimos, Andrew Napauk as guide and Tom Quarick, who claimed to have told Daniel B. Libby and Otto von Bendleben, employees of the Western Union Telegraph Expedition, about gold in 1866 and 1867. Johansen found gold on what was later called Ophir Creek and returned there with sluice boxes. For some inexplicable reason, however, he abandoned all of his equipment near the Casadepaga River. (15)

Meanwhile, prospecting was going on in the Canadian Yukon and "Klondike" became a name that electrified the world. In San Francisco, Daniel Libby, caught up by the excitement, organized a party to return to his prospecting grounds of 30 years earlier. In the fall of 1897, he and H. L. Blake, L. F. Melsing and A. P. Mordaunt hired Dexter's former guide, Napauk, for prospecting the Niukluk and Fish rivers, and then returned to Cheenik for the winter. In April, 1898, with the help of Tom Quarick, they built a mining camp which they called Council City and established the El Dorado Mining District, apparently without any knowledge of the Fish River Mining District which had been formed in July, 1881, by the Omilak miners.

At least four prospecting trips were made from Council into the surrounding area during the early part of 1898, and one of these jaunts pointed the way to the gold rush when an Eskimo showed Libby and his partners gold from the Nome area. Blake and several others followed the tip that same year and this resulted in the exciting but somewhat sordid tale of the discovery on Anvil Creek. (16)

The sudden engulfment of the entire peninsula by prospectors in 1899 and the new importance of land as property caused Dexter to worry about the title to his Cheenik trading post, which included the building put up by Green in 1882 and still claimed by him although it had been abandoned since 1891. Cheenik had grown from two dwellings to a fairly large settlement by 1899 because the Eskimos from the surrounding area were drawn to Dexter's post. The establishment consisted of a dwelling 70 by 22 feet, a "store" 16 by 16 feet, a fish house 12 by 14 feet, a log house 16 by 16 feet which was occupied by Dexter's Eskimo mother-in-law, two small gardens and "other buildings."[17]

Dexter appealed to Sheldon Jackson for help in obtaining information in Washington about his status as owner. Jackson's reply has not come to light but it apparently was favorable because Dexter lived in Golovin, formerly Cheenik, as a trader for many years until his death.

After the big gold rush to the Seward Peninsula subsided and mining became a more or less routine business, another attempt was made to work the Omilak Mine. In 1906 the Granby-Alaska Company was incorporated for that purpose. Mining equipment, an electric power plant and a sawmill were sent to the mine, which was leased with an option to buy. Miners sunk a 200-foot shaft, blocked out some ore, and drove a 500-foot tunnel toward the ore deposits during a year of development work, but no ore was shipped. Work was suspended in 1907, but a little mining was again done in 1910.[18]

In 1909 a U.S. Geological Survey party visited the mine and reported that none of the veins was "of sufficient size to warrant mining," and, "Considering the number of years the ground has been held and the large expenditures that have been incurred, the amount of development work is astonishingly small." The reports said that half a mile or so below the mine were a repair shop, electric plant, assay laboratory, electric sawmill, stable, "and other things usually found only at large producing mines," as well as a river steamer, which had never been used.

Henry P. Chandler, who worked with the Granby-Alaska Company in 1906-07, said that at the mine itself there was a bunkhouse, a shaft house, a blacksmith shop and a powder house. About a mile from the mine down the South Fork of Omilak Creek (erroneously called Mosquito Creek on U.S. Geological Survey maps) was "Lower Camp," which had a bunkhouse, a storehouse, an electric power plant, a stable and a steam sawmill. A wagon road connected Omilak with the Fish River where a storehouse called "Buster House" was built.

About 1907, the Seward Peninsula and Southeastern Railway Company, which was planning to build a railroad from Nome to Council, also proposed a 44-mile extension from Council to Omilak, but construction of the railroad never got started. On April 4, 1908, Wallace Johnson was appointed postmaster at Omilak, evidently in the expectation of a revival of activity there, but the office never opened and the appointment was rescinded the following year.

After more than a decade of idleness, the galena ghosts came to life again in 1922 when Mr. Green, who had not been heard of for years in the Nome area, returned to further develop the Omilak property. He had some 300 tons of supplies and equipment but nothing came of the venture. More than 40 years after the original discovery, Green gave up for the last time.

The prospects for the Omilak grew steadily dimmer as mining costs increased through the years. World War II interrupted most mining on Seward Peninsula, and some of it never did revive. In 1965 the Omilak and 30 other tracts of foreclosed mining claims were sold at public auction in Nome by the Alaska Division of Lands.

The great rewards that had once been expected of the mine had not materialized, and the $50,000, or perhaps even $100,000, worth of silver taken from the mine was but a drop in the bucket compared to the millions in gold from the rest of Seward Peninsula. The efforts had been no less, however, and the name Omilak will always be a reminder of the first Eskimo experience in mining as skin boat after skin boat full of ore floated down the Fish River for the smelters of California.

Notes

1. Dall's scrapbooks are in the archives of the Smithsonian Institution Libraries, Washington, D.C., and Jackson's are in the Presbyterian Historical Society manuscripts, Philadelphia. Also helpful was a scrapbook of the Life-Saving Service (1879-1882) in Record Group 26 (Records of the U.S. Coast Guard), National Archives, Washington.

2. Mendenhall, 1901, pp. 189, 201, and plate 21; Collier et al., 1908, p. 15.

3. No Captain Gallagher is listed in "Returns of Whaling Vessels Sailing from American Ports...1876-1928." Reginald B. Hegarty. Gallagher was possibly a trader.

4. In 1909, A geological Survey bulletin listed official assay returns from the mine as ranging from $38.10 to $137.29 silver value per ton, and from $20.08

to $61.52 lead value per ton. (Smith and Eakin, 1910,
p. 348). This entire report is duplicated in U.S.G.S.
Bulletin 449 (1911). The Omilak mine is also mentioned
in other bulletins, for example Nos. 314, 480, 533, 622,
649, 662, 722, 933A and 1246.

5. Information about 1881 events is taken from The
San Francisco Chronicle, May 4, 1881, The Oakland Daily
Evening Tribune, October 21, 1881; Harrison, 1905, pp. 48,
130; Collier et al., 1908, p. 14; Smith and Eakin, 1910,
p. 345, and Henry P. Chandler, personal communication.

6. The Oakland Daily Evening Tribune, October 21,
1881; Logbook of the Corwin, entry for September 17, 1881
(National Archives, Record Group 26, Records of the U.S.
Coast Guard).
     Eleven years after Gallagher's discovery, a story was
circulated that a man named Hoffner had discovered the
mine after Eskimos gave him bullets made from pure silver
(Unidentified newspaper account, dated October 22, 1891,
Dall scrapbooks, Vol. 18, p. 133). Walter Hoepfner
(Hoffner) went down with the schooner Alaska in 1883 (Healy,
1889, p. 81.)

7. Jacobsen, 1884, pp. 154, 222, 258, 267, 268, 271,
186.

8. Information for 1883 is taken from Smith and Eakin,
1910, p. 345; Healy, 1889, pp. 8-9; Logbook of the Corwin,
1883; and Letter, M. A. Healy to Charles J. Folger, dated
St. Michael, August 9, 1883, National Archives, Record
Group 26, Alaska File. Healy gives the names of the
missing men in his report, but of the original 10 stockholders, apparently only Babb was aboard.

9. Healy, 1889, p. 9.

10. Letter, Healy to Folger, dated San Francisco,
October 6, 1884, National Archives, Record Group 26,
Alaska File; Healy, 1889, p. 9; and Logbook of the Corwin,
1884.

11. Information about 1885 is from M. A. Healy,
1887, pp. 6, 13.

12. Smith and Eakin, 1910, p. 348; Porter, 1893,
p. 236; Spurr, p. 125.

13. Information for 1891 and 1892 is taken from The
San Francisco Chronicle, August 5, 1892; Unidentified
clipping in August, 1892, Sheldon Jackson scrapbook, Vol.
22, p. 160; Logbook of the Bear, 1892; Letter, Healy to
the Secretary of the Treasury, dated Sausalito, January
21, 1892, Record Group 26, National Archives; and The San
Francisco Examiner, January 23, 1895.
     According to Harrison (1905, p. 273) John A. Dexter

first came to Alaska on the steam whaler Grampus, but the
Grampus was not in the Arctic until 1886. Henry G. Dexter
was the captain until 1889 (Hegarty, 1959).

14.   Files of the Division of Geological Survey, State
of Alaska, College, Alaska. Two bulletins of the U.S.
Geological Survey reported that in 1898 the company became
the Russian-American Mining Exploration Company (Collier
et al., 1908, p. 14, and Smith and Eakin, 1910, p. 345).

15.   Castle, 1912, pp. 8-9.

16.   Ibid., pp. 10-11; Collier et al., 1908, pp. 16-18;
Spurr, 1899, p. 125; Carlson, 1946, p. 261; Blake, 1900,
p. 2.

17.   Letter, Dexter to Jackson, dated Golovnin Bay,
September 10, 1899, Correspondence MF 137, Presbyterian
Historical Society.

18.   Information for this period is from Smith and
Eakin, 1910, p. 347; Ricks, 1965, p. 48; Files of the
Division of Geological Survey, College, Alaska; The Nome
Nugget, July 30, 1965; and Henry P. Chandler, personal
communications.
The largest stockholders of the Granby-Alaska Co.
were a Mr. Burnam of Portland, Maine; Young of Saint
Stephen, New Brunswick; and Miner of Granby, Quebec. They
were also interested in the Granby Mine in British Columbia.
I am very grateful to Henry P. Chandler of Tuftonboro,
New Hampshire, for maps, photographs and information about
the mine in 1906-1907 and the 1920's. Mr. Chandler, who
was at Omilak during 1906-07, remained in the Teller and
Nome areas until 1914. He continued to correspond with
Seward Peninsula miners after he left Alaska to engage
in mining in the western states and later to work for the
U.S. Bureau of Mines in Washington, D.C.
I also wish to thank Mildred Brown, College, Alaska,
and David M. Hopkins, Menlo Park, California, for their
help in supplying geological reports, and Don Grybeck of
College and Thomas P. Miller of Anchorage for photographs.

IX

THE MAKING OF A LEGEND:
CHARLIE AND MARY ANTISARLOOK'S REINDEER HERD[*]

Mary Antisarlook Andrewuk--usually known as Sinrock Mary--was the most celebrated Eskimo woman of her day, but it was a pinnacle that she had reached only through a series of fortuitous events and subsequent stories written about her. The publicity given to this woman in Alaskan writings has been out of proportion to the attention given to her husband, Charlie Antisarlook, from whom she inherited a herd of reindeer under American, not Eskimo, inheritance laws and thereby became the "Reindeer Queen." One of the reasons for her greater fame is that she outlived her husband by 48 years, thus casting his role in a shadow. The purpose of this paper is to balance the scales and present the background to Mary's unique place in the history of the Alaskan reindeer industry.

Mary's good fortune came about with her marriage to a man who was in the right place at the right time. Charlie's trip in 1890 as interpreter aboard the revenue marine cutter Bear set the stage for his acquisition of reindeer through a unique enterprise: the importation of Siberian domesticated reindeer to be owned by Eskimos for the purpose of "raising" them into civilization and keeping them from starvation. This project was conceived by Sheldon Jackson, Presbyterian missionary and general agent of education for Alaska, while he was aboard the Bear in 1890 to establish schools in northwest Alaska.

Both Mary and Charlie were born at a propitious time to become famous in recorded annals. Mary was born in Saint Michael, a cosmopolitan settlement that had been established in 1833 as a redoubt by the Russian-American Company. After the purchase of Alaska by the United States in 1867, it became a busy American trading center, where she met people from many foreign lands as well as native Alaskans from distant villages. Charlie was born in the Nome area of a family that traveled extensively for trade: to Saint Michael, Siberia, but especially to Port Clarence, where they awaited the arrival of the "whaling fleet" every summer about the fourth of July. Both could speak fair English, a skill that gave them an advantage in dealing with the white man.

---

* Unpublished.

118

Mary, who was also known as "Reindeer Mary" and
"Russian Mary" was a newsworthy subject to the early mining
days of Bering Strait because of being a woman in a
frontier land--and an Eskimo woman at that--whose wealth
and imposing presence (in 1902, a writer called her "tall
and powerful, weighing nearly three hundred pounds"),(1)
set her apart from the mass of poor, anonymous Eskimos
who roamed the streets of Nome and up and down the coast
after the discovery of gold in 1898. However, she would
not have endeared herself to her own people, as she did,
had she not possessed virtues that here highly esteemed
by the Eskimos: a good nature, helpfulness, and generosity.
She thus combined a commercial success highly regarded by
the whites with a role most valued in Eskimo culture.

Mary, who apparently acquired her English name from
Americans who were unwilling to use either her Russian
name, Palasha Makrikoff, or her Eskimo name, Changunak
(or Sangruyak), was born of Russian and Eskimo parents
at a date unknown even to Mary herself. In a short,
unpublished article written by her niece, Esther Oliver,
about 1937, it is said that she was born in "1860-1870,"
but I was told in 1964 in Unalakleet by Eskimos who had
known her that she was born in the 1850s. When she died
on 22 November 1948, Stephen Ivanoff, a well-known Eskimo
trader of Unalakleet, who was 74 years old at the time,
quoted her age in the Nome Nugget as almost a hundred years.(2)

The names "Mary" and "Charlie" were bestowed upon many
an Eskimo by the early traders and miners of western Alaska,
causing untold confusion among all those so-called. One
of the women who has been confused with Sinrock Mary is
Alakiak, after whom the gold-rush town of Marys Igloo was
named. That Mary, who was sometimes called "Kougarok Mary,"
was also well-known and highly regarded as a generous and
compassionate woman during the gold rush. Born about 1878
near present-day Nome, Alakiak was taken to Port Clarence
by relatives when she was left an orphan. In 1901
prospectors, pushing into the Kougarok country, chose a site
for a town near "Mary's igloo," 50 miles north of Nome,
where, according to a newspaper item of 1901, "Many's the
poor fellow under obligations to this Eskimo woman for food
and shelter during...those severe winter storms. She has
become one of the best and certainly the most favored member
of her race among the whites."(3)

Sinrock Mary had led an uneventful existence until she
met her second husband, Antisarlook (anasaluk) who had come
to Saint Michael for a visit. Both had been married before:
Charlie, to a woman by the name of Aminguk, also from the
Nome area, and Mary, to a Russian from Saint Michael
(Charlie left his wife for Mary). After their marriage in
1889, they moved to Cape Nome, but Mary, who had grown up
in the comparatively urban Saint Michael, was in for a
cultural shock. She used to tell the school children of
Unalakleet, with considerable disbelief, that "there were
no white people there. Not any groceries, either. Their

food wasn't like what the Eskimos [of Saint Michael] work hard [for wages] to have." Instead, she said, those Eskimos of Cape Nome, lived on "real simple food" like tomcods, whale meat and blubber, seal oil and seal meat, rabbits, and ptarmigans."(4)

They did not stay at Cape Nome very long, and we first learn about them in contemporary written sources a few months later--in the summer of 1890--when Captain Michael Healy of the Bear hired them at Port Clarence to be interpreters for the summer's cruise. An entry in the logbook of the Bear for 4 July reads: "Took on board Indian interpreters Charley and his wife Mary to act as interpreters in taking census and establishing schools."(5) Several publications state that they were hired as interpreters for the buying of reindeer in Siberia, a story that Mary herself was in the habit of telling, but this was not so, since Jackson had not yet conceived of his reindeer project by the time they were engaged as interpreters, and no reindeer were purchased that year. On this trip, Jackson's first to the Arctic to oversee the building of schools at Cape Prince of Wales, Point Hope, and Point Barrow, he precipitously began his plans for importing reindeer after Healy had talked to him about his own ideas concerning such a project. A part of the cruise of the Bear that summer was devoted, therefore, to the investigation of the possibilities of buying reindeer in Siberia.

Mary and Charlie helped to take the census at various villages along the coast of Alaska, and also got a glimpse of Siberia when the Bear stopped at both Little Diomede Island in the Bering Strait and at a village at East Cape, Siberia. They were discharged on 31 July off the Seahorse Islands, but taken aboard again on 2 August to take the census at Point Barrow, according to the logbook. On 3 August, "Indian interpreters Charley and Mary left the vessel [off Cape Smythe House of Refuge] discharged from date."

Mary and Charlie had decided to spend the winter at Point Barrow, and Healy promised to take them to Saint Michael in the summer of 1891. On 14 August, according to the logbook of 1891, they boarded the Bear at Point Belcher because Point Barrow was icebound. But they did not return to Saint Michael, since Jackson apparently persuaded them to disembark at Cape Prince of Wales to assist the teacher, W. T. Lopp, whose co-teacher, Harrison Thornton was returning to the States for the winter. On 26 August, while en route to Siberia, Jackson wrote to W. T. Harris, the Commissioner of Education, that he had "engaged a native man and his wife who is a good interpreter and cook to remain with Mr. Lopp this winter..."(6) Whereupon, they left the Bear on 30 August 1891.

In the meantime, however, they traveled on the Bear to Siberia and were present when the first of sixteen

reindeer were purchased on 27 August at a village called
Enchowan. These sixteen deer were not obtained for
Jackson's project but only "to answer the question [posed
by Jackson's many critics] whether reindeer could be
purchased and transported alive." All sixteen were placed
on the Aleutian Islands on 21 September as the Bear
steamed for home.[7]

It is doubtful that Charlie and Mary were on the Bear
to interpret in 1891 because they could speak none of the
Siberian languages, and Siberian interpreters were used,
even in 1890. Yet, according to Mary's story, when Jackson
was negotiating with the Siberians, he apparently asked her
to interpret, which she was unable to do, "so she cried
when she couldn't understand or do any interpreting."
Then, when she cried, "the Captain [Healy] slapped her on
the face." In 1890, when the Bear stopped at the villages
along the west coast of Alaska to take the census, Mary
had been impressed by how "very polite or good natured" the
people were. But "when they get to Siberia [in 1891] people
were not polite. They were wild and they never smile."
Nevertheless, she reported favorably that the owner of the
reindeer lived in a very fine place, and had many deer
skins hanging up to dry. The first reindeer that were
purchased--two spotted and two black ones--were brought
to the Bear by "a poorly dressed" man without a nose
whistling at them.[8]

The logbook for the following day, the 28 August,
recorded that at "6.30 [a.m.] Lieut. Jarvis left vessel in
launch to bring on board reindeer purchased yesterday....
1.30 Lieut. Jarvis returned in launch with four of the
reindeer purchased yesterday....the four reindeer were taken
on board as an experiment. More could have been purchased
if desired."

The Bear returned to Cape Prince of Wales where Charlie
and Mary were discharged in the care of Lopp. They remained
there until February 1892 when it was learned that Mary's
mother had died at Saint Michael. Lopp let them go to Cape
Nome "where Charley's people lived...as they had not seen
their people for two years and were homesick." In Lopp's
report to the American Missionary Association of the
Congregational Church, which had a contract with the Bureau
of Education for the Wales school, he wrote that they had
been "fair cooks and housekeepers, honest and faithful and
could speak English."[9]

In 1892 Charlie and Mary were on hand at Port Clarence
to meet the congregated ships, especially the Bear, for on
25 June Healy "delivered to Mary, native interpreter,
articles received in San Francisco."[10] They were also
present on 29 June when Jackson selected the "watering
station of the whaling fleet" at Port Clarence, a half mile
from the Eskimo village of Sinramiut, as the site for the
reindeer station. A flagpole and two tents were erected,
and provisions and supplies for the station were unloaded

from the steamer Newport. The events of this day have been
preserved in a number of photographs taken by Miner W.
Bruce, who had been hired as the first superintendent of
the Teller Reindeer Station, as it was called after
Senator Henry M. Teller, of Colorado. One of the photographs shows the tents, supplies, and a group of ten
Eskimos, one of whom, I am sure is Mary (sitting on a box),
and probably Antisarlook, although we do not know which one
he is since he has never been identified in a picture. This
apparently is the first published photograph of Mary, who,
in later years, was a favorite subject of photographers.[11]

On 4 July the first reindeer were landed on the beach
and a building, 20 by 60 feet, was built by carpenters from
the Bear. Four herders were brought from Siberia that
summer to take care of the reindeer, and "several Eskimo
men...were to learn the trade of herding reindeer."[12]
One of these men was Charlie Antisarlook.

Charlie's stay during the year 1892-93 was not an
especially happy one, mainly because of Bruce's apparent
antagonism toward Mary. Perhaps Bruce's differences with
Healy--and subsequently with Jackson--were at the root of it.
Healy had decided that Bruce and his assistant, Bruce
Gibson, were to be fired because of alleged misbehavior,
selling of whiskey, and hatching up a private scheme to buy
Siberian reindeer, which would have been competitive with
Jackson's project. In a letter to Jackson, Healy confessed
that his "opposition [to Miner Bruce] began after one or
two days in his company."[13]

Since Jackson at that time was highly beholden to Healy
(as skipper of the Bear) for the success of his project, he
discharged Bruce and Gibson and replaced them with Lopp,
who had no experience with reindeer herding (but
neither had Bruce or Gibson). At any rate, Bruce said that
he had to discharge Charlie from the station because of his
"half-breed Russian wife. She had been among the whites
both at St. Michaels [sic] and Point Barrow [in 1890-91],
and knew just enough English to make mischief among the
natives. She behaved in such a manner that the only thing
to do to avert dissatisfaction among the natives was to
discharge her husband which was promptly done."[14]

Although Bruce had discharged Antisarlook, he was on
hand again when Lopp arrived to take over the reindeer
station in July 1893. Charlie was apparently determined to
take advantage of Jackson's promise that the Eskimos were
to own reindeer by making himself visible and available at
every opportunity. He knew, probably more than any other
Eskimo, what grand opportunities might lie ahead for a man
who owned reindeer. He was probably the only Eskimo man who
knew, and got along well with, from the very beginning,
all three key figures of the reindeer business--Healy,
Jackson and Lopp, as well as all of the officers of the Bear.
His ability to communicate in English was undoubtedly a
significant factor at a time when there were few Eskimos

who could even speak the pidgin English of the time.

A few weeks after Lopp's arrival at the reindeer station he wrote in his diary that "Kamuk and wife and Charley and Mary want to stay all winter," and the next day he hired them. By August 26 they had completed building a "shed" to house the herders, and a log house, 12 by 15 feet, for Charlie and Mary, since Charlie was apparently given special privileges. Lopp wrote to Jackson that Charlie was "anxious to get a herd of deer, and is willing to stay and trust to your generosity for his reward. Of course, I can only promise him 2 deer for the first year, but he thinks you will give him more than 2 if he stays here and does his duty. Charley is almost as good as a white man to have around--in some ways much better."(15)

Up to the time of Antisarlook's death in 1900, almost all of the reports and correspondence refer to only "Charlie," "Charlie and wife," or "Charlie and Mary." But in 1893, Mary J. Healy, Michael Healy's wife who sometimes accompanied him on the Bear, wrote about Mary without reference to her husband: "Mary adopted a little baby boy 5 months old whose mother was going to kill it. She carries it on her back, and takes the best care of the little thing. It is the third she has saved from death." This baby was undoubtedly Sigayuk, or George Antisarlook, who was born in 1893.(16) From all reports, he was the favorite of the eleven or twelve children that Mary adopted or cared for during her lifetime.

Lopp's diaries show an increasing interest in the reindeer by the Eskimos in 1893 and 1894: On 3 September, "Sovowhase [Soovawhasie] a young man from C. Nome enters herding school," and on 2 February 1894, "Charlie's brother [unnamed] brought two new herders from Unalakleet, and one from [Golovnin] Bay--Martin [Jacobson], Herbert [Tatpan] and Oo-kwit-koon." In all, there were approximately fifteen herders at the station in 1893-94.(17)

Yet, almost two years after the first reindeer had been landed at Port Clarence, no Eskimos owned a herd of reindeer, although several had earned a few through apprenticeship. Coupled with the discontent that this created among the herders was the inability of the Eskimos to get along with the four Siberian herders. The two events, however, that brought Antisarlook close to his dream of owning a herd was, first, the arrival of Laplanders in July to herd the reindeer, the Siberians having been sent back home because they proved temperamental and insubordinate. Most irksome to the Eskimos was a provision in the Laplanders' contracts that gave them all the reindeer they wanted for clothing and meat, a stipulation that the Eskimos could scarcely have greeted with joy since up to that time they had not been permitted to kill any reindeer.

Antisarlook was probably responsible, in part, for some of the resentement toward the Lapps, for William Kjellmann,

who had recruited the herders in Lapland and had become
the third reindeer superintendent, wrote in his annual
report of 1894-95 that "the Lapp herders did not receive
the warmest welcome from the people who are supposed to
have influence among the Eskimos." To the Eskimos, the
Laplanders, from a distant land, were not only usurping
their rights, but were putting the independent Eskimos
in a subservient position. Furthermore, their reportedly
surly dispositions differed greatly from the Eskimos,
who, at least outwardly, always seemed happy and cheerful.
A newspaper article of that time reported the four
Lapland children as being "not a very jolly crowd. They
are phlegmatic, careworn and silent, like their fathers
and mothers, and never smile."(18)

The second was a gift, not a loan, of a hundred head
of reindeer to the Congregational mission at Cape Prince
of Wales, to which Lopp had returned after his one-year
stay at Port Clarence. These two events exacerbated the
dissatisfaction among the Eskimos and created somewhat of
a backlash for the entrepreneurs of the reindeer business,
for to the Eskimos it meant that the reindeer had not,
after all, been imported for their use, as Jackson had told
Charlie ever since 1890.

Jackson, therefore, was compelled to fulfill his
promises for he finally realized that the Eskimos had
become "somewhat skeptical concerning their being permitted
to ultimately own the reindeer." Yet, even while planning
the loan of a hundred deer to Charlie and "his friends,"
he tried to persuade him to stay at the reindeer station
for another year at a salary of fifteen reindeer instead.
At last, he decided on the loan, entrusting "three or four
of the most experienced native apprentices with a herd of
115 reindeer [actually only a hundred since fifteen were
already owned by the apprentices]." Under terms of the
agreement they were to repay the one hundred deer after a
five-year period; were not to kill any bearing females; and
the herd was to be open to government "inspection and
control." On 5 September 1894, Antisarlook signed the
agreement (as An te si look) for his four co-owners: "I
zik sic, Kok to wak, I up puk and Soo vawha sie."(19)

Jackson was less than honest when he wrote that he had
loaned the first herd of reindeer to "the most experienced
native apprentices," for of the five men whose names were
on the loan agreement, only two of them, Antisarlook and
Soovawhasie, the eighteen-year-old lad who had come to the
station the year before, had any experience with reindeer.
The other three, "Iziksic (Asiksik, Antisarlook's brother,
"the old trader"), Koktowak (Kuktiuk), another brother, and
Iuppuk apparently began herding reindeer after the agreement was signed. Furthermore, William A. Kjellmann, the
third reindeer superintendent in as many years, who was an
experienced reindeer man from Norway, said that he had had
to dismiss Soovawhasie in December (before Antisarlook took
possession of the herd) because he did not take an interest

in the reindeer and had been found guilty of a few small thefts. "His qualifications seem to fit him better to become a great doctor [i.e., shaman] in this region rather than a herder. The Eskimos say that he was born to be a doctor, as they know from certain marks on him."[20]

The choice of Charlie to be the recipient of the first herd to fulfill Jackson's promise was inevitable, but according to Kjellmann he did not seem to be physically equipped for the strenuous life of a herder, since "on his arrival at the station he was quite ill and puny, and hence I could not set him at any hard work. He was soon to take a herd of his own, and he needed all the strength he could gather before taking charge of his own herd."[21]

Not until 1 February 1895 was the herd moved, mainly because Charlie went to Cape Prince of Wales for the annual trading and dancing festival. In the meantime, he had pursued the usual activities around the station, as recorded in the daybook kept by T. L. Brevig, assistant superintendent, teacher, and minister to the Laplanders: Charlie and Mary went to Point Spencer to see their brother; Charlie took care of deserters from whaling ships in his house; and Charlie looked for lost reindeer. On 2 November 1894 Brevig wrote that "the day opened with a catch-as-catch-can fight between Mary and Nah yuk. Charley tried to mediate peace and was sent sprawling to bed by his 'better half,' and her opponent sent sprawling to the floor headforemost."

Shamanism was still an important part of Eskimo life on Seward Peninsula at that time, and Brevig, the minister, had an opportunity—though at a distance—to see a performance that included Charlie. On 9 December he wrote that "the leading shaman had a confab with the spirits to-night. He had four fires burning in a square and reposed himself in the middle, groaning and sighing. Four new doctors were with him guarding the fires; Charley was one of them." The curious Laplanders were warned by Mary not to look at the fire. Thorwald Kjellmann, William Kjellmann's father, went out to watch, but the "guards" immediately vanished, leaving the shaman alone. Thinking that he was a sick man, Kjellmann spoke to him, but did not receive an answer. The next day, Charlie and Mary asked Kjellmann if his feet were stiff or swollen because he had spoken to the shaman.[22]

The first week of January 1895 saw feverish preparations among the Eskimos of Teller Reindeer Station in anticipation of the trip to Cape Prince of Wales for the annual festivitie Such intervillage get-togethers, often called the Messenger Feast, were the highlights of the dark winter season all along the coast of western Alaska during the shortest days of the year. One village—or at least the headman of the village—invited the inhabitants of another village, or villages, which ordinarily celebrated together year after year. That year, Kingegan, the village at Cape Prince of

Wales, was host to the villages of Sinramiut on Port
Clarence, Kauwerak (east of Port Clarence) and small
villages nearby. People with dogteams came daily to the
reindeer station and to Sinramiut village beginning the
second of January until all had arrived so they could
travel the 50 miles to Wales together. By the time they
left before daybreak on 6 January, 300 persons and 82
sleds had gathered. They were led to Wales by official
messengers, dressed in feather headdresses and fancy
clothing, and by Charlie, who was one of "the leading
men."(23)

Charlie returned from Wales on 19 January, and by the
30th most of the herders and Laplanders had been sent out
to the herd to help him choose the animals for the move
to the Sinuk River near Cape Rodney. On 1 February,
Charlie received his equipment, and prepared to leave the
next day with his deer despite a blizzard. About noon
on 2 February, a clear day but with the snow still flying,
Charlie and his family set out, accompanied by Aslak Somby,
a Laplander, and two Eskimos, Moses and Ahlook.(24)

Charlie's main home was on the site of an old village
near the mouth of the Sinuk River. Sinuk is the usual
spelling for "Sinrock," and is a more accurate rendition
of the Eskimo word singuk (or chinik in Yupik) meaning
point, a name that has been given to a number of Eskimo
villages in western Alaska. "Charlie's place" quickly
became a popular way station for winter travelers along
the coast. They had scarcely got settled, when in late
February, David Johnson, a Convenant missionary from
Unalakleet, arrived at Sinrock with two interpreters en
route to Teller Reindeer Station, Cape Prince of Wales,
and Kotzebue Sound, where he planned to establish a mission.
Because the herd was without a manager experienced with
reindeer, Somby and his family returned on 5 April to
help Charlie at fawning time. By 20 May, Charlie's herd
had been increased by 77 fawns.(25)

During the following year, the herd was again attended
only by Charlie and his herders, but another Laplander was
sent for the fawning season of 1897. In April, Kjellmann
visited the herd and learned that it was usually kept near
Charlie's house on the coast where there was no moss.
Consequently the herd was in poor condition. The herders
told him they had to stay near the ocean to fish because
"Antisarlook did not give them any [food], and they had to
scratch for themselves. When I arrived the apprentices
were feeding on the bark of willows, as the herd was too
far from the coast for any fishing to be done." He ordered
a deer to be slaughtered so they would have something to
eat. Charlie and his family were fishing about ten miles
east of Sinrock, and Kjellmann, "upon going to this camp...
took him to task for the poor condition and treatment of
the herd and apprentices. [Charlie] complained of the hard
winter and said he had all he could do to support himself
and family; that there had been no catch of seal, and last

summer's fishing had failed." Kjellmann counted 193
animals "besides the fawns born during the spring," and
although he said that the "herd was poor and not well
managed," he considered the forty-one percent increase
in reindeer in two years to be "a good percentage."(26)

Jackson's inconsistencies and rather unfeeling attitude
toward the Eskimos, and his unremitting drive to build up
reindeer herds for the missions was clearly obvious that
year by his request that Charlie pay back his reindeer
loan two years before the date specified in the contract
when there were only 278 animals in the herd.(27)   There
was no official explanation for this move, nor any report
on Jackson's visit to Charlie on 18 September 1897 (as
recorded in the lobgook of the Bear), but it undoubtedly
was for the purpose of asking him to return the deer.
Although Jackson might have considered Kjellman's report
an excuse for taking them back--Charlie's agreement read
that a hundred deer could be reclaimed at any time if they
seemed to be in danger of being lost "through neglect or
mismanagement"--Kjellmann had not recommended such a
course, especially when the fawning seasons had turned out
so successfully.   There is no doubt that the deer were
taken back to augment the herd at the new station of Eaton,
established near Unalakleet in 1897, and named after
General John Eaton, former Commissioner of Education.   Dr.
A. N. Kittilsen, the superintendent, took 120 reindeer
from Charlie (53 males, 65 females, and three fawns),
leaving him about 160; yet he had been loaned only a hundred,
and had owned outright fifteen more from his work at Teller
Reindeer Station.(28)

An even more bizarre turn of events came in the early
part of 1898 when the government "borrowed" every one of
Charlie's remaining reindeer to save a number of whalers
(not Eskimos) who allegedly were starving at Point Barrow,
their vessels having frozen in the ice pack.   When this
news was learned, the Bear was pressed into service from
San Francisco, and sailed to the edge of the ice at
Tununak on the Kuskokwim delta.   From there, Lieutenant
D. H. Jarvis traveled by dogteam to Sinrock to persuade
Charlie to loan his deer to save the whalers, arriving on
19 January 1898.   In his report of the "Overland Expedition,"
Jarvis wrote that he "had looked forward to this day so
long that now it had come I almost shrank from the task it
brought.   [Antisarlook] and his wife were old friends...but
how [was I] to induce them to give up their deer and convince
them that the Government would return an equal number at
some future time...These deer were their absolute property.
The Government had only a few weeks before taken from
Antisarlook [sic] the original number it had loaned to him
because of his good service and character, and had left him
the increase, which were now his...and the people gathered
about him, were dependent upon the herd for food and clothing

After explaining to Charlie that he had not come to
take the deer by force, but that he should decide of his

own free will and to trust the government to return them and to give him "ample and suitable reward," Charlie and Mary "held a long and solemn consultation, and finally explained their position. They were sorry for the white men at Point Barrow, and they were glad to be able to help them; they would let me have their deer, which represented their all, on my promise of return, if I would be directly responsible for them...I readily agreed to this, for I fully appreciated their goodness and the justice of their position. They were poor except for the deer herd, which was all they had to depend upon. They had grown quite a village about them, all in the service of the herd, and if I took the deer and 'Charlie' away, these people were likely to starve unless some arrangements were made for their living." He arranged for them to get provisions until the Bear's scheduled return in the spring.

Jarvis said that there were 138 deer in the herd, five of which belonged to the herders. He purchased these for about $15 apiece. Under terms of the loan, Charlie's herd was to be paid back in the summer of 1898 "together with the estimated increase in the herd for the coming spring, about 80 fawns, thus making 213 reindeer in all to be replaced."(29)

Antisarlook was paid $30 a month to go with his herd. He was accompanied on the drive by Dr. S. J. Call, surgeon of the Bear, and several assistant herders, one of whom was a young man from Wales named Utenna (George Ootenna) who later became a well-known reindeer owner in his own right. At Cape Prince of Wales, this contingent of the drive met Lopp's herd, which was also borrowed, and on 3 February, 448 reindeer and a train of dogteams started for Point Barrow. Almost eight weeks later, on 29 March, Jarvis' contingent was the first to arrive at Point Barrow, Lopp, Call, and Charlie coming soon after. They were greeted with astonishment, almost as apparitions ("had we come up in a balloon?" was asked), since it was not known that news of the wrecked whalers had reached the outside world. But ironically, after the great expense of sending the Bear on special duty, and the sacrifices and heroic efforts of the reindeer drivers, Jarvis learned that "there had been no great suffering and that for the present there was no great need."(30)

Reindeer herds for missions were again of first importance in disposing of the animals that were not needed, after all, for the whalers. Although 180 deer were eventually killed for food at Point Barrow, there was a surplus of animals after fawning time in 1898. Therefore, 391 reindeer were loaned to the Presbyterian mission at Point Barrow and thirty-four were driven to Point Hope for the Episcopalian mission. Apparently at no time was it thought expedient to let Charlie drive reindeer back to Sinrock, and when the first deer were returned in 1898, they were given to Lopp, not Antisarlook.(31)

Jackson's imperious plans to give reindeer to missions

deprived a poor family of a herd that could have been
returned within a few months. Although Jarvis had given
Mary orders for food during Charlie's absence, it was not
always easy to travel the 45 miles to Teller or the 75
miles to Golovin. When Francis Tuttle, captain of the
Bear in the summer of 1898, met Mary and others seal
hunting on Sledge Island, he wrote that "Mrs. Artisarlook
[sic] said they had nearly starved since her husband left
as seal and fish, their principal food had been very
scarce. I gave her ample provisions to last three months,
and promised to bring her husband back from Point Barrow."
Charlie arrived home on the Bear on 24 August, along
with "10 bags flour, 10# coffee, 1 box lead, 500 cartridges
(.44), 2 boxes tobacco, 2 boxes bread, 50# soap, 1 Bbl salt
Beef, 1000 primers and 1/4 lbs. powder."(32)

The reindeer needed to repay Antisarlook and Lopp
had to be purchased in Siberia because Jackson did not
want to deplete either the government or the mission herds,
but in 1898, they were able to buy only 159 deer, which
were given to Lopp as the first payment of the debt.
Antisarlook did not receive any until 13 July 1899 when
83 animals, which had been purchased by the crew of the
Bear, were landed at Cape Riley in Port Clarence and
driven overland to Charlie by Per Larsen Anti (a Laplander),
Tautook (an Eskimo herder), and two assistants. In 1899
because the debt had risen to more than 900 reindeer,
according to the terms of the contracts, two more ships
were pressed into service. The Thetis, a navy ship was
reoutfitted, and the J. S. Kimball Company of San Francisco
furnished a vessel under contract. But even with three
ships, only 322 reindeer were purchased, and since any
more delay would increase the debt, it was necessary to
repay the remainder of the deer from government and mission
herds, which Jackson had tried to avoid. During the winter
of 1899, Dr. F. H. Gambell of Eaton Station returned the
rest of Charlie's deer. "Charley and Mary were very much
delighted over the fact that I had brought them so many
[286] deer," he wrote Jackson. "They wanted me to get
them a teacher for their children next year [as there]
were 18 children who would go to school."(33)

Charlie was adequately paid for his work on the long
trip and subsequent stay at Point Barrow. Supplies were
unloaded for him from the Bear on 25 July, 4 August,
12 September, and 26 September 1899; and on 2 July 1900,
he received the "remainder of stores."(34)

Seward Peninsula, in the summer of 1899, was not a
good place to raise reindeer because prospectors had spread
out in all directions after the discovery of gold on
Anvil Creek. All winter long in 1898-99, people from the
Klondike and Alaskan points poured into the new mining
camp of Anvil City, later named Nome. In the summer of
1899, after the news had reached the "outside," an
estimated 20,000 people came by ship to a spot where, a
year earlier, there had been only a seasonal fishing camp.

In this one town lived, for a short while, almost ten times
the entire population of Seward Peninsula, an area of
about 25,000 square miles. On 26 July 1899, Jackson
described Nome as "a conglomeration of tents, with half
a dozen houses or shanties, and two or three iron ware-
houses in process of erection by the transportation and
trading companies. The ocean front is staked out with
claims for from 10 to 20 miles."(35)

Despite the prospectors who had found Charlie's place
a convenient roadhouse and his reindeer tempting targets,
all was going well for the herd and the people at the
little settlement of Sinrock when tragedy struck in the
summer of 1900. On 15 July, less than two weeks after
delivering the final payment to Charlie for his work in
the reindeer drive of 1897, the Bear returned to Sinrock
because Captain Tuttle had heard that Charlie was a very
sick man. The logbook for that day reads, "Visited and
prescribed for Charlie Artisarlook, his wife, and six
other natives."

Charlie died on 30 July of measles or pneumonia in
the epidemic that swept western Alaska that summer.(36)
The Nome Daily News of 2 August 1900 reported his death
with the headlines: "Reindeer King Dead. Charlie
Antisarlook, Richest Eskimo of Northern Alaska." His
wealth, the article said, included a herd of reindeer
numbering "probably 500" and "a number of mining claims,
some of which are said to be promising."(37) Mary's
inheritance, however, was not as large as usually thought
--not 500, or even 400, the number most commonly quoted,
but only 272. According to the Commissioner of Education
Report for 1900-01, the Sinrock herd in 1900 was divided
as follows: "Mrs. Charlie Antisarlook (a native woman)
in charge. The herd numbers 360, of which Mary, widow of
Charlie, owns 272; her sister-in-law, widow of Achickchick
[Asiksik], owns 45; Sagoonuk [Simon Sagoonik] (son of
Achickchick, aged 16 years), owns 10; Kotak [Koktowak,
Kuktiuk] (Charlie's brother, aged 21), owns 12; Angalook
[Ongalook, Oliver Anawrok] (Charlie's brother, aged 16),
owns 9; Assebuck [Accebuk] aged 18, owns 6 and Kokenyok
owns 6."(38)

Charlie's death was the real beginning of Mary's fame
--and of her troubles, especially the growing menace of the
white prospectors' shooting and scattering the herd.
Shortly after Charlie's death, Lieutenant Jarvis drove the
herd to Cape Douglas, about 30 miles northwest of Sinrock,
hoping that Mary, too, would move there, but Jackson,
fearful that "the miners will rob her of the whole herd,"
wanted her to move to Teller where she could place it in
the government herd.(39)

There were other reasons, too, why the people over-
seeing the reindeer industry wanted her to move from
Sinrock. Living near Nome, Mary was easy prey to unscru-
pulous white men who offered her liquor and wanted to marry

her to get control of her herd. Captain Tuttle wrote to Jackson in 1900 that he had "found her in Nome in tow of a Swede, who I heard intended to marry her to get the herd."(40)

Apparently the "Swede" did marry her, although no such union was reported in any writing of the time. Nevertheless, in a letter, in the National Archives, Brevig wrote to Jackson on 4 March 1901 that Mary "is now married to Mr. Anderson the Finn who was with her last summer, and he is now assuming control of the herd." He also said that Mary had moved her herd to the Kuzitrin River and would not take any advice. "As anyone trying to do anything with the herd exposes himself to a lawsuit from Mr. Anderson [so] I have written to Judge Noyes and asked for an injunction restraining Mary and others from disposing of or interfering with the deer until your arrival in July, and a guardian can be appointed for the heirs, as Mary is not entitled to more than 1/6 of the deer at the utmost." A handwritten note at the top of the first page of the letter says, "Dr. Harris [Commissioner of Education] thinks it is a good thing that Mr. Anderson has married Antisarlook's widow. Being a Finn he will appreciate the value of the deer and take good care of them. N." However, when Mary E. Hart, a newspaperwoman, visited Mary at Sinrock later in the year, there apparently was no husband around.(41)

Mary finally decided to move her herd to Unalakleet, nearer her old home. She started out from Sinrock in December 1901 with the reindeer under the supervision of a Laplander named "Rauna" (Johannes Aslaksen Rauna), whom she had hired as head herder. As if she had not had enough troubles, this move led to a lawsuit, filed by J. T. Lindseth for wages supposedly due him on the move to Unalakleet, and a jury trial in 1904. The seeds for this suit were planted when Rauna abandoned the herd at the Nome River, then went back to the bright lights of Nome, "commencing to drink and fight and thus was put in jail for cutting another fellow with knife," according to A. E. Karlson, the Covenant missionary at Unalakleet.(42) Lindseth, who had been hired to work at Eaton Station in 1900 by Jackson, but was no longer employed there, went to the herd, took charge of Mary, got Rauna out of jail, and installed him again as head herder. Jackson had been enthusiastic about Lindseth because he was as optimistic about the success of an Alaskan reindeer industry as he was, but his enthusiasm for Lindseth waned because of his alleged drinking and illegal selling of liquor at the station, and had him discharged.

From the Nome River Lindseth took Mary and the Eskimos with her to Unalakleet ahead of the herd; Rauna and the remainder followed at a slow pace. They were so long on the way that Mary became alarmed, and wanted to go back along the route, but Lindseth insisted on going instead. He sent a note to Karlson asking for power of attorney so

that he could take complete charge of the herd and sell
some of the reindeer. Karlson told him that he did not
have the authority, and when Mary came to Unalakleet from
Eaton the next day, he learned that she was completely
unaware of Lindseth's request, and had not authorized him
to act for her. Lindseth, however, decided that he did
not need power of attorney; on 18 January 1902, he wrote
to Jackson that he was "now in charge of [Mary's] deer and
am acting for her on all business transactions."(43)

When the reindeer finally arrived in Unalakleet on
27 February Karlson advised Mary to count them and to her
dismay she found that there were only 320 instead of the
400 that she thought she had started out with in December
1901. On inquiry it was learned that both Rauna and
Lindseth had sold reindeer to various people along the
way.(44) Mary's herd was combined with one belonging to
Per Spein, a Laplander, and all were driven to good
pasturage near Tolstoi Point. In August of that year
Jackson made an agreement with Mary designed to protect the
herd for her and her heirs: "the Government [will] control
her deer for ten years and agrees to give the Government
for their care and attention 25 female deer a year." She
was also given a log house--to be moved from Eaton to
Unalakleet--to live in.(45)

Shortly after the deer had arrived in Unalakleet,
Lindseth claimed that Mary owed him a salary for driving
them from Nome River to Unalakleet but Mary refused to pay
on the grounds that he had offered to accompany the herd
voluntarily since he was going to Unalakleet anyway. On
6 March a meeting was held in Unalakleet to inquire into
Lindseth's claim. During the meeting Mary agreed to pay
him three reindeer to settle accounts, although she objected
to the expenses that Lindseth had run up en route. (At
that time reindeer were being sold to miners as draft
animals for $100 apiece, and shortly before she had left
Sinrock, Mary had sold two for $150 apiece.) Lindseth
accepted the three deer, but still was not satisfied and
demanded an additional fifteen as salary. This number
was reduced to ten during the meeting, but Mary refused to
pay. "It was finally agreed upon to refer the salary
question to Dr. Sheldon Jackson when he returns hither."(46)

Lindseth, not willing to wait four months until
Jackson's visit, went, on the following day, to the United
States Commissioner, F. T. Merritt, in Saint Michael and
brought suit against her. Soon after, Karlson wired
Merritt that he thought the suit should be dropped because
Mary had not only taken care of Lindseth's expenses with
the three deer, but the herd was under the control of the
government. Merritt wrote back that since the suit was
already filed--anyone could file a suit, he said--he could
do nothing until both sides had been heard. He had not yet
served the papers after a lapse of six weeks because he
could not find anyone who was traveling to Unalakleet, and
he did not wish to incur the expense of sending a deputy

marshal. Once the summons had been served, he continued, she would have to state her defense (by proxy, if necessary), but he hoped that the case would be settled out of court.[47]

Mary's defense was three-fold. In the first place, she said that she had not hired Lindseth, but that he had accompanied her by his own choice. Second, he had sold her deer without permission en route from the Nome River to Unalakleet; and third, he had plied her with whiskey all of the time that he had been with her and had stolen money. In a letter written for her by a man named McCoskrie, she said that Lindseth "kept buying and giving [me] whiskey all the time and it set [me] crazy. So he could steal [my] money and deer." She said that she had $600 when she left Sinrock; spent $200 for food, and thought that Lindseth had stolen the rest.[48]

In 1902, another man, Anders Johnson, also claimed that Mary owed him wages for taking care of the herd for a month before it was combined with Spein's. Jackson, writing to Karlson, said that Mary "denies that she owes him anything, claiming that he was employed by Lindseth and not her, and that Lindseth has been amply compensated by the amount he stole from her."[49]

In August 1902 Jackson wrote to Lindseth threatening him and Rauna with a suit because of "dishonorable and dishonest" dealings, and a trial in which "you may both be thankful if you escape a long imprisonment." Jackson also threatened to sue Lindseth if he did not pay for the "government supplies" he had procured from Karlson.[50] Lindseth was not intimidated, and would not drop his suit against Mary.

As late as 26 September 1903 Jackson was urging that the suit be settled out of court. He was convinced that Lindseth would lose, not only because of his allegedly dishonest dealings with the herd, but because he "may be landed in jail for selling liquors [illegally] that winter that he was at Eaton Reindeer Station; also for giving liquors to the natives...on the way between Nome and Unalaklik." To resolve their differences, he suggested that Mary pay him five deer in settlement rather than continue in a suit that might drag on two or more years, and "keep her stirred up in the meantime."[51]

Lindseth would not accept the five reindeer, and the suit continued. His claim was for $553.45, including eight per cent interest from 15 December 1901. The case was heard on the opening day of the February term in 1904 in the Federal District Court of Nome. Despite the many people and large amount of correspondence involved, as well as the uniqueness of an Eskimo defendant in a civil suit, the case received very little public attention. But when the case was decided, the Nome Nugget of 17 February reported under the heading "The District Court" that the "first case on the docket was that of J. T. Lindseth vs. Mary

Mary Antisarlook in 1901

Antisarlook, commonly known as Sinrock Mary. This was an action to recover $553 for services alleged to have been rendered defendant by the plaintiff. The case went to the jury yesterday afternoon, a verdict being rendered for the defendant. Judge Bruner represented the latter, and George D. Schofield the plaintiff."(52)

May had to borrow money for the lawsuit from Dr. C. O. Lind, who had succeeded Dr. Gambell at Eaton Station, and Lopp, whom she had not paid back by 1910. In a chatty letter written by Galen B. Fry, a resident of Klery Creek, Kobuk River, to Lopp, he suggests that in spite of the debt, he should "treat the old girl kindly for she was

raised a pet."[53] But by the time that the jury had
found for Mary in 1904, the herd was safely in her own
hands. She had even weathered the peril of another marriage
on 2 August 1902 to Andrew Andrewuk, an Eskimo, who might
have wanted to gain control of her herd. To the contrary,
the Fifteenth Reindeer Report stated that Andrewuk "takes
no active interest in the reindeer" (page 26).

Nevertheless, she may have been closer to disaster
than she realized five months earlier when she entered
into another "marriage." On 8 March 1902 Lindseth wrote
to Karlson that he had heard that "Mr. Heckman from Chinick
Golovin Bay is to bee [sic] here shortly and is to get
married to Mary of Sinrock." Yet, three days before, on
5 March, E. S. Walker, stationed at the Saint Michael
military post, had written to Jackson: "Mary married Chas.
Hichman a saloonkeeper of Chinik and...she gave him a bill
of sale for her herd. The marriage ceremony was performed
by Young, the mail carrier from Unalaklik to Chinik. It
took place at Unalaklik. Of course it was a mock ceremony
but Mary probably thought it all right."[54] Even at
Unalakleet, away from the mainstream of prospectors and
miners, Mary and her herd seemed to be fair game for the
would-be reindeer merchants.

Seven years after Charlie's death, the legitimacy of
her inheritance was brought into question by Kuktiuk and
Ongalook (Oliver Anawrok, Esther Oliver's father), Charlie's
brothers. In a complaint filed with the Reindeer Service
in 1907 they said that they, not Mary, should have
inherited the herd under Eskimo inheritance laws. This
disposition was not challenged at the time of Charlie's
death, probably because the brothers were young. (Ongalook
was only about 15, and Kuktiuk, 21). If Eskimo law had
prevailed, Mary would have been left empty handed. W. T.
Lopp, who was superintendent of the Bureau of Education in
charge of reindeer in northern Alaska in 1907, said in his
report of this claim, "according to the old Eskimo custom,
they would have inherited all of them and the widow none,"
and although the brothers, as well as "Sagoonuk" (Simon
Sagoonik), Charlie's nephew, then owned a few deer, they
had earned them through apprenticeship. "I explained to
them that they should have presented their claim in 1901,
but that the [United States] laws governing inheritance
gave these deer to Mary and her adopted children. One of
the children is the sister of these two brothers and the
other is the brother of the cousin, Sagoonuk. The third is
a half-breed Portugese [sic; Segayuk]. I pointed out to
them that most of her deer would be inherited by their
blood kin, and promised them to try and persuade Mary to
do something for them; before I left, Mary promised to give
these herders, Koktouk [kuktiuk], Angalook and Sagoonuk
each two female deer next June."[55]

Although Mary did not have the tens of thousands of
deer that various writers have asserted, the ownership of

several hundred animals made her a wealthy woman at a time when most of the Eskimos were living in a subsistence economy. But this wealth would have been meaningless if she had not shared it, according to Eskimo custom, with the less fortunate. Known to have a "big heart," she tried to help anybody in need.

The Eskimos deserted Sinrock when Mary left, and a correspondent for the Nome Nugget lamented after a trip there in the spring of 1902 that "the smiling face of Mary, and the Eskimo bairns that were usually around there" were gone, as were the good old days of '99 "when Mary played the accordion, the mushers tripping the light fantastic with the native beauties, while some cheechako [newcomer] passed the hootch around."(56) But Sinrock was not forgotten. Although Mary lived there for only seven years, or less than a tenth of her long lifetime, the name Sinrock Mary followed her and forever commemorated the place where her good fortune began.

Notes

1. Feature article by Mary E. Hart in The Nome News, 17 October 1902.

2. Esther Oliver, "Story of Sinrock Mary," W. T. Lopp Papers, University of Oregon Library, Eugene.
Mary's Russian name was given as Palagai Makrikoff in Mary Hart's feature article of 17 October 1902, but Palasha Mikrekoff in a list of names compiled by Lucy Petrie of Unalakleet (private archives). Mary's Eskimo name was given to me variously in the Unaluk dialect of Unalakleet as Chunuak, Chunugak, and Changunak; but Sangruyak in the Kauwerak dialect, according to Ruth Nunasalook Kakaruk (Mrs. Johnny E. Kakaruk) of Teller, whose grandfather was Asiksik, Charlie Antisarlook's brother. Lucy Petrie's complete name for Mary was "Andrewuk, Palasha Mikrekoff Chang-oonak."
In an article in Kwikpagmiut (1976: 90), published by the lower Yukon River schools, Mary's Eskimo name is given as "Sineraq," which, of course, is not correct. This name was either an attempt on the part of the writer to render "Sinrock" more "Eskimo," or it was confused with the name of Mary's sister, whose Eskimo name was Sineraq. Sineraq was the first wife of Guy Kakarook, the watercolorist of the late nineteenth century.
All information not documented in this article was obtained in the course of field research covering the years 1963 to 1978. I received genealogical information about Mary, Charlie, and their relatives from Simon Sagoonik (nephew of Charlie Antisarlook); Marion Mayugiak Gonangnan (wife of George Sigayuk Antisarlook, her second

136

husband); Ruth Kotongan and Ruth Kakaruk (granddaughters
of Asiksik, Charlie's brother); Nany Anawrok (wife of
Oliver Ongalook Anawrok; Ongalook took his father's name
as a surname, but Nanny was often known as Mrs. Oliver);
Martha Nanouk (step-daughter of George Antisarlook); and
Peter Nanouk (nephew of Andrew Andrewuk, Mary's husband).

3. The Nome News, 13 December 1901. Mary Alakiak was
the mother of William Oquilluk, author of People of Kauwerak.

4. Esther Oliver, "Story of Sinrock Mary." This short
handwritten manuscript in the University of Oregon Library,
does not carry an author's name, but is attributed to
Esther Oliver, the daughter of Ongalook (Oliver Anawrok),
Charlie Antisarlook's brother, about fifteen years his
junior. In this "story," Esther Oliver realized that much
of the information she wrote from the talks that Mary told
the school children of Unalakleet was not accurate, for
she complained, "I never can get a good story from Sinrock
Mary. When I ask her to tell me, she talks of this and
that....She tells it mixed." Unfortunately, almost all
information about Mary in articles and books written since
the 1930s is erroneous, sometimes taken from Mary's garbled
reminiscences, sometimes deliberately exaggerated.

5. The logbook of the Bear for 1890. The logbooks of
the Bear are located in the U.S. National Archives, Record
Group 25, Records of the United States Coast Guard.

6. Letter, Sheldon Jackson to W. T. Harris,
Commissioner of Education, dated 26 August 1891, Arctic
Ocean, Sheldon Jackson Collection, Scrapbook 26,
Presbyterian Historical Society, Philadelphia.

7. Jackson's detailed report of the 1891 cruise of
the Bear and reindeer negotiations is in Education Report
1894 (see Bibliography for complete citation), but he never
mentions Mary or Charlie. Nor does he mention them in his
report of the cruise of 1890 (Education Report 1893).

8. Oliver, "Story of Sinrock Mary."

9. Lopp's report in American Missionary, December,
1892, page 386.

10. Logbook of the Bear, 1892, U.S. National Archives,
RG 26.

11. Third Reindeer Report, opposite page 19. The
annual "reindeer reports" are referred to herein by number.
For a complete citation see the Bibliography.

12. Ibid., page 16. For a discussion of the importation
of domesticated reindeer see Ray, 1975, Chapter 17.

13. Letter, Michael Healy to Sheldon Jackson, dated 30 July 1893, the Bear, Point Barrow, Sheldon Jackson College manuscript collection, Sitka.

14. Third Reindeer Report, page 72.

15. Lopp diary for 1893, Lopp Papers, University of Oregon Library; Lopp to Jackson, 17 August 1892 in Third Reindeer Report, page 133.

16. Letter, Mary J. Healy to Sheldon Jackson, dated 25 August 1893 in Third Reindeer Report, page 138.

17. Lopp diaries for 1893 and 1894, Lopp Papers, University of Oregon Library; Fourth Reindeer Report, page 72.

18. Fifth Reindeer Report, page 65; unidentified newspaper, 10 June 1894, Dall Scrapbooks, vol. 21, page 64, Smithsonian Institution Archives, Washington, D.C. The Eskimos were not the only ones who disliked the Laplanders. William Kjellmann, complaining of Healy's harsh treatment of all at the reindeer station, wrote Jackson that Healy would not permit Charlie to board the Bear one time "because he had a Lapplander cap on"; and the Commissioner of Education, W. T. Harris, wrote that "Captain Healy could endure the natives well enough but he could not endure the immigrants." (Letter, Kjellmann to Sheldon Jackson, dated 5 September 1895, Madison, Wisconsin, U.S. National Archives, RG 75, Records of the Bureau of Indian Affairs, letters received; Letter, W. T. Harris to Reverend C. J. Ryder, dated 14 May 1896, RG 75, letters sent, Vol. 14, page 18). All RG 75 citations herein are from Records of the Bureau of Indian Affairs.

19. Fourth Reindeer Report, pages 46, 66-67, 84; Fifth Reindeer Report, page 15.

20. Fifth Reindeer Report, page 70.

21. Ibid.

22. Ibid., pages 97, 98, 102, 104, 108, 111.

23. Brevig, 1944, pages 93-94.

24. Fifth Reindeer Report, page 115.

25. Ibid., pages 117, 120, 123. Brevig mistakenly calls David Johnson, George, in his daybook journal.

26. Seventh Reindeer Report, pages 54-55.

27. Education Report 1898, page 1646.

28. Eighth Reindeer Report, page 9.

29. Agreement signed by Jarvis at "Point Rodney," 20 January 1898, Report of the Cruise of the...Bear...(1899), page 144. On page 90 of this report, it says that 220 were due Charlie.

30. Ibid., pages 57, 81-82.

31. A complete accounting of the reindeer is given in Report...of the...Bear (1899), page 143.

32. Uncatalogued letter, Francis Tuttle to the Secretary of the Treasury, dated 23 June 1898, U.S. Rev. Steamer Bear, Norton Sound, Alaska (found, in 1972, between pages of the logbook of the Bear for 1898, U.S. National Archives, RG 26); logbook of the Bear, entry for 24 August 1898.

33. Ninth Reindeer Report, page 19; letter, Jackson to F. H. Gambell, Assistant Supt. Eaton Reindeer Station, dated 18 September 1899, RG, letters sent, Vol. 23, pages 339-41; letter, Gambell to Jackson, dated 4 January 1900, Eaton River Station, RG 75, entered in letters sent, Vol. 26, pages 112-14; Education Report (tenth reindeer report section), 1901, page 1771.

34. Logbooks of the Bear for 1899 and 1900.

35. Ninth Reindeer Report, page 42.

36. The Nome Daily News, 2 August and 10 August 1900.

37. Two articles in the Nome Nugget for 2 August 1901 reported--in rather disparaging terms--that Charlie left two widows. There is no evidence that he had two wives simultaneously, but there were at least two widows at Sinrock, one of whom was the wife of Asiksik, Charlie's brother, who also died in the epidemic.

38. Education Report 1902, page 1483.

39. Education Report (tenth reindeer report section) 1901, page 1768; letter Jackson to William A. Kjellmann, dated 10 September 1900, RG 75, letters sent, Vol. 27, pages 1-5.

40. Letter, Francis Tuttle to Sheldon Jackson, dated 27 September 1900, the Bear, St. Michael, RG 75, letters received. The Nome Nugget also reported a fanciful tale of Mary's leaving Sinrock because the ghost of a dead herder was stampeding the herd at night and scaring the herders (issues of 11 October and 7 December 1901).

41. Nome Nugget, 4 October 1901.

42. Letter, A. E. Karlson to Sheldon Jackson, dated 1 April 1902, RG 75, letters sent, Vol. 37 unpaged. Corres-

pondence about the Lindseth lawsuit, which would ordinarily
be found in "letters recieved," are inserted unpaged in
"letters sent," Vol. 37.

43.   Letter, J. T. Lindseth to Sheldon Jackson, dated
18 January 1902, Eaton, RG 75, letters sent, Vol. 32, pages
361-62.

44.   Twelfth Reindeer Report, page 15.   Only ten of the
deer sold were actually accounted for.

45.   In 1906 W. T. Lopp was made superintendent of the
Bureau of Education in charge of reindeer in the northern
Alaska district.   In his annual report of 1907, dated 26
March 1908, he wrote that he had released Mary from the
contract of paying 25 deer for a ten-year period.   Because
the deer were transferred at the same time that she had
sold female deer to the government, for two years, she did
not realize that she had paid the government for supervising
the deer, and seemed ignorant of ever having entered into
such a contract (RG 75, letters received).

46.   "Minutes of meeting held for the purpose of inquiring
into the affairs of Mary Sinrock vs. J. T. Lindseth," 6
March 1902, Unalakleet, RG 75, letters sent, Vol. 37 unpaged.
The participants in the meeting are not named, but the
minutes are signed by A. E. Karlson, and C. E. Ryberg, who
was a Congregational minister.

47.   Letter, F. T. Merritt to A. E. Karlson, dated 21
April 1902, Saint Michael, RG 75, letters sent, Vol. 37
unpaged.

48.   Letter signed by Mary, "her mark," written by
"McCoskrie" to Sheldon Jackson, dated 8 June 1903, Penny
River, RG 75, letters sent, Vol. 37 unpaged.   This is
apparently James W. McCoskrie, who was a "friend of the
Eskimos" (see Nome Nugget, "Eskimos on Sandspit," 3 August
1904).

49.   Letter, Sheldon Jackson to A. E. Karlson, dated
20 August 1902, steamship Ohio, Covenant Church Archives,
Unalakleet.

50.   Sheldon Jackson to J. T. Lindseth, dated 15 August
1902, RG 75, letters sent, Vol. 33, pages 201-2.

51.   Letter, Jackson to Dr. C. O. Lind, 26 September
1903, RG 75, letters sent, Vol. 37, unpaged.

52.   I have tried unsuccessfully to find a transcript
of the trial.   Apparently one was never made.   Dr. C. O.
Lind, who had succeeded Dr. Gambell at Eaton Station, wrote
to A. J. Beecher, a court reporter at Nome, asking for a
transcript.   On 20 June 1904 Beecher answered that upon
"receipt of $75.   I will be pleased to send you this
transcript by Registered mail."   When I saw this letter in

the Covenant Church Archives, Unalakleet, it was still in its envelope, and a note on the envelope was written: "Keep for Mary's protection. The Records were never transcribed at that time nor a month later, and when I met Butcher [Beecher] in Nome it was agreed that he never does transcribe the same. C. O. Lind, July 20, 1904."

53. Letter, Jackson to Karlson, dated 16 August 1906, Washington, D.C., Covenant Church Archives, Unalakleet; letter, Galen B. Fry to W. T. Lopp, dated Klery Creek, Kobuk, 1 July 1910, Lopp Papers, University of Oregon Library.

54. Letter, J. T. Lindseth to A. E. Karlson, 8 March 1902, RG 75, letters sent, Vol. 37, unpaged; letter, E. S. Walker to Sheldon Jackson, 5 March 1902, letters received, #4939.

55. "Report of W. T. Lopp, December, 1907," RG 75. Mary was also faced with a claim by an apprentice who had not been paid for his services. Lopp wrote in his diary for 6 November 1904 that "Kiunok a modest young man herded deer for Charley 5 years and saved the herd while all Charley's boys were sick. Then when they got better he went to care for his own father and when he returned Mary gave him the cold shoulder. So he has rec'd no deer. During the 5 years he rec'd one deer artega [parka], 1 seal pants, 1 drill pants, 1 seal boots" (Lopp Papers, University of Oregon library).

56. Nome Nugget, 2 June 1902.

X

PICTURE WRITING FROM BUCKLAND, ALASKA[*]

For untold millenia throughout the world, from Pleisto-
cene times up to the present, drawings have been used to
convey an idea. Alaska has shared this bounty in a number of
forms: engravings on ivory and bone by the northern Eskimos;
paintings on wooden ware and gutskin by the people of southwest Alaska; petroglyphs of Kodiak Island and vicinity; and
a "picture writing" that was devised toward the end of the
nineteenth century for recording trading accounts and
remembering Bible verses in both north and southwest Alaska.
The meanings of the petroglyphs and ivory engravings remain
unknown, despite attempts at deciphering them, but a few of
the painted designs representing ancestor exploits are still
remembered, as are some of the symbols used in picture
writing.[1]

Picture writing came into being in direct response to
non-native trade and religion, and though the ivory engravings
and paintings on wood were obvious antecedents, this writing
was largely influenced by the books and magazines brought by
traders and missionaries. Unlike the graphic designs of
northern engravings and southwest paintings the picture
symbols represented foreign objects, words, and ideas--not
episodes of Eskimo life--and were executed almost entirely
on paper.

The drawings in trading accounts (See Figure 1) were
usually so realistic that there was little doubt as to what
the symbols stood for. This was not true of the picture
writing used for religious purposes. Many seemingly realistic
drawings did not represent the object drawn. For example,
the drawing of an eye did not mean an "eye." Instead, it
stood for the word "astonished" because "the eye has an
astonished look."

There were three regional styles of picture writing for
the Scriptures and hymns: Kuskokwim, Kotzebue, and Buckland,
the Kotzebue style apparently having evolved from Buckland.
The Kuskokwim picture writing was invented[2] by an Eskimo
man, Uyakok, who was born about 1870 in Akiachak on the
Kuskokwim River. He was the son of an influential shaman and
was beginning to follow in his father's footsteps when he was
converted to Christianity. Moravian missionaries visited

---

* <u>Arts and Culture of the North</u>, Summer 1981, pp. 339, 341-44.

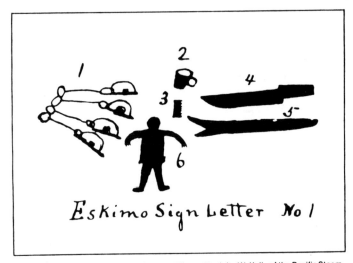

Figure 1: Pictured is a letter requesting supplies sent to John W. Kelly of the Pacific Steam Whaling Company by members of his hunting parties. ". . . means that one man (6) wants four steel fox traps (1), one drinking cup (2), one paper of needles (3), one knife (4), and a package of leaf tobacco (5)." —Sheldon Jackson: *Report on Introduction of Domestic Reindeer into Alaska* (the fourth reindeer report). Washington, 1895. pp. 48-49.

Uyakok's home shortly after they had established the Bethel mission on the Kuskokwim River in 1884, and encouraged him to become a "helper" to spread their teachings to the villages.

Helper Neck, as he became known, was one of the most enthusiastic and devoted helpers who devised a picture writing to record Bible verses and related material, not only as a memory aid, but to use--as he had seen his mentors do--for his own preaching. (Two other Kuskokwim Eskimos, Kavaraliaq, and Wassilie, were also pioneers of picture writing, according to Alfred Schmitt.)(3) Although Helper Neck could neither read nor write English or Eskimo in conventional form, he went even further and invented a shorthand system (see Figure 2) composed of Eskimo phonetics, English words, and arbitrary symbols. In his history of the Moravian missions, Wendell H. Oswalt wrote that Helper Neck's feat was "no less impressi"

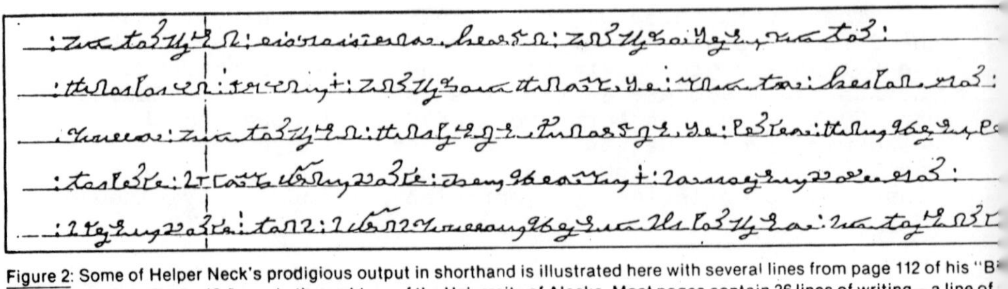

Figure 2: Some of Helper Neck's prodigious output in shorthand is illustrated here with several lines from page 112 of his "B" thick ledger book, 7½" x 12," now in the archives of the University of Alaska. Most pages contain 36 lines of writing—a line of to each space—but Neck managed to get 72 lines of very small script on some of the pages.

than that of Sequoya," the Cherokee Indian man who invented
a writing system.(4)

Sometime after 1900 another picture writing originated
in northern Alaska where the Eskimos speak Inupiaq rather
than Yupik of the Kuskokwim area. At Buckland, on the
southern shore of Kotzebue Sound, Koliraq Ruth Ekak, whose
father--like Yuakok's--was a shaman, succumbed to Christian
teachings that were brought to Kotzebue by Quaker missionaries
in 1897. Koliraq was a visionary in a most modern sense,
and in 1899, she and her husband, Ekak, went to Unalakleet,
where the Swedish Covenant Church had established a school,
so that their only child, Tusagovik, or Lily, could learn to
read and write and "teach our Eskimo people the word of God."
They walked the entire distance of 150 miles from Buckland
during the winter, their few dogs pulling all their worldly
goods.

I spent several days in the summer of 1968 with Koliraq's
daughter, Lily Savok, in both Nome where she lived, and in
Kotzebue where she was attending a Friends conference. When
Lily explained the origins and meanings of the picture writing
for me she tended to give her mother, who became a Quaker
missionary in the Kotzebue Sound area, a large part of the
credit for developing the picture writing, and said that the
writing was not fully in use until 1914. But Lily, as a
precocious child, apparently had begun to draw mnemonic
picture signs when she was a pupil in Unalakleet. In an
interview printed in a church publication, Lily said that she
taught her parents the Scriptures as soon as she had learned
them in school (her mother sometimes attended class with her),
"but it was hard for them to remember. I began to write the
verses in picture words which made it much easier."(5)

The steps involved in describing the symbols--from
choosing the verses to drawing the pictures, writing the
English and Eskimo texts, and recording the explanations--
proved to be far more time-consuming than either of us had
anticipated. However, I obtained enough verses to give a
glimpse of a fascinating excursion into grammatology,(6)
undertaken entirely by the Eskimo people themselves.

As on the Kuskokwim, the Scriptures were learned first in
Eskimo, the symbols, with a few exceptions, being derived from
that language. Mrs. Savok was very much surprised to learn
that Helper Neck had devised a similar kind of writing, but
she was certain that neither she nor her mother had seen
examples of his work. Both the Kotzebue and the Buckland
picture writing differ from the Kuskokwim in several respects,
the most important being an economical use of symbols and a
less literal use of action figures. Each symbol of the
Kotzebue-Buckland writing represents only one word or phrase,
whereas the Kuskokwim drawings are equated with syllables, and
in the Eskimo language that can add up to a considerable number
of pictures. In the Kuskokwim writing several action figures
were sometimes used to express an idea, which was contained

Figure 3: Picture writing of The Ten Commandments in regional styles of Buckland and Kuskokwim

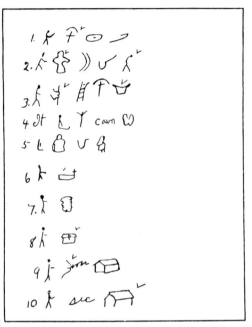

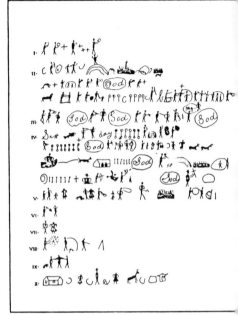

A. Buckland[A]
Lily Savok
English Explanation Below

B. Kuskokwim[B]
Helper Neck
English Explanation Not Available

1. Thou shalt have no other gods before me.

Man points to another: "God is a cross beneath a rainbow," and the check mark makes it negative; "me" is an oval enclosing a dot, meaning "in this world," "in the mind," or "me"; the last symbol is the "front end of a boat," but the phrase *agayutiqago* means roughly "God in mind"; therefore, the symbol for "me" follows the symbol for "God"

2. Thou shalt not make any graven image and bow thyself to them.

"Making parka, or image," check mark makes it negative; parallel lines means "a likeness"; "a dipper of soup, which in Eskimo sounds almost like 'and'"; a man bowing, negative check mark

3. Thou shalt not take the name of thy God in vain.

The hand shown is "in strong taking hold," and the check mark makes it negative; "in Eskimo, when coming down stairway, same word as 'name' so a stairway is shown; "God is a cross beneath a rainbow"; a dishpan, but since the check mark makes it negative, it is an empty vessel, or "in vain"

4. Remember the sabbath day to keep it holy.

The first two letters of *itkagaluwu*, or "remember" the sitting figure is resting (sabbath); a nest in a tree is a word that sounds similar to "day

in Eskimo; "Cown" are the first letters of *kaunayilago*, or "keep it last symbol, for "holy, was my mother's own symbol"

5. Honor thy father and thy mother.

The first drawing is just a symbol; drawing of a man for "father" woman wearing a parka with a hood for "mother"

6. Thou shalt not kill.

A post-European grave, a symbol that was also used for "death

7. Thou shalt not commit adultery.

"A symbol for life, only in a rough way"

8. Thou shalt not steal.

The box indicates treasure, but the negative check mark "ma not"

9. Thou shalt not bear false witness against thy neighbo

Mouth speaking, with negative check mark; a house, in this meaning neighbor

10. Thou shalt not covet anything that is thy neighbor's.

"Sic" is a reminder for the phrase, *siknatiyuminaichin* a house negative check mark

[A] Obtained by Dorothy Jean Ray

[B] George Byron Gordon obtained this example in 1907 from a person he does not identify, but who undoubtedly was Helper Gordon wrote in *In the Alaskan Wilderness* Philadelphia, 1917, p. 138: "The author of this document . . . relying entirely on hi resources, afterwards discovered that he needed a more rapid method of writing to keep up with the spirit of the time, a gradually developed a system of shorthand by using the picture writing as a basis."

in only one figure of the northern writing. Until there is
evidence to the contrary, I am inclined to believe that Mrs.
Savok originated and developed her picture writing
independently. (See Figure 3.)

Writing the Scriptures demanded a more complicated
system of symbols than the trading accounts, which needed only
nouns. The meanings and process of choosing symbols were
decidedly imaginative, but the selection was not systematic,
and each symbol had to be learned separately. Once it was
selected, however, it was used consistently, not only by the
originators, but by others who learned the symbols.
Occasionally, a person created a symbol that "belonged" only
to him or her. (The majority of users in the north were
women.)

Although the Buckland symbols were conventionalized in
both style and meaning, they were used only as memory guides
and not to write to other Eskimos. Only selected verses and
hymns were coded; there was no attempt to write out the entire
Bible. From the verses that I recorded, I have been able to
organize the symbols into nine categories based on derivation.

Action figures (stick figures in various postures;
Christian symbols; Mnemonic symbols (arbitrary symbols used
simply to remember a word, but used consistently for that
word, such as the symbol for "he" or "she"); Mnemonic letters
(the beginning letters of an Eskimo word, written in English
letters, for example, "Cown" to remember kaunayilago, or
"keep it"); Realistic forms (for example, the drawings for
father, mother, and house); Rebus (a picture of a word that
represents another word with a similar sound; for example,
drawing of a dress for "always," because the word for dress
sounds like always in Eskimo); Schematic diagrams (for
example, a pole drawn to a line representing the sky means
"height"); Metonymy (drawing of an object used to represent a
word with comparable attributes, for example, "in vain" is
represented by an empty dishpan); Synecdoche (use of part of
an object to represent a whole; for example, a feather to
represent an angel, that is, a feather from the angel's wing).
Drawings of each example mentioned are shown in the accompanying
illustrations. (See Figures 4, 5, and 6.)

The drawings are exactly as drawn for me by Mrs. Savok,
and although I recorded most of the verses in Eskimo, that
language is not necessary for an understanding of the symbols,
except where noted.

The Alaskan picture writing is a thing of the past, but
it would not surprise me if some older person might still use
it. The originators are all dead. Helper Neck died in 1925
at about 55 years of age. Ruth Ekak died in 1945, age unknown,
but over 70; and Lily Savok, in 1980, at age 84. But their
missionary work has been carried on by their children: Lloyd
Neck in the Moravian Church and Fred Savok and Ruth Savok
Outwater in the Covenant Church.

<u>Figure 4</u>: Explanations of Bible Verses

And into whatsoever house ye enter, first say, Peace be it this house.

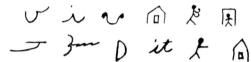

Luke 10:5—And ("a dipper of soup, which in Eskimo sounds almost like and") into (English alphabet "i" for in) whatsoever ("in imagination, we made it like a dishpan, meaning, 'put together'") house (a house) ye ("all of you") enter (person going in a door) first ("front part of a boat") say ("make a sound"; a mouth and sound issuing from it) peace (this is a symbol for a bow, or *keluinuq*, "a word that sound like peace, or *kiuniuq*) be it (part of Eskimo phrase to remember "be it") this (a person points to *this* house) house (house)

He only is my rock and my salvation; he is my defence; I shall not be greatly moved.

Psalms 62:2—He (a symbol to remember the words, he, she, him, and her) only (*kisimi*, meaning "one." "It is also used for 'but,' but you have to understand Eskimo for it") is my rock (person pointing to self, and drawing of a rock) and ("a dipper of soup, which in Eskimo sounds almost like and") my (person pointing to self) salvation ("net saved Eskimos in famine time by getting fish"; this symbol was also used for save) he (a symbol to remember the words, he, she, him, and her) is my (person pointing to self; also used for "I"; sometimes the word "is" is represented by a small dot) defence (ON signifies the first two letters of the Eskimo word, *annukviga*, meaning "place of safety") shall not be greatly moved (N is the first letter of the phrase, *nukti minechna*. The undulating line means that it is moving, but the check mark above it means "it is taken away." Therefore, the movement is taken away, so it does not move. A circle is the symbol for weight, great, greatly, and world)

And ye shall know the truth, and the truth shall make you free.

John 8:32—And ("a dipper of soup, which in Eskimo sounds almost like 'and'") ye ("all of you") shall know (*naleq*, "which is white, pretty skin in winter," is similar to *nalungichiga*, 'to know'") the truth (just a symbol) and the truth (see above) shall make you free ("a man is chained to a ball, but the check mark above his head takes it away," so he is free).

Weeping may endure for a night, but joy cometh in the morning.

Psalms 30:5—Weeping (a person's face with tears) may (there is no word in Eskimo for may, so an "m" is used) endure ("hang on to it," the center is held by two opposing ropes) for a night ("it's dark") but (see under Psalms 62:2) joy (person with arms upraised "is happy") cometh (the symbol expresses the thought of "going that way and coming back; therefore, "cometh") in the morning ("the sun is coming up," therefore, "morning").

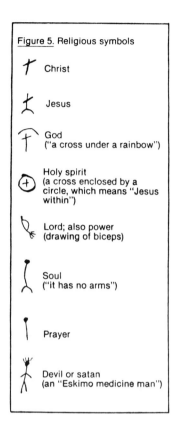

Figure 5. Religious symbols

Christ

Jesus

God
("a cross under a rainbow")

Holy spirit
(a cross enclosed by a
circle, which means "Jesus
within")

Lord; also power
(drawing of biceps)

Soul
("it has no arms")

Prayer

Devil or satan
(an "Eskimo medicine man")

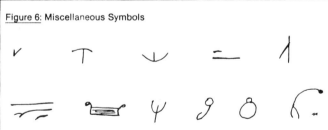

Figure 6: Miscellaneous Symbols

Top line: A check mark (means no or not; makes a negative). Height or heaven ("a pole up to
the sky.") Depth (drawn opposite of height.) Passeth ("the bottom line passes the top line.")
Trust ("leaning on a pole.")

Bottom line: Lowliness ("the world is lower than heaven.") Meekness ("because the middle is
lower than the ends.") Justification (drawing of a bow and arrow, "because the Eskimo word
meaning hit the target sounds almost like it.") Reward (a hook "because the word meaning
hook sounds like it.") Good (an apple "because it is *naguruk*, or good.") Love or charity ("the
person has pity on the little one.")

Notes

1. I. J. Gelb, in A Study of Writing (University of
Chicago Press, 1963, p. 29), calls the terms ideographic and
pictographic (and consequently, picture writing) as used for
American Indian writing misleading because the symbols are
entirely different in inner structure from other systems
such as Egyptian and early Sumerian. Since he favors the
reconstruction of the history of writing on inner characteristics of a system, and not on the outer characteristics
(on which he says American Indian and Eskimo writings are
based) he has substituted a more specific, and less confusing,
term, "descriptive-representational device." This does
more nearly describe these particular symbols, but for a
more euphonious--albeit less accurate phrase, I shall
continue with "picture writing" herein.

2. Of course, the picture writing was not really
"invented," but that is as good a word to use in this
article without sounding strained or cumbersome.

3. Alfred Schmitt, Die Alaska Schrift und ihre
Schriftgeschichtliche Bedeutung, Simons Verlag/Marburg, 1951,
p. 22.

4. Wendell H. Oswalt, Mission of Change in Alaska, the
Huntington Library, San Marino, California, 1963, p. 100.

5. From an unidentified church publication, Youth,
No. 24, about 1965(?).

6. Grammatology is the name given to the "science of
writing" by Professor Gelb (1963, p. 23).

XI

LAND TENURE AND POLITY OF

THE BERING STRAIT ESKIMOS[*]

The Eskimos have been popular subjects for writers
from the time of first discovery in their various homelands
of Greenland, Canada, Alaska, and Siberia, but rarely do we
find a discussion of their political organization in the
many publications ranging from narrative accounts to
anthropological monographs. On the contrary, writers consistently imply that the Eskimos have no political
organization, and some have flatly stated that they have no
territorial concepts, boundaries, leadership, or law.[1]

Political organization has been traditionally interpreted in terms of a complex, and usually large, state or
nation. Consequently, whenever a different or simplified
form of government fails to fit the preconceived pattern of
highly developed governmental machinery and concomitant
trappings, it is either overlooked, or interpreted within
another aspect of culture such as religion, kinship,[2] or
social organization. By disregarding such topics as leadership, law, or group solidarity as parts of political
organization, where they properly belong, the Eskimos have
been deprived of a fundamental part of their culture: the
relationship of a group to a specific territory with its
processes of control both within and beyond its boundaries.
Political organization thus defined is applicable to any
Eskimo group, no matter how simple or complex its government.

Anthropologists have recently shown increasing interest
in describing and analyzing primitive political organization
as a separate unit of study within a culture. Many valuable
contributions have been made during the past two decades in
books and papers presenting thoughtful, theoretical dis-
cussions of this field of anthropology,[3] but Eskimo studies
have not yet reflected these new insights, even though
problems of land-community relationships, tribal identification, residence and citizenship, implications of war, and
the like are most provocatively present. In this paper I
present data and interpretations which I hope will help
turn the tide. My subject people are the twelve political
units in the Bering Strait area of Alaska. I shall touch
upon leadership, territorial occupancy, and tribal identity
and concepts.[4]

---

* Journal of the West, July 1967, pp. 371-94.

What I shall call the political unit here has been
termed the political community by other writers, but both
refer to a group of persons with a common residence and
conceptual, if not hard and fast, boundary lines. A
discussion of even the basic subject of tribal boundaries
has been hopelessly crippled by the accepted notion that
all Eskimos could wander wherever they wished because no
group claimed land exclusively, and therefore could not have
boundary lines. E. Adamson Hoebel, in a textbook about
primitive law, peremptorily states that Eskimo land "is and
ever remains no-man's land in an absolute and unconditional
sense....Anyone, whatever his local group, may hunt where
he pleases, for the idea of restricting the pursuit of food
is repugnant to all Eskimos, except to some extent in
Western Alaska."(5)

I have found this was not true in the Bering Strait
region, and I doubt in other Eskimo areas. Every tribe of
the Bering Strait was as aware of its boundaries as if fences
had been erected. Furthermore, there was no "unused land,"
and none of the so-called "vacuums" that have sometimes been
thought to exist elsewhere in aboriginal North America. The
use of empty, unoccupied lands in the North has been repeatedly
made by unobservant writers, who neglected to mention inten-
sive seasonal fishing, caribou, bird, and small animal hunting,
berrying, or egg and vegetable gathering activities which
at one time or another involved nearly every square mile of
territory.

I have singled out several other statements by Hoebel,
not only because they in no sense apply to the area under
consideration, but because in their context they are understood to pertain to all Eskimo cultures. There are, however,
many different Eskimo cultures, and one statement cannot
stand for all. A brief statement after each quotation
summarizes its irrelevancy for the Bering Strait area, and
will be dealt with more fully below.

"The Eskimo is what some would call an anarchist. He
has no government in the formal sense, either over a territory
or at all."(6) This statement is too broad. The Bering
Strait Eskimo did not live in anarchy; he lived in a well-
ordered society in which a chief and often a council played
an important role. The influence of their government
extended over a definitely bounded territory within which
the inhabitants were directed by a system of rules and laws.

"Magic and religion rather than law direct most of their
actions."(7) Although it has also been inferred by other
writers that religion was the only force that kept Eskimo
behavior in line, an Eskimo's spiritual transgressions were
in no way connected with intratribal or intertribal law and
order, but with spheres over which man had no control--the
weather, the game supply, or illness--and it was only within
those that the shaman, or religious leader, performed.
Transgressions against society were met with political
judgment, and those against the spiritual, with religious
judgment.

"Contacts between local groups are fleeting and temporary. No superstructure of social organization embracing several local groups has ever come into being."[8] In the Bering Strait area, contacts between local groups were frequent and long-lasting, and were formalized through tribal political alliances entered into for subsistence and defense purposes.

Both Verne F. Ray and Anthony F. C. Wallace have used the term, confederacy, for what I am calling an alliance, in their respective papers, "The Columbia Indian Confederacy: A League of Central Plateau Tribes" and "Political Organization and Land Tenure among the Northeastern Indians, 1600-1830." The composition, aims, and actions of the Bering Strait alliances were strikingly comparable to those in the ethnic confederacies discussed by Wallace. However, because of the greater informality of the Bering Strait confederacies and the shorter time encompassed in my data about them, the term alliance appears to be semantically more appropriate.[9]

Another common misconception about Eskimo political organization has been that the local group was a kinship group, pure and simple. Local groups or villages did not exist on the basis of kinship, but on the basis of common residence and citizenship conferred by physical association of the group with a certain area. Though a woman might be born in Wales, she became a Kauwerak citizen when she married a Kauwerak man and lived in Kauwerak, and kinship had nothing to do with it. Likewise, a man who was permitted to live permanently in a village or tribal territory other than his place of birth was considered to be a citizen of his adopted home. Temporary fishing or hunting camps have been composed entirely of kin, but the kinship composition was merely coincidental with the political unit. Relationships with the permanent home village, as well as with other temporary hunting camps, had to be explained in terms of locality and polity.

The Bering Strait Area

The area under consideration extends from the southern shore of Kotzebue Sound to the southern shore of Norton Sound, and includes all of Seward Peninsula, the shoreline of Norton Sound as far south as Pastolik, and the islands off the mainland, which are Little Diomede, King, and Sledge. The geographical limits comprise many heterogeneous political units, and are coincidental with the extent of my field work. This paper could be confined to one large amicable cooperative political unit that included the tribes of King Island, Little Diomede Island, Wales, Port Clarence, Kauwerak, Nome, Sledge Island, and Fish River, but I am extending it to contiguous groups with which I am familiar. By including these random groups, which have political organizations like the core unit, it is hoped that reexamination of other Eskimo polities will be encouraged.

Information presented here pertains principally to the early nineteenth century, although remnants of aboriginal political organization were still in force as late as 1898-1900 during the Nome gold rush. The first tangible representative of the United States government to the Bering Strait area was the revenue marine steamer, Reliance, which sailed to Kotzebue Sound in 1878. Not until 1880, however, were routine yearly cruises to the Arctic established. This government was apparent only during the three or four months of ice-free seas, so the Eskimos did not become aware of new political mechanisms at work until the miners and merchants stayed the year round.

Eskimos of the Bering Strait area did not form one large tribe or political unit although for the most part they spoke mutually intelligible dialects. There was one generalized settlement pattern, but three subsistence patterns, which I have called the Whaling Pattern (whale, walrus, seal, and fish), Caribou Hunting Pattern (caribou, fish, seal, and beluga or the white whale), and Small Sea Mammal Pattern (seal, beluga, fish, and caribou).[10] Every subsistence pattern contained within it all of the region's available food products except whale, walrus, and occasionally beluga. Each larder also included many berries, water-fowl and game birds, squirrels, rabbits, eggs, and vegetable and root products. The principal tribe of the Whaling Pattern was Wales, and of the Caribou Hunting, Kauwerak. A typical example of Small Sea Mammal hunters was Shishmaref.

The settlement pattern was a large village and several smaller ones located on a large river or coastal area within several hundred square miles of territory. The villages were periodically deserted for seasonal activities of fishing, berrying, trading, or caribou hunting, but Wales with its more than five hundred inhabitants was never completely empty. The political unit, which included these settlements within its specific territorial boundaries, was also coincidental with the tribe. The name of the principal village usually furnished the tribal name.

Although the smaller villages usually had the suffix, "-miut," which meant both people of, and place of, such as Katinyamiut (people or place of Katinyak), a small village on the upper Kuzitrin River, their inhabitants were also considered to be Kauweramiut, or people of the territory of Kauwerak, the capital village; or those from the village of Tapkakmiut (people or place of Tapkarak or Tapkarzrak on the coast south of Wales) were also Kingingmiut, or people of the territory of Kingegan, or Wales as it is now called. The tribe in the Bering Strait area was, therefore, not synonymous with one village as occasionally reported from other Eskimo areas, but included several other villages within a large territory. The tribe as used in this paper does not correspond to older tribal designations, which in Alaska, were usually linguistic, not political, classifications. Until the end of the 1800's maps of tribal terri-

tories were constantly revised, but even the most detailed
maps presented only generalized linguistic data, and not
actual political or tribal units. Few revisions were made
in the 1900's.[11]

There were twelve tribes and twelve political units
between Kotzebue Sound and Norton Bay, and five neighboring
ones to the north and the south. Their English names will
be used in this paper except for Kauwerak, whose present-
day equivalent of Igloo (from two subsequent villages,
Mary's Igloo and New Igloo in the same area) is sometimes
confusing. Only one name is given if the Eskimo and
contemporary name coincide, or if a generalized name such
as Tapkakmiut was used. These tribes are: Buckland River
(Kangyik); Deering (Inmachuk or Kugalik; in the nineteenth
century this also included people of the Kiwalik River);
Tapkakmiut (in the nineteenth century this included
Shishmaref or Kikkiktuk, Cape Espenberg or Tukutat, and
Goodhope River or Pittak); Wales (Kingegan); Little
Diomede Island (Ingalik);[12] King Island (Ukuivuk); Port
Clarence (principally Sinramiut; also included Nook);
Kauwerak; Nome (the largest village was Ayasayuk at Cape
Nome; also included Sledge Island, or Ayak); Golovin
(Chinik); Fish River (Irathluik); and Koyuk.

North of Seward Peninsula and to the east of Kotzebue
Sound were the Kobuk River and Selawik River tribes, and
to the south of Seward Peninsula and on the east coast of
Norton Sound were those of Shaktolik, Unalakleet, and St.
Michael (Tachek). The tribes east of Solomon and around
Norton Sound to St. Michael were all considered to have been
"Unalit" at one time.

The dialects spoken by the people of Shishmaref, Wales,
Port Clarence, Sledge Island, King Island, Little Diomede
Island, Nome, and Fish River were of the Inupiaq, or
northern Eskimo, language. They were so closely related
that together they can be called the Bering Strait dialect.
In the early nineteenth century the people from Deering
westward spoke the so-called Malemiut dialect, and those
from Solomon eastward along the entire coast of Norton Sound
south of St. Michael spoke variations of Unaluk (spoken by
the Unalit) a dialect of Yupik, the southern Eskimo
language. By the end of the nineteenth century, Malemiut was
spoken as far west as Cape Espenberg on the north and in
various places on Norton Sound.

During the early nineteenth century, the population of
the area between Kotzebue Sound and Pastolik was probably
between 3,000 and 4,000, and of Seward Peninsula and related
islands alone, 2,500. The population was most dense on
the islands, and least dense on the southern coastline of
Kotzebue Sound. The largest villages with their approximate
populations at this time were: Wales, more than 500 in its
two divisions of Kiatanamiut and Agianamiut; Kauwerak (now
abandoned), 75-100; King Island and Little Diomede Island,
both possibly 150; Cape Nome (Ayasayuk, now abandoned), 100.

Leadership

The general form of government in the Bering Strait area was one in which the wishes of the people were carried out by one or more chiefs often working with a council of elders. The chieftainship was an office supposedly filled by the most capable man in the village, and though ideally it was hereditary, any man with the required qualifications could be groomed for its duties. Basic requirements were intelligence, wisdom, unselfishness, fairness, bravery, wealth (or the ability to acquire it), but above all, diplomacy and ability to arbitrate and get along with other tribes.

Every Bering Strait village had one chief, who served as leader of the kazgi or community house,[13] and if there were two kazgis, two chiefs. The name for chief in the Bering Strait area was "omelik," or "rich boss or leader," which in the nineteenth century had greatly expanded its original meaning from "boat [oomiak] owner and leader of the whale hunt." Sometimes the protégé of the principal chief was also considered to be a chief, and if the older man died unexpectedly, the younger man was expected to step into office. Meanwhile the protégé was only an assistant who carried out the desires of the chief. The council appointed a chief if the incumbent died without training a successor. Women were not chiefs, but were sometimes council members. A chief's several wives were considered to have a certain amount of influence behind the scenes.

A man remained in the chieftainship throughout his lifetime, and though his physical strength might wane, his life-long experiences that had culminated in a wise old age were highly valued. A chief had the cooperation of his people; he was loved, respected, and followed. He was a diplomat and an intermediary who helped everyone, but who "made trouble for nobody."[14] Therefore, the shaman or medicine man (angutkuk in the northern Eskimo language), who was often feared, disliked, and viewed with suspicion, was never a chief or political leader. His only qualification necessary for leadership was a certain amount of wealth acquired from doctoring, but his role was in the religious and ceremonial sphere, not the political.

The Kazgi

The kazgi was both a building where discussion of government were undertaken by the chief and the council, and a sodality to which members of the community belonged. Smaller communitites had only one building, but larger ones, like Wales, had several. In the 1850's Wales had four, or two in each village.[15] If a village had a kazgi it was considered to be an autonomous unit and a principal focal point of the tribe, but if it did not have one, it was considered to be a part of the nearest large village in the tribal territory.

If there was only one kazgi in a community, it was
known by the village name, but if there were more than one,
each had a name different from the village. In the 1890's
the two Wales (Kingegan) organizations were known as
Agianamiut and Kiatanamiut, which also served as names for
the separate sections of the Wales community.

In Wales and in small villages with only one kazgi,
residential sites tended to cluster around the community
building mainly for convenience, but on King and Little
Diomede Islands, the residence arrangement near the several
kazgis was without definite pattern. If a kazgi was dis-
banded because of disinterest or dwindling membership the
survivors were likely to attach themselves to another.

The building, which varied from eighteen to twenty-four
feet square, belonged either to the entire community or a
segment of it, and was used for many purposes other than
political business: for men's craft work and manufactures,
for instructing young boys, as a guest house for visitors who
could not stay in a relative's home, and for dances and
festivals when women and girls were admitted.

A man (and sometimes a woman) belonged to a kazgi by
virtue of his father's membership, but in actuality anyone
could belong. In Wales, membership was given to any family
who maintained a stone oil lamp and shared meat with others.
Sometimes membership was given to the poor or to orphans
who contributed labor of keeping the kazgi clean in lieu of
the lamp. Membership was not therefore based on kinship,
although many members were related because of the father-
son relationship and of the tendency to belong to the kazgi
of relatives.

Inside the kazgi, related persons worked in specific
areas that were handed down through the family. The place
of honor was directly opposite the winter entrance, and it
was this area that the chief and his family occupied.

The membership sustained the political privileges of
the chief and supplied members for the council, and though
the members owned the kazgi and contributed labor and
materials for a new building, the chief decided its location
and how it was to be built. The chief of each community
house carried out his normal duties independently, but
worked closely with other kazgi leaders in times of crisis.
He also sponsored festivities like the Messenger Feast in
conjunction with the council and community members. When
there were several kazgis in a village they alternately
played host to the festival as if they were different
villages. The island people who could not come to the mainland for winter festivities thus had their own celebrations,
as did Wales, when not involved in an intertribal exchange.

In the intertribal Messenger Feasts, each of the host
headmen asked a relative in the invited village to provide
him with specific gifts. Ideally, he asked a cross-cousin

who had a joking relationship with him, although in practice
he would ask anyone who would honor his requests. In turn,
the host was to give gifts not ordinarily obtainable by his
cousin within his own resources. Relatives often helped
gather gifts, and this aid, which sometimes became a duty,
was political and not social because the richer a man became
the better he was able to function as a chief.

Chieftainship

    At various times in the kazgi the chief would orate
principles of conduct, which included reminders of the
territorial limits to which a person could safely go, management of intratribal affairs, admonitions about stealing or
committing murder, and such homely details as tips about
survival on turbulent sea ice, in a storm, or about the best
ways to hunt hard-to-get animals. The chief, in conjunction
with the council, made rules and laws, saw that they were
carried out, and arbitrated in both intratribal and intertribal affairs. The chief, however, usually made the final
decision alone, and as Eskimo men often said, "The Chief's
word was law," and the younger men rarely ran counter to his
advice.

    The chief and the council held many meetings to decide
on various courses of action--for division of labor in
cooperative ventures such as construction of a new community
building or a caribou corral; positions to be assumed in
case of threatened attack; procedure of dividing food during
famine; duties to be undertaken at ceremonials; and punishment for crimes. The chief and the council also granted
permission to other tribes for territorial use, and
admonished their own tribal members about trespass into
foreign territory.

    Although details of their legal system cannot be gone
into here, it must be emphasized that the Eskimos of Bering
Strait did not live in "anarchy," and that the political
rules under which they lived were as stringent (and sometimes more so) as in more complex societies. A few general
examples here involve theft, adultery, and murder. Property
was left unattended and unlocked because it was known to be
against the law to steal. Despite this, thefts did occur,
and punishment ranging from restitution to temporary social
ostracism was dealt to the offenders. Ostracism, which in
extreme cases was banishment from a village, may properly
be compared to punishment by incarceration in our own
system today. Banishment, which was levied for repeated
thefts as well as extreme conjugal infringements, could mean
death if the banished person could not find a relative in
another village to harbor him.

    Punishment for murder usually was the killing of the
murderer, actually an execution since everyone knew that it
was to take place. Eskimo punishment was direct and severe;
a man was never given repeated chances to prove innocence
before his execution, nor to go free on a legal technicality

for a known crime. The chief and older men of the council
passed a sentence, but often the younger men were assigned
to carry it out.

Each tribe expected chiefs of other tribes to give the
same advice and information to their tribal members, and
when Siberians or other Eskimos invaded or trespassed on
land in the Bering Strait, the tribes assumed that they had
ignored their chiefs. Despite persistent traditions of
conflicts, the chief ideally tried to keep peace. Once when
some eager young Shishmaref men "wanted to get Siberia,"
their chief told them in strong terms that they were not
to cross the strait for fighting. However, the Eskimos
were expected to defend their land to the death if
Siberians came to Seward Peninsula. The village chief was
usually the war chief, but if he did not wish to serve in
that capacity, the council appointed another man.

In aboriginal times, the chief was the usual guide for
strangers to foreign territory. He had learned the necessary
procedures for dealing with different tribes through both
experience and extensive instruction for his position.
Among other things, he had learned what topics of conversation, personal or tribal, should be discussed or avoided in
every territory, but above all, he had memorized all intertribal events and names of older persons needed to establish
his identity and business. This knowledge was of the utmost
importance, for without it he was unable to acquire
essential rapport. Actually, however, he probably had
become acquainted with various tribes by accompanying an
older chief to the trading markets or to foreign territory.

The legendary inyukutak or "hiding man" of western
Alaska had a great deal of basis in fact, for inyukutak was
usually a stranger who by some quirk of fortune had been
blown away from home on broken ice or had got lost in a
storm. He had to stay out of sight or be killed if he could
not satisfactorily establish his identity and reason for
being in the village. No man went alone as a stranger to
foreign territory in pre-white days. However, once his
contacts were made through his guide, he could then "strike
off on his own."

Early explorers likewise customarily engaged chiefs as
guides, for not only had they established foreign contacts
but were well acquainted with the country. Moreover, they
also were in the best position through their political prerogatives to provide large quantities of food needed by
expeditions. The help given by these chiefs has led to
erroneous assumptions that "chiefs" and "chieftainships"
were created by Europeans who chose atypical Eskimos to
perform various chores. Although this may have been the
case during the latter part of the nineteenth century when
there were more men than chiefs available for work, it did
not apply to the early days when the aboriginal political
organization was still intact.

Despite the often inaccurate information left by early travelers, a few routine observations nevertheless give us glimpses of aboriginal chieftainship. For example, in 1816, Kotzebue dealt with two chiefs who sat apart from a large circle of fifty men on the south shore of Kotzebue Sound. At another time near Cape Deceit, he reported that the commands of a young chief to his men "were punctually obeyed."[16]

Officers of the ships searching for Sir John Franklin between 1848 and 1854 in the Bering Strait area had extensive dealings with tribal chiefs, whose reputation often preceded them. Commander T. E. L. Moore in 1849 permitted his officers to visit "a chief's village at the entrance of Hotham Inlet" to try to get information about Franklin. The old chief "was represented as a man of great influence among these people."[17]

In Bedford Pim's journal, the chief of the Spafarief (Kiwalik) tribe "presided over an extent of country from which the main supplies were obtained and was deemed politic to conciliate him."[18]

Captain Richard Collinson in 1854 reported that he was introduced to Omatoke as successor to Chimuak, a chief who had died since he met him in 1851 in Port Clarence, and when sails belonging to his ship were stolen from their storage place on shore by Eskimos of the nearby village, they were returned by "the interference of the two chiefs."[1

In 1854, Berthold Seemann, commenting on the characteristics of chieftainship, said that all chiefs were hereditary and in an all but forgotten statement reported that their power included "making treaties or granting permission for hunting on the grounds belonging to his tribe."[20]

Tribal Territory and Boundaries

Recognition of boundary lines between Eskimos and Indians has been made by most writers, but rarely between various Eskimo groups. W. H. Dall, in 1870, said that the Indians and Eskimos "exhibit great jealousy in regard to their boundary lines. These lines are generally formed by the summit of the watershed between the small rivers which empty into the sea and those which fall into the Yukon.... Any man of either race found on the wrong side of the line is liable to be shot at sight, and deaths occur every season from this cause."[21]

This statement was applicable also solely to Eskimo groups because their boundaries were equally precise and as jealously guarded. Eskimos of the Bering strait area could not hunt wherever they pleased, but only in their own or their alliance's territory. During caribou hunting they did not move with the herds into neighboring land but stayed within their own sharply defined boundaries. Permission was needed to hunt or fish on foreign territory, even that of an alliance, but it was rarely asked of an enemy tribe. To be caught in territory of an unallied tribe could mean death, for men were often sent out specifically to chase off rumored trespassers.

The following discussion of boundaries and territorial use focuses to a large extent on the Kauwerak tribe. Because of its inland position and importance, it serves as an ideal example of both maritime-land and intertribal relationships. Information about all tribes in the core area as well as others within Kauwerak's range of intercourse is necessarily included.

Kauwerak, the capital village of the Kauwerak tribe, was an eighteenth and nineteenth century settlement on the left bank of the Kuzitrin River in the interior of Seward Peninsula. The village site was on a treeless tundra plain, but a series of waterways offered fairly easy access to the sea and coastal villages, which contributed to Kauwerak's large size. It is said that all of the driftwood used in house construction was brought by skin boat from the coast. Not far distant to the south of the village rise the Kigluaik, or Sawtooth, Mountains, in whose majestic peaks lived the legendary Eagle who brought the Messenger Feast to the Eskimos.

The original location of the village was determined by the presence of a large sandbar, which is now almost obliterated by silt deposited during the past eighty years. This sandbar, the site of excellent fishing, was the only one of its kind for several miles up or down the river. The principal food animal, however, was the caribou, which migrated periodically through the area in winter and were occasionally hunted in summer. In order to utilize the winter caribou migrations to the maximum, the Kauwerak people built settlements with semi-subterranean houses of sod and willow trees on the various parts of the Kuzitrin River and its tributaries. Some of these small villages were considered to be permanent bases, but others were used only seasonally for either caribou hunting or fishing.

By the 1880's most of the caribou had either been killed or had fled Seward Peninsula, and no one alive today has ever participated in a full-scale caribou hunt. For the only first-hand information about winter caribou hunting and permanent interior villages we are indebted to First Mate William Hobson of the <u>Rattlesnake</u>, a ship in search of Sir John Franklin's third expedition during 1854,[22] and for information about villages, tribal organization, and boundaries to the aged grandsons of the last inhabitants of old Kauwerak.

A metes and bounds description of the Kauwerak boundary is presented in a footnote to exemplify the Bering Strait preoccupation with territorial limits. Other boundaries, similarly describable in terms of divides, rivers, and other landmarks, are placed on the accompanying map as accurately

as possible.(23) Kauwerak's most vigorously defended
boundary lines were those to the north between both Shishmaref and Deering, and in the southeast between the Koyuk
River people. At the time under consideration in this paper,
the trespassing of inhabitants of the Goodhope River,
Deering area, and Kiwalik River drainages into Kauwerak
territory was said to have precipitated a number of disputes.
On the other hand, the Kauwerak had been told by their
chiefs, "Do not go on the north side of Aurora Creek if you
want to live," and "do not trespass on the tributaries [of
the north-flowing rivers] because those people [on the north
slope of Seward Peninsula] claim all the headwaters." On
the northeast corner of the boundary, Imuruk Lake was
claimed by the Deering people, although the southern shore
near the lava beds belonged to Kauwerak. All of the lava
beds lay within Kauwerak territory.

"Shishmaref people" often caused trouble by trespassing
into Kauwerak territory, and Kauwerak people into
Shishmaref, notwithstanding their chief's admonishments to
the contrary. Both tribes blamed disappearances of hunters
in the old days to killing by the other tribe over trespass,
particularly in the headwaters region of the Kougarok River
and at Serpentine Hot Springs, an especially desirable area
for herring, tomcod, and smelt fishing, and for caribou
hunting.

On Kauwerak's southeastern boundary, the Koyuk River
people, especially when they were Unalit, aggressively
coveted the Kuzitrin Lake area near the lava beds. The
Kauwerak considered this lake at the eastern extreme of their
territory to be of great importance not only because of
fishing and hunting, but because of its being a source of the
Kuzitrin River, the whole length of which they claimed.

Family Fishing and Hunting Areas

Small areas for fishing and sometimes for hunting were
claimed by families within all tribal territory of the Bering
Strait area. Claims were established at the mouth of almost
every large tributary of large rivers, on various sections
of productive streams like Tuksuk Channel, Agiapuk River,
and Fish River, and in certain coastal areas. Some sites
had been in the same families for many generations, and
were usually patrilineally inherited. Once they were abandoned, they could be claimed by others. Clearly then, the
holdings were strictly by usufruct.

Permission was always asked to use any part of water or
land belonging to the sites, which varied in size from only
a few thousand square feet to the length of an entire creek.
Women of the family gave permission to gather eggs, roots,
greens, and berries, especially salmonberries. The more
plentiful cranberries and blueberries found on hillsides
and hilltops were usually not included within a fishing site.

Permission to fish was accompanied by payment of a certain percentage of fish caught. On the other hand, if a man or a woman asked to help with fishing (or possibly had been asked to help) he would also be paid with fish. At a one-mile-square fishing site at the mouth of North River near Unalakleet, the usual payment to a person for each drag of the seine was as many salmon that could be strung on a large willow branch (usually about five).

On the Kotzebue Sound shore of Seward Peninsula the entire length of a few creeks near the coast was considered to be family areas for both fishing and hunting. Candle Creek (musito'ak, Eskimo potato), a tributary of the Kiwalik River, had "belonged" exclusively to one family for generations for all subsistence pursuits. Other creeks were held under similar circumstances, and great jealousy was exhibited toward their use, not only for fishing, but for snaring birds, squirrels, and hunting caribou. Some families had acquired a reputation for excessive stinginess by refusing permission to use their land. Tributaries of the upper river were not restricted to family use, but were open to all the tribe primarily for caribou and squirrel hunting.

The use of family sites among the Kauwerak did not extend to caribou hunting because most of their land was utilized by the entire tribe for winter caribou hunting in cooperative drives into brush or stone corrals. The caribou drive was used to some extent everywhere on Seward Peninsula, although people living in coastal areas where caribou were less plentiful hunted them individually near the sea or in the interior back of their winter homes.

Tribal Alliances

Tribal alliances had been formed to extend political boundaries for greater flexibility in subsistence pursuits and for enlisting aid against common enemies. During the early nineteenth century primary alliances were in effect between Wales, Port Clarence, and Little Diomede Island; Wales, and the Tapkakmiut tribe of Shishmaref, Cape Espenberg, and Goodhope River; Kauwerak, Fish River, King Island, Port Clarence, and sometimes Nome; Nome, Fish River, King Island, and sometimes Kauwerak; Golovin, Shaktolik, and Unalakleet; St. Michael, Pastolik, and sometimes Unalakleet. A larger alliance between Wales and Kauwerak, the two most powerful nineteenth century mainland tribes particularly applied only to trade and exchange of the Messenger Feast, though families of each tribe used the other's resources. The relationship between these two tribes, however, was often marked by rivalry and animosity, which was not characteristic of the other alliances. Indeed, it seems probable that their friendly alliance had only recently evolved (during the eighteenth and nineteenth centuries) because tradition says that once they were bitter enemies.

The alliances had no formalized intertribal councils,

offices, or meetings, the chiefs and other leading men informally representing their tribes. Permission to use foreign territory was given by its chief through a standing agreement with the tribe, and not by a family, although visiting tribal members were guests of relatives while using another tribe's territory. Individual members could not use foreign territory if not sponsored by a relative. This reciprocity extended territorial usage in three ways: first, it enabled the islanders of Bering Strait to expand their resources by using the mainland; second, it served as a safety device against starvation in any one area; and third, it permitted mainland groups to obtain products difficult to get within their own boundaries.

The expanding of island resources by using the mainland aided both islanders and mainlanders through reciprocal hospitality and exchange of commodities that always accompanied mainland use. King, Little Diomede, and Sledge Islands are small, rocky, precipitous, and almost barren of edible vegetation and productive streams, but though land resources were limited, whales, walrus, and seals were abundant and eagerly sought after by mainland tribes. Reciprocity of territory was only one of various ways devised for exchange of land and sea products. Another was through trade, and still another was through festivities such as the Messenger Feast in which a formalized exchange of products was a prominent feature. This event took place in December at the time of least subsistence activities, but when greatest quantities of food supplies were on hand. Various island families, unable to attend the mainland Messenger Feasts because of sea and ice conditions, took advantage of the land use alternative and sailed their oomiaks to the mainland during the summer to trade, to gather vegetable products, to fish for fresh water fish, and to hunt caribou. They were accompanied to mainland sites by their mainland relatives. An island family who hunted caribou one year might go to a trading market the next, but they always tried to return home by the end of September before the ice formed and the stormy season set in.

The King Islanders took kayaks up the Kuzitrin River to several lakes, including Kuzitrin Lake for caribou hunting. Caribou were driven into the lakes and speared or shot with bows and arrows from the kayaks. The King Islanders also went to Pilgrim Hot Springs on the Kruzgemapa River to gather huge boatloads of greens, and occasionally fished on sites belonging to relatives, particularly in September after they had finished their trading. They sometimes hunted beluga and seal near Cape Douglas during the open water of early summer.

Little Diomede Island people often traveled to Port Clarence for seal hunting and fishing, and were known to go as far inland as the village of Kauwerak to hunt caribou, usually accompanied by Wales people who were permitted to hunt caribou on the lower Kuzitrin. Little Diomede people also went to Wales for fishing, sealing, and crabbing.

Sledge Island, a good walrus and whale hunting area before the 1850's, lay in a political and geographical relationship to the mainland similar to King and Little Diomede islands. Sledge Islanders used mainland territory between Cape Nome and the Sinuk River for fishing, berrying and caribou hunting. When ice conditions permitted, mainlanders went to the island for crabbing, and sometimes to participate in walrus hunting.

When islanders used the mainland it was understood that they were to give products more or less unobtainable in their borrowed territory in return. Such products as walrus hides or seal oil were often traded at that time, but the exchange was commonly in the form of hospitality. Mainland families were permitted to live on the islands with relatives for a winter or longer, the visiting families returning home in the spring after the ice had broken up. They were sometimes accompanied by island relatives who would then reside in mainland villages of their alliance.

Protection against famine was of vital concern even in this area of comparatively rich resources because weather, ice conditions, and localized scarcity of game could bring people to the verge of great need. An important refuge for all tribes within the Port Clarence alliance was Tuksuk Channel, a river flowing from Imuruk Basin to Grantley Harbor. In the lean months of late spring, the Port Clarence people permitted unrestricted ice fishing for tomcods and smelt by people within their alliance. Salmon fishing during the summer was usually restricted to tribal members, although families theoretically could play host to a nontribal relative of an alliance during this important fishing season. However, mainland people usually had sufficient fish in their own streams, and island people were often engaged in trade at places where they were also permitted to fish.

Another alliance sanctuary in times of want was the area immediately surrounding the village of Atnuk on Cape Darby east of Golovnin Bay where people of the Fish and Koyuk river drainages were free to get seals and fish.

The summer trading markets at Kotzebue Sound, Point Spencer in Port Clarence, and St. Michael were places that were sometimes utilized in time of famine, although travel difficulties during the commonly hungry seasons of late winter and spring often prevented long distance jaunts. The trading markets during summer also augmented home resources in a limited way through the local alliance's lending of small areas to visitors for temporary use. Each tribe, even those within the alliance, had its specific camping and fishing spot spaced some distance from another. Travel to a trade market often took many weeks, so the combined trading and fishing made it possible for trading families to augment their home inventories while continuing their normal food getting.

The basis of each trading market, despite its inter-

national aspects, was the local alliance, which furnished
the majority of temporary residents. People from the Kobuk
and the Noatak Rivers went to Kotzebue to exchange inland
products for sea products. Those from Kauwerak took goods
to Point Spencer. St. Michael functioned as a trading post
for numerous items including Indian-made goods, often
traded through northern Eskimos who went to St. Michael.
Indians sometimes went to St. Michael, at least when
Russian trade goods became increasingly available in the
1830's, but were not known to have gone to Kotzebue or Point
Spencer. The Point Spencer market once rivaled the huge
Kotzebue Sound market of the latter nineteenth century.
Traders and their families went to Point Spencer from as far
away as Unalakleet and Point Hope to pitch their camps on a
three-mile stretch of beach for trading and fishing. In
1867, Frederick Whymper, artist for the Western Union
Telegraph Expedition said that "the larger part of the furs
leave the country [through Port Clarence]."[24]

Point Spencer was also the focal point for Port Clarence-
Kauwerak seal and oogruk hunting that began in April, as well
as for combined trading and fishing after the ice breakup in
June. The Kauwerak seal hunters did not always remain for
trading, but returned home to fish for salmon at their family
sites.

Reciprocity between mainland groups was not as crucial
as that between island and mainland because the larger
territories could handle most emergencies. The alliances
provided great leeway, and if caribou hunting had been poor
during the winter, it was consoling to know that seals could
be caught in another tribe's territory in the spring.

Alliances for defense were also important in the Bering
Strait area where villages were constantly preoccupied with
impending conflicts. All tribes within an alliance were
fighting partners, although those most vulnerable to attack
felt greater responsibility toward each other. Hoebel's
comment that "Eskimos fight for grudges but not to acquire
territory,"[25] simply does not apply to Alaska, and needs
reexamination on the basis of more groups than the few
apparently utilized for his conclusions.

The Bering Strait Eskimos certainly fought because of
grudges and the so-called "blood feud," which was really
the sanctioned execution of a succession of murderers, but
the greater part of fighting was over trespass or the
invasion of land.[26] This applied to both Eskimo and non-
Eskimo groups. Eskimos felt greatest apprehension toward
non-Eskimos, who were considered to be chronic and extremely
dangerous interlopers. The enemy of the Eskimos' eastern
territorial boundaries was Indian; on the coast north of
Golovnin Sound, Siberian (both Chukchi and Eskimo). Conflicts
with Indians usually occurred on Eskimo-Indian boundary
lines, and fighting between unallied Eskimo groups also took
place near boundaries. Anxiety toward other Eskimo groups
was not as pronounced as toward non-Eskimos, but disappearances

and unexplained deaths of hunters and travelers were often blamed on other Eskimos because of trespass or deliberate invasion of territory. The abandonment of Kauwerak village during the nineteenth century has been attributed to territorial pressures, apparently from the north and the east, possibly by the Malemiut during their expansion (see below).

Little Diomede Island and Wales were closely allied against Siberians, as were Port Clarence and Kauwerak. Kauwerak and Fish River were strong allies; an often-told "true story" is that Kauwerak people once helped the Fish River people fight Indians who had invaded the easternmost tributary of their river. The various Unalit groups living around Norton Sound, according to tradition, also came to each other's aid more than once when attacked by the slowly-infiltrating Malemiut.

The geographical location of villages and the efficient distant warning system established by cooperating tribes appears to have kept surprise attacks to a minimum, but everyone was alert to strangers, and rumors of impending attacks were a normal part of life. In 1867, W. H. Dall said, "Nearly every year a panic occurs on the Coast or in the interior from some rumor that the hostile race are preparing for invasion and war."[27] Apprehension had not lessened fifteen years later when J. A. Jacobsen reported the uneasiness of the small village, Orowignarik (Ukvignaghuk, east of Moses Point) when word came that the Ingalik Indians of the middle Yukon were on their way to attack.[28] Every possible precaution was taken to minimize sudden invasion. For example, bells attached to ropes were said to have been strung round the village of Unalakleet when attack was thought to be imminent, and Wales people kept watch for Siberian boats from Cape Mountain behind the village.

Every unfamiliar boat was suspect. In early days, it was customary for Siberians to cross the strait accompanied by their island relatives either in their own, or their relative's, skin boats. However, after European trade goods had intensified intercontinental trade toward the end of the eighteenth century, it is said that they often came in their own boats without relatives. Traders and people intent on peaceful missions apparently used identifying insignia. In July, 1791, between Sledge Island and Cape Rodney, Joseph Billings' expedition saw nine natives in a skin boat hoisting a "bladder" on the point of a lance when they neared the sailing ship,[29] and in 1816 Kotzebue met skin boats in Kotzebue Sound flying fox skins on tall poles.[30]

Kauwerak people were always prepared for Siberian invaders, who once supposedly penetrated as far inland as their capital village where oomiak skins had been erected as a barricade. The last encounter of Siberians in Kauwerak territory took place when two men of the "whole army of Siberia" were spared by the Kauwerak chief, who sent them home with a warning for their chief to "stop invading if he wanted his people to live."

Kauwerak's warning system was in effect throughout the
Port Clarence-Grantley Harbor area, which was fairly well
populated in both winter and summer. Strategic spots were
utilized as defense lookouts. A hillside near the entrance
to Imuruk Basin has been pointed out as a place where
Eskimos invariably waited for rumored Siberian invaders.

"Siberians were always trying to get Eskimo land," the
Eskimos say, but evidence is equally clear that the
Siberians were apprehensive of the Americans' wresting
territory from them because it is said they sent spies
periodically to Little Diomede Island for reports of
American invasion plans.

Tribal Readjustments

Actual attacks by Eskimos, Siberians, or Indians are
not of record, but field data and scattered nineteenth
century accounts suggest that various tribal movements during
the eighteenth and nineteenth centuries were accompanied by
strife and bloodshed. Exact movements can be only hypo-
thetically reconstructed because they must be based of
necessity on those scant sources, yet two important facts
emerge: first, every tribe recognized its own territory and
boundaries as well as those of its neighbors, and second,
each tribe was eager to extend its boundaries, and would have
done so if land had not been so carefully guarded.

According to one tradition, all of Seward Peninsula
except a strip on its southern coast was once occupied by
Wales and Kauwerak people. Wales territory extended roughly
from the York Mountains as its southern boundary to Goodhope
Bay as its northern one, and Kauwerak territory comprised all
of the rest of the peninsula to the adjoining Indian
territory on the east and to the coastal strip on the south.
This strip, it is agreed by all, was occupied by Unalit
before and during the nineteenth century, but at what time
they moved from the south, the direction from which everyone
supposes them to have come, may never be determined. During
the nineteenth century they lived as far west as Golovnin Bay
where both the Kauwerak and Unaluk dialects were spoken.
For earlier times, one tradition places them as far west as
Bluff, and still another, at Cape Nome. However, by the end
of the nineteenth century, the Kauwerak dialect was spoken
everywhere in the southern half of the peninsula except in
the area around Golovnin Bay, and in the area to the east of
it where the Malemiut had settled during the middle part of
the nineteenth century.

The relationship of the Fish River Kauwerak speakers,
who occupied the upper river, and the Golovnin Bay Unaluk
speakers, who occupied the lower, is an interesting one
since it does not conform with the usual pattern of Bering
Strait settlement of one tribe's holding an entire river.
This suggests either that the Unalit had taken over the

territory from the Kauwerak just before it was occupied by
Malemiut, or that the Kauwerak had come from the north to
take over the river system from Unalit, possibly in conjunction with the fur trade.

The principal shift in territorial occupancy of the
Bering Strait was that of the so-called Malemiut, who slowly
moved from the Kobuk and Selawik areas to Unalit country
around Norton Bay. This movement, briefly outlined in a
previous paper,[31] apparently started when the Malemiut
began serving as middlemen for the Anyui-Kolyma fur-tobacco
trade market established by the Russians in northern Siberia
in 1789. These middlemen not only went to upper Yukon
Indian territory for furs, but used Unalit coastal land as
a route to the lower Yukon Indian and Eskimo country. When
initial permanent Malemiut residence was established among
the Unalit is not known, but Lieutenant Zagoskin reported
these Eskimos as temporary traders on Norton Sound between
the years 1842 and 1844, recording only the "Unganglimiut"
(the Unalakleet Unalit) as permanent residents around
Unalakleet.[32] Much later, in 1880, E. W. Nelson understood that the southern limit of the Malemiut before the
Russians arrived in St. Michael in 1833 was at the head of
Norton Sound,[33] yet Zagoskin did not use Koyuk, the
Malemiut word, but Kvinhak, the Unaluk equivalent for the
river in that position of Norton Sound.[34] Most informants
think that the Koyuk Malemiut moved there in the 1860's or
1870's.

The Western Union Telegraph Expedition found that the
Malemiut as well as some Kauwerak people had established
seasonal camps at Unalakleet between 1865 and 1867, and it
probably was at this time that the Malemiut began their
coexistence with the Unalit.[35] The 1880 census reported
that the southernmost permanent settlement of Malemiut was
Shaktolik, and that they had a few winter houses at
Unalakleet "within the boundaries of another tribe."[36]
The 1890 census (from information collected about 1883) said
that Egavik (between Shaktolik and Unalakleet) was both
Malemiut and Unalit.[37] By the late nineteenth century,
Unalakleet was composed of peoples speaking two separate
languages represented by three dialects--Inupiaq and two
of its dialects, Malemiut and Kauwerak, and Yupik with its
Unaluk dialect.

This slow penetration was doubtless facilitated by the
smallpox epidemic of 1838, which was apparently confined to
Unalit settlements. Koyuk (Zagoskin's Kvinhak) at the mouth
of the river of the same name, was hard hit; Unalakleet is
said to have had only thirteen survivors, and the small
villages of "Michat, Chiupliugpak, Kuakali, and Kabychluik"
near Kikigtaruk between St. Michael and Unalakleet were
abandoned.[38]

North of Kauwerak territory a similar juxtaposition of
peoples took place according to tradition, but recorded data
are even more scarce than for the early Malemiut-Unalit

relationships. To the Eskimos themselves, the northern coast
of Seward Peninsula held the fewest attractions for living.
This is reflected in the area's relatively small population
and in the commonly held beliefs that people from that area
were constantly agitating to push south into the rich
Kauwerak country. The principal tradition says that the
entire north slope, except for the Buckland River system,
was inhabited before the eighteenth century by speakers of
the Bering Strait dialect. By mid-nineteenth century
"Malemiut" speakers (the name by which all Kotzebue Sound
dialects are now known) had come from the east to settle west
of Deering.

However, another tradition suggests that during both the
eighteenth and the nineteenth centuries the north slope was
occupied by Kotzebue Sound speakers, and that the Shishmaref
people, speaking a Bering Strait dialect, came from the south
to push north the people of Kotzebue Sound. This explanation
is less favored by my informants than the first. Causes
other than the fur trade may have contributed to the dynamic
events of the latter eighteenth and early nineteenth
centuries, for example, the increased use of dog traction
about 250 years ago in that area, [39] which gave the Eskimos
extended mobility for winter-time travel on both land and
sea.

Recent changes in family and community occupancy of the
Bering Strait Eskimos have followed earlier patterns. Shifts
during the twentieth century were partly the consequence of
events over which the Eskimo had little or no control but
they managed nevertheless to join communities within the
tribal, or at least, alliance, territory. The new town of
Nome was the only exception but it was atypical in being
composed of Eskimos from many distinct tribes. Even so, Nome
embraced very few persons from beyond the Bering Strait area.

A few of the more representative examples may be noted:
Islanders from Little Diomede characteristically moved to
Wales or to Teller; people from the Kauwerak area moved to
Teller, as did the King Islanders; dwellers on the Kobuk and
the Noatak have maintained their old villages but visit
Kotzebue for summer fun and fishing.

Nome is an uneven composite of people of Diomede,
Kauwerak, Golovin, King Island, and Nome origin, plus some
others. Many Diomeders were drawn to the Nome area to
market their ivory carvings. A scattering of Kauwerak was
attracted by the cosmopolitan character of the town--its
schools and employment--but some subsequently moved to Teller.
The greatest influx was of King Islanders. Until recently
they came only for the summer. Like the Diomeders they
were interested in a ready market for their ivory carvings,
and a limited summer residence sufficed. However, in 1966,
they moved permanently to the Nome area.

It will be noted that a distinction has been made
between the town of Nome, as such, and the general Nome

area. The town came into being through settlement by
individuals and families, not through community or tribal
relocation. During the many years (after the gold rush)
that King Islanders went as a group to the mainland for the
summer, they maintained their own settlement, "King Island
Village," east of Nome, and physically separated by a mile
of open land. Now that they apparently intend to remain it
appears that this isolation is to be maintained. Likewise,
the Diomede Islanders originally set up their own summer
village, to the west of Nome, but later occupied a tract
adjoining the settlement of King Island Village, but
sharply separated from it. Not only has the principle of
tribal integrity and territorial separation been preserved,
but the political mechanisms of control, including leadership and traditional rules of behavior are specific and
distinct for each of these groups. Both recognize today
the overall superior political power of the United States,
but this has not erased their concepts of separate political
organization as tribes nor the patterns that characterize
the alliances.

Notes

1. For example, Geert van den Steenhoven says, "It is
a well-known fact that Eskimo society has no _political_
organization: there are no formal councils, there is no
central power, there is no question of state or government."
The Caribou Eskimo know "only a minimum of private property,
no land-ownership in any form, no state, no tribes, no
chiefs" (1959, p. 14 and Appendix A, p. 6).
Wendell Oswalt reports of the Kuskokwim Eskimos, "In
the era immediately preceding historic contact, village-
wide organizations of any nature were singularly absent.
There existed a state of contained anarchy, in which no
individual or organized group of individuals controlled any
activities in the name of the community. Napaskiak was of
course a physical village clearly separated from similar
settlements along the river, but there was nothing in the
nature of a governing body" (1963b, p. 64).
About the North Alaskan Eskimos (principally Point
Barrow), Robert F. Spencer states: "a political structure
was lacking" (1959, p. 444).
And, Kaj Birket-Smith in a book that is supposed to
deal definitively with the Eskimos concludes, "Thus among
the Eskimos there is no state which makes use of their
strength, no government to restrict their liberty of action.
If anywhere there exists that community, built upon the
basis of the free accord of free people, of which Kropotkin
dreamt, it is to be found among these poor tribes neigh-
bouring upon the North Pole. There is no rank or class
among the Eskimos, who therefore must renounce that satis-
faction, which Thackeray calls the true pleasure of life,
of associating with one's inferiors...Trapping grounds and

hunting fields are the property of all and none, res nullius, which not even the 'tribe' can lay claim to" (1959, pp. 144, 145).

2. Pospisil 1964.

3. For example, Fortes and Evans-Pritchard 1962; Mair 1962; and Schapera 1956.

4. Because of the limitations of this paper, a discussion of legal mechanisms cannot be included.

5. Hoebel 1954, p. 79.

6. Ibid., p. 81.

7. Ibid., p. 70.

8. Ibid., p. 67.

9. V. Ray 1960; Wallace 1957.

10. D. Ray 1964b, p. 62.

11. Prior to Ivan Petroff's map of 1880 in Report on the Population, Industries, and Resources of Alaska (1884) no maps had tribal or linguistic boundaries drawn on Seward Peninsula. Maps by the explorers, Frederick William Beechey, Joseph Billings, James Cook, and Otto von Kotzebue noted only physical features and a few villages.
Lieutenant L. Zagoskin (1847) included a map that had the Malemiut Eskimos ("dwellers of skin tents") holding the entire peninsula.
H. J. Holmberg made a map in 1854 from written sources, but placed inhabitants only on a small piece of the peninsula's southern shore. These were the "Anlygmuten," which probably means the Unalit (1855).
W. H. Dall's map of 1875 had the "Kaviak" (his interpretation of Kauwerak) inhabiting the entire peninsula (1877). In his Alaska and its Resources (1870) he proposed calling this land mass "Kaviak Peninsula," which, however, was named Seward Peninsula after the man most instrumental in purchasing Alaska from Russia.
E. W. Nelson's map in The Eskimo about Bering Strait (1899) is essentially the same as Petroff's map, and these two are the ones most often followed today.
John W. Kelly made detailed maps of a small area of Seward Peninsula and country to the north. One is dated 1889 in his "Eskimo Vocabularies" (Wells and Kelly, 1898, p. 1242) and 1893 (Jackson 1895, p. 90).

12. Only Little Diomede Island is included here. During the nineteenth century, Little Diomede was considered to be allied with Alaska, and Big Diomede, with Siberia. However, according to Albert C. Heinrich, who has done considerable research on Little Diomede, the two Diomedes were once considered to be one community, and have five small

villages, four of them on Big Diomede (1963a, pp. 394, 398).

13. The word, <u>kazgi</u>, has been reported variously from different dialects and by different writers as kashgi, kazegi, kazhgi, kalegi, lakgi, and karegi.

14. Hereafter all uncredited quotations are from my informants. This paper is based on statements obtained from forty-five Eskimo informants during three seasons of field work on Seward Peninsula and contiguous areas including the Kobuk River and Saint Michael.

15. Trollope 1854-1855.

16. Kotzebue 1821, pp. 208, 235.

17. Moore 1851.

18. Seemann 1853, p. 135.

19. Collinson 1889, pp. 332-33.

20. Seemann, p. 60.

21. Dall 1870, p. 144.

22. Hobson 1854-1855.

23. Beginning at a point on the southeast corner of Imuruk Lake, thence southerly along the eastern side of the lava beds to an unnamed peak due east of Mount Boyan, thence westerly along the main ridge of the Bendeleben Mountains, which ridge separates the waters of the Fish River from the Kuzitrin River, thence through the pass called Ukinaruk to the western extremity of the Bendeleben Mountains, thence southerly to a large lake on the divide between the head-waters of the Kruzgemapa River and Sherrette Creek, thence westerly along the southern ridges of the Kigluaik Mountains to the headwaters of Canyon Creek, then northerly and northeasterly along the mid-channel of said creek to its mouth in Imuruk Basin, thence northeasterly across Imuruk Basin to the mouth of the Agiapuk River, thence northerly along midchannel of said river to a point two miles due east to the mouth of Boulder Creek, thence northwesterly across the low ridge separating the waters of the American River and the Nuluk River to a point two miles above the mouth of the most northerly tributary of the Nuluk River, thence easterly to Portage Creek, thence across said creek, thence easterly across the most northerly tributary of Rock Creek, thence easterly across Star Creek at about two miles from its source, and easterly to Taylor mining camp, thence southerly along midchannel of the Kougarok River, thence easterly along midchannel of the North Fork of the Kougarok River to the source of French Creek, thence along the ridge separating the drainages of Aurora Creek and Lorna Creek to the confluence of said creeks, thence easterly along the mid-channel of Aurora Creek to a point due south of Aurora mining

camp, thence easterly along midchannel of the Noxapaga River
and Muskellunge Creek to a point on the southwest shore of
Imuruk Lake four miles northeast of Camille Cone, thence
southeasterly to the point of beginning.

24. Whymper 1869, p. 163.

25. Hoebel 1949, p. 399.

26. The majority of their traditons and folk tales of
killings also reflect this concern, but often have a similar
anatomy in that they deal with "large" villages or tribes
of "long ago," all end with the miraculous survival of only
one or two persons to carry on traditions, and the village
or the tribe telling the story is not the aggressor.
Disciplining of children was also done through threats
about enemies.

27. Dall 1870, p. 144.

28. Jacobsen 1884, p. 294.

29. Sauer 1802, pp. 243, 248.

30. Kotzebue 1821, p. 208.

31. Ray 1964b, p. 87. The map that accompanies the
present paper pertains to the early nineteenth century
before the Malemiut had moved permanently to Norton Sound.
Occupancy of the Fish River drainage is problematical. The
rest of the boundaries and tribal distributions are those
within the greater consensus, as already discussed.

32. Zagoskin 1847, pp. 47, 65-67, 76.

33. Nelson 1899, p. 24.

34. Zagoskin 1847, p. 109.

35. Dall 1870, p. 24.

36. Petroff 1884, p. 126.

37. R. Porter 1893, p. 130.

38. Zagoskin 1847, p. 61.

39. Giddings 1964, p. 114.

XII

NINETEENTH CENTURY SETTLEMENT AND SUBSISTENCE
PATTERNS IN BERING STRAIT[*]

I. General Considerations

The settlement pattern of the pre-European Bering
Strait Eskimo was basically the same throughout the entire
area although subsistence patterns and ethnic groups varied
from place to place. This paper will examine the relationship of subsistence patterns to the settlement pattern and
population, and determine what aspects of the patterns lent
themselves to resolving problems of change in the nineteenth century.[1] Detailed information about the various
areas and villages will be discussed following this general
presentation of the factors involved.[2]

The term Bering Strait Eskimo, which includes almost
all of the inhabitants living between Kotzebue and Norton
sounds, is used here interchangeably with Seward Peninsula
Eskimo because the boundaries of social, kin, and ceremonial
interaction formed a comparatively homogeneous unit of
culture within the peninsula. (The people of the area
shown in Map 4, however, were culturally more related to
Kotzebue Sound than Bering Strait.) The majority of
inhabitants spoke two dialects of the Inupiak language,
(1) Central Bering Strait with two subdialects, Kauwerak
(Dall's erroneous Kaviagmiut), and Wales (Kingikmiut), and
(2) Malemiut. The southern coast of Seward Peninsula was
inhabited by speakers of Unalit, a Yupik language. In the
nineteenth century, as a result of the Siberian fur trade,
the Malemiut had moved southward from Kotzebue Sound to
settle among the Unalit (singular, Unaluk), who, prior to
that time, occupied the entire coast and river systems
between Golovnin Bay and Saint Michael (Ray 1964a).

The Bering Strait area was noted for both its great
herds of caribou and vast migrations of walrus and whale in
the nineteenth century. Thus, the hunting of these dis-
tinctive animals evolved separate subsistence patterns,
engaged in by different groups. All of the inhabitants of
the area, however, depended on seals and fish for basic
foods. Fowl and eggs formed a large part of the diet at
certain times of the year, and berries, roots, and greens
were utilized to a greater extent than in most Eskimo areas.

---

* From Arctic Anthropology, Vol. 2, No. 2, 1964, pp. 61-94.

The general settlement pattern of the Bering Strait Eskimo was a large village with several small linguistically related villages located within a radius of 20 to 30 miles. Sometimes the settlements were located along a river, such as the Kuzitrin; sometimes on the ocean, as at Cape Prince of Wales. The intervening territory was considered to belong to the village cluster for hunting and fishing, an arrangement that included, ideally, the islands in reference to the mainland. The inhabitants of the smaller villages participated with the capital village in intergroup activities, together forming a unit for the reciprocal trading ceremonies (the so-called messenger feast) with other similar groupings. Each large village had one or more leading men who, in capacity of traditional chieftain, acted decisively in times of danger, and had the aggressive role in intertribal ceremonies, trade, and everyday pursuits.

Almost all of the villages were inhabited in the winter, and occasionally in the summer. Winter villages and summer fishing camps were located inland as well as on the coast. However, a fishing camp, unless doubling as a winter village, was not considered a permanent home. In the Bering Strait area, great importance was attached to a home village, and no matter what moves the inhabitants made during the year, one village was considered to be their "permanent" village. The term "permanent" in this paper is more or less synonymous with a year-round village, and is always considered thus in a village with a kazgi. On both the coast and inland, the home village was the winter village, although the inland caribou hunters spent a relatively short time in their home village than those on the coast.

The terms "inland" and "coastal" here mainly refer to winter activities of the individual villages; it does not indicate that the inland inhabitants remained only in the interior, or coastal inhabitants only on the coast. Inland dwellers went annually to the bays of their rivers for fishing or seal and beluga hunting. Occasionally entire families traveled a long distance from their home village for a joint fishing and trading venture. The practice of fishing a long way from home undoubtedly became more common after Siberian and American trade goods were obtained in large quantities.

The single most important institution that designated the degree of permanence and prominence of a village was the kazgi, or ceremonial house. The kazgis of Seward Peninsula were structures large enough to accommodate inhabitants of visiting villages. Wales had four kazgis when first mentioned in the literature in 1854 (Trollope 1854-55: 863) but two were abandoned during the latter part of the nine-teenth century. King Island had two or three kazgis (Curtis 1930: 103; Heinrich 1963d: 388); Little Diomede had two, and Shishmaref had two (Keithahn 1963: 104). The following villages had one each (south to north): Ignituk, Chiukak, Ayasayuk, Kalulik, Amilrak, Sinramiut, Kauwerak,

Pitakpuk, and Buckland (Makkukruk). The following villages
probably had a kazgi: Koyuk, Chinik, Nusok (Nook),
Kividluk, and Deering (Kipalut). In all cases except
that of Ignituk, which was near Chiukak, and Nusok, which
was near Ayasayuk, these villages formed a definite focal
point for the surrounding territory.

Although the settlement pattern was the same everywhere
in the nineteenth century, there were three principal
subsistence patterns: (1) whale, walrus, seal, and fishing,
to be called the Whaling Pattern; (2) caribou, fishing, seal,
and beluga, to be called the Caribou Hunting Pattern, and
(3) seal, beluga, fishing, and caribou, to be called Small
Sea Mammal Pattern. (These do not include trade food.)
These subsistence patterns were not correlated with any one
dialect or language group. The groups and their dialect
affiliation in the Whaling Pattern were Little Diomede and
Wales (Central Bering Strait: Kauwerak subdialect). Those
of the Caribou Hunting Pattern were Buckland, Deering, and
Candle (Malemiut, at least in the nineteenth century,
although Candle might have been Kauwerak) and Kauwerak
village and north central Seward Peninsula (Central Bering
Strait: Kauwerak subdialect). The Small Sea Mammal Pattern
included the areas of Golovnin Bay (Unalit), Teller (Central
Bering Strait: Kauwerak), and Shishmaref-Espenberg (Central
Bering Strait: a variation of Kauwerak).

The subsistence patterns had three important aspects:
(1) the mobility of the inhabitants seasonally for food
getting; (2) the flexibility of the food quests, and
the variety of principal foods utilized within one subsistence
area, which led to: (3) the many alternatives offered in
all subsistence patterns, but especially the Caribou and
Small Sea Mammal patterns. The Eskimos of the Whaling
Pattern were oriented to the sea more than were those of
the other two patterns. Caribou and salmon were of little
importance compared to sea mammals. However, both products
were obtained through trade or travel to other territory.

Winter caribou hunting was most important to people of
the Caribou Hunting Pattern. In the spring, however, the
caribou hunters went to the bays or coastal areas of their
rivers for beluga and seal hunting. For example, the
Buckland people went to Eschscholtz Bay from their mountain
winter caribou corral, Attenmiut (probably Zagoskin's
Aiashadak-koshkonno); the Candle (Kugaluk) people went
downriver on the Kiwalik from their caribou grounds. The
Kauwerak people went to Tuksuk Channel and Agiapuk River
for fishing and to Grantley Harbor for beluga and seal
hunting from their inland villages on the Kuzitrin.

The Eskimos of the Small Sea Mammal Pattern lived
mainly on seal and beluga, but also traveled short distances
inland for caribou hunting. Caribou sometimes came in the
winter to their coastal villages, particularly if the
tundra pastures were snowfree. Thus it can be seen that
almost all of the Seward Peninsula Eskimos in the eighteenth

century had a diet that included caribou meat. The caribou began to decrease in the 1870's, and by the 1880's almost all had left the peninsula. The inland villages disappeared and the inhabitants moved elsewhere.

Population

The major consensus in the literature about this area is that early pre-European population had been large, the population decreasing drastically after the arrival of Europeans, especially the first whaling ship through Bering Strait in 1848. Without a doubt the introduction of firearms had a direct bearing on the disappearance of the caribou, and commercial whaling on the decrease of whale and walrus, but the Eskimos did not, as asserted, decrease in direct proportion to the decrease of game. When late nineteenth century observers remarked upon deserted villages along the coast they assumed that all of them had been occupied simultaneously and abandoned suddenly. For example, Sheldon Jackson, eager to melt the hearts and pocketbooks of Americans for his reindeer project in 1890, proposed that the Alaskan Eskimos, a remnant of a once-glorious nation, were dying of starvation. Jackson used fallacious corroborating material to emphasize his theme. One of his examples was Frederick William Beechey's mentioning a large village of "1000 to 2000 people on Schismareff Inlet; it has now but three houses" (Jackson 1893: 1292). At Jackson's time this village had a population of 80 persons with probably 15 houses (Lopp 1892: 390).

What Beechey actually said about this village (Kikiktuk, now called Shishmaref) was this: "We noticed...a considerable village of yourts, the largest of any that had yet been seen" (1831 volume I: 247). Because this was Beechey's first anchorage on the Alaskan mainland, he had had little opportunity to compare villages. Beechey went on to offer an estimate of population for the area between Port Clarence and Point Barrow: "about 2500, including Kow-ee-rock [Kauwerak]" (1831 volume II: 568). Beechey furthermore said that he had taken into account the seasonal habits of the people and the deserted villages, which he presumed would be inhabited in the winter. It is significant that 21 years before the first whaling vessel sailed through Bering Strait Beechey said, "[the estimate] may serve to show that the tribe [Eskimo from Port Clarence to Point Barrow] is not very numerous" (ibid.).

Although many sweeping, unsupported statements have been made about the dwindling of a once large population, an analysis of actual population estimates proves this to be false. Even the most grandiose of estimates proves to be reasonable, or even low, and the result is that contrary to traditional belief, the population had increased, or at any rate had maintained itself right up to the twentieth century. It is common knowledge that the Eskimo population is increasing today.

One of the first population estimates for Alaska that included Seward Peninsula was made by Petr I. Popov, who was sent to Fort Anadyr in Siberia in 1711 to collect furs as taxes from the Chukchi. He learned that the population of the big land across the strait (probably an extensive territory) was 6000. However, it is notable that the Chukchi considered the comparatively small figure of 6000 to be very large--more than three times that of the Chukchi (Müller 1761: xxv).

In 1854, the surgeon, John Simpson, like Beechey, offered a conservative estimate of population for the Colville River-Bering Strait-Norton Sound area of 2500, and "probably little more than 2000" (1854-55: 919).

William H. Dall, in 1870, said that the population was: 1500 for "Kaviak Peninsula" (Seward Peninsula), 1000 on the coast of Norton Sound (including territory as far south as Saint Michael), 100 on Sledge Island (which seems rather high), 150 on the Diomedes, and 1000 on the Arctic coast. He did not mention King Island. Thus, the area all the way from Saint Michael to the Arctic coast had a total population of only 3750 (1870: 537).

The 1881 cruise of the Thomas Corwin produced an estimate of "three thousand [Eskimos] on the northwest coast of America, from the Colville River, on the east, to Bering Strait, including the islands therein, on the west" (Hooper 1884: 101).

The 1890 census reported that the "Seventh District" (all villages from Sea Horse Island, east of Point Barrow, to the "Norton Sound settlements", i.e., to Saint Michael) had a total population of 3222, which included at least 333 commercial whaling men, as well as 267 inhabitants of Saint Lawrence Island. Subtracting these, the total is 2525 (Porter 1893: 8 and 162. Saint Lawrence is not included in other estimates, except possibly Popov's).

The 1890 census also counted the inhabitants by tribes as well as by area, arriving at a total of 2650. "Nuwuk, 143; Unaligmiut, 110 [underestimated]; Kingegan, 652; Mahlemiut, 630 [overestimated]; Kaviagmiut [i.e., Kauweramiut], 427; Tikera, 295; King Island, 200; and Utkeaq, 193" (ibid.: 154).

Thus, the population estimates between the years 1827 and 1890 for northwest Alaska from Point Barrow as far south as Saint Michael ranged between 2000 and 3750. However, my conclusion on the basis of published figures for separate villages during the latter decades of the 1800's (when the Eskimos were supposedly dying out) shows that Seward Peninsula alone had a population between 2000 and 2400. This is substantially higher than many former estimates made for the entire area as far north as Point Barrow. The population, therefore, had not decreased after the mid-1800's, and any prior conclusions to that effect were

erroneous and based on emotion or misinterpretations of
population readjustments.

Settlement Readjustments

Several population shifts that occurred during the last
half of the nineteenth century probably presented a picture
of population decrease to uncritical observers. The
population apparently had been stable for centuries in view
of the early conservative population estimates as well as
evidence that subsistence areas were sustaining their
safe limit of population, although I have not worked this
out numerically.

One of the most important adjustments of ethnic groups
was that which followed the Malemiut movement southward
beginning during the last decade of the eighteenth century.
The movement, initiated long before the caribou disappeared
from northwest Alaska, was a result of Kotzebue Sound and
Port Clarence Eskimo-Chukchi trade in furs, which were
destined for the Anyui trade fair on the Kolyma River in
Siberia. The first Malemiut traders went to the Yukon, but
subsequent ones branched out to southern Seward Peninsula
and eastern Norton Sound into Unalit territory after kinship ties had been established and the caribou had disappeared.

The Malemiut infiltration into Unalit territory was
accomplished first by roving groups who returned yearly or
bi-yearly to Kotzebue Sound. Even at its height it was
not a solid taking over of territory, but occupation of
abandoned sites, or settlement among the Unalit. Writers
like Henry Woolfe have spoken of the rapacious methods of
the Malemiut, but with the exception of a few gruesome
folk tales, there is no substantiation (for example, see
infra, Koyuk-Golovin area: Nuviakchak).

A second reason for population readjustment during
the nineteenth century was the disappearance of the caribou.
This disappearance, however, was not a cause for the caribou
hunters' invasion of another tribe's territory. The
Malemiut and Kauwerak Eskimos of the Caribou Hunting
Pattern continued to live in the same general area after
the caribou left. They moved to alternative villages,
both coastal and inland, of their original territory,
and pursued alternatives already existing in their pattern.
This also applied to the transplanted Malemiut in eastern
Norton Sound in the 1860's.

With the exception of the southward movement of the
Malemiut, there is no historical evidence that Seward
Peninsula groups moved to other tribal territory. I was
told that a family left Wales in "prehistoric times"
(prior to the nineteenth century) for Point Barrow because
one of their members committed a murder. (This move has
also been suggested by Curtis (1930: 136) because of bitter
inter-family feuds, and by Jenness (1928: 73) because of

harassment by Siberian raiders.)[3] No matter how dire
subsistence conditions became in the nineteenth century,
there was no need for a family or village to move outside
its own subsistence pattern. The use of both land and
sea was involved in each pattern, and the large hunting
and fishing areas could be utilized by any one of the
villages belonging to the dialect group or tribe. Furthermore, every village's safety was reinforced through an
intricate kinship system and reciprocal trading arrangements. Thus, numerous alternatives through flexibility of
the subsistence pattern, mobility within their territory,
kinship relations, and trade were always available during
crises. At times of famine everywhere, the kinship and
tribal boundaries expanded to allow greater latitude of
interaction.

Small villages sometimes were abandoned to be relocated
nearby within the same subsistence pattern, and continued
to be known by the same name. This was true of Shaktoolik,
Angutak, and Bluff, for example. This was not true for
the largest villages such as Ignituk, Ayasayuk, Kingigan,
Kauwerak, and Kikiktuk (Shishmaref). When they were
abandoned, as were Ignituk, Ayasayuk, and Kauwerak, they
remained so.

Other reasons for the abandonment or readjustment of
villages in the nineteenth century besides the infiltration
of the Malemiut and the disappearance of the caribou are as
follows. A village example is given for each.

1. Abandonment of a village because of a few deaths.
Complete abandonment for this reason took place only when
the village was very small--one or two houses--or had a
very small population (Port Clarence: Kogrukpak). After
the 1838 smallpox epidemic, the 13 survivors of Unalakleet
--at that time a small village--moved from the left bank
of the river to the right bank. Two known devastating
epidemics occurred after the time encompassed by this paper,
the 1900 measles and pneumonia epidemic, and the 1918
influenza epidemic. I have found no evidence that the
smallpox epidemic of 1838 reached north of Unalakleet,
although it may have (Section II: Koyuk).

2. Death of the entire village population from
illness, starvation, or poisoning. The death rate from
what probably was botulism poisoning apparently was very
high prior to European contact (Koyuk-Golovin area: Kiuk.
Three families died of food poisoning in 1901, at which
time the village was permanently abandoned). Starvation
sometimes occurred when weather conditions made hunting
impossible for long periods of time.

3. Storms and seismic sea waves (tsunamis) affected
unsuitably located coastal villages. About 1830 a tsunami
swept over a large portion of the western Alaskan coast.
I have learned of four examples of its destruction, but
undoubtedly other small villages were affected (see

Safety Lagoon, Golovin, Little Diomede Island; and farther
south, Shaktoolik; see under Safety Sound-Cape Douglas
Area: Settlements).

     4. Village sites often wore away because of river
action or natural erosion. Shaktoolik had moved at least
three times in the historical period, and as late as 1931
village leaders asked advice about moving five miles
downstream because the river had eaten away the bank
(Anderson and Eells 1935: 95). Buckland has moved because
of river erosion, and Unalakleet, today, is subjected to
severe wear.

     Chungauroktulik, a village on Golovnin Bay, reportedly
was demolished by a landslide.

     5. The semi-subterranean houses often became
uninhabitable because of dampness and repeated inundations
in the spring. New houses often were built in the same
village without demolishing the old. Because of this
practice, many villages looked larger than they were.

     6. Some small villages moved periodically because the
inhabitants wanted a change. This apparently was a common
practice in the Solomon River and Golovin area where a
village, considered to be a permanent one, would be
inhabited for a few years until the inhabitants (often one
or two families only) got tired of their old "village,"
and built a new one.

     7. Several informants, particularly from the Buckland
and Koyuk-Golovin areas, said that before their grand-
fathers' time, villages often were destroyed by Indians,
and occasionally, other Eskimo groups. Substantiation
is thin and the majority of "true" stories appear to be
folk tales. A story rarely ends without the miraculous
escape of one woman, one woman with a child, or an orphan.
Furthermore, no villages of the Wales and Port Clarence area
were lost to what has been considered annoying attacks by
the Chukchi.

     8. Twentieth century village changes: The gold rush
of 1898-1900 brought the first major dislocations to the
Seward Peninsula Eskimos. After the first surge of 30,000
gold seekers had turned the country back to the Eskimos,
and despite the establishment of mines over most of the
area, the old patterns continued with minimal changes.
Even the magnet of Nome and the measles and pneumonia
epidemic of 1900 did not noticeably disturb the old subsistence and settlement patterns for two decades. For a
few families, however, the reindeer industry provided a new
subsistence pattern. The final dislocation for the
majority was due to the influenza epidemic of 1918 when
hundreds of Eskimos south of Shishmaref and north of Saint
Michael succumbed. Almost all of the remaining small
villages became extinct. "They all died in the flu" is
said about Ayasayak, Sinramiut, Sinuk, and many more.

By that time, however, other non-Eskimo changes--
especially establishment of schools--had appeared to make
the abandonment of the remainder of the small villages
desirable. Certain villages grew because of the school,
but others because new job opportunities developed in the
changing economy. The aboriginal large village-small
village settlement pattern disappeared. Instead, the large
isolated village, often with part-Caucasion population,
became dominant.

II. Village Analysis

I have divided Seward Peninsula into five main
subsistence and geographical areas. These correspond
roughly, also, to linguistic units. The areas are:
(1) Koyuk-Golovin; (2) Safety Sound-Cape Douglas;
(3) Port Clarence-Kauwerak; (4) Wales-Diomede islands-
Shishmaref; and (5) Southern coast of Kotzebue Sound.

Each area is discussed with reference to food resources,
linguistic affiliation, population, and pertinent historical
or descriptive information about individual villages. All
areas and settlements are presented from south to north,
proceeding clockwise around Seward Peninsula. All settlements existed in the eighteenth and nineteenth centuries,
and were compiled from maps, publications, manuscripts,
and informant data. I obtained settlement data from
informants mainly in 1955, 1961, and 1964 from 35 Eskimos
representing all areas of the peninsula, including the
culturally related Unalakleet. Twenty-one of my informants
were over 60 years old, and only five were under 50.[4]

Comprehensive mapping could not have been done without
informant data because printed sources, as a rule, mention
only the largest settlements, and exact locations are
usually problematic. Furthermore, a name such as Hobson's
"Pittock River" (the Goodhope) could not have been
identified from published sources as it does not exist in
print. All information was placed immediately on U.S.
Geological Survey quadrangle maps.

When citing villages from publications I have retained
the original spelling. Otherwise, I use spelling as
standardized through informant data, prior widespread
usage, or the United States Board of Geographic Names.
Golovnin is the spelling for the lagoon and the bay;
Golovin, for the village.

The Eskimo pronunciation is italicized in its initial
major occurrence in the text. I transcribed the words
phonetically, but they are here presented as phonemically
as possible in ordinary type. Therefore, the a is generally
pronounced as ah, the u as oo, i as ee, e as ay, o as oh
(Koyuk is pronounced Koh-yuk, not Koiuk), and the ng
usually as ŋ . The ch is the English ch. Occasionally the

i should be pronounced as the high, open front vowel I, and the u as the mid open central Ω but in this paper, for the sake of uniformity, I have not used separate symbols for them.

A detailed map could have been made from informant data alone. Interest in geographical information is general among the Eskimos, though there are few specialists, and they are becoming fewer. The specialists know every foot of ground, every gulch, streamlet, and rock pile. Typically, an informant told me: "Before 1900 [the gold rush and measles and pneumonia epidemic] there were lots of little names between Chiukak and Ignituk," a distance of only ten miles. Nevertheless, because of the large area involved, I am sure that there are a number of camp-sites or prominent traditional landmarks that I did not get. All large rivers had many camps, some utilized generation after generation, some abandoned, and some newly established in the nineteenth century. The general pattern of settlements and the naming system of all areas, however, are easily discernible.

Koyuk-Golovin Area

This cultural and linguistic area could include with justification all of the territory as far south as Unalakleet, including Shaktoolik and Cape Denbigh. For purposes of this paper, however, the first village to be treated in detail is Koyuk at the head of Norton Sound. All villages are in Unalit unless indicated otherwise.

The social and subsistence activities of the people living between Shaktoolik and Koyuk were oriented around Norton Bay. To some extent this was true as far south as Saint Michael, because the people traveled extensively from there to the northernmost boundaries of the Koyuk-Golovin area and beyond. Subsistence patterns were essentially the same from Golovin to Unalakleet. Unalit speaking people occupied the coast from Saint Michael to Golovnin Bay in the eighteenth and nineteenth centuries, and only at the beginning of the nineteenth century did the Malemiut begin to settle among them. At the time of the smallpox epidemic of 1838, there were no Malemiut in Unalakleet, but by mid-nineteenth century a small percentage were both Kauwerak people and Malemiut. By 1911 there were 16 Unalit, 14 Kauwerak, and 10 Malemiut families (informant data). E. W. Nelson said that in 1880 Shaktoolik people were mainly Unalit (1899: 252) but the 1880 census reported it to be the southernmost Malemiut village (Petroff 1884: 126).

Although seasonal pursuits were carried on with a 25-mile radius as a rule, certain persons, and sometimes whole families, traveled north to Kotzebue Sound and south to Unalakleet, and even Saint Michael. Zagoskin said that "Ikalikhvigmiut" (Fish River village or Irathluik) was a depot for great cargoes of furs going to Port Clarence

from the south (Zagoskin 1847: 109) and when H. F. Dyer
visited the village of "Erathlicmute" at the mouth of the
Niukluk River on January 11, 1867, he found that the
inhabitants "had all gone to Unalakleet" (The Esquimaux
1867: 35).

Travelers followed well-known trails both winter and
summer. Overland winter trails led to Kotzebue Sound from
the eastern shore of Norton Sound along the coast and
thence to the Koyuk River via the East Fork of the Koyuk
and the West Fork of the Buckland. Another trail to
Kotzebue Sound led from the Koyuk along the hillsides to
the east, and thence down the Wilson Creek tributary of
the Kiwalik River. "Coralling caribou" people occasionally
went by sled from the upper Buckland to the Kiwalik, Koyuk,
and Golovnin Bay.

The Kiwalik River could also be reached from the Fish
River via a low divide north of the Omilak mines across
the Tubuktulik River and the Koyuk, thence down a tributary
of the Kiwalik (Brooks 1901: 216).

An old trail up the Fish and Niukluk rivers and across
a divide to the Kruzgamepa (locally called the Pilgrim) was
used subsequently by many white men, among them Thomas
Bourchier and Bedford Pim of the Franklin search, the
Western Union Telegraph Company men, Johan A. Jacobsen,
and gold rush prospectors.

Winter trails between Shaktoolik and villages on the
north coast of Norton Bay cut almost straight across the
bay. In summer, however, the umiak route closely hugged
the shore since the Norton Sound boatmen did not boldly
strike across large stretches of water as did the well-
known northern seafarers of Diomede, Sledge and King Islands.
Indians occasionally came to the villages of Norton Sound
by canoe in summer and by sled in the winter. Norton Bay
is called kungikuchuk ("big inlet") by the Eskimos.
Spruce is found along the Koyuk, Fish, Niukluk, and many
small rivers.

Food resources

Walrus and whales were absent in this area. Seal
hunting was important, and caribou hunting was exceptionally
good in the hills between the Inglutalik and Koyuk rivers.
Beluga were plentiful at the mouth of the Inglutalik River
and in Golovnin Bay. Fish were important everywhere, and
the mouth of almost every river was a potential, if not an
actual, campsite. Some places were known to be better
than others; for instance, coastal fishing near the town
of Moses Point was known always to have "the best fishing,"
and Fish River was "always to be depended on." Short
rivers could supply the needs of only a single family, but
large rivers like the Koyuk and Fish rivers supported many
camps. The Fish River Eskimos, whose principal aboriginal
food was fish, had an abundance of salmon, as well as

whitefish, trout, grayling, and pike.

Large herring were especially plentiful around
Golovnin Bay. A perpetual spring on the Kwik River west
of Bald Head is said to have furnished a limited amount of
salmon all year round.

Thousands of ducks and geese were caught on Golovnin
Bay in the spring, and innumerable flocks of ptarmigan
were snared in brushy areas everywhere in the winter.
Eggs, hunted both on cliffs and on the tundra, were an
important part of the diet. Berries, Eskimo potatoes, and
various greens were extensively utilized.

Population

The population of this area probably did not exceed
400.

The 1880 census presents figures for only five villages
of the Golovin area and six villages for the Norton Bay
area north of, and including, Shaktoolik. The Golovin
villages were: "Atnuk, 20; Ignituk, 100; Chiookak, 15;
Okpiktolik, 12; and Tup-ka-ak, 15" (Petroff 1884: 11).

Norton Bay villages were: "Shaktolik, 60; Oonakhtolik,
15; scattered villages, head of Norton Bay, 20; Ogowinagak,
20; Kvikh, 30; and Nubviakhchugaluk, 20" (ibid.).

The total is 327, which did not take into account the
inhabitants of the Fish River drainage or the villages at
the head of Golovnin Lagoon, the addition of which might
raise the total to over 350.

The census figures for 1890 were presented wholly by
Henry D. Woolfe, a correspondent for the New York Herald.
His material is often unreliable. He gathered the
population figures only two or three years after the 1880
census, which restricts any meaningful use of them. The
total population for this area, including Shaktoolik, adds
up to 418 (Porter 1893: 3). He gave population figures
for only a few villages. He lumped most of them into
"Norton Sound settlements" with a population of 283, of
which 164 were "native" Eskimos and 119 "foreign" Eskimos,
and "Golovin Bay [sic] settlements" with a total of 76,
broken down as follows: "Golofnin Bay, 25 total; 12
native Eskimos and 13 foreign Eskimos; Ignitok, 64 total,
38 native, 26 foreign; Singick, 12 total, 5 native, 7
foreign; Atnik, 34 total, 21 native, 13 foreign" (ibid.: 8).
In a different place, however, he says, "Golofnin Bay
includes native villages of Siningmon [Chinik?], Netsakawik
[Nutsvik, i.e., White Mountain], Ukodliut [Ikathluik], and
Chilimiut [Kulumuvik?]" for which he gives no population
figures (ibid.: 162). ("Foreign" Eskimos were those born
elsewhere, and apparently included visitors as well as
spouses.)

The 1890 census also presented a section without
population figures: "Norton Sound settlements comprise a
large number of small settlements as follows: Orowinarak
[Ukvignaguk, Isaacs village], Quikak [probably Kuinihak],
Aniluk [Atnuk?], Angaktolet [Ungatulik, Inglutalik River?],
Quiuk [Koyuk], Newothliket [?], Konerkat [?], Impuit
[Ignituk?], Origneak [same as Orowinarak?], Keek [Kuik],
Upiktalik [Okpiktulik], Ongatuk [Angutak], Unamahok [?],
Ikekik [Egukachak?], Arinik [?], Natoket [?], Kyuktolik
[this is the same village as Nubviakhchugaluk, 1880
census: see Nuviakchak], and Taphok [Tapkak]" (R. Porter
1893: 162). Several of these villages, it will be noted,
are west of Golovnin Bay.

At that same time, Shaktoolik had a total of 38
persons, 25 of whom were "native" Eskimos, and 13
"foreign." Unalakleet had a total of 175 persons, 100
of whom were "native," and 75 "foreign."

Archaeology

For general summaries of the Bering Strait area see:
Henry B. Collins, Arctic Area, 1954; J. L. Giddings and
others, "The Archeology of Bering Strait," 1960.

One of the oldest Alaskan sites to date was excavated
at Cape Denbigh by Giddings (1951, 1964) who also excavated
at Koyuk, and McKinley Creek in the Golovin area. He made
a reconnaissance of the intervening territory. In 1929
Collins excavated briefly at Cape Denbigh and Koyuk.

In 1926 Aleš Hrdlička made a superficial archaeological
reconnaissance of the entire coast by boat, going ashore
only occasionally (1930, 1943).

Settlements

1. Koyuk (probably a Malemiut word). The old village
of Koyuk was located on the right bank of the Koyuk River.
In the 1880's Edwin Engelstadt's trading post was located
on the left bank. D. Jenness called Koyuk village,
"Inglestat" (1928: 79).

The Western Union Telegraph men called it Konyukmute
(The Esquimaux 1867: 33) and Kioukmute (Taggart 1953: 154).
Koyuk apparently is Zagoskin's Kvynkhakgmiut, an Unalit
word (1847: 109). This suggests that the Malemiut had not
yet settled there. In 1865 William H. Ennis said that the
village had been deserted for 13 years because of sickness
and death (Taggart: ibid.). The date is too late to
refer to the 1838 smallpox epidemic if his reported time
lapse is correct. However, if the epidemic did reach
Seward Peninsula it is possible that the Malemiut replaced
the stricken Unalit and reinhabited the village.

In January 1881 J. A. Jacobsen said that all of the
houses were vacant because the people were hunting or
trading (1884: 297).

The population in 1880 was 40 if "Kvikh" in the census refers to Koyuk (Petroff 1884: 11). Kvikh may have referred to Kuik (see below).

1a. Koyuk River. At the confluence of the East Fork (Iluanivit; Eritak by Jacobsen) with the main stream of the Koyuk was a summer fishing site called Iluanivit ("place where the smelts run"). Jacobsen mentioned this place, deserted in the winter, to be Itlauniwik. He also mentioned that the principal route from the East Fork to the Buckland was down Pujulik (Puyulik--"river with smoke") Creek, a tributary of the West Fork of the Buckland, a well-traveled route before the caribou disappeared. According to informants, travel ceased during their grandparents' time, which accords with Lieutenant E. P. Bertholf's observations in 1897. He found several clusters of old abandoned huts along the same route, with which his Eskimo guide appeared to be thoroughly familiar, "for he wound in and out among these hills, and generally managed to keep to a pretty level road. We crossed and sometimes followed for a while quite a number of small streams, all of which I learned were tributary to either the Koyuk or the Buckland river." The guide had names for all of the settlements, but Bertholf did not report them. When he tried to get an explanation for the inhabitants' moving, the guide said that "he guessed they wanted to go somewhere else" (1899: 110).

Brooks, in 1900, said that he came to only one permanent fishing cabin on the Koyuk (not the East Fork, but the main stream) after leaving the mouth. This cabin was 4 1/3 miles downstream from Knowles Creek, about 108 miles from the mouth (Brooks 1901: 199).

A fishing camp known as Uksakuknuk was located about 3/4 mile upstream from Dime Landing. In 1900, this camp and another known as Nulaguk ("place to rest" on Kenwood Creek) were used by one family.

2. Kuiguk ("big river"). A summer village for fishing and berrying near the mouth of Kuiuktulik River.

3. Ukvignaguk (usually printed Ogowinagak or Orowinarak). This is "Isaac's village," after which Isaacs Point was named. Isaac, a Malemiut trader, had settled down here after many years of trading between Kotzebue Sound and Saint Michael. In the 1880 census the population of the village was reported to be 20 (Petroff 1884: 11). In 1882, the total population of 26 persons lived under one roof. All were related in some way to Isaac (Jacobsen 1884: 240-41).

4. West side of Bald Head. In 1778 Captain James Cook saw a number of dwellings on the west side of Bald Head (1784 volume II: 477), but apparently he was referring to Kuik (Giddings 1964: 179). In Unalit, Bald Head is known as Uluksak, for the slate found there.

5. <u>Kuik</u> ("river"). An ancient village was located at the mouth of Kwik River on the right bank. A later village, also abandoned, but still shown on maps, was built on the left bank and is now used as a berry picking camp. The survivors of the 1900 measles epidemic died of food poisoning.

6. <u>Tubuktulik</u>. This village (Tubukhtuligmiut), reported by Zagoskin as being a very large settlement, was located at the mouth of the Tubuktulik River (1847: 109). One informant said that long ago Tubuktulik was a large village with a kazgi, but that most of the village had washed away. Other informants remember it only as a summer fishing village, as did W. C. Mendenhall (Brooks 1901: 215). Mendenhall said that a total of 50 to 100 Eskimos had assembled for fishing at the mouths of the "Kwiniuk, Tubutulik [sic], and Kwik rivers," before the measles struck in 1900.

7. <u>Kuinihak</u> ("new river"). The village was located about two miles from the mouth of the Kwiniuk River on the left bank near the present village of Moses Point. It has also been called <u>Paimiut</u> (Unalit for "mouth"). Moses Point was named after an Unalit man, who had been given the name of Moses during the gold rush. Jacobsen called this village Kjuwaggenak on the Quinekak River (1884: 254).

Between Kuinihak and Nuviakchak a small settlement, <u>Milianotulik</u>, on Iron Creek (Miniatulik) was supposed to have existed.

8. <u>Nuviakchak</u> ("young girl" or "virgin"). Located near present-day Elim, Petroff's and Nelson's maps record Nuviakchak as Nubviakhchugaluk and Nubviukhchugalik ("place of the young girl"). Jacobsen calls it Newiarsualok, or Cap Jungfrau (1884: 291). The 1880 census recorded a population of 30 for this village (1884: 11), but the 1890 census omitted it. However, the 1890 census listed a "Kyuktolik" among "Norton Sound settlements," undoubtedly the same village, as seen from the following folk tale.

At some time before 1880 a number of Unalit men from as far south as Shaktoolik attacked a Malemiut family, who had wrested the site of Nuviakchak from their Unalit kinsmen. The Unalit killed all but a beautiful young daughter, who was then raped by the men, tied by the arms and legs between four kayaks, and torn into four pieces when each man paddled in a different direction (informant data; Jacobsen 1884: 255). The area around Petersen Creek, less than two miles from Elim, is still known by the name, Kuyuktalik, or sexual intercourse. According to informants, it was there, and not at Elim (Nuviakchak) where the girl supposedly was raped.

When Nelson visited Nuviakchak in 1880 he said that

the houses were large and well-made, with floors of hewn planks (1899: 252). Informants said that between 1900, when everyone died of measles, and 1913, when the village was reinhabited by Unalit from Golovin, and named Elim, its three cabins were used only for temporary shelter during fishing and sealing seasons. In 1882 Jacobsen remarked about the extraordinarily good sealing there (1884: 254).

9. Fishing sites between Nuviakchak and Atnuk: There were no permanent settlements between Nuviakchak and Atnuk, possibly because of the characteristically hard winds and steep banks. However, the sites used for berrying, sealing, and fishing during the nineteenth century were ancient. They are still used today: Nutikut (at Walla Walla), Kotikutuk, Tivithluk, Kukuktaolik, Kangekachakpuk, and Ichet. Occasionally, informants said, a single family might remain at one of the places for a large part of the year.

10. Atnuk ("hunting bag strap"). This village, sometimes pronounced Utnuk, was favorably located on Cape Darby, which is called Kikiktaualik in Unalit. During times of famine, groups from all over came to get food. In the nineteenth century, caribou, following the high ridges of the Kwiktalik Mountains, came down to Atnuk. Atnuk has also been recorded as Ocnocamute and Att-nagha-mute (The Esquimaux 1867: 35, 37); Athnock-e-mute (Taggart 1954: 164-65); Atnykgmiut (Zagoskin 1847: 109) and Adnek (Jacobsen 1884: 289). It was a permanent winter village despite Zagoskin's assertion that it was the summer camp of Golovnin Bay people. On his map he located Atnuk adjacent to Tubuktulik Creek, more than 40 miles east of Atnuk, but omitted a settlement at Atnuk (ibid.: 111).

The first recorded visit to Atnuk was that of Thomas Bourchier on March 26, 1851. It was, he said, "the large native village called Atnuk" (1852: 889). In June 1866 Otto de Bendeleben said that the men in his party came to the "large village," which was very old and densely populated at one time, but 15 years before, "a disease caused great mortality among the natives" (The Esquimaux 1867: 37). That date would have coincided with Bourchier's visit, but how accurate is Bendeleben's elapsed time of 15 years is unknown. This also coincides with the illness in Koyuk reported by Ennis, also of the Western Union personnel (see #1: Koyuk).

Informants say that in prehistoric times Atnuk was a large, permanent village, located on both sides of a small stream locally called Cold Creek. Also, in the distant past, a folk tale says that the Indians wiped out all of Atnuk, with the exception of one little boy. Later, the site was reinhabited.

Petroff, in the tenth census reported Atnuk's population to be 20 (1884: 11) and the eleventh census reported 34, of which 21 were native to the village (R. Porter 1893: 3).

11. Chinik (or Chingnak), "point of land." This village, usually spelled Cheenik on old maps, was the site of present-day Golovin. The entire coastline of Golovnin Lagoon and Bay was extensively utilized for beluga hunting, seal hunting, many kinds of fishing, and duck and goose hunting. The majority of names on the map in this area pertain to fishing camps that had been occupied for many generations by the same family. Permission was needed by others to fish there.

Zagoskin erroneously gave Chinik the name Ikalikhvigmiut which Hrdlička copied. Zagoskin actually was referring to Irathluik, located at the confluence of the Niukluk with the Fish (Irathluik) River, but placed it incorrectly because of imperfect maps at his disposal in Saint Michael. Hrdlička, in copying the location and name, made a point of saying that Chinik, today's Eskimo name for Golovin, was erroneous. Zagoskin placed a "Cheenik" where "Mission" (of the Swedish Evangelical Covenant Church of America) is now located on maps, between nos. 12 and 13 on Map 1. The Eskimo name for Mission is Tuklaktoik, but the point of land has been known as Chingnak.

Chinik (Golovin) was a very small settlement during the nineteenth century until the gold rush of 1899-1900. In 1880 the developers of the Omilak silver mine, the first commercial mining venture on Seward Peninsula, made Chinik their headquarters. John Dexter, a sailor turned Omilak miner, later established a successful trading post in the 1890's.

12-17. Fish River trail and camps. (The name of Fish River in Unalit is Ikathluik; in the Kauwerak dialect, Irathluik.) The winter trail from Golovnin Bay to Kauwerak village had been in use for centuries. In 1821 Khromchenko erroneously reported a continuous waterway between Golovnin Bay and Port Clarence, which was placed on maps as late as 1898 (Nelson 1899: plate II), but in his report for 1822, Khromchenko clearly explained that the trail consisted of two rivers with a portage at the headwaters.(6) Nine miles of mountains separate the headwaters of the two rivers.

13. Nutsvik or Nutchvik ("place where one can look all over"). Between Chinik and Irathluik were several well-established fishing camps, including Nutsvik, now called White Mountain. Until the gold rush days, Nutsvik had only one permanent dwelling, but was a vantage from which people scouted the occupied and unoccupied river camps (Andrews notebooks). Bourchier in 1851 came to the "hut called Natch-wik" (1852: 889). White Mountain expanded during the gold rush as a river port. Later, a native boarding school was built.

14. Irathluik (also known as Ikathluik). Bourchier in 1851 visited both Irathluik and Chinik, which Zagoskin had confused (see #11: Chinik). Informants say that the village was also known as Niuklukpaga ("mouth of the

Niukluk" in Kauwerak language). However, one informant
said that Irathluik was located northwest of present-day
Council, at the mouth of Ophir Creek, obviously an error.

Five miles above the mouth of the Niukluk on the Fish
River was another small settlement known as Chauiapak.
Also, at the mouth of Cache Creek, a tributary of the Fish
River, there was a large seasonal fishing camp.

15. Keluniak. This camp, near Council, has also been
spelled Kig-lu-ni-ar-puk (Bourchier: ibid.) and
Kelungiarak (Jacobsen 1884: 272). Established as a
seasonal camp for Irathluik people, it had but a single
dwelling in both 1851 and 1883. Anachauik was the name
for the camp at the mouth of Ophir Creek.

16. Tashagaruk. Bourchier in 1851 also stopped at
a hut called Tashagaruk, 14 miles upstream from Keluniak
(Bourchier: ibid.). Unlocated.

17. Kuksuktopaga. This settlement on the Niukluk
apparently was used both winter and summer. Both
Bourchier and Jacobsen reported it to have two houses.
Bourchier spelled it Coxatapaga, and Jacobsen, Kaksertobage.
Today's spelling, Casadepaga, refers to the river (mined
in the early 1900's), which flows into the Niukluk. From
Kuksuktopaga the route to Port Clarence led over the
divide between the Niukluk and Kuzitrin rivers. (The
villages on the Kuzitrin will be discussed in the Kauwerak
section.)

Several other fishing camps along the Fish and Niukluk
rivers were utilized yearly by families living in tents.

18. Chungauroktulik and Popikiuk (nos. 1 and 2 on
Map 1) were often occupied the year round. Chungauroktulik
was wiped out by a landslide. Popikiuk's inhabitants died
in the 1900 measles epidemic.

Jacobsen mentions passing two inhabited villages,
Singakloget and Ojeralik, on his way from Chinik to Ignituk
in 1882 (1884: 259). Possibly they were Chungauroktulik
and Popikiuk.

19. Other camps of Golovnin Lagoon and Golovnin Bay
were known by the following names (nos. 3-14 on Map 1):
(3) Igluchauik; (4) Kulumuvik; (5) Kukok; (6) Uiaalik;
(7) Chingikchauk; (8) Malimiuk; (9) Kikchauik; (10) Nunanuhak
(11) Kingukpuk; (12) Chimuklik; (13) Kailiovik; (14) Kuichak.
At McKinley Creek, where Giddings excavated the site of
Gungnuk (1964: 197), there was only a family fishing site
during the nineteenth century. Nunanuhak and Malimiuk were
known to be ancient fishing sites. Malimiuk later became
a reindeer herder's camp. Chinikchauk was famous for its
excellent berry grounds.

20. Ignituk. This was the largest village of the

Golovin area. Zagoskin erroneously placed <u>Chiukak</u> (#23) at the site of Ignituk, and located a "Knichtagmiut," (name unrecognizable to Eskimos) on the opposite side of the peninsula from Ignituk. Apparently this referred to Ignituk. Hrdlička copied both errors and said further (on the basis of Zagoskin's information) that the name Chiukak should not be applied to the real Chiukak farther north, but to Ignituk. The names Ignituk and Chiukak have always been used for the respective villages. Despite Hrdlička's reconnaissance of 1926, he relied almost exclusively on maps (often with erroneous data) and hearsay information for his village names and locations.

Ignituk was often host to the messenger feast and feast to the dead, reciprocally celebrated with the Shaktoolik people. Festivities were also celebrated locally with Cape Nome people. In 1882 Jacobsen visited Ignituk where 200 Eskimos had gathered to celebrate a feast to the dead, which he describes in detail (1884: 259-267).

Otto de Bendeleben reported in 1866 that the women of this village were exceptionally beautiful, and that the chief, Aya-pana, was an energetic trader for the Russian-American Company in Saint Michael (<u>The Esquimaux</u> 1867: 37). E. W. Nelson said that in March 1880 he saw about 150 people at this village: "It was built at the mouth of a small canyon leading down to the sea, and the lower houses were on the upper edge of an abrupt slope 40 or 50 feet above the beach, where were arranged on sleds the kaiaks of the villagers ready for seal hunting on the sea ice. The houses had plank floors and broad sleeping benches. They were built with a small, square anteroom, which was used as a storeroom for provisions, and from it a passage about 3 feet high and 10 to 20 feet in length led to the round hole giving access to the living room" (1899: 252).

The tenth census reported the population to be 100 (Petroff 1884: 11) and the eleventh census, 64, of which 38 Eskimos were native to the village (Porter 1893: 3).

21. <u>Ipnuchauk</u> ("little bluff"). Little is known about this village, but it is thought by Eskimos today to have been "a pretty big village once, and inhabited all year." This might be "Chaimut" referred to by Zagoskin (unknown today) but copied by Hrdlička in 1926.

22. The coastline between Ignituk and Cape Nome was rich in birds, bird eggs, fish, and squirrels. Between Kayona Creek and Square Rock, a distance of two miles, smelt fishing was exceptionally good. In 1880, E. W. Nelson said that a number of small houses were located all along the coast between Ignituk and Cape Nome for use by people fishing or snaring marmots. "These summer houses, or shelters, were conical lodges, made by standing up sticks of driftwood in a close circle, with their tops leaning together, forming a structure like an Indian tipi

....A narrow vacant space between two of the logs, forming the wall, served as a doorway" (1899: 253).

23. Chiukak ("in front"). Zagoskin and Hrdlička erroneously placed Chiukak at Ignituk. Baker said that "Knecktakmiut," or Ignituk, appeared on the Western Union Telegraph Expedition map of 1867 in the position of Chiukak (1906: 181). I have been unable to locate this map, but there is no doubt that the Western Union men followed Zagoskin's incorrect information.

Informants consider Chiukak to have been large. Prior to the gold rush they thought it had four or five houses. A gold prospector, M. Clark, reported that "[Cheokuk] was at one time a populous center of the Eskimos. A great many deserted igloos remained and only a few bore marks of recent habitation, but their burial grounds reached away back to the tundra on both sides of the stream (1902: 72). However, the 1880 census reported "Chiookak" to have only 15 inhabitants (Petroff 1884: 11).

24. Egukachak. This village, located near Bluff, was a focal point for single families who came there in sailing umiaks during the summer. The settlement pattern between Ignituk and Safety Sound differed from the general Bering Strait pattern in that almost all "villages" were composed solely of family groups, who would live at a site for a few years, and then move to another in the same subsistence area. "These villages moved around a lot," an informant said, although the settlements were considered to be permanent.

25. Tapkak. This small settlement derived its name from tapkak, meaning "sandy straight line beach," a name encountered frequently north of this area (see also #45, #53, and #57). Many twentieth century maps refer to this area as Topkok, with a specific location of Topkok Head. Petroff in 1880 said that "Tup-ka-ak" had a population of 15 (1884: 11). The eleventh census reported Tapkak to have a population of 51, 23 of whom were native to the village (R. Porter 1893: 3).

26. Okpiktulik ("place of many willows"). This village, situated at the mouth of present Spruce Creek, was known for its unusual quantities of driftwood earlier in the century. Informants say that long ago there were as many as 10 houses there, but Petroff reported only 12 persons in 1880 (1884: 11). Zagoskin's Ukvikhtuligmiut and Hrdlička's Ukvikhtulig (from Zagoskin) are not at Tapkak, as indicated on their maps. Hrdlička said that Okpiktulik was a "dead village at Topkok Head" (1930: 200).

27. Angutak (Solomon). The area around Solomon was also considered to be an excellent fishing and squirrel-hunting area, and Unalit from Golovnin Bay traveled seasonally at least that far west. The villages of this area also "moved around" as in #24. The family groups

probably did not represent a large population. In the
nineteenth century, the language spoken from Chiukak to
Cape Nome was a subdialect of Kauwerak, known locally as
Chiningmiut.[7]

Safety Sound-Cape Douglas Area

Safety Sound is the official name on maps, but Safety
Lagoon is used locally. King and Sledge islands are included in this area. During the nineteenth century the
inhabitants spoke the Kauwerak dialect, although those in
the southern portion might have spoken Unalit earlier.
One of the folk tales of this area describes the populating
of King Island by mainland people. A man from Kauwerak
village hooked a large fish, which dragged him to sea. The
fish stopped about 40 miles from land and turned into a
rock, or King Island. Later, a girl from the same area ran
away to the island, found a mate, and began to populate
the island (Curtis 1930: 105).

Food resources

The mainland coast, outside the migration path of
walrus and whale, had less food resources than the Golovnin
Bay or Port Clarence areas. However, the King Islanders
depended heavily on walrus and actively pursued whales.
Even Sledge Island, only 20 miles from the mainland in this
area, was noted for its large herds of walrus in the mid-
nineteenth century. Apparently whaling had also been
carried on, because William B. Van Valin, teacher at Sinuk
on the mainland, found a shaman's whaling kit of figures
and amulets hidden in a rock pile on Sledge Island (1941:
47-48). These two islands, with their comparative wealth
of food, accounted for almost half of the area's population.

Despite the lack of easily obtained walrus and whale,
there was abundant caribou, ptarmigan, fish, and seal for a
limited number of mainland families. The area also had
good supplies of ground squirrels, rabbits, and bear. One
man told me that a village would not be established in that
area unless ptarmigan and rabbits were found nearby. Because
rivers were not large like the Koyuk and Fish, the majority
of fishing was done at the mouths; only a few camps were
found upstream on the Nome and Snake rivers. Salmon,
trout, and grayling were the principal fish. Beluga were
caught, as a rule, only near Cape Nome and Cape Douglas.
In the spring, ducks, geese, and swans were plentiful,
particularly in the Safety Lagoon area. Blueberries,
salmonberries, and the juicy, smooth, blackberry ("aziak")
were found in abundance. The inhabitants of this area also
ate a great deal of roots and greens.

Population

The total population of this area, including King
and Sledge islands, was about 320. Almost one half lived
on the two islands. The mainland population was not large
for the area involved.

The 1880 census presented the following figures:
"Imokhtagokshuk [Safety Lagoon], 30; Chitnashuak [Snake
River], 20; Ayacheruk [Cape Nome], 60; Oo-innakhtagowik
[Nome River], 10; Aziak [Ayak, Sledge Island], 50; village
opposite mainland, 10; Ookivagamute [King Island], 100;
Nook at Cape Douglas [this is not Nook, but Kalulik], 36"
(1884: 11).

The 1890 census: "Cape Nome, a total of 41; 25 native,
and 15 foreign Eskimos. Sledge Island, a total of 67; 43
native and 24 foreign" (R. Porter 1893: 8).

W. H. Dall in 1870 said that there were 100 natives
on Sledge Island (1870: 536). Informants do not believe
that the population was ever that high; perhaps some of
those counted were visitors on the island. Dall's Seward
Peninsula information was often inaccurate.

The 1890 census reported King Island to have a
population of 200, of whom 87 were native and 113 foreign
(ibid.). The Esquimaux reported 250 people to be there
at one time in July, 1867 (1867: 41). Captain Michael A.
Healy's population figures for King Island in 1888 totaled
200, 33 of whom were males and 45 females under 21 years
of age (Jackson 1893: 1273).[8]

Archaeology

Little archaeological work has been undertaken in
this area. In 1926 Hrdlička made a brief reconnaissance
of the Safety Lagoon area (1930, 1943) and F. Hadleigh-West
excavated a site in 1961.[9]

Settlements

28. Nuk ("headland," locally spelled Nook). The name
Nook is applied today to an aggregate of fishing camps on
Safety Lagoon, but old maps and censuses refer to only one
village, Imokhtagokshuk, unfamiliar now as a village name.
It may have referred to Safety Lagoon itself, or to the
settlement called Mupterukshuk. The name for water in the
Igloo dialect is imuk, and for swampy or wet, imuruk, a
name applied to the majority of coastal lagoons of Seward
Peninsula. Imokhtagokshuk, with a population of 30, was
reported by Petroff in 1880 (1884: 11) and subsequently
copied by several maps, including the Hydrographic Map of
1890-1892.

Two other villages, Mupterukshuk and Nusok, have been
reported for the Safety Lagoon area in the nineteenth
century. Mupterukshuk was a small village in which an
informant, born in 1877, said he moved from Situk (see
below) when a small child. He does not recall the name,
Nusok, but thinks it may be Nook. Prospectors in 1898-99
reported staying at a village of this name near Port Safety
(Clark 1902: 66-67; Nome News 6 March 1901). Mupterukshuk
was west of Nook.

The Nook area apparently had been occupied for many centuries despite its vulnerability to storms and tides. For example, about 1830 a seismic sea wave swept over Safety Lagoon, washing out hundreds of skeletons, which prospectors found heaped on the beach in 1899. Anokteo, an old man of Port Safety, told M. Clark in 1899 that he remembered his father reaching down into their house to grab him by the hair when the water rushed in. They rode out the swell in an umiak (1902: 212). This great seismic sea wave also pushed large chunks of ice over Chinik (Golovin), destroying it (Castle 1912: 13). It swept away a whole village on the Diomedes (Hawkes 1913: 382).

When Hrdlička personally inspected the area he said, "Here a clear illustration is had of what changes in a short time on sites of this nature may be wrought by the elements. Fifteen years ago, according to eye witnesses, there were still many burials and skeletal remains scattered in the rear of the Nook village, which faced the coast. Then in 1913 came a great southwestern storm, which at Nome, aside from causing other havoc, ripped up the town cemetery and carried away coffins with bodies, scattering them over the plains in the rear. After that storm not a vestige remained of any of the burials or bones near the large Nook village--everything had been carried away or buried under sands, and the pits of the houses themselves were largely filled in" (1943: 87).

The many storms required that many more houses be built than necessary under ordinary conditions. Hrdlička counted about 30 depressions, which he said appeared to be two villages (possibly one had been abandoned and the other built later, or possibly they were of two different ages), but there are actually hundreds of depressions, probably representing many villages of different ages. For instance, in a four-mile stretch, three small villages (Mupterukshuk, Situk, and Nook) existed simultaneously at the end of the nineteenth century. Nook now stretches over a mile long area. Hadleigh-West excavated one house in the Nook area, and found side blades and end blades of flint related to the Norton culture, 2500 years old (Nome Nugget 13 November 1961).

29. Situk, Ayasayuk, and Kebethluk. Two permanent villages were located at Cape Nome: Situk ("beluga") and Ayasayuk ("pushed out, but not detached") usually spelled Ayacheruk on maps. Situk, the smaller of the two was located on the east side of Cape Nome on high dry ground. Ayasayuk, located on the west side, apparently was also called Kebethluk. This village was mentioned by Lieutenant D. H. Jarvis (1899: 50) and has been confirmed as a name by an informant 87 years old. Younger informants do not know this name, and refer to the village in this position as Ayasayuk, which is also the name applied to the headland known as Cape Nome.

Jarvis said that Kebethluk had "comfortable log houses ...quite a large village," (ibid.) which fits the description

of Ayasayuk. Ayasayuk was reported having a population of
60 in the 1880 census (Petroff 1884: 11). In 1850 Captain
R. Collinson said: "...we were within two miles of the
shore to the west of Cape Nome, under which we saw a large
native encampment" (1889: 83). Several years before
Zagoskin had mapped the village as "Azachagyagmiut" (1847:
111). The 1890 census said that "Cape Nome includes
native villages of Kogluk [Kebethluk?] and Ahyoksekawik
[Ayasayuk]" (R. Porter 1893: 162).

My oldest informant said that when he was a boy,
inhabitants of Situk were moving to Kebethluk and
Mupterukshuk. However, Situk was still a living village
in February, 1899 when prospectors made their camp near it
(Clark 1902: 66-67). As late as 1901 the Nome News
reported that an Eskimo man had killed his wife at
"Seatok" (6 March 1901).

Beluga, tomcod, and squirrels were abundant near Cape
Nome, and caribou and salmon within a reasonable traveling
distance. In the summer the inhabitants scattered in
family groups up and down the coast, particularly around
Safety Lagoon and toward the Sinuk (Singak) River. In early
summer families from as far away as Sinuk, 36 miles north,
congregated at Cape Nome for beluga hunting.

30. Nome area. The name "Nome" was first known on
the British Admiralty maps of the 1850's. The most
reasonable explanation of its origin resulted from a query,
"Name?" for a cape on a map. The cape now known as Cape
Nome had been called Cape Tolstoi by the Russians (Zagoskin
1847: 109).

Uinaktauik. This is the name of the Nome River as well
as a summer fishing camp. It might have been the winter
settlement of a family or two. Petroff reported the
population of "Oo-innakhtagovik" in the 1880 census as 10
(1884: 11). Today a dozen or more families have summer
fishing camps there. Some are year-round residents.

Sitnasuak. "Chitnashuak," a village on the Snake River,
known by the same name, had a population of 20 according to
the 1880 census (ibid.). Nome now straddles the river. The
consensus today is that the Nome River long ago was a better
salmon fishing stream than the Snake. About two or three
miles out into the sea from the Snake River, however, is
found superb king crab fishing, which begins when the ice
freezes solidly enough for safe travel, usually by January.
The mother of one of my informants passed the Snake River
in an umiak en route to Kotzebue Sound from Golovnin Bay
in the 1880's. At the mouth she saw what she thought were
four huts. "They turned out to be two summer huts, and
two piles of crab shells, though." Captain Ellsworth West
in 1894 saw a "small huddle of summer huts" at the same
place, and went ashore to bargain for salmon (1949: 10).

31. Small villages and camps between Snake River and

Sinuk River: Summer fishing camps or small year-round
settlements were found at all stream mouths between these
two rivers. Those considered to be year-round villages
were: (a) Nagaluk ("lower ground"), five miles west of
Nome; (b) Sitnasuakak ("little Snake River") at the mouth of
Penny River where seal and duck hunting and fishing were
especially good. This site is still occupied during the
summer. Another man of this area gave an Unalit pronunciation, Chiknachauik, to this river; (c) Kailiosuak or
Kayalashuak ("one who rides a kayak") also spelled
Kieyusuok (McDaniel 1946: 15), located at the mouth of
Cripple Creek. It once had five houses.

Camps were: (a) Kungskuik at the mouth of Quartz
Creek, a favorite seal hunting camp; (b) Two miles east
of Quartz Creek, several Eskimos had a fishing camp near
some ancient dwellings in 1900 (ibid.); (c) Rodney Creek
once had three houses, supposedly for seal hunting and
fishing;(d) Sonora Creek, which reportedly had some ancient
igloos, was a summer camp in 1900.

32. Singak (Sinuk), meaning "point." The village and
river names are now spelled Sinuk on maps; therefore, that
spelling will be used here. It has also been called
Sinrock. The Esquimaux spelled it Singigungmiut (1867: 29).
Sinuk, located on the left bank of the Sinuk River, was a
very old, but probably small, settlement aboriginally. It
was sometimes occupied the year round. The headwaters
area of the Sinuk River was said to have been excellent
pasturage for caribou herds. Fishing was carried on both
summer and winter in the lower river. The inhabitants of
Sinuk and Ayak (Sledge Island) traveled back and forth
constantly. Sledge Islanders went regularly to Sinuk for the
excellent fishing and berrying in late summer, and crabs were
brought from Sledge Island to the mainland in the spring.

The belief that Sinuk was once a large village
aboriginally apparently stemmed from the early days of
reindeer herding when it became the headquarters for the
first Eskimo-owned reindeer herd in 1895. Charlie Antisarlook (Antesiluk or Anachaluk) built a large herd from an
original loan of 100 reindeer. When Antisarlook died in the
1900 measles epidemic, his widow, Sangruyak (Reindeer Mary
or Sinrock Mary), a Russian-Eskimo woman, continued the
herding. After the reindeer herds became established at
Sinuk (though Mary Antisarlook moved hers farther south),
a Methodist mission and public school were established on
the right bank of the river. The 1918 influenza wiped out
the village.

33. Ayak ("pushed off and detached"). Ayak, or Sledge
Island, has often erroneously been called "Aziak," the name
for blackberry. Captain James Cook named it after a sled
that he found on the beach, August 5, 1778 (1784 volume 2:
442). Beechey called it Ayak correctly, as did Kotzebue
and Sauer, but the early Russians began the incorrect use of
the name (Zagoskin 1847: 111). Dall and Petroff on their

maps copied it as Aziak, as did Nelson, whose map is
essentially that of Petroff's.

Informants indicated that within memory only one
village (on the east side) had existed there. Hrdlicka
mentioned two "dead villages," but he did not visit the
island (1930: 89). The United States Coast and Geodetic
Survey Bulletin 40 reported the village to be on the east
side (1901: 46). When E. W. Nelson visited the island in
July, 1881, he said that "the winter village was perched on
a steep slope, facing the sea [away from the land and
facing west?], and well above the water. The houses were
set one back of the other on the slope of the rocky talus
that extends up to the top of the high bluff; they were
built on the plan of those at Cape Nome...except that the
storeroom usually opened on a level with the ground in
front, instead of through the roof. In July, 1881, this
village was almost deserted, as the people were on the
adjacent mainland engaged in salmon fishing" (1899: 254).

From a photograph reproduced in the Report of The
Cruise of the U.S. Revenue Cutter Bear (1899: 125) it
appears that the village was situated on the east side.

Petroff reported the population in 1880 to be 50
(1884: 11). In 1890 the population was given as 67, of
which 43 were native to the island, and 24 foreign (R.
Porter 1893: 8). The 1890 census said furthermore:
"Sledge Island includes the village of Ahyak and three
small settlements on the main land opposite: Senikava
[Sinuk], Sunvalluk [Sitnasuak?], and Okinoyoktokawik
[Uinakhtaguik]" (ibid.: 162). Dall, in 1870, said the
population was 100, a figure possibly obtained from the
Western Union Telegraph contingent at Port Clarence (1870:
536).

Walrus hunting was once of great importance. On June
27, 1842, Zagoskin said that the roar of hundreds of
walruses around his ship off Sledge Island was deafening
(1847: 56).

34. Cape Rodney area. Cape Rodney (named by Captain
Cook) always had been utilized for seasonal fishing and
hunting, but informants said there never had been a village
with permanent houses. In 1791 both Sarychev (1806 volume
2: 46) and Sauer (1802: 245) reported that summer dwellings
were erected in several places in the vicinity of Cape
Rodney.

In 1827 Captain Beechey landed near "several yourts
[tents or driftwood huts?] but the people had fled upon their
arrival. He also saw several herds of caribou browsing on
the tundra a short distance from the beach.

E. W. Nelson erroneously called Cape Rodney, "Kaluligit,"
which is the name for Cape Douglas (1899: 499).

Pingo ("mound"), at the mouth of Igloo Creek, was supposed to have been a village of several houses long ago, but no one has lived there within memory.

35. Singiyak. This village of about six houses was located at Cape Woolley and was occupied until the 1918 influenza wiped out the entire village. I was told that Peter X. Peterson, a white fox rancher, lived on top of the ancient village. This is the site to which the King Islanders would like to move permanently (see #38).

36. The lagoons between Cape Woolley and Cape Douglas: Various places were occupied for fishing, but the main station was located at the mouth of Tisuk River. The name Kuzruk was also given me as a name for this place.

37. Kalulik ("rocks on the beach"). This village at Cape Douglas was very old, and had a kazgi, according to informants. W. T. Lopp said it had ten houses in 1893. It was the residence of a famous shaman, Oh-tai-luk (1893 diary). Earlier, in 1867, The Esquimaux reported that at "Kalulingmiut" there were two deserted houses and an inhabited one occupied by Utamanna and his 17 relatives (1867: 29). The village had five houses after 1900.

E. W. Nelson erroneously places "Nook" here instead of at present-day Teller. The cartographer apparently located the dot at the beginning of the word, Nook, instead of at the end (1899: pl. 2).

38. Ukiuvuk. King Island is a precipitous, craggy island, which in the past was unsurpassed for walrus and whale hunting. In the nineteenth century the village was located on the south side of the island. In the summer the inhabitants lived in square parchment skin houses on stilts, and in the winter, rock houses. In 1880 there were about 40 houses (Hooper 1881: 15). Until Sheldon Jackson began his propaganda about "starving Eskimos," these people were always described as being prosperous (see, for example, Petroff 1884: 10).

The King Islanders were (and are) superior kayak makers and paddlers. Some traveled widely both in kayak and umiak to Unalakleet, Kotzebue, and Siberia (informant data; Muir 1917: 119; Bannister 1942; 229). Entire families made periodic trips to the mainland long before Europeans arrived. After Nome was founded they journeyed there for the summer's longshoring and ivory carving. Recently many of the islanders have remained in Nome all winter instead of returning to the island in the fall as was their former custom. At this writing, several of their spokesmen are urging the United States government to relocate them at Cape Woolley.[10]

Port Clarence-Kauwerak Area

Kauwerak-speaking people lived in this area, which was subjected to concentrated intercourse with Europeans earlier than any other area. From 1849 until 1853 at least four ships of the Franklin search came to Port Clarence. For five consecutive winters a ship remained in Grantley Harbor. Men of the Plover and the Rattlesnake built houses on the spit across from Teller, and made many trips to Kauwerak and other inland villages for fun and food. They also traveled to Wales, and to Golovnin Bay and Saint Michael via the Kruzgamepa-Fish River trail. Many Eskimos visited the ships out of curiosity as well as to trade.

Whaling north of the Bering Strait began about the same time as the Franklin search (1848), and ships occasionally found it convenient to get water and driftwood at Port Clarence, particularly after the U.S. Revenue Marine Service established a coal stockpile on Point Spencer in 1884. A number of informants have told me that international trading fairs were held at Point Spencer long before those at Kotzebue Sound. A three-mile stretch would be covered with skin tents, umiaks, and hundreds of Eskimos who came from as far away as Siberia and Saint Michael. When the people left at the end of summer, not a tent pole remained. The Diomede and King islanders also came to the area to hunt and fish with their relatives.

Forty Western Union Telegraph Company men established headquarters called Libbysville across from the present town of Teller in 1866. They remained until July, 1867, when the project was abandoned. In the spring of 1867 starvation faced the men, who separated to various points for hunting or to be near Eskimos who were as badly off as they. When Libbysville was vacated, the men presented the houses and a number of unneeded items to leading men. The telegraph wire was left behind to be used for a variety of purposes such as bracelets and the Shishmaref reindeer corral many decades later (Keithahn 1963: 89).

Food resources

This area had large herds of caribou in the past, particularly north and east of Kauwerak village. Productive fishing was undertaken at almost all times of the year, but particularly in the spring in Tuksuk Channel and in summer and fall in Imuruk Basin and Grantley Harbor, and tributary rivers. Ptarmigan in the winter, and ducks and geese in the summer were plentiful. There was no walrus or whale hunting in this area, although sea mammal products were obtained by trade. Even the inland people made umiaks of walrus hide for travel on the rivers and ocean. Beluga and spotted seal came into Grantley Harbor to be taken in nets near the entrance to Tuksuk Channel. In winter and spring seals were sought at Point Spencer, and by the middle of May many of the inland people had arrived for hunting. However, some families from Port Clarence and Grantley

Harbor also went to Cape Douglas for sealing. As early as April fishing sites were occupied on Tuksuk Channel. As in Golovnin Bay, most of the river fishing sites were blanketed with proprietary rights, having been handed down from father to son generation after generation (Larsen 1951: 70; Ray field notes; Weyer 1932: 207). Permission was needed to fish in particular spots. This was also true on the Agiapuk and Kuzitrin rivers. Wales people also came to this area to fish, and Port Clarence people, in turn, went as far north as Palazruk for winter sealing. The general annual fishing pattern was to fish first in April for whitefish in Tuksuk Channel, in July and August for salmon in various other rivers, and just before freezeup in the fall (September) for herring and tomcod. Great quantities of fish, mainly whitefish, were obtained both summer and winter in the lower Kuzitrin. Flounder were got in quantity near the large spit across from Nook in early summer where a dozen fishing parties might be located along its length.

Population

The total population for this area was about 350.

The 1880 census gave only two figures, a total of 236 as follows: "Kaviazagamute [Kauweramiut], L. Imorook, 200," and "Siniogamute [Sinramiut], Port Clarence, 35," but it is stated in another section about Port Clarence that "three or four Innuit villages are located here" (Petroff 1884: 9 and 11).

The Sinramiut population of 36 is probably conservative, because in 1854 Trollope reported "Sin-na-ra-mute" to have a population of 40 or 50 (1854-1855) and in 1892 the population was reported to be 100 living in 10 houses (Bruce 1894: 43).

The 1890 census reported the "Kaviagmiut" to be 393, and Port Clarence Eskimos to be 236 "native Eskimos," and 249 "foreign Eskimos," making a total of 878 Eskimos (R. Porter 1893: 3, 158). Even with the deduction of the 249 foreign Eskimos, apparently in the area to trade with the whalers, the total of 629 is too high for the area. The figure, 393, obviously included inhabitants of both Port Clarence and Kauwerak, because a population count of 1892 by Miner Bruce, who knew the area well, totaled only 360. Mr. Bruce was the first superintendent of the Teller Reindeer Station, located near the village of Sinramiut. He estimated the "Sinarmetes" to be 100; the Noongmetes [Nook, and apparently inclusion of several other small villages in Grantley Harbor], 60; and "Kyazermetes" [Kauweramiut], 200 (1894: 74).

The 1890 census also reported: "Port Clarence includes the small native settlements of Chainruk [Singaurak], Nuk, Kovogzruk [Kauwerak], Toakzruk [Tuksuk], Anelo [?], Sinnepago [Sinramiut?], Kalulegeet [Kalulik at Cape Douglas], Metukatoak [?], Kaveazruk [Kauwerak?], Kachegaret [?], and Perebluk [?]; also, the whaling steamers J. H. Freeman and

Grampus, the barks Reindeer and Bounding Billow, and the brigs F. A. Barstow and W. H. Meyer" (R. Porter 1893: 162).

Informants have estimated the population of inland Kauwerak people from 70 to 150. Hobson's report in 1854 indicated that he saw 100 persons between the ship and the uppermost village on the Kuzitrin, but he failed to mention the population of two villages. Undoubtedly many of the people considered Kauwerak their permanent home.

In 1827, Captain Beechey estimated 400 persons in the Port Clarence area, which undoubtedly included Kauwerak because of his interest in, and awareness of, the place (1831 volume II: 568).

Archaeology

Several reconnaissance trips have been made in the area, but no extensive excavations undertaken. Hrdlička in 1926 made a cursory survey of the area (1930: 200-202). In 1929 Henry B. Collins excavated at Kauwerak, which proved to be an eighteenth or nineteenth century site (1930; personal communication). In 1949 Helge Larsen located an Ipiutak site at Point Spencer, and made a reconnaissance of the Port Clarence-Kauwerak area (1951: 70).

Settlements

39. Igluakik (or Amilrak) and Kaga. At least two villages were located on Point Spencer. Igluakik, with four houses and a kazgi, was on the west side about halfway on the spit. Another village, Kaga, was located on a broad bay at the end of Point Spencer.

The Esquimaux in April, 1867 reported a village, "Amilrokmiut...midway between Cape Spencer and Cape Douglas" (1867: 29). Amilrak means narrow; Igluakik and Amilrak are the same village.

The earliest notice of habitations on Point Spencer was by Beechey in 1827: "by the remains of some yourts upon [the north end of Point Spencer] has at one time been the residence of Esquimaux" (1831 volume II: 544).

40. Siberian raids. Although the Wales and Igloo people were friendly neighbors in the eighteenth and nine-teenth centuries, I was told that long ago they were enemies. That possibility, however, does not seem as real to them as the depredations supposedly committed by marauding Siberians. They say that both Chukchi and Eskimos planned and carried out attacks all the way from Cape Prince of Wales to the village of Kauwerak (Collins: personal communication; Hrdlicka 1930: 117; Ray: fieldnotes). It is difficult to believe that the Siberians could have carried their raids so far inland, past the constant concentration of people both winter and summer between the outer harbor of Port Clarence and Imuruk Basin. Nevertheless, several informants told me that

watchmen sometimes were stationed at the mouth of Tuksuk Channel to watch for invaders, and that a cave was in readiness for women and children. (No one can find the cave today.) Within Imuruk Basin itself is a prominent rocky hill called Kakriogvik, where, it is pointed out, Igloo people made flint points while watching for Siberians. A man 68 years old (in 1964) said that "a lot of Siberian skulls" were piled up when he was a child, and still another said that "Siberian skeletons are still to be found there." Siberians were supposed to have fought as far inland as Kauwerak.

Although many persons are eager to discuss the "Siberian wars of long before the whites," all contemporary accounts appear to have the same flavorful origin. It is impossible to assess the severity or frequency of the alleged raids.

41. Akavingayak and Ikpiung. Akavingayak was located on the southwest side of a bluff between Fox and Nickel Creek, and Ikpiung, at the mouth of Fox Creek.

42. Mizek ("low swampy place"). This settlement on a spit near Point Jackson had "quite a few houses at one time," but they were in constant danger of inundation. In the 1890's the Reverend T. L. Brevig said that four families lived at Point Jackson (1944: 255).

43. Sinramiut and Taksunuk. The village, Singak (also spelled Synok, Sinuk, but usually Sinramiut) was the largest village in Port Clarence. I shall use the name Sinramiut for this village to distinguish it from Sinuk, farther south (#32). Beechey, who visited this village, mentioned a kazgi and burial ground (1831 volume 2: 542). The Sinramiut traveled extensively to both Kauwerak and Wales, and exchanged the messenger feast with both. Often when Kauwerak was invited to Wales, people of Sinramiut were also invited. One of Sinramiut's main sealing camps was at Kingauguk toward Wales. In 1892 Sheldon Jackson and Captain Michael Healy of the Bear landed the first Siberian reindeer a short distance east of this village, where the Teller Reindeer Station was established.

44. Ikpiumizua and Ikpigilauk. Southeast of Sinramiut were two small villages each composed of a family or two: (a) Ikpiumizua ("end of the tundra"), and (b) Ikpigilauk ("in the middle"). In 1894, one winter house and 10 or 12 summer fishing camps were located on Ikpigilauk's sandspit (Jackson 1895: 46).

45. Salinuk, sometimes called Nuk (usually spelled Nook). This small village was located on the site of present-day Teller. The name, Nuk, also referred to the spit on the North side, across from Salinuk. The first appearance in the literature of this name was in September 1827 by Beechey who said, "Upon the low point at the entrance of the inner harbour, called Nooke by the natives,

there were some Esquimaux fishermen...,these...were...King-
a-ghe [Wales people]" (1831 volume II: 543).

Nook's population in the 1880 census was 36, although
Petroff erroneously located the village (as did Nelson) at
Cape Douglas (1884: map). It was not mentioned in the 1890
census. In 1892 the village had three winter houses
(Jackson 1895: 46).

The coast east of Teller was called Tapkak (see also
#25, #53, and #57). William Hobson in 1854 proceeded from
the Rattlesnake via Topp-cutatawne (Tapkak), a village
between the ship's anchorage and Tok-sook (Tuksuk) (1854-55).
Topp-cut-atawne probably referred to an old village site at
the mouth of Dese Creek.

46. Tuksuk Channel. Beechey in 1827 explored Grantley
Harbor as far east as "Tokshook," at which entrance he saw
a village. He also said that there were two other villages
on the "northern and eastern" shores of the harbor. He
called the village on the northern shore, "Choonowuck,"
which undoubtedly was one of two small villages both called
Singaurak located on either side of the mouth of Tuksuk
Channel (1831 volume II: 541).

North of the mouth of Tuksuk was a small village,
Kasilinuk ("burns in the mouth," i.e., Offield Creek, which
sometimes tastes bitter). This settlement was often
inhabited summer and winter.

On April 6, 1851, Thomas Bourchier said that the ice
was completely gone from midchannel: "parties of natives
were numerous on both sides, attracted by the abundance
of fish [whitefish]" (1852: enclosure 15). Today's salmon
fishing sites, said to be a result of population adjustments since 1900, follow the hereditary pattern of fishing
sites on the Kuzitrin and Agiapuk rivers where the earlier
salmon fisheries were located. The Tuksuk sites are now
occupied usually during the salmon fishing season of July
and August. From Grantley Harbor to Imuruk, they are as
follows:

Singaurak (two separate camps; old igloos near the
northernmost one. Singaurak is a coastal name, meaning
channel.) (1) Musu ("Eskimo potato"); (2) camp name not
given; (3) Kazgun ("seine"; two camps of the same name
are opposite each other); (4) Akulesak ("something in the
middle"); (5) Titkaok ("eye shade"); (6) Itak (not a camp,
but the location of the only known pictographs on Seward
Peninsula); (7) Kingnugat ("caches in the ground"); (8)
Asagorak; (9) Alianak ("lonesome place"); (10) Ipnuk.
Kangarak is an old permanent settlement, "a genuine old
village," near which is located a present-day fishing site.

47. Kauwerak. This village was the second largest on
the mainland of Seward Peninsula. From it came the tribal
name, Kauweramiut ("people of the gravel bar") erroneously

reported by many, including W. H. Dall, to be Kaviak or
Kaviagmiut. Dall understood that the village was called
"kaviak," or the Unalit word for red fox, instead of
"kauwerak" or the Kauwerak word for gravel bar, or sandbar.
(See Ray 1964a and "The Kheuveren Legend" (Ray 1976, in
this book) for history of this village.)

The following spellings refer to the village of Kauwerak:
Kow-ee-ruk (Beechey 1831 volume II: 568); Kaviak (Zagoskin
1847: 109; Dall 1870: 162); Cove-e-aruk and Cuv-vi-e-rook
(Hobson 1854-55); Kavyiak (Kellett 1851); Kaviarazakhmute
(The Esquimaux 1867: 35); Kaviazagamute (Petroff 1884: 11);
Kowieruk (Collins 1937: 238); Qavjasamiut (Rasmussen 1941:
8); Qaverak (Larsen 1951: 70). In English orthography,
Beechey's and Collins' spellings would be as suitable as
mine. The a and ee sound before the r is variable in
Igloo speech, and used interchangeably. The "v" is usually
used by Malemiut speakers, not Kauwerak.

One of my informants, whose grandfather lived in
Kauwerak as a small child, said that Kauwerak had started
"maybe sometime at the end of the 1700's or maybe earlier"
when a family moved there from another inland village
seeking a good fishing place.[11] Within a few years they
were joined by others. Specific dates by informants are
always subject to reevaluation. The lateness, however,
coincides with Collins' information that the site was not
old. He said: "The site consists of a midden about 12 feet
high, 200 feet long by 20 to 50 feet wide. There were 16
house pits on the surface of the midden. None of these was
excavated; the only digging I did was along the face of
the midden. Parts of the midden have undoubtedly been washed
away...While we were there a storm raised the water almost
half way up the midden. The midden was very poor in artifacts,
compared with those at places like St. Lawrence Island,
Wales, etc. A few decorated artifacts were found, all having
modern designs of Y figures and alternate spur. A few
pieces of iron were found about three feet deep in the midden.
Unfortunately we found no harpoon heads or other really
diagnostic artifacts, but on the whole I would say that the
material excavated would be 18th or 19th century, though
older material should be found deeper in the midden. Sea
mammal bones were scarce, caribou abundant" (personal
communication).

In 1854 Mate William Hobson, en route from the
Rattlesnake's anchorage in Grantley Harbor to Chamisso
Island in Kotzebue Sound, said that Kauwerak had seven
houses, "all large." His list of inland villages compiled
on that trip is the only one made at first hand to my
knowledge. Villages in the Chukchi language on Kobelev's
map (Pallas 1783 volume 4: pl. 1) and on the 1794 edition
of James Cook's map apparently were obtained in Siberia.
Hobson arrived at Kauwerak on Feburary 11 and returned
March 23. On both dates the inhabitants were away hunting
caribou (this, and the following information is compiled
from this report, 1854-55, and informant data).

48. Inland villages reported by Hobson on the Kuzitrin River; (Many of the village names are spelled several ways in the report because of the vagaries of handwriting. I have chosen only one. The villages italicized are pronunciations obtained from informants.) The name, Kuzitrin (kuzikliun, "new channel"), which is now applied to the main channel of the river and several small tributaries, was once applied only to the "new river," which broke through into its new channel within memory of informants' great grandparents.

February 12: Shungiowret, 30 inhabitants, two small dirty huts, "but the people seem tolerably well off." This is Sungiyorat ("little bends"), about three miles east of Marys Igloo on the old channel of the Kuzitrin. (Shungiowret was also inhabited on Hobson's return in March.)

February 13: Kek-to-alek (Kektoashliuk, "place where it breaks"). (On his return March 24 the river close to the village was dammed.) Kaktoashliuk was once located on both sides of the river, less than a mile upstream from Marys Igloo, called Aviunak, a late nineteenth century settlement. Bourchier in 1851, en route from Norton Sound to Grantley Harbor, came to a village, Muk-nuk, and then to Tik-to-aluk (Kektoashliuk). Muk-nuk apparently is Atnuk, approached, informants say, by way of a pass called Ukinarak between the headwaters of the Niukluk River and Belt Creek.

On the same day, February 13, after only a 2 1/2 hour journey, Hobson arrived at Noo-kei-row-elek, which had two inhabited huts and 15 inhabitants. (This village was also inhabited March 24 on his return.) Informants did not recall a village by this name, but said that a village, Alakasak, was located south of Kingmemsieua near Shelton.

February 14: During the day he passed two separate, inhabited huts. (On his return, March 23, he called one of the huts, "Oa-te-ue," located between Kogrupack and Nookeirowelek. Oateue may have been Atnuk, the handwriting of "n" appearing as "u.")

February 15: Hobson passed Ko-gru-pack (Kogrukpak), but did not stop. This was a village at the mouth of Kougarok Creek.

February 16: He stopped at Obell, a village of three huts and about 50 inhabitants after traveling only six miles. (On his return March 21, Obell was deserted because of the death of several persons.) This might have been Asuk on the Belt Creek flats.

February 17: At his next stop, Peo-loe-low-reuc, he found one large hut and several "more or less ruinous in the vicinity." There were about 25 persons, well off. Perhaps this settlement was at the mouth of Bonanaza Creek, which, however, is recalled as being named Katinyak or Katinyamiut.

(On his return, March 22, about one hour's travel north of
Obell, Hobson passed two hunting huts, which he did not
mention on his first trip.)

On February 18 he arrived at Show-e-yok, a village of
four huts, set in pairs almost like two distinct villages.
The inhabitants were well clothed. This village is Soiyuk
("Eskimo drum," named after a drum-shaped lake) on the
upper Kuzitrin. Inuingnuk ("no more people") was another
small caribou village above Soiyuk. (This may not have
been the original name of the place, but one applied after
it was abandoned.)

Hobson left Showeyok on February 20, camped out that
night, and on the 21st passed a small abandoned hut called
E-tum-ner-it on a small tributary of the Kuzitrin, which
probably was the Noxapaga River. From there he crossed to
the watershed of the Pittock (Goodhope) River, which will
be discussed in the Cape Espenberg Section.

49. Kingauguk ("nose point"). The coast westward
from Sinramiut was utilized more for winter sealing than
summer fishing. The farthest west sealing station of
Sinramiut village was at Kingauguk, or Cape York. A well-
traveled trail connected the two villages. (The village
at Cape York was not located on the Kanauguk River as
sometimes thought.) In 1854 Captain Trollope reported
Kingauguk as "King-a-wie" or "King-how-common," which had
three dwellings (1854-55: 913).

50. Agolik. Enroute to Kingauguk was a shelter
cabin at the mouth of Lost River known as Agolik. This
cabin was known, also, to the Franklin search people.

Wales-Diomede Islands-Shishmaref Area

Included in this section is the coastline from
Shishmaref to Cape Espenberg called Tapkak. Territory
traditionally thought to belong to Wales extended from
about 25 miles south to about 25 miles north of Wales.
Shishmaref territory began at the northern boundary and
extended almost to Cape Espenberg. Although the consensus
is that Shishmaref had been populated in the past by Wales
people, the dialect spoken from Shishmaref to Cape Espenberg
was closer to Kauwerak speech than Wales. The people themselves called the speech Tapkakmiut. People of this
dialect apparently lived as far east as the mouth of the
Goodhope River in the nineteenth century, but it is beyond
the recollection of anyone today whether they might once
have populated the entire northern half of Seward
Peninsula. By the nineteenth century the area as far
west as Deering (extending out from the inner bays of
Kotzebue Sound) was populated by Malemiut speakers.

The southernmost whaling area of the Alaskan Arctic
was in the Bering Strait. The Diomede islands and Cape
Prince of Wales were ideally located for the pursuit of

the whale. The vast herds of migrating walrus usually passed through the strait between May 15 and the end of June. With seal and ugruk plentiful, the population of the comparatively small area of Bering Strait itself reflected the great wealth of natural resources. The inhabitants were known to be fearless men of the sea and ice. They also hunted polar bear when ice conditions were favorable. Their technology in material culture was unsurpassed in the Eskimo area, and elaborate ceremonies grew up around whale hunting. Their tools and art reflected plentiful raw material and a substantial amount of leisure time.

Caribou thrived inland in great herds, but the Wales and island people concentrated on sea mammals. Therefore, only a few families from the areas to the north, particularly around Shishmaref, carried on inland caribou hunting. Salmon were not caught in the rivers between Port Clarence and Cape Espenberg. (They were, however, found in the rivers of Kotzebue Sound.) Tomcod were caught through shore ice everywhere along the coast, and flounders were found in specialized shallow waters.

Because of the variety of subsistence patterns between Wales and Cape Espenberg, I will discuss them briefly in conjunction with the villages.

Population

The total population of the Wales area (25 miles north and 25 miles south of Wales), including Little and Big Diomede islands, was about 850. North of the northern boundary to Espenberg, including Shishmaref, were about 200 more persons.

The village of Kingigan (Wales), the largest Eskimo village in Alaska during historical times, made up the largest part. Until recently its population was around 500, but not 800 or 900 as sometimes suggested (Keithahn 1963: 10; The Esquimaux 1867: 15).

The following population figures for Wales are taken from official reports and first-hand accounts:

1854: (Trollope: 1854-55) About 200 or 250 in each village. Wales was a settlement of two separate villages. Agianamiut on the south and Kiatanamiut on the north.

1866: (The Esquimaux 1867: 15) 900 Eskimos.

1880: (Petroff 1884: 4) 400. This is low.

1890: (R. Porter 1893: 3) 488. The population of 652 was also reported on page 154.

1891: (Lopp and Thornton 1891: 366) 539 inhabitants.

1892: (Lopp 1892: 390) "In March there were 527 people living here. In spring and fall this is probably increased to 560 and 560."

1895: (Jackson 1895) 539.

Population figures for Little and Big Diomede islands are as follows:

1779: (From a census taken by Ivan Kobelev in Pallas 1783 volume 4: 107; a translation of this is also found in Masterson and Brower 1948: 94). Little Diomede had 85 men and 79 women, and Big Diomede, 203 men and 195 women in two villages.[12]

1850: (Collinson 1889: 74) The two Diomedes were said to have a total population of 300.

1870: (Dall 1870: 536) 150 persons were said to live on the "Diomedes."

1880: (Petroff 1884: 4) "Inalit, E. Diomede Island, 40."

1881: (Muir 1917: 218) "West Diomede...perhaps a hundred."

1890: (R. Porter 1893: 8) "Ignaluk [Little Diomede], 85 total, 45 men, 40 women, 44 native Eskimo and 41 foreign Eskimo."

There are very few population figures for the coast known as Tapkak from Shishmaref to Cape Espenberg. An estimate of about 200 can be made for the area from about 25 miles north of Wales to near the mouth of the Goodhope River on Kotzebue Sound including Shishmaref. This is based on actual figures obtained by W. T. Lopp in 1892. About 50 of the 200 "belonged" to Kingigan. During the winter of 1892 Lopp said that in seven settlements he counted 200 persons, 80 of whom lived in "Kegiktuk" or present-day Shishmaref (1892: 390). This is the village that Sheldon Jackson said Beechey reported to have had 1000 to 2000 inhabitants. Shishmaref was not reported in the 1880 or 1890 censuses.

In addition to the 50 Wales speakers and the 80 inhabitants of Shishmaref, another 100 persons probably lived between Shishmaref and Cape Espenberg (including Espenberg) although this estimate may be high. There was only one large village, Kividluk, between Shishmaref and Cape Espenberg, supposedly with seven houses in 1892 (Jackson 1895: 97). This meant that it might have had a population of at least 50 if all houses were occupied.

Archaeology

Hrdlička continued his 1926 survey in this area (1930, 1943). D. Jenness carried on investigations at Little Diomede Island and Wales in 1925 (1928), and Collins in 1929 (1930; 1937). The Stoll-McCracken Arctic Expedition investigated briefly in the Bering Strait area (McCracken 1930; Weyer 1932).

Settlements

51. Anaktoaluk. An old village, extinct in the nineteenth century, Anaktoaluk is said to have existed at the mouth of the Anikovik River. The village of York is now located there. The village of Kingauguk (#49) was used jointly with Port Clarence people.

52. Palazrak. This was a small year-round village about 3 1/2 miles southeast of Tin City, said to have had six or seven houses once. In 1894 the winter population was 40 (Brevig 1944: 95). An informant thought that the village was placed about two miles too far to the northwest on the USGS map of 1950.

53. Tapkarak. In winter, sled travel was heavy between Wales and Palazrak (Tin City). By spring a deep road had been carved into the beach (Thornton 1931: 131). The Eskimo Bulletin for 1895 referred to Tapkarak as "Tapkarzruk suburb," one of the best king crab fisheries of the area in February and March. Tapkarak probably had a permanent population of 20.

In winter, seal hunting was pursued at the local permanent villages. However, with the coming of spring the inhabitants moved into tents toward Cape Prince of Wales for walrus and whale hunting.

54. Umeveyuk. This place between Palazrak and Tapkarak, thought to have been an ancient village site, was a reindeer herding camp in the 1890's. Mr. Lopp called it Oomeveeruk (letter to Mrs. Thornton, 13 March 1935).

55. Kingigan ("high," now called Wales). The two villages at Cape Prince of Wales were collectively called Kingigan, but known individually as Agianamiut (south village) and Kiatanamiut (north village). Zagoskin called the collective village Nykhtakgmiut on his map, saying it was a camp, and Tapkhakgmiut (Shishmaref), an "important" place (1847: 109). Hrdlička said that Wales was "Old Nykhta" on Zagoskin's map (1930: 202). Wales was the busy winter capital for sea mammal hunting, but was inhabited also during the summer. Some of the inhabitants moved out of the village during the summer to fish in neighboring rivers or to go to Port Clarence or Kotzebue Sound in conjunction with trade.

Three reports have called Cape Prince of Wales by variations of a Chukchi name. Sauer called it "Kygmil" (1802: 257), Kobelev, in his map, "Kigygmin" (Pallas 1783 volume 4: pl. 1), and Cook's map of 1794, "Kisigmin." (See Ray 1964a.)

When Beechey inquired at Port Clarence about the Wales village he understood the two villages there to be called Eidanoo, and King-a-ghe. King-a-ghe was supposed to be an inland village. No one has been able to explain the strange word, Eidanoo. It is not an Eskimo word. Someone has suggested that it was a corruption of the English, "I don't know," but the Eskimos at that time did not know enough English to differentiate between yes and no.

56. The Diomede islands (imaglit: "They of the sea," Heinrich 1963a: 380). Little Diomede Island has only two sites suitable for villages. The present village is on the west side. The other site on the east apparently never was utilized (ibid.: 394-395). Big Diomede, as noted in Kobelev's population figures, had two large inhabited villages in 1779 (Masterson and Brower 1948: 94). Kobelev called Big Diomede, Imaglin, and Little Diomede, Igelyin.

Besides whale and walrus, the Diomede Islanders ate immense quantities of birds and bird eggs. They were great travelers to both Siberia and the Alaskan mainland, and built large, sturdy umiaks. Diomeders occasionally wintered at Wales. They traded with both continents, and after the Russian fur trade began in earnest during the latter half of the eighteenth century, often joined the Chukchi in trading for skins at Kotzebue Sound. Umiaks were constantly plying back and forth between Alaska and the Diomedes, and King and Diomede islands. Travel on ice was risky, and rarely done, despite reports by today's Eskimos (usually from other parts of Arctic Alaska) of exploits by their countrymen's ancestors. It cannot be denied that the hunters of the Bering Strait area, including King Island, were expert weather and ice men; they often risked their lives in every kind of sea and ice conditions to puruse the whale, walrus, and seal. It also has been said that especially brave men, well versed in sea currents and wind, had been known literally to hop an ice cake for a trip to an island or the mainland. But crossing the strait on ice even to Little Diomede could be undertaken only when a favorable combination of extreme temperatures and calm weather had formed the jagged and quixotic ice into a solid crust. The ice in the strait is usually a mass of moving peaks and valleys. Even at its best, a dangerous breakup might occur without warning. In 1897, the Eskimo Bulletin reported that since 1890 the Eskimos had been able to cross only once on the ice (in 1892), and that "few natives now living and no whites have ever made this 50 mile trip on the ice" (1897: 2). In 1892 the winter was unusually cold with no thaws. The fall was late and the spring was early. "In February and March the straits were blocked up with smooth ice fields from the North. Five [from

Wales] with dog-sleds went across to East Cape for
tobacco" (ibid.).

57. The coast from Wales northeast to Cape Espenberg
is composed of a series of salt water lagoons and small
fresh water lakes. The coastline trends acutely northeast
from the strait and the coastal waters are very shallow for
many miles out to sea. This area abounded in ducks, geese,
and swans. Young men chased fledgling ducks on the lakes
in kayaks. The farther that people lived from the strait
in the Seward Peninsula area, the more they depended on
seals, fish, birds, or caribou rather than walrus or
whales. In the Shishmaref area ugruk was of paramount
importance.

Almost all of the villages in this section to Cape
Espenberg were winter villages, which were often used in
summer. Although the general name for the inhabitants of
the coast from Ikpik to Espenberg was Tapkakmiut, the
Shishmaref people were also known as Kikiktamiut.

58. Pinguzurak ("little knoll"). This first village
north of Wales was also known by the name of Sezromenik
("clump of tundra"). During the summer in pre-European days
strong runners chased caribou herds into the lagoons where
men in umiaks speared them.

59. Singaurak, often pronounced Singlorak ("little
channel") and Mitletavik. These were neighboring villages
on a long spit of land of Lopp Lagoon. Singaurak was
situated on the ocean side and Mitletavik on the lagoon
side. Lopp called Singaurak "Synowrook" (1893 diary).
Singaurak had three houses in 1892 (Jackson 1895: 97), but
informants said that it had more than ten houses and a
kazgi before that. Apparently a village, "Mugistokivik,"
which appears in the location of Mitletavik on the USGS
quadrangle map (1950) was unknown by that name. This
locality and "Flounder Flat," an area across from Teller,
were two of the most productive flounder grounds of the
peninsula.

60. Agudlauak. This village, also called Oswoodlawok
(Lopp 1893 diary) and Ah-Gude-Le-Rock (Gibson map) was
located north of Singaurak on the ocean side. The immediate
vicinity was noted for goose hunting. In 1892, "Ah-gwood-
la-wok" had three houses (Jackson 1895: 79).

61. Mitletak or Mitletavik. Some confusion exists
about the two villages called Mitletavik. This village,
also called Mitletopik, goes by the name of Mitletukeruk on
several maps, including USGS 1950. Informants say this is
wrong. Lopp established a mission at "Mitletok" in 1897
with an Eskimo missionary in charge. Collins excavated
at this village in 1928 (1937: 261-264).

62. There were a number of small villages between
Mitletak and Shishmaref considered to be year-round settle-

ments. They were always occupied during ugruk and seal hunting seasons: a) Isak, an old site; "Ezooah" in 1892 had three houses (Jackson 1895: 97); b) Ikpik was also an old village, supposedly with a kazgi; c) Imiengnak (also spelled Imangnaq and Ima-anok) had one house in 1892 (ibid.); Sinyasut, placed five miles too far north on the USGS map according to informants, had four houses in 1892 (ibid.); (e) Itibluk; (f) Owevuk (uivuk?) had four houses in 1892 (ibid.).

63. Kikiktuk ("island," the original name of Shishmaref). The subsistence pattern at Shishmaref was typical of the coast from Ikpik to Cape Espenberg. In September groups moved to various rivers (particularly the Serpentine near Shishmaref) for whitefish, grayling, and tomcod fishing. Herring, caught for dog food, was the last big run of fish before the river froze. No salmon entered the rivers of this section. Vegetable foods were emphasized, and cranberries, blueberries, and salmonberries were gathered and stored in seal pokes. By the middle of October the people were back in their villages, preparing for seal hunting. They caught tomcods through the ice and hunted seals during winter. Ugruk appeared about the first of May, and by June the people had dispersed in small groups in ugruk camps for many miles along the beach. The ugruk was the mainstay of the entire stretch of coast, the hunters sometimes going as far as 30 miles offshore on the ice with their rugged sleds. By late June they resorted to hunting ugruk and seals in umiaks. In the middle of July they went up the Serpentine and other rivers to lakes where men in kayaks chased ducks ashore to the waiting boys and women. They hunted all kinds of waterfowl including cranes and swans, and gathered eggs on the tundra (the above information has been summarized from field data; Keithahn 1963; and Mayokok 1959).

The site of Shishmaref apparently had been occupied for many centuries. In 1816 Kotzebue explored the village, which was built in a straight line along the shore. "We had already got upon the roof of the jurtes, without meeting with any people; fresh traces, however, which we saw everywhere showed us, that they were more fearful than their dogs, and had fled at our approach" (1821: 199-200). In 1926 Hrdlička examined several old sites near Shishmaref, the most important being east of the present village. Unfortunately, the site (like that at Cape Woolley) had been leveled by a fox farmer, which threw Hrdlička into a deep melancholy (1930: 202; see also Keithahn 1963: 91).

64. Fishing villages near Shishmaref were: (a) Ipnorak at the mouth of the Serpentine River; (b) Nonatak; and (c) Lungyat. Iyet ("cooking pot") was the name for Serpentine Hot Springs, utilized as a camping area.

65. In the eighteenth and nineteenth centuries scattered small villages northeast of Shishmaref to Cape Espenberg were occupied for winter sealing always, but

have been used recently for summer ugruk hunting and
trapping. An early day impression has survived that the
area had always been uninhabited. Petroff's and Nelson's
maps do not indicate any villages between Cape Prince of
Wales and Espenberg, but apparently this was due to lack
of information.

In 1854 Trollope observed that "The country between
King-a-ghee and Schismarief Inlet is not much inhabited.
It is called the Tass-cockte [Tapkak] country, and is
frequented for hunting and shooting" (1854-55: 917).

In July 1816 Kotzebue said as he proceeded northward
from Wales: "Many habitations which cover the coast,
indicate a numerous population" (1821: 199), and as he
sailed northward from Shishmaref: "[the coast] appeared
to us to be very much inhabited, as we discovered numbers
of subterranean dwellings" (ibid.: 206). In 1897
Lieutenant D. H. Jarvis put it more realistically: "There
are numerous remains of old villages all along the coast,
but that are now deserted, I believe to be due not so much
to the fact that there are less people, as to the desire to
change a situation when the houses get into bad repair..."
(1899: 60).

The area north of Shishmaref for a distance of about
25 miles was exploited intensively. Several places were
used permanently as ugruk camps: (a) Akunik; (b) Siluk
(a small year-round place, very old); (c) Akoliksat; and
(d) Enagruk. North of this is an inlet known locally as
James Moses Bay, used for caribou hunting from kayaks in
the nineteenth century.[13] Wild fowl were abundant.

66. Kividluk and Singyak. These were two year-round
villages. Kividluk (sometimes spelled Kevedlok on maps)
had seven houses in 1892, and possibly a kazgi (Jackson
1895: 97). Singyak had only one or two houses within
memory, but has ancient house depressions. Those living
in Kividluk went to Likliknuktuk, #69, for fishing and
sealing.

Between Kividluk and Cape Espenberg a number of camps
were regularly established for spring seal hunting. Sometimes the residents went to the lakes back of the coast
for fishing. Trapping was done there in the twentieth
century.

Lopp, in February 1898, traveled past a village,
"Sedlemeet" (going north) the day before he arrived at
Cape Espenberg. This might have been near Singyak because
he called Kividluk, "Kivuklouk" (manuscript log of 1898
reindeer drive). It may have been at the mouth of the
Kitluk River.

Southern Coast of Kotzebue Sound

The area from Cape Espenberg to the Buckland River in
the northern part of Seward Peninsula was occupied mainly
by persons speaking the so-called Malemiut dialect in the
nineteenth century. The direction of communication for
these local groups was toward the northern shores of
Kotzebue Sound rather than southward, although in later
years some Malemiut speakers began to drift along the
coast toward Wales as well as inland toward Unalakleet.
E. S. Curtis (1930: 168) recounting a folk tale about the
messenger feast said, "The people of one of the large
Kotzebue [Sd.] villages [Cape Espenberg?] always spent the
summer fishing, and in hunting whale, seal, and caribou along
the coast near Shishmareff, extending their operations nearly
to Cape Prince of Wales." The tribal affiliation of the
"Kotzebue village" is not identified. Present-day persons
insist that the entire coast from the strait to beyond
Espenberg had been inhabited in early days by Central Bering
Strait Eskimos, and only recently by Malemiut speakers at
the northern extremity.

Food resources

Whale and walrus were not present in Kotzebue Sound, but
seal and beluga were important. Caribou hunting was widespread in the early days. Fowl and eggs were found in
abundance on Chamisso Island, Puffin Rock, and in other
cliffy areas, as well as the tundra. Salmon and tomcod
fishing was often conducted year round at a village considered to be the "permanent" village. Vegetable products
and berries were not as common as farther south, but nothing
edible was left uneaten. On Chamisso Island grew an
especially succulent variety of wild celery.

The yearly round of activities was the same pattern
as described for Buckland #76.

Population

Population figures for this area during the eighteenth
and nineteenth century are scarce. Those that do exist
indicate a small population during that time, probably about
200. The area between Cape Espenberg and Deering
fluctuated greatly during caribou and sealing seasons.
Deering people sometimes went all the way to Tapkak at Cape
Espenberg for sealing. The center of population appeared
to be on the Buckland River during these two centuries,
despite the wealth of archaeological material found at
Deering.

The 1880 census indicated only three villages from Cape
Espenberg to Buckland: Ta-apkuk [Tukutat: Cape Espenberg]
had a population of 42, Kugalukmute [Candle] had 12, and
Kongigamute [Buckland River] had 90 (Petroff 1884: 11).
The 1890 census recorded only 51 persons at Cape Espenberg
(Porter 1893: 8).

Archaeology

At Deering is a site related to the Point Hope Ipiutak
and excavated by H. Larsen (1951). Also, on Trail Creek,
a tributary of Cottonwood Creek, which in turn empties into
the Goodhope River, is a series of caves in which Larsen
found arrow points used in caribou hunting (1950; 1951).

Settlements

67. Tukutat. This village was located at the mouth
of Espenberg River (Inuiknik, "no more people"). Kotzebue
did not visit this village, but was told about it. At
Cape Deceit he met a group of Eskimos, the chief of whom
took a pencil "and really drew the cape at the southern
entrance of the sound, which he represented as a bending
point of land. Upon this he drew a number of habitations,
which he called Kegi [probably Kotzebue's rendering of
kikiktuk, "island"] whither he, in a friendly manner,
invited us" (1821 volume I: 235).

Beechey in September, 1826 anchored near the tip of
the cape where he said he saw many poles stuck into the
ground, several huts and burials, but no people (1831
volume I: 328).

Tukutat was reported as "Ta-apkuk" in the 1880 census.
Tapkak referred, however, to the summer camp south of
Tukutat. The census reported a population of 42 in 1880
(Petroff 1884: 4), and 51 in 1890. Of the 51, 23 were
"native" to the village, and 28 were "foreign" (R. Porter
1893: 3). In January, 1897, when Lieutenant Jarvis passed
through "Toatut" he reported two houses with a population
of 22 (1899: 61). Captain C. L. Hooper's observation of
20 houses in 1881 is inconsistent with the small population
and may have been a misprint. Many of the houses may have
been uninhabited if his report is correct (1884: 38).

68. Tapkak. This seasonal camp, located south of
the cape, has also been reported as "Paapkak."

69. Seasonal sites. There were no settlements considered to be home, or permanent, villages between Cape
Espenberg and the mouth of the Goodhope River. The most
used fishing and sealing sites were: (a) the mouth of
Agaklik River, south of Tapkak; (b) Nugnugaluktuk, at the
mouth of the stream draining one of the lakes called
Kealik; (c) a site on Kougachuk Creek; (d) Ungmalaukpuk
on the north side of the broad bay at the mouth of the
Nugnugaluktuk River; (e) Tugmagluk on a southern point of
the bay; (f) Likliknuktuk to the west of Tugmagluk, on
another point. This was thought to have been a winter
village, also. The lakes to the west of these abounded in
fowl, particularly eider ducks. Old depressions are located
at both (e) and (f).

During Kotzebue's stay on Kotzebue Sound he visited the camp of a single family on the north shore of Nugnugaluktuk River, probably near Ungmalaukpuk. When Kotzebue's sailors returned to get him, the family became frightened, and packed up and paddled to the south cape (1821 volume I: 226). Soon afterward Kotzebue saw eight sailing umiaks setting out from Cape Deceit. When they drew near he saw that each umiak contained 12 men (ibid.: 232).

70. Pitak or Pitakmiut. This village is located at the mouth of the Goodhope River. Hobson traveled to Kotzebue Sound from Port Clarence via the Kuzitrin and Pittock Rivers (see also #48). Although Hobson mentioned a village (deserted because of three deaths) near the ocean, it is not possible to locate it from his description. It probably was Pitak. By his own estimate he was about 36 miles west of Cape Deceit. Pitak inhabitants spoke "part Deering and part Pitak," a Bering Strait dialect, at the end of the nineteenth century.

71. Villages on the upper Goodhope River and surrounding area: The watershed of this river was the caribou grounds of a group of persons whose home village was Pitak. Perhaps they were Kauwerak speakers in the eighteenth and nineteenth centuries. In 1854 after Hobson had left Soiyuk (#48) and had struck a tributary of the Goodhope, he came to a settlement that he called Kip-lik-tok. It had four huts and a large supply of caribou meat. The village cannot be located from Hobson's description, but present-day Eskimos think it was Pitakpuk, on the upper Goodhope. A number of large house depressions, including a kazgi, are located on flat ground near the river. Another area, possibly a settlement, upstream from Pitakpuk at the confluence of Placer Creek with the Goodhope was called Mitliktogvik ("place where people meet").

On the west shore of Imuruk Lake was a settlement called Mitlakmiut, located on top of a hill near a spring. Piles of old caribou horns are still to be seen in this vicinity. Southeast of Imuruk Lake are many small lakes with "millions and millions of grayling." Collectively, the lakes are called Silukpuktut. They are near extensive lava beds.

72. Uyauks, Siknaugrurak, and Toalavik. A small village, Uyauks, was located at the mouth of Clifford Creek, and another, Siknaugruruk, at the mouth of Rex Creek. Toalavik was situated at the mouth of Sullivan Creek. Beluga hunting was good in the shallow water between Toalavik and Elephant Point. When Hosbon traveled this stretch of coast in February and March, he did not see anybody between the mouth of the Goodhope River and Cape Deceit.

73. Kipalut. This small village was located at Cape Deceit near the present village of Deering. Hobson

mentioned a village, Kip-pel-lik here. In February, 1854, the village had two good huts (one inhabited) and two in poor condition. The present village of Deering is located at the mouth of the Inmachuk River, but an ancient village called Ipmachiukmiut has been excavated behind Deering. Most of the old village inhabitants died in the 1900 measles and pneumonia epidemic (Andrews notebooks).

In 1914 a committee of Deering residents, under the guidance of the Bureau of Education and the Quaker missionary, chose a site on the Kobuk River where they built a new town called Noorvik ("transplanted"). A reservation 15 miles square was granted for this still-thriving village (U.S. Bur. Ed. Bull.1916 #47: 50). The decision to move was, in part, suggested by the depletion of the salmon fishery due to mining operations, although natural resources of the area after the caribou disappeared had been less productive than the rest of the peninsula. Deering did not die as a village, however, and is still inhabited.

74. Kugruk. An old settlement was located on the right bank of Kugruk Lagoon. At Willow Bay close by is a favorite fishing camp. These two camps possibly are the two mentioned by Beechey in September, 1826: "at the mouth of two rivers in the first and second bays to the eastward of Cape Deceit there were several spars and logs of driftwood placed erect, which showed that the natives had occupied these stations in the summer for the purpose of catching fish, but they were now all deserted" (1831 volume I: 325).

75. Kiwalik (Kuwaluk) River. The concentration of population was small in Spafarief Bay until mining brought Candle into existence in 1900. Beechey saw only one party of Eskimos, whose dogs were pulling an umiak along the beach. The 1880 census indicated that "Kugaluk" (Kuwaluk), eight miles upstream from the outer bay had a population of 12 (Petroff 1884: 4). This probably was the village of Muzitoak ("place of the Eskimo potato"), at the mouth of Candle Creek, considered to belong to one family. From information received at Saint Michael in 1842, Zagoskin said that "Kualiugmiut" at the mouth of Spafarief (Kiwalik) River was "large" (1847: 109). In 1881 when crew members of the Corwin went up the Kiwalik River, they saw at the mouth a deserted hut (Muir 1917: 122), probably the fishing site called Kikiktuak, near the recent town of Kiwalik.

In early days the inhabitants of this area lived on seal, rabbits, ptarmigan, fish, edible roots, greens, berries, but especially, caribou. Caribou were hunted in areas restricted to the tributaries of the Kiwalik River. There is evidence that creeks belonged to certain families, and that specific areas of tundra were considered as belonging to one family for their hunting and fishing. The caribou corral of Unalikchauk (location unspecified) at the head of the Kiwalik was said to belong to one family.

76. Kangik (Buckland River). The Buckland River
people spoke a dialect of Inupiak that was popularly called
Malemiut. In the nineteenth century they combined caribou
hunting with sea mammal hunting and fishing. In the early
nineteenth century, their large inland village of Attenmiut
called Aiashadakkoshkonno by the Athabascan Indians
(Zagoskin 1847: Map) was undoubtedly their largest winter
settlement for caribou hunting. Their largest downstream
village was Makkukruk, or Kangik. One of my informants
said that Makkukruk usually had 10 or 15 families living
in it, but when Jacobsen visited "Makakkerak" in 1882,
he said that it had only one dwelling. Henry D. Woolfe,
who also traveled to Buckland at about the same time,
reported the village of "Mahkachrak" to have one house
(1894: 181). A village with semi-subterranean houses existed
formerly near the site of old Buckland as well as at Igloo
Point (Lucier 1954: 215). Buckland village has moved
several times because of erosion problems.

The principal lower river village near old Buckland
village apparently was primarily a summer village, which
probably enabled the 1880 census (taken in the summer) to
report "Kongigamute" to have a population of 90. Although
Beechey had ascended the Buckland River for some distance
in September, 1826, the first record of a village on the
Buckland was made by officers of the Herald, searching for
Sir John Franklin.[14] In 1849, Captain Kellett reported
that his men (having spent the first night at Elephant
Point), stayed the second (September 10) at a large village
of 22 tents and 150 people (1850: 21). Reporting the same
event, the author of Euryalus[15] said that this village,
called "Neitawigmeot," had 11 tents and 60 natives on the
evening of their arrival. However, within "minutes,"
there were 17 tents. By the next morning there were 22
tents and 120 people, 30 less than reported by Kellett
(1850: 250). All were on their way up the Buckland,
called "Salmon River" by the author.

Beechey saw only tents on Elephant Point (Singyak,
apparently an ancient site, and nineteenth century campsite) in September 1826 (1831 volume I: 322). In 1489 the
author of Euryalus said that on Elephant Point were
several "erangs" [tents?], and "about 20 natives on the
spot where remains of deer and porpoises had been met with"
(1860: 256).

In 1880 Captain C. L. Hooper said that no one lived
permanently on Eschscholtz Bay (1881: 24). E. W. Nelson
said that Elephant Point apparently had been a village
site before he visited it in 1881 (1899: 264), although
Kotzebue, in 1816, said this about it: "There were two
small huts, near our landing-place, which were raised
several feet, supported by four pillars, and covered with
morse-skin [walrus skin]. These huts did not seem
constructed so much for continual residence, as for magazines for their instruments, and hunting utensils" (1821
volume I: 218).

When Jacobsen left "Makakkerak" in 1882, he came to the village of "Inuktok" (Inyuktuk, "people killed") on Igloo Point, which also had only one dwelling (Jacobsen 1884: 303). Inyuktuk refers to a deadly fight with Selawik people. Only a mother and her baby were saved.

Charles Lucier, who spent the winter and spring of 1951 at Elephant Point, briefly summarized the subsistence pattern of the Buckland River Eskimos but did not name or locate any settlements: "About nine months of each year, September through early June, are spent up river fishing and hunting. The most permanent Buckland village is situated outside the down river or northern margin of spruce timber. Here, in the fall and early winter, the inhabitants formerly lived in semi-subterranean moss-covered houses...Later, usually in January, the Kangyikmiut moved up river to their camp at the caribou corral. From here, hunting parties ranged widely over the interior of Seward Peninsula in search of caribou, small game and fish. Shelter on hunting trips was provided by the 'itchalik,' a hemispherical skin tent supported by a framework of arched willows....When spring neared, the Kangyikmiut moved gradually down river, stopping at fishing and hunting camps on the way. By June, they reached Eschscholtz Bay, the easternmost extension of Kotzebue Sound. In early summer they fished and hunted sea mammals, especially the white whale (beluga)....by late August they were ready to go up the Buckland River in skin boats to their fall fishing sites" (1954: 215).

Although caribou hunting meant moving over a large territory, it did not mean ranging unrestrictedly over "the interior of Seward Peninsula." As brought out previously in the discussion of all other groups, including the caribou hunters of the Nome area, Kauwerak, Shishmaref, and Candle, the territory occupied by any one group was restricted to their main river and its tributaries. The Kangyikimiut were no different from any other Seward Penin-sula group in that respect. They had their restricted tribal area, and remained within it. Only when they branched out with trade goods in the early nineteenth century did they trespass on other tribal territory. It was a special kind of trespass that enabled them to settle down in Unalit territory after certain other requirements of social relationships had been complied with.

77. Upper Buckland River villages: The use of permanent dwellings on the Buckland and its tributary streams were apparently in wider use than indicated in the above summary. In 1882 Captain Jacobsen, en route to Kotzebue Sound from Koyuk via the Koyuk and Buckland rivers, came to the village of "Kajak" on the "Unalitschok" River (West Fork of the Buckland). The village had three permanent dwellings, two of which were inhabited (1884: 302. Woolfe reported "Kyack" to have two houses--1894: 181). Other villages besides Kayuk were located on "tributaries of Buckland, Unalechock and Iethe'took...Kaiyowrook

(1 house) [Kilulik?] and Toopkich (3 houses)" (ibid. Unlocated). A settlement known as Kuluvachak was located near the mouth of the North Fork of the Buckland, and Kaluguachik [location unspecified], a caribou camp on Buckland headwaters. A family moving from Makkukruk to Kaluguachik had to camp three times en route. When Lieutenant Bertholf followed the Koyuk and Buckland river route to Kotzebue Sound from Norton Sound he passed several clusters of abandoned houses (see #1a).

Conclusions

Settlement and subsistence patterns crosscut linguistic and tribal affiliations. The linguistic divisions of this area were comparable to what could be called tribal divisions, and the villages sharing a dialect constituted a loose but definitely recognizable polity. Village and tribe were synonymous in some parts of the Eskimo world, but not on Seward Peninsula.

In the late eighteenth century and early nineteenth century, the northern Inupiak dialects extended eastward on Seward Peninsula to Golovnin Bay and possibly only to Cape Nome to meet the Unalit speakers (Yupik language). This general dialect, Unalit, extended as far south as Saint Michael. At this same time the Inupiak speakers inhabited the northward flowing rivers into Kotzebue Sound at the inner eastern part of Seward Peninsula, and the Unalit speakers occupied the southward flowing rivers (Inglutalik, Tubuktulik, Koyuk, etc.) into Norton Sound.

Although there were only four general linguistic groupings in the area, the following subdialects were (and are) differentiated: Koyuk (Unalit in the eighteenth century; Malemiut and Unalit in nineteenth century); Golovin (Unalit and possibly Kauwerak in the eighteenth century; Unalit and Kauwerak in the nineteenth century); Solomon and Nome ("Chiningmiut," a Kauwerak dialect); Port Clarence and Grantley Harbor ("Sinramiut" similar to standard Kauwerak); Kauwerak village and all Kuzitrin tributaries (Kauwerak); King Island (a Kauwerak dialect; Cape Douglas similar to King Island); Wales (Kingikmiut or Wales dialect); Little Diomede (similar to Wales dialect); Shishmaref ("Kikiktamiut," a Kauwerak dialect; it was also called "Tapkakmiut," which, furthermore, was spoken all the way from Shishmaref to Cape Espenberg); southern shore of Kotzebue Sound (probably Kauwerak speech in the western part during the eighteenth century. "Malemiut" prevailed during the latter part of the nineteenth century. This was further subdivided into the dialects of Kiwalik (Kuwaluk), Deering, and Buckland. On the Goodhope River a mixture of "Deering" and Tapkakmiut was spoken.

With the exception of Malemiut (Inupiak) and Unalit (Yupik) the dialects of the Bering Strait were mutually intelligible, and can be called collectively Central Bering Strait. Subdialects are differentiated only by non-phonological characteristics, occasional variant allophones, and occasional word substitutions. Malemiut had several permanent sound shifts, and many differences in meanings, but was usually understood by Central Bering Strait speakers. From an informal survey of all my informants, the consensus was that the Malemiut language would be easiest for an English-speaking person to learn, Unalit, the hardest.

Unalit, the northernmost Yupik dialect, was also spoken by many Central Bering Strait persons living on its northern border, but the language presented difficulties to the majority of Inupiak speakers. Many linguistically perceptive southern Inupiak speakers, however, were able to speak Unalit after a short exposure to it. This was not true of other Yupik dialects such as Nunivak Island, which was not only unintelligible to Inupiak speakers, but difficult for northern Unalit speakers as well.

From an analysis of the settlement patterns, subsistence patterns, and linguistic groupings, it appears that the various groups inhabiting and laying claim to their land at the end of the nineteenth century, had lived in that area at least since the beginning of the eighteenth century. The exception was the southward transfer of a number of Inupiat, popularly called Malemiut, during the nineteenth century. (Zagoskin said that the Unalit word "Malemiut" meant dwellers of skin tents" (1847: 107). Only one Malemiut speaker could give me an Inupiak meaning for it: "to the leeward.")

Relationships with contiguous groups and those with whom the messenger feast was celebrated were usually good, but boundaries were solidly respected. Cooperation between groups was reinforced by the messenger feast celebration in which both kinship and political interaction was at its optimum. Especially was this true between King Island, Kauwerak, Sinramiut, and Fish River, and between Wales, Sinramiut, and Kauwerak.

Between more distant groups (or those not involved in the messenger feast exchange) interaction was reduced, and often dangerous. No person would enter another Eskimo group's territory without having relatives there to identify him, or without a guide to take him there. Friction arose most often in Bering Strait between (1) Siberians and American Eskimos, (2) Eskimos and Indians, and (3) Contiguous groups of interior Seward Peninsula over caribou territory trespass. Boundaries were so rigidly and jealously guarded, particularly in the interior of the peninsula, that an Igloo man (from information given him by his grandfather) was able to mark with precision the boundaries of all Seward Peninsula groups. "To cross them," he said, "at certain places, and without certain reasons, invited death." The boundaries followed mountain peaks and water-sheds of large rivers as well as certain arbitrary points established through traditional use.

A group wishing to use another's land for fishing or hunting had to obtain permission from that group, and permission was usually granted. However, it was rarely asked unless there was certainty of being granted. Nineteenth century observations that Eskimos could hunt and fish and travel anywhere they wished was based on incomplete evidence. The assumptions that Eskimos were free to go wherever they wished for subsistence purposes were grossly erroneous.

However, from the historical facts of the Siberian-Alaskan fur trade at the beginning of the nineteenth century, and the comparative ease with which a few Inupiat began moving southward into Unalit territory, it appears that special conditions provided for unusual intertribal flexibilities. The act of trading apparently included special privileges and immunities. However, this probably did not exclude the importance of even minimal kinship ties as a base for these prerogatives. When a few Inupiat from the Kotzebue Sound area began moving southward, some taking the Buckland River route, and others the Kobuk route to the Yukon and thence to Unalit territory via various portages, they were traveling to enemy territory, so to speak, but within a newly acquired role as tobacco and fur middleman between the native Siberian tobacco traders.

The Siberian-Alaskan fur trade began after the establishment of the Anyui Trade Fair (on the Kolyma River) by the Russians in 1789 solely for the purpose of trading tobacco to the Chukchi for Alaskan furs (Wrangell 1840: 114-119). It is possible that the movements of Eskimos became greater than ever before after Russian tobacco became of prime international importance (though probably not until 1790), because rarely had an item of trade been so fervently desired or sought (See Ray 1975b: 97-102 for a brief discussion of tobacco introduction into Alaska).

Eskimos from Kotzebue Sound, Port Clarence, Kauwerak, and King, Diomede, and Sledge islands were the Alaskan middlemen, but the Kotzebue Sound and the Kauwerak traders were the original fur traders to the upper Yukon after the demand for furs became of commercial importance. Only a few traders made the perilous journey to the upper Yukon via the Buckland River, but by the 1840's Zagoskin was able to discuss their common comings and goings. Zagoskin's "Malemiut" included, however, all of the Bering Strait people, including the Sledge and King islanders, who, after the establishment of Saint Michael in 1833, made frequent trips to the post.

The early Malemiut traders did not remain permanently in Unalit territory until long after Saint Michael, the farthest north trading post at that time, was established, and more than 50 years after the inauguration of the tobacco-fur trade. Only after the Malemiut were convinced that they could trade as profitably with the Russians of

America as with the Russians of Siberia did they remain permanently in Unalit territory. As Saint Michael grew as a trading post, the Bering Strait middlemen switched their allegiance to the Russian traders in Alaska. As late as the 1860's, however, some (like Isaac, or Kaleak, of Ukvignaguk--#3), were still loyal to their Siberian contacts at Kotzebue Sound, considering both Kotzebue Sound and Saint Michael as home, but some (like the aging Alluiyanuk) had settled down permanently in the Unalakleet area. Alluiyanuk, from somewhere on the Kobuk River, had been the only member of his family to go south where he married a Koyuk girl, later moving to Saint Michael. He had five sons and a daughter, all of whom remained in the Unalakleet area. One of his great-granddaughters told me that he was the <u>first</u> Malemiut to go to Saint Michael (Dall in 1867 speaks of old "Alluianok" several times in <u>Alaska and Its Resources</u>.) In the 1880's when Isaac was getting old, he also decided to settle down in Unalit territory, establishing the "village" of Ukvignaguk on the north shore of Norton Sound where no prior settlement had existed.

Alluiyanuk's descendants today comprise a substantial proportion of the southern Malemiut population, having intermarried meanwhile with Kauwerak and Unalit speakers of that area. (It is of interest that in the Unalakleet area where the Unalit and Malemiut languages once were most common, the Kauwerak language is now preferred. The Unalit language is disappearing and the Kauwerak language is superseding all.) Several other traders, likewise, remained permanently in Unalit territory. In the 1890's a few more families came south to join their relatives.

The findings in this paper relate to a specific period in the history of the Bering Strait Eskimo, but are significant for areas far beyond the boundaries of this study. Population adjustments in contiguous areas were governed by the same factors operating in terms of local conditions. The changes that took place in the nineteenth century were a result not only of internal modifications (such as loss of caribou), but because of Euro-Asian influences. That the most severe causes of change--the disappearance of the caribou and the readjustments of an ethnic group due to trading activity--did not cause internal disruption is because of the dynamic aspects of Bering Strait culture: the great value put on initiative, the ability for adaptation, the constant emphasis on intratribal tranquillity and interpersonal relations, the presence of a number of prevailing alternatives in the subsistence quest, and the flexibility of the settlement pattern with the subsistence pattern. The diverse use of their territory and its products, and the intertribal safety measures through such mechanisms as kinship and social and trading exchanges as found in the messenger feast enabled them to accept change without moving out of their traditional territory or boundaries. At the particular time under consideration, the unusual change of territory by the Malemiut was caused by events outside the Eskimo's own, traditional culture.

Notes

1. The word "village" in this paper is used inter-changeably with settlement, modified as indicated in the various sections.

2. There are four sectional maps on which most of the settlements described herein are located.

3. After this paper was published I read the report of a visit to "Kigigmen" (Wales) by Ivan Kobelev, who was attached to the expedition of Joseph Billings in 1791. In this report he said that he arrived there on 11 June 1791, but found the village deserted, surmising they had left because of famine. He also said that he had learned that Siberians had attacked the village and taken women and children prisoners, and so they may also have left because of fear. He said that 20 skin boats and approximately 150 men had gathered for a "campaign" to a northern area called "Tapkhan" (tapkak, the name for the coast between Wales and Cape Espenberg) (Chernenko 1957, pp. 131-32).

4. The informants were: Mrs. Rita Ahmasuk, Mr. and Mrs. Sam (Viola) Ailak, Mr. Bert Bell, Mrs. Emma Black, Mr. and Mrs. Mischa (Louisa) Charles, Mrs. Thelma Christoffersen, Mrs. Nellie David, Mrs. Beatrice Davis, Miss Mollie Dexter, Mrs. Minnie Fagerstrom, Mrs. Topsy Horen, Mrs. June Jackson, Mrs. Margaret Johnson, Mrs. Jessie Jorgenson, Mr. David Kakaruk, Mr. and Mrs. John E. (Ruth) Kakaruk, Mr. John A. Kakaruk, Mr. Peter Kakaruk, Mr. Dan Karmun, Mr. Mike Kazingnuk, Mr. Robert Mayokok, Mr. and Mrs. James (Bessie) Moses, Mr. Taylor Moto, Mrs. Rose Omelak, Mr. William Oquilluk, Mr. and Mrs. Simon (Edith) Sagoonik, Mr. and Mrs. John (Lily) Savok, Mrs. Florence Taft, and Mrs. Emma Willoya.
Informants in Unalakleet and St. Michael, not included in the 35 who contributed geographical information, but who furnished additional valuable information about Malemiut-Kauwerak-Unalit relationships were Mrs. Nannie Anowrak, Mrs. Thora Katchetag, Mrs. Marian Gonangan, Mr. Alec Miyomic, Mrs. Martha Nanouk, and Mr. and Mrs. Harry (Carrie) Soxie.
Mrs. Ruth Ost Towner gave me unlimited help during the gathering of material.

5. Zagoskin's settlements of northern Norton Sound are often erroneous because he obtained all of his information from visitors at Saint Michael. He also did not have a good map on which to locate them.

6. Khromchenko 1824, pt. 11, p. 247.

7. Chiningmiut, or singingmiut, was an old term that differentiated certain coastal peoples from others living inland.

8. Ivan Kobelev's visit to the American mainland in 1791 also resulted in the first census of King Island. He said that there were about 70 males and adolescents and 100 females and young children. Ten persons from Kauwerak were visiting the island at that time, but he did not say whether they were included in the population figures (Chernenko 1957: 134).

9. Subsequent to the publication of this paper, John R. Bockstoce undertook extensive investigations in the vicinity of Cape Nome (see Bockstoce 1973).

10. This plan was never carried out. Instead, most of the King Islanders moved into brand-new homes built for them in Nome, and by 1967, the island was completely abandoned except for periodic hunting.

11. For further information about the origin of Kauwerak see "The Kheuveren Legend" (Ray, n.d.).

12. In 1791 Kobelev again visited the Diomede islands. He reported the population of Big Diomede to be 103 males and adolescents, and approximately 115 females and young children. On Little Diomede he counted 45 males and adolescents and 55 females and young children (Chernenko 1957: 131).

13. James Moses became very well known as Kivetoruk Moses, the artist, in the 1960's and 1970's.

14. Prior to the publication of this paper I had not read the accounts of the voyage of the Blagonamerennyi, which was one of two ships that explored the north Alaskan waters during 1820 and 1821 under the direction of Mikhail N. Vasiliev and Gleb S. Shishmarev. The two accounts are by Karl K. Hillsen and Aleksei P. Lazarev, both officers on the Blagonamerennyi, who recorded the first notice of a large encampment of people at Elephant Point in 1820. When asked where they lived, the people pointed to the Buckland River. The population of the camp was reported to be 200 by Hillsen, but 300 by Lazarev (See "Early Maritime Trade with the Eskimo of Bering Strait and the Introduction of Firearms" for more information).

15. In an article about the Franklin search ship, Herald, the following note is made about the authorship of the book, Euryalus: "Euryalus, published anonymously in 1860, has in a later edition been attributed to William Chimmo, another midshipman in H.M.S. Herald, whose drawings illustrate the book. Miss Burns [the author of the article], now in England where she is continuing... research in naval history pertaining to the Pacific coast, concludes that the book may be a compilation of two journals, Chimmo's dry record enlivened by the breezy diary of Pim which was known to his companions" (Burns 1963: 13).

XIII

ESKIMO PLACE-NAMES

IN BERING STRAIT AND VICINITY* (1)

In Bering Strait, Alaska, naming of places in the
Eskimo language stopped almost entirely at the end of
the nineteenth century, although Eskimos continued to
occupy the land of their ancestors. The Bering Strait
Eskimos lived mainly along 1,044 miles of coastline
(including offshore islands) between the mouth of the
Buckland River and the village of St. Michael, with two
tribes living inland away from the sea.[2] The territory
of each tribe, except that of islands and several coastal
areas, included tributaries and watersheds of one or
more large rivers, one or more permanent villages, and
many seasonal camps. Almost every feature had a name.

The use of general or modified appellatives like
"river," "big river," "mountain," "island," or "little
island" for principal topographic features along all of
the western Alaskan coast has produced a duplication of
names, which suggests that Eskimo nomenclature was very
simple and elementary. On the contrary, this was only part
of an extensive toponymic system (there was also an
abundance of descriptive and specific names) and had considerable cultural significance, for the duplication of
names indicated the existence of individual tribal
identities along an extensive coastline once thought to be
occupied by only one huge "tribe." In other words, the
repetition of names was not an indiscriminate, unimagina-
tive naming by a single group, but was the consequence of
numerous tribes having organized constellations of place-
names within separate boundaries, each with its own
"mountain," its own "bay," and particularly, its own
"river."

Place-names and personal names of Bering Strait
Eskimos represented spatial and temporal continuities
that functioned in different, though not mutually exclusive,
spheres of Eskimo life. Personal names with their name-
souls were related to the supernatural, but place-names,
which had no souls, belonged to the natural world. A
personal name assured its user of a secure place in
society (the personal naming practices linked past and
future generations through re-use of specific names) and

---

* Names, Vol. 19, No. 1, 1971, pp. 1-33.

often, protection from harm. [3] Place-names systematized
territorial features within a tribe, and provided the
Eskimo with continuity to the land from time immemorial.

In the old Eskimo religion, every human being had
several souls, two of the best defined being a life-soul
and a name-soul. After death the life-soul disappeared
forever, but the name-soul wandered about until it was
again bestowed upon a friend's or a relative's new-born
baby, quite often a grandchild. Personal names always
left the body of their own volition, but were restored
to another human abode through human intervention. Place-
names were immobile, and remained at their designations
until forgotten.

Whereas human beings and some animals possessed
souls, inanimate objects had spirits. However, a place-
name that was the same as an object did not contain a
spirit, because the object's spirit was a generic one that
infused a category of objects, and was not an individual
spirit. So far as Eskimos know today, these spirits had
no connection with the name of a place. A toponym that
referred to animals or birds important in religion or
mythology had no magical connotations. The fickle line
between reality and folklore wavered indiscriminately
between fact and fiction. Though a place might be named for
a legendary creature, the name was only a statement of
geographical identification within a specific tribal area;
yet most narrators of folk tales used specific village
names to place their stories in as real a context as
their everyday world.

Places were not named after human beings, inasmuch
as association of a personal name with a place-name was
conceptually improper, but a person and a place might
coincidentally have the same name. A huge common pool of
names was available for both personal and place-names, and
considerable overlapping occurred. Most personal names
were taken from nature or noteworthy events, and a baby
born in an isolated place sometimes received a name from
his birthplace if there were no names of recently-deceased
persons available. The specific place-name then entered
the realm of personal names and was not used again as a
toponym. However, there was no prohibition against using
a similar name for a place if it was taken from another
source, but this was rare, for once a place-name was known
to have been appropriated for a human being, it was
thought unwise to utilize it in a toponymic context because
of the name-soul. An Eskimo could have as many as a dozen
names, but others knew him by only one at a time, usually
his first. A place also had only one name, although various
parts of a large village or an island could have additional
identifying names.

Place-names, including individual campsites, were
considered to be as permanent as the land to which they
were attached, and, as far as we know, the majority of

Eskimo place-names that I have recorded were in use at the time of first European contact in the 1700s.[4] Informants could recall only a few names that had been applied to places during their lifetime, and documentary evidence supports their statements that most Eskimo place-names were "prehistoric."

During the eighteenth century, Russians in Siberia obtained a few Alaskan names from the Chukchi tribes of northeast Siberia and from Diomede islanders living in the Bering Strait between Siberia and Alaska. Shortly after the Russians arrived in eastern Siberia in 1648 they eagerly set about learning more about a big land said to lie east of Siberia, but the defiant Chukchi kept them more than 500 miles away from the Strait for many years. In 1711 Ivan Lvov, a cossack from Yakutsk, recorded the first Alaskan name of any kind when he traveled to the Chukchi Peninsula for information about geography and trade. Lvov placed a sausage-shaped island on his map in the position of Alaska on which he inscribed, "The land is big, and people live there who in Chuktosky language are called Kigin Eliat." This Kigin Eliat, which the Chukchi had presumably learned through the island people, is probably none other than kingigan, the Eskimo name for Wales.[5]

In 1765 Nikolai Daurkin, a Chukchi who had been reared as a cossack in Yakutsk, placed several more Alaskan native place-names on an annotated map. This map and another made by Ivan Kobelev in 1779 are two of the most exceptional maps to be made for any part of Alaska, though both were drawn without first-hand observation of places recorded. Daurkin's map[6] is considerably distorted, but he mentioned four Alaskan names, three for the first time: he called kingigan Kigmil, and recorded Tikegan (tikera, "finger," present-day Point Hope), Okibyan (ukivuk or uivuk, King Island), and Kheuveren (kauwerak, a famous old village on the Kuzitrin River).

When I began my research, Kobelev's map was the only extensive compilation of Bering Strait native place-names in existence. Other explorers recorded a few names here and there, but none approached Kobelev's feat of locating 69 Seward Peninsula settlements (61 with names) on a map made by Eskimos during a visit to Little Diomede Island.[7] In contrast, Captain James Cook, the first European to chart the west coast of Alaska and to step ashore on the Alaskan mainland north of the Aleutian Islands a year before Kobelev's visit, recorded only one Eskimo place-name, Chaktoole Bay (near the present village of Shaktoolik) on the entire western Alaskan coast.

Kobelev's settlements conform to their actual geographical locations to a remarkable degree, and more than half of the names correspond to those known today. This is an exceptionally high percentage in view of the impediments these names encountered en route toward

identification. The words were originally recorded in
Cyrillic from Eskimos who did not speak the dialects represented in the village names (Kobelev spoke Chukchi and
may have used interpreters). The names were then transcribed (we hope from legible writing) into German
orthography, many words retaining Chukchi suffixes -an or
-un, which Kobelev recorded or substituted for Eskimo -ak
or -uk. Eskimo has also changed as does any language, and
students of their own tongue say that words used only a
generation ago are sometimes difficult to understand.
Informant recall varies from area to area and I have a few
areal gaps. For example, of Kobelev's seven settlements
on the Goodhope River I am familiar with only one.

The villages on Kobelev's map that can be identified
from my records are, north to south:

Tuguten: possibly tukutat near Cape Espenberg,
    although not in the right place.
Kygichtan: kikiktaruk, present-day Kotzebue.
Leglelachtoch: likliknuktuk, a campsite on Goodhope
    Bay.
Pyktepata: pitakpaga, old village at the mouth of
    the pitak, or Goodhope River.
Tschinegrün: singyak, an old village between Cape
    Espenberg and Shishmaref.
Chibamech: kividluk near singyak.
Topak: tapkak, by which name the entire coast from
    Cape Espenberg to the vicinity of Wales was known
    (see discussion of tapkak).
Chikichtei: kikiktuk, the name of Shishmaref and
    Sarichev Island.
Agunich: akunik, an old village near Shishmaref.
Negnegnaroch: nonatak; ipnorak? camps on Shishmaref
    Inlet.
Agulich: agolik, an old village, but is misplaced.
Kigygmin: kingigan or Wales.
Imaglin: imaklik, Big Diomede Island.
Iagilin: ingalik, Little Diomede Island.
Tepchagyrgurt: tapkarak, south of Wales.
Puleragmin: palazrak, south of Wales.
Paitamat: paituk, or Baituk River.
Itschigaëmag: ikpiumizua, a village on Port Clarence.
Nugmat: nukmiut or nuk, Teller.
Ukipen: ukivuk, King Island.
Tschekevui: tuksuk, Tuksuk Channel?
Fl. Cheuweren: kauwerak.
Agibanich: akavingayak, a camp on the southern shore
    of Port Clarence.
Chalamachmit: kalulingmiut or kalulik, Cape Douglas.
Ejech: ayak, Sledge Island.
Tschagnamit: singiyak, Cape Woolley, or possibly
    singak, Sinuk River. Kobelev's spelling is similar
    to that of Lieutenant L. Zagoskin's for "coastal
    people," or Chnagmyut in 1844.[8] See also page 14.
Chailchotschoch: kayalushuak, Cripple River and small
    abandoned village north of Nome.

Tschugnutschumi: sitnasuak, Snake River and small
  village.
Antschirag: ayasayuk, Cape Nome and large village
  below the cape.
Memtachagran: mupturukshuk, a small old village
  south of Cape Nome.
Amutach: angutak or Solomon.
Achrutulach: okpiktulik, Spruce Creek and camp
  east of Solomon.
Tschiwach: chiukak, old village between Spruce Creek
  and Golovin.
Nituch: igⁿituk, a large old village between chiukak
  and Golovin. The current pronunciation may be
  slightly different from the eighteenth and early
  nineteenth centuries since Zagoskin also recorded
  this village as Knykhtakgmyut.[9]
Iglumit: iglu, Corwin's Cove near Golovin.
Tschinik: chinik, Golovin.
Annure: atnuk on Cape Darby (it has also been
  spelled Annuk on later American maps).
Kuinegach: kuinihak, Moses Point; possibly, Koyuk.
Kuimin: possibly Koyuk?

Difference in pronunciation of similar place-names
along the Alaskan coast reflect the numerous dialects of the
two mutually unintelligible Alaskan Eskimo languages,
Inupiak and Yupik, also called the northern and southern
languages. Both mean "real, or genuine, people," derived
from the respective words for "[Eskimo] person," inuk and
yuk. The well-known word Innuit comes from the northern
stem and means "mankind of all races." The geographical
division between the two languages at the time of first
white contact on Seward Peninsula (in 1778) was at Golovnin
Bay, 80 miles east of Nome, where Unaluk, a dialect of
Yupik, was spoken, but the Unipiak boundaries shifted south
during the historical period so that Unalakleet, once an
Unaluk-speaking village, became trilingual with the addition
of Malemiut and Kauwerak speech.[10] People who spoke
these languages had immigrated south sometime during the
early nineteenth century, the Malemiut occasionally
traveling as far south as the Kuskokwim River, but they
settled permanently only around the coast of Norton Sound
in abandoned camps or occupied Unalit villages. However,
with few exceptions, these places kept their original
Unaluk names, apparently through efforts of local inhabitants.
The area around Shaktoolik, which was once an Unalit settlement later known as a "Malemiut village," still retains a
large number of original Unaluk place-names, and Malemiut
informants eagerly pointed out numerous names that were
"real Unaluk words," as noted in the discussion of
individual place-names.

Differences in dialect of contiguous tribes speaking
the same language are usually prosodic with some phono-
logical changes. Between languages, however, there are
syntactical and many lexical differences. A shift of
phonemes like the voiceless alveolar spirant and the voice-

less alveopalatal spirant in Kauwerak and other northern
dialects to the voiceless alveopalatal affricate in Unaluk
consistently marks the difference between the two languages
in the Norton Sound area, as represented in words like
singak, chinik; shaktulik, chaktulik; or soiyuk, chauiyak.

I recorded names and meanings for about 275 places
and an additional hundred names without meanings in the
course of anthropological inquiry into nineteenth-century
political organization, tribal distribution, and settlement
and subsistence patterns during the summers of 1961, 1964,
and 1968.[11] It is now impossible to get an exhaustive
listing of place-names because many names are already beyond
recall, and because the time required for a complete
recording of all meanings and names of hills, mountains,
creeks, rivers, lakes, ponds, bays, localities, villages,
and camps would be prohibitive. Yet a large enough sample
was obtained to draw conclusions that might apply to other
Eskimo areas.

The names were transcribed phonetically from about 50
bilingual (Eskimo and English) speakers who provided
meanings in English. Unlike the Yukon-Kuskokwim Eskimos
whose principal language is still Yupik, most of the
inhabitants of the Bering Strait are bilingual. Exceptions
are some older mainland Eskimos and King and Diomede
islanders who do not speak English, and many young people
who do not speak Eskimo. Because this paper concentrates
on Eskimo knowledge of place-names and meanings and their
place in Eskimo concepts, and not linguistic analysis, I
have used only names and explanations supplied by informants.
Many meanings are obviously not literal translations, but
are what the words meant to each person. Every meaning
applies specifically to one location, and multiple meanings
are those given by more than one informant. I have suggested
a meaning only when it was unknown, and none has been taken
from another printed source except for explanatory notes.
Place-names without meanings have been omitted unless an
informant said that it was "only a name." Although it is
rather easy to guess the meaning for almost any Eskimo place-
name, native speakers are reluctant to offer one if it is
not in a form that makes sense to them. This caution was
apparent everywhere from Kotzebue Sound to St. Michael, in
responses from the 50 major informants as well as other
persons. Most Eskimos cannot provide meanings for printed
Eskimo names if they have been erroneously recorded, are in
non-English orthography, or are in an unfamiliar dialect.
The fairly large percentage of names with obviously known
roots that have "no meanings" indicates semantic caution and
comparatively little interest in etymological relationships.
On the other hand, there is a fierce pride in preserving
their language, even by those with the least interest in its
history.

The names are presented in simplified form that could
be useful for maps. This scheme, however, omits a number of
significant differences in pronunciation; for example, that

between the voiceless velar stop and the voiceless uvular
stop, both indicated here as k̲, and between the high back
vowel and mid-central vowel, both represented by u̲. The u̲
in the suffix -uk̲ is sometimes pronounced as in the English
word, "luck," but the u̲ at the beginning or in the middle of
a word (ungalaklik, nuk̲) is pronounced as in "spook." The
ng used here is usually pronounced as in "sing," not
"linger"; the a (atnuk, atuik, kukak), as in "father"; and
the o (Koyuk, okpiktulik), as in "lone." The Eskimo
Language Workshop (for the Yupik language) at the University
of Alaska has been faced with similar problems of
simplifying orthography for published material. They have
decided on a c to represent the ts, ch, and sh sounds. The c
would not be appropriate here because the latter two consonants,
as we have already seen, often signify a difference in
language, not only dialect. Therefore, I have used the
diagraphs ch and sh to differentiate the two.

Names and meanings are discussed under two general
classifications, topographic features and settlements, sometimes interchangeably because of a primary organization of
etymological relationships, but the names are not always
repeated in an alternate category. If the name of a place
is spelled phonetically in their map names of today, I have
not added my phonetic version.

The Names

Land features

Two terms differentiated Eskimos living on the coast
from those who lived inland away from the sea: tapkakmiut
("people of the sandy shore-line," -miut means people)
and singingmiut ("people of the coast or watershed").
North of the Bering Strait area, inland people were called
nunamiut ("people of the land"), but this name did not
apply to Seward Peninsula tribes living in the interior
on the Kuzitrin and the Fish rivers. The best known
tapkakmiut pertained to people living on the shore of the
Chukchi Sea between the old village of ikpik (north of
Wales) and Cape Espenberg. The word tapkak is also found
in other areas of the Bering Strait in a more narrow sense:
a small area and old village near Solomon was tapkak
("sandy beach") or Topkok on maps, and near Shaktoolik
another tapkak ("hard tundra along the coast") ended at a
campsite known as tapkamisua ("end of the coastal tundra"),
or the Eskimo name for foothills. However, this name
refers to the end of flat ground, not to the beginning of
hills as in English. The Foothills Roadhouse was a popular
stopping place for dogteams carrying mail in the early
part of the twentieth century. This place was first
reported as Tor-qua-me-su-a in 1851 by Thomas Bourchier of
the parties searching for Sir John Franklin in the Bering
Strait area between 1848 and 1854. Taupanika was located
on A. Petermann's map, "Wrangel-land" (1869) and the 1880
census said that Tup-hamikva had a population of ten.[12]

A fourth tapkak ("sandy beach") is the present Eskimo
name of Stebbins, now located on a straight stretch of
coast south of the nineteenth century village site of atuik
("bent point"), situated at the foot of a bluff, Tapkarak
("small tapkak") was a winter village on the coast south
of Wales.

Higher land along the coast was often called ikpik,
a word used mainly in coastal situations. The best known
ikpik was located at the southern end of the tapkak area
near Shishmaref, and spelled Ikpek on maps. This word has
been translated as "bank along the shore," "high ground,"
and "foothills." An area on the Unalakleet River is called
ikpiluk, explained both as "bank" and "a big bank, open,
and one can see far off." Two small villages on the coast
near Teller were ikpiumizua ("end of the tundra", i.e.,
pertaining to the bank) and ikpiglauk ("in the middle [of
ikpik]"). Coffee Point in the St. Michael area is known
as ikpakpuk ("big cliff as it comes down to the lowland").

Related words are ipmachiuk ("bluff"), the name for
Deering at the mouth of the Inmachuk River on the north
coast of Seward Peninsula; ipnuchauk ("little bluff"), an
old village north of Rocky Point in the Golovin area; and
ipnorak ("rocky wall"), a camp on Shishmaref Inlet.

Singingmiut or chiningmiut (depending on the language)
was used to differentiate coastal from inland people between
Cape Rodney and Rocky Point, and along portions of eastern
Norton Sound. This is Zagoskin's "tribal" word, "Chnagmyut,"
which he also explained as "coastal people."(13) This word
refers specifically to coast or edge along the sea, but also
means watershed, as found in the name singloak, a Tuksuk
campsite that was once the site of an old village reported
as Choonowuk by William Frederick Beechey in 1831.(14) The
name is considered to be "somehow a coastal word put on an
inland camp." It is found also in the part of Wales village
called singuarangmiut ("people of the lagoon," situated near
Wales River or singluraruk), once occupied by reindeer
herders. In 1968, George Ootenna, 92 years old and one of
the first herders, was the only inhabitant of singuarangmiut.
There was also a singaurak, situated on Lopp Lagoon.

The word singak or chinik, depending on the language,
is usually applied to low, well-drained ground, and is
the Eskimo name for Brevig Mission, singak or singingmiut
(often spelled Sinramiut, "outlet of the lagoon"), Golovin
(chinik), and an old village, singak, situated at the mouth
of the Sinuk River near Nome. In 1867 The Esquimaux said
that the latter, Singigungmiut, was nearly deserted in
April, the inhabitants having gone to Aiyakh (Sledge Island)
to hunt "mukluks" (i.e., oogruk or bearded seals).(15)
Golovin or chinik ("point" or "spit") is usually spelled
Cheenik on maps, and was first reported as Tschinik by
Kobelev in 1779 and as Chinik by Vasilii S. Khromchenko in
1822.(16) "Small spit" or chinikchauk is the name of South
Spit opposite chinik, a camping and berry-picking area.

"Point" is also the name of Cape Woolley (singiyak), Elephant Point (singyak), Safety, east of Nome (chingyak), and a few camps like chinikpuk ("big point") in the St. Michael area, chingyak at the mouth of the Sineak River[17] near Shaktoolik, and singyak, a year-round village between Shishmaref and Cape Espenberg. A Malemiut man who now uses a Shaktoolik River camp called chinikluak, an Unaluk name, did not know its exact meaning.

Places whose names were derived from singak were usually situated on flat ground near sea level. Comparable high places were sometimes called nuk or nuwak, although low, flat places that were spits of land also bore this name. Two well-known Nooks are at Safety Sound and at Teller, the latter probably the Nugmat of Kobelev's in 1779. The Safety Sound Nook today is a summer camping area of about 30 cabins stretching for several miles along a long, thin spit that separates Safety Sound from Norton Sound, but the original nuk was only a camping site for inhabitants of the old village of ayasayuk at the base of Cape Nome. In this case, nuk meant "the farthest point out [on the spit]," about five miles east of Cape Nome.

Tolstoi Point in the Unalakleet area is nuwak ("point"), and Black Point and Hunting Point in the St. Michael area are nuwak ("nose") and nuk ("spit or headland"), respectively. A village on Cape Denbigh was known as nuklik ("high bluff," "farthest out point of bluff"), and mapped by Zagoskin as Nuklit in 1842-1844, but he placed this settlement much farther north on Cape Denbigh than Nukleet, an archeological site occupied from about the thirteenth to the eighteenth centuries. However, Zagoskin may have been told about an area once pointed out to be as "Nuklik Point" on the east side of the Reindeer Hills near the head of the Sineak River, north of the coastal Nukleet site. The archeologist J. L. Giddings was also aware of the dual use of this name.[18]

The Kauwerak section of Unalakleet on the river bank was called nukaluk ("where is a point"). A winter caribou village on the Kuzitrin River was called "Nook owelek" by Mate William Hobson of the ship Rattlesnake searching for Franklin in 1854,[19] a name derived from nuk. Informants said that the name is now unknown, but the settlement may have been located where the river is cutting out a site called alakasak.

Similar points and headlands were called a variety of names. Wales was called kingigan ("high," "high bluff") because of Cape Mountain; Cape York near Wales and its old village were called kingauguk ("nose point"); Point Dexter on Norton Bay is egrak or ekuk ("end"); Blueberry Point near Unalakleet is called igvayahak ("come to see other side"), and Rock Point near St. Michael is nakinguk ("[point] on low ground"). A point on Stuart Island at Stephens Pass is called chiukak ("in front"). Ptarmigan Point (ingikut) on the north shore of Imuruk Basin is "just a name," but seems to be related to the name for "mountain".

Two prominent capes, Point Romanof, south of St. Michael, and Cape Nome, are known by approximately the same name, azyateyuk and ayasayuk (also given to me as ayacheruk). Zagoskin recorded Point Romanof as Cape Azachagyak in 1844,[20] and Kobelev's name for Cape Nome was Antschirag in 1779. The meaning given for Point Romanoff was "sheer cliff", and for Cape Nome, variously as "brace," "broke off and did not move from shore," "stopped at edge of water," or "lower cliff than Sledge Island," in other words, a sheer cliff on the mainland. Sledge Island, or ayak,[21] means "pushed out" or "comes out to the edge of the water, broke off, went out, and stopped." Kobelev mapped Sledge Island as Ejech. A part of Cape Nome in profile is almost a straight cliff to the sea, as is the higher end of Sledge Island.

Another very old site excavated by Giddings on Cape Denbigh is the site called Ayatayet, also pronounced ayatayuk. This name is probably related to ayasayuk and azyatayuk (Cape Nome and Point Romanof), but there is no explanation for the coincidence of a nuklik near ayatayuk and a nuk near ayasayuk.

The names pingo and pingak are used variously for "mound, "small hill," and "knoll." In the Nome area, pingo ("mound") was a camp near Igloo Creek. In the Wales area pingu ("mound") and pinguzurak ("poor little knoll"), were old villages. Near Golovin, pingukpuk ("big mound"), in the vicinity of an old reindeer cold storage plant, was a good black cod fishing spot in April when cracks appeared in the ice. Pingak ("knoll") near Koyuk was a place where they marke reindeer in the early 1900s. Pingak ("mound") near present-day Stebbins was an old hunting and fishing camp which was later called Sourdough Village during the gold rush because of successful homebrew operations. This pingak was the home of immigrants who came from Nelson Island about 1915, and whose descendants now comprise a substantial part of the population of Stebbins. Related names are punuk ("little hill or "little bluff"), a small hill between Christmas Mountain and the Shaktoolik River where the foothills begin; pinungulak ("black cliff," i.e., a "volcano"), a wood-gathering area, and punut ("cliffs"), the name of North Point, both on Stuart Island.

Near the mouth of the Kuzitrin River in ancient times lived an aggregation of mythical malevolent beings called pingumiut ("mound people") because they lived in small mounds. Not so far away on the north side of Birch Hill lived another equally dangerous group named itukiamiut or "hollow people" because they lived in hollows (i.e., ituka, "man-made hollow") These were not Eskimo settlements.

Long ago every hill and mountain had a name. Stuart Mountain near St. Michael is ingektuk ("mountain"), but another "mountain," or ingiktak near Unalakleet has been described as "a good mountain." The latter is one of the few places known to have been named within memory when a well-known old woman, Mrs. Ivanoff, picking berries many

years ago exclaimed about the blueberry-covered mountain:
"Ariga! una ingiktak!" In the Bolovin area, a mountain
that sheltered another group of malevolent beings, the
ingekpumiut, was called ingekpuk ("big mountain"). The
McDonald Mountains toward the Yukon River were ingikpait
or igikpait ("big mountains or hill"), where the Malemiut
of Unalakleet hunted caribou at the end of the nineteenth
century.

Hills and mountains also had descriptive names. Two
mountains near Unalakleet are known by Kauwerak names,
iknikuerik ("sharp, steep mountain") and kigtuyet ("highest
among several"). A related word is the name of the
Kigluaik Mountains (kigluaik or kigluait, "sharp peak,"
"sharp peaks"), located in the original home area of the
Kauwerak dialect. This name was placed on a map for the
first time in 1898 by the U. S. Coast and Geodetic Survey.
A sedimentary series was named the Kigluaik series in 1900
by the U. S. Geological Survey.[22]

Also in the Unalakleet area are chulunguchunat ("lots
of little hills"); chungegathleye ("hill, steep, slanting
down"); iguikpuk ("big hill") or Traeger Hill; kanayaget
("perhaps it means edge of the hills where people go down
to the flats"), the low hills in front of "air force hill,"
known as okpiaktalik ("willow place"); neskochungut, or
"little heads" because of various rock formations; and
pitikshuik ("place of shooting") because caribou were chased
up the sides in the old days to be shot with bow and arrow.
The mountain at the White Alice site near the Unalakleet
River, known both as putut ("piled rocks," or "arch where
rocks are put") and putulgit ("rocks with a hole"), was
named in this way: "On Putut years ago people would walk
to the highest nose; one man put a rock there, and then
another would walk through and put another rock so they
know how many had walked through; and young people later,
years ago, made it into an arch, and therefore it is called
putut."[23]

The present village of White Mountain (it was once only
a campsite) and hill on which it is located are known as
nutchvik (in Unaluk) and nutsvik (in Malemiut), meaning
"place where can look a long way," or "place where can look
all around." Crater Mountain in the St. Michael area is
also called nutchvik (or nutsivik by some Malemiut speakers),
"where look around [for caribou in the old days]."

Stephens Hill near St. Michael is chinikthlik ("sharp
point" or "big point"); the Tolukowuk Bluffs east of
Klikitarik are called tulokouk ("where crows are"); and
Tomcod Hill in the Golovin area is irathluit or "fish" (it
is near the Fish River).

A group of mountains in the Kuzitrin area, located
near Noxapaga, is known as kelulinuk ("last river back"),
and Marys Mountain on the Kuzitrin River is aviunak ("black
whale") because the mountain looks like a whale. One of my

informants said, "If Mary's Igloo [an abandoned village that began during the gold rush near the house of a friendly Eskimo woman, Mary, who later married Oquilluk] had an Eskimo name, this would be it." Star Mountain (not located for me) in the Koyuk area was also called "black whale" or akvugunuk.

In the Shaktoolik area, a hill that looks like a pot is called utkusingnak (a Malemiut word), and Christmas Mountain is uluksruk ("stone for ulus") because slate used in making points and knives is found on the mountain. The Eskimo name of Bald Head west of Koyuk is also uluksak ("slate") because of the stone found there.

A number of hills and mountains were named after prominences that resembled parts of the human body. A hill in the Unalakleet area is sunguk ("forehead"), and mountains behind St. Michael are uvzait ("breasts"). Niuthlyungnauak, a hill near Rocky Point, nuthlunak (The Sisters) near St. Michael, and nuthluk (First Portage on the Unalakleet River) refer to "buttocks." The rocks that suggested the name for First Portage have disappeared. A village nuthlutaligmiut is discussed in the settlement names.

Islands

Islands were often called simply "island" or kikiktuk. This is the name for Whale Island near St. Michael, Besboro Island between Unalakleet and Shaktoolik, and Sarichev Island and its village now called Shishmaref. The latter was recorded first by Kobelev in 1779. Stuart Island or kikiktapuk ("big island") was recorded by Khromchenko as Kikh-takh-pak in 1822 for the first time.[24] Cape Darby is kikiktaualik or kikiktoaluk ("like an island" or "has an island", i.e., is a peninsula), and Klikitarik, the map name for an abandoned nineteenth-century village, kikiktaruk or kikiktauk ("a little island" or "island"). The old village of kikiktaruk had a roadhouse for early twentieth-century mail carriers whose pronunciation of this word permanently changed it to Klikitarik with a long a, now used by the Eskimos themselves for the old site. Zagoskin reported it as Kikkhtaguk with a population of 28 in 1842-1844.[25] In the Kuzitrin River a little island is called kikiktaruk ("small island"), and near St. Michael the name of a seal hunting camp is kikauuat ("little islands").

An island that was the home of an autonomous tribe never had a variant name of kikiktuk: Sledge Island was ayak; Little Diomede Island, Ingalik ("just a name"); Big Diomede, imaklik ("of the sea"); and King Island, ukivuk ("just a name"). Island names within tribal territories, particularly when there was more than one island. Names of some of these islands are, on the Kuzitrin River, amituk ("narrow strip"), which apparently refers to the narrowness between island and beach, and anguaktusak ("where was a boat paddle race," i.e., in the nineteenth century, two oomiaks would race upstream to the village of Kauwerak, each

starting on opposite sides of the island); near St. Michael,
mit-thak ("eider duck") or Eider Duck Island,(26) o-ovignak
("pile of [Alaska] cotton") or Beulah Island,(27) and
ungalukamiutkiklaouak ("south island"), a small island about
one and three-fourths miles southwest of the mouth of
Stuart Island Canal.

Water

     St. Michael Bay was called tachek ("bay"), which also
was the name of the old village on the northeast point of
St. Michael Island, of St. Michael Island, and of St.
Michael Mountain. The village was also called tachekmiut,
Golovnin Bay was also known as tachek (first recorded as
Tachik by Khromchenko),(28) but Norton Bay was kungikuchuk
("big inlet," "end of a big inlet," "end of a big bay").
Apparently this word could also mean "big peninsula." The
word kungik (as in Unaluk) and kangik (Malemiut) means "end
of a river," by which name the Buckland River and its
principal village were known. Kangik was located about 30
miles up the Buckland from Eschscholtz Bay where the estuary
begins to widen. However, kangik means more than just mouth
of a river, and often means "a little harbor" when applied
to water, but "reindeer or caribou corral" when applied to
land. A locality near Shaktoolik was called kungiyuk
("corner") and another near Unalakleet was kangirak
("shelter" or "corralling place"). The latter name was
also given to good berry grounds behind the corral, which was
situated on a slough. Two localities near Unalakleet are
kangirak ("corner") and kangiraktovik ("place of corral" for
reindeer or caribou; informant was uncertain as to which
one). Kangiraktovik is north of the Unalakleet radio towers.
Kangikuk ("corral corner [for reindeer]") is a fairly recent
name near Rock Point Hill in the St. Michael area, and
kangaruk ("just a name") is an old village and present campsite on the northwest shore of Imuruk Basin.

     Often the mouth of a river or a village at its mouth
were called "mouth of [river's name]" as in the following
examples: shaktulempaga ("mouth of Shaktoolik River");
niukliupaga ("mouth of the Niukluk River"), a fishing camp
in the Fish River area; kugrupaga ("mouth of the river"),
a campsite in the Wales area; itkirunpaga ("Birth Creek
mouth"); and paimiut ("people of the mouth," Unaluk dialect),
the old village name of Moses Point (I have been told that
this place was also called kuinihak or kuinhamiut, also in
the Unaluk dialect).

     The name Chaktoole Bay reported by Captain Cook has
subsequently been spelled Shaktoolik in the Malemiut
dialect. The original Unaluk word apparently pertained to a
large coastal area near the mouth of the Shaktoolik River
if the meaning refers to the enormous piles of old and
bleached driftlogs cast up along the beach, as some people
think. There is no consensus as to the meaning of the word.
It is considered by most to be "only a name," but others
have ventured the following explanations: "old wood just

lying on tundra," "all mixed around" (i.e., because chaktak means "spread out"), and "jumbled driftwood." However, another meaning given me by a very old woman was "people moving around; not stay in any place long." No one seems to be satisfied with any of the meanings. It is interesting that Thomas Bourchier of the Franklin search parties reported this name in the Unaluk dialect as Chuk-to-aluk as late as 1851.[29] Apparently the Malemiut pronunciation had not entirely superseded the original one at that time.

Only one river in a tribal area was called merely "river" or "big river." The most famous Alaskan river, the Yukon, was once called Kwikpak or Kwichpak (kuigpak, "big river"), which is the Eskimo name for the lower portion occupied by Eskimos. However, the Indian word for the upper part is now applied to the entire river. The Kobuk River (kowuk or kopuk), north of the area discussed in this paper, also means "big river" in the dialect variously called Kobuk or Malemiut, and may have an etymological relationship to the present name of Koyuk on Norton Sound. The Kiwalik River (kualuk) means "big old river." This generic name for stream was also used as Kwik River and its old village of kuik ("river") on Norton Sound; for the village of Haycock, kuarak ("little creek"), but is "not an old name" (near Koyuk); in kuinhamiut ("river people"), an area near Koyuk; and in Poker Creek kuik ("river"), in Powers Creek, kuihuk ("creek," "nice creek") and fishing camp at the mouth, and in Kowegok Slough, kuegvak ("imitation river") in the Unalakleet area. Beeson Creek near Shaktoolik is kuiyahak, said to have been named by people from Nelson Island, north of Kuskokwim Bay, during the early nineteenth century. The name of Beeson Slough is kuyuksak. The Chiroskey River's name in Eskimo is kuikuvloak, but is considered to be "only a name."

The name Koyuk (village and river) is a puzzling one. It apparently has lost all meaning. It is not only "just a name," but a "queer name." Possibly it is a combination of kuiyuk or kuinihak, which are Unaluk words, with kopuk, a Malemiut word, to produce Koyuk after the village was resettled by immigrants from the Kobuk River sometime after the smallpox epidemic of 1838. It may also have resulted from cartographic mutation. Zagoskin recorded an Unaluk name, Kvynkhakmyut (probably kuiniukmiut) on the river Kvynkhak in the position of Koyuk River and village in the 1840s.[30] In 1867 Otto de Bendeleben of the Western Union Telegraph Expedition said that the "deserted village [inhabitants apparently away fishing] of Konyukmute [was] the prettiest part of the country I had yet seen." A map printed at the time of Alaska's purchase in 1867 called this river Koipak apparently from information received from Western Union personnel. Frederick Whymper, artist for the expedition, spelled it Koikpak on his map published in 1869, but W. H. Dall, another expedition member, first used the present spelling Koyuk on a map in 1875.[31]

Descriptive names were also popular for rivers and

creeks. The principal river of the Kauwerak area is the
Kuzitrin, <u>kuzikliun</u> ("new river"), although early Russian-
Chukchi sources suggest that this river may have been called
<u>kauwerak</u> (from the village name) during the eighteenth
century. Older Kauwerak people say that their grandparents
can remember the new channel starting in the river. A smaller
stream in the area still bears the name Kaviruk, as <u>kauwerak</u>
is pronounced in other dialects. A large river that joins
the Kuzitrin is the Kruzgamepa (<u>kuzgemapa</u>, "one of two
rivers"), now officially known as the Pilgrim River.[32]

Other rivers in the Teller-Kauwerak area are Agiapuk,
considered to be "just a name", but an informant thought
it might mean "big one opposite [the Kuzitrin]"; a slough
called <u>akluk</u> ("bear"), so named because a woman once met a
bear there and hit him on the head with a root pick; the
Bluestone River, <u>klupalvakluzet</u> ("lots of maggots");
<u>erokpik</u> ("bedroom pot") because the dark water that comes
from an island tastes "funny"; Offield Creek and campsite,
<u>kasilinuk</u> ("bitter" or "burns in the mouth"), a creek which
is "sour and limey, and very hard"; Tuksuk Channel, <u>tuksuk</u> or
<u>tukshuk</u> ("narrow canyon wall", "narrow entrance", or
"passage [as in a semi-subterranean house]"), first reported
by Kobelev as Tschekevui in 1779; and <u>tuno</u> ("back"), an
unlocated river north of the Agiapuk.

In the northern half of Seward Peninsula are Candle
Creek and old camp or village, <u>musutoak</u> ("has lots of
[Eskimo] potatoes"); the Espenberg River, <u>enuiknik</u> ("no
more people"); the Goodhope River and village at its mouth,
<u>pitak</u> ("big bend," "hollow place"), name first reported by
Kobelev (1779);[33] the Nugnugaluktuk River ("cape shaped
like a goose"), which flows into Goodhope Bay; Kugrapaga
River ("river runs down to the sea"); Nuluk River ("just a
name"); Upkuarok Creek ("great pathway"); Pinguk River
("knoll"); Baituk River, more correctly pronounced <u>paituk</u>
("inheritance"), first reported by Kobelev in 1779; and
Kanauguk River ("nose point"). The last four are in the
Wales area.

In the southern part of Seward Peninsula, the Eskimo
name of Tisuk River was said to be <u>iukevik</u> ("wind goes
through the valley"); Cripple River and old village are
both known as <u>kayalashuak</u> ("person who rides kayak"), the
Chailchotschoch of Kobelev's; Spruce Creek near Solomon is
<u>okpiktulik</u> ("place of many willows"), reported by Kobelev
as Ochrutulach; and Hastings Creek near Nome is <u>uvgun</u> ("cut").
The Tubuktulik River, meaning "where are many whitefish" was
also the site of an old village, Tubukhtuligmyut, reported
by Zagoskin in 1842-1844. He said that it was "heavily
populated."[34] The East Fork of Koyuk River (and a
campsite) were named <u>iluanivit</u> ("place where smelts run"),
and one of its tributaries, <u>puyulik</u> ("river with smoke").
The Fish River is <u>irathluik</u> in Unaluk dialect and <u>ikathluik</u>
in Kauwerak ("place where fish are"), because of a rainbow
trout spawning area near the nineteenth-century village of
<u>irathluingmiut</u> above Council. The Niukluk River means "one

[river] toward the west," and was first reported by Thomas
Bourchier of the Franklin search party as Nu-kluk in 1851.[35]
A nearby creek is ovuknasik or "creek where many willows
grow." A slough, timauiyaak ("go over short cut") was
named because kayaks could slide easily over the slough from
the ocean to the Koyuk River at high tide.

The mouth of the Snake River or sitnasuak forms the port
of Nome, and the mouth of the Nome River, uinaktauik, four
miles east of Nome, is the location of a number of summer
fishing camps. Sitnasuak is another word that has lost its
meaning, but one person thought that it could have been
derived from sitnani ("along the edge" plus the suffix -suak,
which "makes it not the smallest river"). Kobelev's name
was Tschugnutschumi. Sitnasuak was also pronounced
chitnikchauk in Unaluk by a very old man born at Cape Nome,
and is a word possibly related to chinik or chiningmiut
("coastal people"). Another old informant told me that all
Nome area people were called chiningmiut in early days.

Penny River, the next river west of the Snake is called
sitnasuakak ("little Snake River," "smaller hunting ground
than Nome," "little pet of the Snake River"). I have been
unable to learn the meaning of Nome River or uinaktauik. The
population of Snake River village, "Chitnashuak," was 20
according to the 1880 census, and of Nome River,
"Ooinnakhtagowik," ten.

Along the east coast of Norton Sound, the Inglutalik
River (inglutalik in Unaluk and iglutalik in Malemiut) is
said to mean "like a house" because "it was named after a
hump that looks like a house." Camps at its mouth were also
known by this name. The meaning of the Ungalik River and
camp, unguktulik (also known as Bonanza in English) is
uncertain, but it is probably related to ungalaklik or
Unalakleet, which means either "one river to the south" or
"from where the south wind blows." (See further discussion
of Unalakleet in list of settlements.) Ungalik is an
erroneous rendition of unguktulik. "Oonakhtolik" had a
population of 15 in 1880. Strawberry creek and fishing camp
near Shaktoolik are anuketulik ("always windy"), a "real
Unaluk word" in an area later settled by Malemiut. The
Egavik River is igavik ("place to cook"), a name also
applied to a very old Unaluk settlement where people cooked
caribou bones in clay pots with hot rocks for tallow.

In the Unalkleet area, the South River is angmanik
("open place") and the North River and a camp and old cache
site at its mouth is nigukmuthluk (also pronounced
nigazmuthluk), which means "northway." Rabbit Creek is
sagvagiktoak ("swift water," "swift ripples"); Blueberry
Creek and fishing camp at its mouth are both known as
choatulik ("blueberry place"); and names of two small creeks
are sikseriak ("where go hunting squirrels") and kukahak
("is in the center," "in between") or Center Creek and camp,
recently named by Frank Degnan, mayor of Unalakleet.
Auchelik Slough is tunuuiung ("short cut to river"), now

considerably dried up and no longer used as a short cut. A
camp here is tunuuikchagyak. The meaning of the creek
aniula, which supplies water to Unalakleet, was unknown to
several informants.

Toward St. Michael, Taket Creek is tatitak ("named
after the little fishes"); Coal Mine Creek, which has an
especially good deposit of clay near its mouth, is kipiukiovik,
meaning "mixing around clay"; Glacier Creek is koluktuk
("water gushing down"); and Poker Creek, kiku ("clay").

The name imaruk (imaguk) meaning "body of water
surrounded by land, but smaller than the sea," has found its
way on modern maps as Imuruk Basin south of Grantley Harbor
and as Imuruk Lake in the interior of Seward Peninsula.
Imuruk Basin was first reported by William Frederick Beechey
in 1826 as "Imaurook."(36) The ocean around Nome was called
taiukpuk ("big salt"), but could also be called imakpuk
("big body of water"). Many lakes all over the Bering Strait
area were called by some form of imaruk, but others were
known by descriptive names. In the Kauwerak-Teller area there
is narvasiuk ("narrow long lake") or Kuzitrin Lake and ikutuk
("not very deep"), into which caribou were driven between
piles of rocks and then speared by men in kayaks.

In the Unalakleet area, Coral Lake is narvukluk ("big
lake"); and lakes without English names are alutalik ("there
is hole," "something that never freezes in winter" [there
might be some kind of animal that keeps it open]), ingmanuk
("big lake half dried"), northeast of Coral Lake, and
unaksiklelik ("where few trees grow"). Near Cape Espenberg
are nervakik (big fish lake") and salipuktut ("Lakes of the
grayling"), where there are "millions and millions of
grayling."

Liebes Cove in the St. Michael area is called mahak
("little water") and was once the site of an old village,
mahagmiut, and later, a trading post. Mahak is often used
when speaking of wet spongy tundra, which indeed has a
"little water" between the millions of soggy tussocks.

Localities

A number of localities and areas had names, and those
that I have learned about include varied descriptions. In
the Teller-Kauwerak area, pamnikotut ("many blackberry
bushes") was the name of a berry-picking area near Tuksuk
Channel; itak ("[red] color"), was the site name on the
Tuksuk of the only known pictographs in the Bering Strait
area; kiklukrakavit ("place where get rock tool material")
was an area where people looked for sharp-edged rocks; and
uksotuk ("many willows") was a place on the northern shore
of Imuruk Basin where Siberians and Seward Peninsula
Eskimos were supposed to have fought long ago.

On King Island, an area was called tununak ("north
[back] side"), and near Shaktoolik, taguyavik ("look back

to see how rough it is") was applied to a part of the shore,
but described in terms of the water which was very rough
when windy. In the early twentieth century, nupaklapuk
("long pole") was given to an area where a reindeer herder's
platform was erected to look for reindeer near the
Shaktoolik River.

On the northern shore of Norton Sound an area around
Paterson Creek near Elim is called kuyuktalik or "sexual
intercourse," a name that commemorates a tragic folktale.
Long ago, it is said, Shaktoolik men attacked and killed a
Malemiut family that had moved into an Unaluk site, known
ever since as nuviakchak ("young girl" or "virgin"), because
here the beautiful young daughter was raped and afterwards
tied to four kayaks, which then paddled off in different
directions. The 1880 census recorded the village of
Nubviakhchugaluk with a population of 30. This name is
translated as "place of the young girl," but I was told that
the rape and murder took place at kuyuktalik, a few miles to
the west. The 1890 census reported the name Kuyuktolik
somewhere in this area.[37]

In the Unalakleet area, akpausouik ("raceway") was a
circular part of the channel on the lower Unalakleet River
where foot races took place on the ice; angzuik ("where put
boats in") was a place where boats were beached on the
Unalakleet River to get to berry grounds; kungikuvik
("place where you leave your sled") was a small area on the
Unalakleet River where Nallagorak, a reindeer herder, left
his sled when he went to Eaton Reindeer Station on the
Unalakleet River; manganik ("kind of a low place") was an
area on the upper Chiroskey River where Unalakleet people
hunted caribou; nalroknekpuk or nalognunik ("long stretch,"
"straight"), was a long straight stretch of water on the
Unalakleet River; and pataukak (a word that means roughly,
"have to go real fast, it's so swift" or "to go upstream
in a hurry so fish won't escape"), is an identifying name
for part of the Unalakleet River. Imguyutuk ("needle and
sewing kit") is the name for a huge vertical folded and
twisted rock formation that plunges into the ocean near
Egavik. According to a folktale, a husband beat his wife,
who ran away with her imguyutuk. In her anger she threw
it against the rocks, which immediately took on the folds
and seams of the semicircular fur sewing bag.

Near St. Michael the area at the southern estuary of
Stuart Island Canal is known as kuiupaingaungalulenginuk
("mouth of river near south island") where people net whitefish, and a stretch of beach and water on North Bay of Stuart
Island is called magnavigamiut ("where they fish tomcods").
Uianskit ("come up out of hole") is a locality name on the
west slope of West Hill on Stuart Island.

Settlements

Settlements, both permanent villages and campsites, had
an even more varied spectrum of names than physical features,
which also applied to inhabited places. The settlement names
complete the place-names from this area, and are given in
alphabetical order because of related words. Settlements that
have already been discussed are omitted unless material has
been added in this section. Kotlik and Pikmiktalik, two
villages south of the area of this study are included because
of trading relationships with St. Michael during the nineteenth century and because of the interesting meanings of the
names.

agashliuk (said to mean "point where people lived") was
remembered as a place very near present St. Michael where Yukon
people and Malemiut lived together when they stayed during the
winter. Zagoskin said that Agakhkhlyak, meaning a place
suitable for a settlement, was also called Tachik.(38) This
has already been discussed under the name tachek, which is
St. Michael's Eskimo name today. I was told that by 1890
there were two different villages, tachek and agashliuk, but
that agashliuk was the older.

agianamiut ("opposite"), the south village on the lower
slope of Cape Mountain, and kiatanamiut ("front"), the north
village on the flats, were the two principal parts of the
village of kingigan or Wales. In 1826 Beechey learned at
Kotzebue Sound about two villages at Cape Prince of Wales,
"Iden-noo" and "King-a-ghee,"(39) but Eskimos have no
explanation for Iden-noo today. It may have referred to
agianamiut. A third part of kingigan is called singuarangmiut
(see under land features), and a fourth, an archeological
site, is kurigitavik ("to run aground going up the river"),
the river being singluraruk, or Wales River. Singuarangmiut
is on the north side of the river across from kiatanamiut.

aktuingnuk, a camp on the Shaktoolik River, now occupied
by a Kauwerak man. This is a real Unaluk word "with no
meaning."

akulesak ("something in the middle" or "two things for
one item"), a camp on the Tuksuk Channel.

akulik or akulit ("in between"), an ancient camp named
this because it was located between iglutalik (Inglutalik)
and Koyuk. This is the Akulik River.

alianak ("lonesome sad place"), a camp in the Teller area.
"This is not as bad as if it would be if very lonesome; then
it would be alianakpuktuk."

alunak ("lonely"), a beluga hunting camp in the
Shaktoolik area.

amilrak ("narrow"), an old village on Point Spencer,
mentioned by Western Union Telegraph personnel in 1867 as

Amilrokmiut.[40] Amilrak also pertains to Point Spencer itself.

   angakukshrak ("old lady"), a Kauwerak word for a Unalakleet camp. It was established on top of an old camp, and named because an old woman was buried there.

   angvanigrak ("used to be open before"), a "real Unaluk word" in the Shaktoolik area; name of a spring seal hunting camp.

   aningnugituak, a camp in the Golovin area. The informant did not know whether the name meant "not flowed away" or "not taken from the house."

   apachoamnuna ("Apachoak's place"), a recently named cabin in the Unalakleet area.

   aparakalik ("belongs to Aparak"), a recent name applied to the cabin of the Eskimo preacher (aparak), Jacob Kenick, by Shaktoolik people when he moved to Nunivak Island to preach.

   asagorak ("just a name"), a camp on Tuksuk Channel.

   atnuk ("big heavy pack strap," sometimes pronounced utnuk), a well-known nineteenth-century village on Cape Darby. This was also the name of a small village, atnuk ("hunting bag strap") on the upper Kuzitrin River. The Cape Darby atnuk was recorded as Atnykgmyut by Zagoskin.[41]

   atuik ("bent point"), the old village of Stebbins situated near a cliff, and first reported by Khromchenko as Tauk in 1822.[42]

   ayasayuk or ayacheruk (for meanings see under capes), an old village on high ground above the beach at the base of Cape Nome. In the 1880 census, Ayacheruk had a population of 60. See also Nome in this section.

   chauiyak ("tambourine drum"), a camp on the Unalakleet River named after a drum-shaped slough behind it. The same name in the Kauwerak dialect (soiyuk) was used for an old winter caribou village near a drum-shaped lake on the upper Kuzitrin. This village, Show-e-yok, was visited by Mate Hobson during the Franklin search.[43]

   chiukak ("in front"), a large nineteenth-century village in the Golovin area.

   Igloo. This name appears frequently on maps for either Marys Igloo or New Igloo, both on the Kuzitrin River. It is not an Eskimo place-name. The village was established when white miners staked out a townsite around Mary's house in 1901. Marys Igloo never had an Eskimo name, but the word aviunak would fit, as we have already seen. New Igloo came into being when dissension between Lutheran missionaries and Catholic priests at Marys Igloo during the early 1920s resulted in the Lutherans pulling their church and school downstream on the snow to a new site.

iglu ("house"), a camp in the Golovin area at Corwin's Cove.

ikitluk ("place where it has been burned"), a camp on the Shaktoolik River, another "reak Unaluk word."

ikyulpak ("mouth of hard wood creek"), a small permanent village at mouth of Telephone Creek, a tributary of the Fish River. This is also the name of the creek and refers either to crooked trees from which bows were made, or because "the creek has a lot of trees."

imiengnak ("[lake] drained out"), an old village in the Wales area. The Eskimo Bulletin, published in the Wales school, called it Im-ang-nok in 1902.(44) See also a lake, ingmanuk.

inuingnuk ("no one there, all gone"), an old site near the lava beds in the Kauwerak area; iniukthluit ("group of houses" from ini meaning houses), an old site near the Unalakleet air field. (This is in the Kauwerak dialect; in Unaluk, the name would be nugluthluit); inyuktuk ("where people are gone, have been killed"), a site on the Buckland River; and inuiknik ("no more people"), old site on the Espenberg River. Kobelev placed the name Inigrain north of Kigygmin (kingigan). No one in the Wales area has heard of such a place. Since one of the names for houses in the Wales dialect is ini, it could have referred to a group of houses, or possibly the abandoned segment of Wales called kurigatavik. Perhaps Inigrin is Beechey's Iden-noo.

isak ("end [of Island]"), a camp located near the end of a spit in the Shishmaref area. Ezooah had three houses in 1892.(45)

iyet ("cook pot"), Serpentine Hot Springs, east of Shishmaref. People camped here to cook in the springs.

kaglik ("where they seine"), a camp on the Unalakleet River, an "Unaluk-Malemiut word."

kailiovik ("where there are always waves"), a camp in the Golovin area.

kalulik ("rocks on the beach"), Cape Douglas and old village. In 1867, The Esquimaux said that Kalutingmiut had one dwelling and 18 inhabitants.(46) This is probably Kobelev's Chalamachmit of 1779.

kangshluk ("lots of milling tomcods"), an old village in the Shaktoolik area. The site is very old and is considered to be the predecessor to Shaktoolik, but shaktulempaga is said to be older than kangshluk.

kaokpak ("large valley," Kauwerak dialect), a camp on the ocean near Unalakleet.

kasigirat ("spotted seal"), a point at a spring camp in the Teller area; kasigeyet ("spotted seal") are camps for berry picking in the Koyuk area.

katinit or katinyak ("rivers come together"), an old village in the Kuzitrin area at the confluence of the American and Agiapuk rivers.

kauwerak ("gravel bar"), a large eighteenth and nineteenth century village on the Kuzitrin River. This has been erroneously reported many times from other dialects as kaviak, especially from St. Michael where kaviak means "red fox." This place was recorded first as Kheuveren on Daurkin's map of 1765, but Beechey was the first (1827) to record it as it is pronounced, or Kow-ee-ruk. I have not used the more accurate phonetic spelling kaoeruk throughout this paper because the easier-to-read Kauwerak has been established in print.(47)

kauingnuk ("red"), a fishing site in the Golovin area.

kazgun ("seine"), a camp at the mouth of the Bluestone River.

kektoashliuk ("place where it breaks"), old village on the Kuzitrin River, two miles above Mary's Igloo. This place was inhabited at the time of the Franklin search and was called Kik-to-alik in the reports.

kinat ("resembles a face"), a camp and name of Isaacs Point. See also ukvignaguk.

kingigan. See agianamiut. The name was reported by Daurkin in 1765 and Kobelev in 1779.

kingmemsieua ("front of the hills" or "end of the low hill"), a camp four miles above the present Kuzitrin River bridge.

kingnugat ("caches in the ground"), a camp on the Tuksuk Channel.

kotlik ("pants"), a village located on the Yukon where the river branches like a pair of trousers. This small Eskimo village in 1868 was also the home of a Russian man when W. H. Dall first reported the name of Kutlik.(48)

kukak ("middle"), a camp in the Golovin area, named after a creek that flows from a hill.

kuksuktopaga ("where there are white hills"), an old village at the mouth of kuksuktuk or the Casadepaga River. The name is derived from the hills becoming white from the reflection of early morning sunshine on white rocks at the river mouth.

kupraouik ("whaling net place"), a camp for catching beluga, or white whales, in the Golovin area.

malikfik ("go after seals with spears"), a camping site in the Shaktoolik area. The name is preserved in Malikfik Bay.

mitletavik ("piece of coastland where they get flounders"), a nineteenth century village in the Wales area.

mekliktlik ("place of good water," "good clear water"), a camp near Unalakleet on the ocean, named after a nearby stream.

mitliktogvik ("place where they meet"), a nineteenth century camp or village on the upper Goodhope River.

mizek ("low, swampy place"), a small village in the Teller area.

mizuk ("swampy place"), a camp on the Fish River.

mukluktulik ("where bearded seals are"), a Koyuk fishing site.

muptegagat ("cache") in the Shaktoolik area, a camp for fall seal hunting. An Unaluk word.

mupterukshuk ("cache" or "white man's house"; informant was uncertain of the specific meaning), an old village near Cape Nome, apparently Kobelev's Memtachagran.

musu ("Eskimo potato"), a camp on Tuksuk Channel.

muzitoak ("place of the Eskimo potato"), a small settlement at the mouth of Candle Creek.

nagaluk ("lower ground"), an abandoned camp, five miles west of Nome.

nagoyatulik ("place where seagull nests"), a camp on Reindeer Cove near Ungalik where people camped to gather seagull eggs. There is also a nagoyatulik at Tolstoi Point.

nagoyumkuti, a name that pertains specifically to a sandbar where seagulls congregate in great numbers on the Unalakleet River, but is also the name of a campsite across the river on a bluff of Oliver Hill. A man was named after this place, and he is now called Kuti.

naplathlasit ("where Lapp [herders] were"), a site of an old Unaluk fishing camp in the Unalakleet area. The Unaluk name had been forgotten so the Eskimo name for nearby Eaton Reindeer Station was given to this camp about 70 years ago.

niklatulik ("where fish are"), a camp in the Koyuk area.

   ningnugarak ("cottonwood"), a camp on the ocean north
of Ungalik.

   Nome. This is included here because suggestions have
been made over the years that the name was derived from am
Eskimo word, which it is not. The town of Nome is situated
on very flat land ten miles west of Cape Nome, and was
named after the cape in 1899. The original name resulted
from a query "Name?" entered on charts of the British
Admiralty Office concerning the cape during the search for
John Franklin. Inquiries were not about the Eskimo name, but
the European "Cape Tolstoi," which had been bestowed by
M. B. Tebenkov in 1833. (Today there is another Tolstoi Point
south of Unalakleet).

   Holmer has conjectured that "Nome...situated on Cape
Nome [which it is not]...may very well at one time have been
named something like 'the port, village or place of the
headland [or nuk]."(49) Cape Nome and its old village have
never been called nuk, the name ayasayuk (or one of its
variant pronunciations) having been used from time beyond
memory. Beechey learned at Kotzebue Sound about a placed
called "I-art-so-rook"; Zagoskin reported in his list of
settlements that "Azachagyagmyut near Cape Tolstoi [was] well
populated"; and Kobelev's Antschirag of 1779 probably referred
to this cape.(50) Cape Tolstoi had appeared on various maps
before Cape Nome (Cape Name?) was readily adopted from British
Admiralty Chart 2172 in 1853.(51) Today ayasayuk or Cape Nome
is never confused with nuk or Nook, by which name the fishing
camps on the spit, five miles to the east are still known;
nor is ayasayuk confused with "Nome's own name, sitnasuak."

   nunamitkoa ("end of the world"), a Unalakleet River camp
of the nineteenth century named because the fishing camps
ended there at that time. The name is still used although
camps now extend much farther upstream.

   nunanuhak ("new place"), a camp near Golovin.

   nuskonakamiut ("place where tree stumps are", a campsite
near St. Michael.

   nuthlutaligmiut ("floating bottoms up"), an old village
near the gold rush boat works of St. Michael. It is said to
come from the following folktale: "Once when high water came,
long before you or I were born, and all the people went to
the hills, one man [apparently the chief] had left his knife
in the house and said to the young men, 'I'll give you a wolf
skin or a daughter if you'll get my knife.' One of them
volunteered, and got to the house just as the wave receded.
He made it, and got the knife, but was caught by another wave
on the way back, and he was floating face down with his
bottoms up when the people returned, and this is what the
word nuthlutaligmiut means."

   nuviachuk (Unaluk), nuviakiak (Malemiut), and
nuviachugaluk ("young lady," "virgin," and "poor young lady")

would be the Eskimo name of present-day Elim, which was
established in 1914 by missionaries of the Swedish Covenant
Church to escape the strong winds at Mission (tuklaktoik) on
Golovnin Bay. For the complete story see kuyuktulik,

nuviulnuk or nuviungnuk ("no point"), a small nineteenth century village near the Russian trading post of
Golsovia south of Unalakleet. It is now abandoned, but two
or three Kauwerak families lived there at the turn of the
twentieth century. The name is preserved today in
Nunovulnuk Harbor. Zagoskin reported Cape Nygvylnuk and the
Nygvylnuk River.(52)

omailuk is the name of the first mine on Seward
Peninsula, developed in the 1880s for lead and silver. It is
spelled Omilak on maps. The word omailuk means "it is heavy,"
and refers to heavy chunks of galena once collected by
Eskimos as curiosities. A relative of umilyuk's, the Eskimo
winter watchman for the mine, suggested that his name also
might have been the origin of the name.

paikchuk ("give away"), a camp in the St. Michael area.
This is erroneously printed as Myoukchouk Point on maps.
See also Baituk River.

pikmitalik ("ground is twisting"), the village
Pikmiktalik, the name derived from a folktale in which
"medicine people" caught foxes, wolves, and wolverines in
man-made holes surrounding the village to make "medicine
at night." Zagoskin recorded the village as Pikhmikhtalik,
its first appearance in print.(53)

puibluk ("high bluff"), an old camp on the Tuksuk
Channel near Deadman's Point. In 1903, it was reported that
"Dunnak went [in October 1902] in to Bee-o-block to build
his father a house."(54)

pupik ("tail of a bird"), a camping spot and good
pickerel fishing area near New Igloo east of Teller.

salinuk ("south [below] side of bay"), the real name of
Teller, which is often called Nook, a name that rightly
belongs to the opposite, or north spit. These spits divide
Port Clarence and Grantley Harbor. Beechey reported the name
Nooke in 1831.(55)

situk ("white whale," or beluga), a small village near
Cape Nome. The Nome News, on March 6, 1901, reported that
an Eskimo man had murdered his wife at Seatok.

sivuloamkuzga ("Siviulak's place"), a Shaktoolik River
camp named in the early twentieth century when Siviulak went
the wrong way near this place while boating. It is now
occupied by another family who has retained the name.

sungiyorat ("little bends"), a winter caribou village on
the old channel of the Kuzitrin River. Reported as

Shungiowret by Mate Hobson of the Franklin search party.

tekikoyaktulik ("many turns [in the river]"), an egg hunting camp near Ungalik.

tingmiakputulik ("place where big eagles live"), a small village (possibly only a camp) at the head of Fish River, named after the mythological Giant Eagle.

tirakpuk ("big sand bar," "long beach"), a Unalakleet River camp. This is a Kauwerak name that has been used for at least 70 years.

titkaok ("eye shade"), a camp on Tuksuk Channel named after a rock hsaped like an eye shade across the river from the camp.

tufchaak ("to go over to the other side"), an ancient village site near Shaktoolik.

tugmagluk ("camping place"), a camp in the Deering area.

tuklaktoik ("talk as through a megaphone"), a camp in the Golovin area. This is the Eskimo name for Mission where the Swedish Covenant missionaries settled after the evils of the gold rush precipitated a move in 1902 from their original headquarters in Golovin. In 1914 they left Mission for Elim.

tutlatulik ("loon duck"), a camp for fishing and fall seal hunting in the Shaktoolik area (another "real Unaluk word").

tutupamtuma or tutupatumpa (explained as "horseshoe" for the first, "horse's hoof" for the second), a camp on the Unalakleet River.

uiaalik ("rocky," "there are rocks"), a camp on Little Rocky Point, about three miles south of South Spit on Golovnin Bay.

uksakuknuk "(looks like a stomach"), a camp on the Koyuk River named after a lake that looks like a stomach.

ukivuk or uivuk ("only a name"), King Island and its village, first reported as Okibyan by Daurkin in 1765. This island was one of the first places in northwest Alaska to receive an English name (Captain Cook in 1778). The first names obtained from Alaskan Eskimos themselves were Ukipen by Kobelev on Little Diomede Island in 1779, Ookivok by Khromchenko at Golovnin Bay in 1822, and Oo-ghe-a-boak by Beechey in 1826 at Kotzebue Sound, apparently from visiting Wales people.[56] Since then the name has been recorded many times, usually as a variation of Khromchenko's, but sometimes of Beechey's. No meaning, however, has been published, and all but one of my own inquiries brought the response, "it's just a name." The exception was "winter" or "winter place," suggested by a Cape Prince of Wales man. This meaning and a

spelling similar to Beechey's has also been noted in a
doctoral thesis by Sergei Bogajavlensky: ugiuvuk, or "winter
home," given by a King Island woman. Apparently no one else
on King Island had connected ugiuvuk with ugiuk ("winter"),
but after learning of the relationship, others agreed that
this might well be the meaning of the name. As Bernard
Katexac, the well-known King Island printmaker wrote me
while I was trying to nail down this meaning, "Ugiuk-puk--
big winter, may mean big time of winter in that part [he was
in Seattle at the time], but actually to us, Ukiuvuk is just
a name for the island."(57)

ukvignaguk or "Isaac's village" on the north shore of
Norton Sound is "just a name." In the 1880 census, Ogowinagak,
the home of Kaleak, an Eskimo trader for the Alaska Commercial
Company, had a population of 30, all in one house.

uluksruk ("slate"), a camp on the upper part of the
Unalakleet River. This camp is also called Whalebacks in
English because of "a man that lived close to Whaleback
Mountain [apparently a cripple]."

ungalaklik, Unalakleet, or Unalaklik, as it is usually
spelled on early maps. There is no agreement as to the
meaning for this old village, which had only 13 survivors
after the smallpox epidemic of 1838.(58) In 1880
"oonalakleet" had 100 inhabitants; it now as about 600.
Ungalaklik might mean "from where the south wind blows,"
"the way the [Unalakleet] River flows south to the ocean,"
or "where the Unalit live." Knud Rasmussen, the Greenland
ethnographer said in 1924 that it meant "farthest south."(59)

utukuk ("old," "Old point"), a camp in the St. Michael
area where many hunters lived together at certain times of
the year.

Some Observations

Naming of places in the Eskimo language is a thing of
the past in the Bering Strait area despite a limited use of
old native place-names, which, too, are slowly succumbing to
English. The preponderance of non-native place-names reflects
the concentrated explorations during the nineteenth century
and the consuming presence of the gold rush at the beginning
of the twentieth.

Native names have been used on printed maps less often
here than in any other Alaskan Eskimo area, and there are
few places that are translations of the Eskimo name, notable
examples being Blueberry Creek near Unalakleet, Eider Duck
Island near St. Michael, Fish River, and the local use of
Sawtooth for the Kigluaik Mountains. Locally, most large
geographical features and settlements are now called by their
non-native names, and only three villages of 17 with a
population of 25 or more have retained an Eskimo name--
Koyuk, Shaktoolik, and Unalakleet. In contrast, almost all

settlements on the Kuskokwim and Yukon rivers and their
deltas have Eskimo names.

The current state of place-names was well expressed by
Mrs. Martha Nanouk, a Unalakleet resident. "We don't use
Eskimo names now. I'm even getting doubts. They don't say
it, period, now. When Grandma [Marion Gonangan, her mother,
76 years old in 1968] goes, will be hard to remember. Now
just using English words. For example, all creeks were named,
but many have been forgotten, or else the name is remembered,
and creek only heard of and not located."

The name for a place could be taken from any source
except a personal name. Those recently named after persons
would have been prohibited during the nineteenth century
because of the name-soul. Within a tribal boundary, large
geographic features were often given generic names, but
descriptive or modified generic names were applied to other
similar features to avoid duplication. This was a necessary
and practical scheme because Eskimo travel was undertaken
from point to point (there were few spatial abstractions) and
names had to be explicit if people were to know where they
were going and how to communicate directions to others. There
fore, names of cardinal points were rarely used, and usually
only when referring to other tribes beyond the local territory
such as Unalit "south wind people," or possibly, "south
coastal people"), and not for specific places. Names that
employed directional terminology, i.e., "in front," "in
front of," "in back of," "opposite," "end of," or "below,"
were used in conjunction with already known topographic names.

Eskimos of this area did not rely on wind as an
ordinary travel aid, with the exception of people sailing
to islands, or seal and walrus hunters on the ice and water.
They traveled mostly on rivers or hugged the coast instead of
striking across, say, Norton Sound or Port Clarence. Even
at the height of caribou hunting, these Eskimos did not
follow the herds for long distances, but hunted them from
permanent inland villages as the herds migrated into their
territory. Thus, they had no general need for meteorological
abstractions, but relied on names and visual aids, which were
augmented in the winter, when snow covered the usual land-
marks, by stone or driftwood markers.

A major settlement usually bore the same name as a nearby
geographic prominence--river, island, or cape. Smaller
settlements and campsites as well as hills, lakes, and
rivers had great leeway in descriptive names taken from
eventful happenings or natural characteristics. Names of
settlements always belonged primarily to the location site,
which could encompass a whole island like Sledge Island, a
small area like Cape Nome, or a tiny area for a campsite. A
village that was considered to be a permanent base home had
two name forms, the site name, and the site name plus the
suffix -miut ("people"). The latter form was the correct
name for an inhabited village, such as chiningmiut for chinik
or katinyamiut for katinyak. However, with the arrival of

English speakers among the western Eskimo, the isolating
characteristics of English began to alter the agglutinative
nature of Eskimo names so that most villages were reported
by the site name. Occasionally, early writers recorded
villages in the current, correct usage like "Kaviarazakhmut"
(kauweramiut), "Erathlicmute" (irathluingmiut, Fish River
village), and "Aiyakamut" (ayakmiut, Sledge Island village) (60)
but now, being abandoned, they are rightly called by the site
name.

Although any geographic feature could be called after
its generic name, coastal features bore this kind of name
more often than others. For example, almost all coastal
islands were given some form of the word "island," or kikiktuk.
Exceptions were the descriptive names of islands that
constituted the home of a single tribe.

Names of birds, animals, fish, and plants were used less
often than descriptive topographic terms, and names of sea
mammals and fish were more popular than land animals, which
were rather rare except for caribou corral names. These
names did not necessarily refer to the use for the site
(i.e., "blueberry place" was a fishing-camp, not a berry-
picking camp), yet the name was usually used relative to the
subsistence quest. No names utilized a fur-bearing animal
of commercial importance. The commercial fur trade of the
Bering Strait (in foxes, land otter, muskrat; the fur seal
and sea otter did not live there) began on a large scale only
after the Anyui trade market was established by Russians on
the Kolyma River in Siberia in 1789. The absence of such
names suggests that most Eskimo names known today had been in
use before the inauguration of the fur trade, and that these
animals had been of little importance in aboriginal economy.

A number of names are still "only a name," even when the
derivation seems obvious to a person with limited knowledge
of the Eskimo language. It is probably irrelevant to a
place--and perhaps to our study of Eskimo cognizance--whether
or not a word can be rendered literally, but Eskimos regard
place-names in two categories today: those with meanings and
those without meanings. Therefore, derivations of names like
Koyuk, Shaktoolik, and Unalakleet, which are only names, had
not been seriously questioned until my inquiries. These
three names, incidentally, are located in territory that has
been occupied for more than a century and a half by speakers
of a foreign Eskimo language, a probable reason for the loss
of meaning.

As European names spread throughout Alaska with its
increasing population and industry, the few remaining Eskimo
toponyms will undoubtedly be forgotten or replaced by other
names. Eskimos constitute almost 80 per cent of the
population of Bering Strait, yet superimposition of foreign
names, including surnames, seems to be an unavoidable
consequence of political and social dominance by another
ethnic group. However, many names are still retrievable

even if the so-called Eskimo wilderness has been dramatically
tamed and systematized through compasses, printed maps,
airplanes, a few roads, and numerous electronic devices.
And though the names are no longer needed for spatial
orientation or even communication, in effect, they once held
a tribal territory together, provided mnemonic guides for
travel and for utilization of resources, and forged a
permanent and identifiable bond with the land.

Notes

1. Research in 1968 was supported by a grant from the
Penrose Fund of the American Philosophical Society.

2. The Bering Strait of my research covers a much
larger area than the narrow Strait itself, and includes
the Seward Peninsula and the coastal area, Norton Sound,
as far south as Stebbins, an area of about 28,500 square
miles with an estimated population of 5,237 in 1967. Cf.
Federal Field Committee for Development Planning in Alaska,
1967, pp. 23, 24.
    Eskimos occupied all of the Seward Peninsula and the
eastern shore of Norton Sound to the crest of the mountains;
the opposite side of the divide was occupied by Indians.
Interpretations and conclusions in this paper pertain
principally to nineteenth century political units, which have
now been superseded by the sovereignty of the United States.
Linguistic groupings today (except for the Nome area) still
coincide with dialects of the late nineteenth century.

3. These relationships and other aspects of personal
naming among the Bering Strait Eskimos are discussed in a
paper by Albert C. Heinrich (1963b).
    Many Eskimos still receive personal Eskimo names in
addition to English ones, but places rarely get a new
Eskimo name today.

4. The date of first white contact depends on a
particular area in the Bering Strait. In 1732, Mikhail
Gvozdev and Ivan Fedorov were the first Europeans to
discover Alaska near what was later named Cape Prince of
Wales in 1778. Gvozdev and Fedorov talked to the people of
Big Diomede Island. In 1778, Captain James Cook stepped
ashore on Sledge Island, Cape Denbigh, and at a place near
present-day Elim. In 1779 Ivan Kobelev visited both of the
Diomedes.

5. Efimov, 1949, p. 114. The name Kigin Eliat is
taken from Efimov's Russian transliteration of Lvov's
handwritten notations on the original map. Lvov's map
was discussed, but not illustrated, by Gerhard Müller,
Siberia's first historian, in Sammlung Russischer
Geshichte, Vol. 3, 1758, p. 53. This volume was translated

as Voyages from Asia to America (London, 1761). In both
editions the name is written "Kitschin Eljat." The Chukchi
called the inhabitants of Alaska KI'IMI'IT, or "inhabitants,"
and called the land itself, KI'IMIN according to Bogoras,
1904, p. 21. This might have been the source for Kigin
Eliat, but I think it was derived from the site name for
Wales. The name "Kynynsty," which is placed on a 1700 map
in Remezov's Atlas could possibly refer to Wales (Efimov,
1964, Map 48).

Meanings of native names are not given in this introductory discussion because they are explained later under
the names themselves.

6. Masterson and Brower, 1948, p. 27n; Fedorova,
1964, p. 97. Masterson's account contains a translation
of Daurkin's report as summarized by Peter Simon Pallas
in Neue nordische Beyträge zur physikalischen und geo-
graphischen Erd- und Völkerbeschreibung, Naturgeschichte,
und Oekonomie (St. Petersburg and Leipzig, 1781), Vol. I.
Pallas did not illustrate Daurkin's map, and Fedorova
illustrates only a small portion of the Seward Peninsula
area. However, it has been published in its entirety by
Grekov, 1960, p. 209, but the reproduction is so poor that
it is difficult to read most of the names even with a
magnifying glass.

7. Kobelev's map was published originally by Pallas
in Vol. 4 of Neue nordische Beyträge (1783), and reprinted
by Masterson and Brower. The same map with names in
Russian was published in 1784 and reproduced by M. B.
Chernenko on page 125 of his article about Kobelev (1957).
Pallas used Norton Sound to separate Kobelev's village
into two groups, a northern section that appears to cover
the entire Seward Peninsula, and a southern section coter-
minous with the Yukon and Kuskokwim deltas, from 120 to 300
miles south of the first. By comparing names I discovered
that all were Seward Peninsula settlements, the two original
groups having been divided by Port Clarence, Grantley Harbor,
and Imuruk Basin. Pallas had an opportunity to look at
Captain Cook's charts, with the newly-discovered Norton
Sound, as they traveled by courier across Siberia from
Kamchatka to London in 1778-1779. Therefore, his substitution
of this body of water for those near the middle of the
Peninsula (and which Cook did not see during his explorations),
threw Kobelev's map completely out of joint. Kobelev also
drew many "undiscovered" bays, islands, and rivers, likewise
unnoticed by Cook.

8. Zagoskin 1967, p. 103.

9. Ibid., p. 126.

10. Unaluk is the singular form of Unalit, the name
for people who lived around Norton Sound. Unaluk is used
when speaking of the language; Unalit, of the people.
I have been unable to get a meaning for the word

Malemiut. It was first recorded both as Maleygmyut and
Naleygmyut by Lieutenant L. A. Zagoskin between 1842 and
1844 during his travels in the St. Michael area and on the
Yukon and Kuskokwim rivers. Zagoskin said that it meant
"people who dwell in blanket-yurts" (Zagoskin, 1967, pp.
103, 124, 291), and applied to those northerners who
traveled around the south. This word did not originate
in the Norton Sound, apparently. All three dialects in
Unalakleet use palatgak for tent; at Elim, kanuk; and
farther north, tupek. However, John Hinz, in discussing
grammar of the Kuskokwim language, with which I am unfamiliar,
lists nalik as "a tupee" (1944, p. 196), and this probably
is the origin of the word Malemiut, written originally as
Nalegmiut. Zagoskin did not explain his use of both
spellings, so possibly the word could also have been derived
from the word, maliga ("follow") because the northerners
were both traders and caribou hunters. However, Zagoskin's
own meaning provides an ultimate source.

11. Most of the settlement names from my research on
Seward Peninsula in 1961 and 1964 were placed on maps and
analyzed in terms of subsistence and configurations in
"Nineteenth Century Settlement and Subsistence Patterns in
Bering Strait" (1964b).

12. Thomas Bourchier, 1852; A. Petermann, 1869, Vol.
XV, table 2; Petroff, (Tenth Census) 1884, p. 11. All
references to the Tenth Census of 1880 hereafter refer to
page 11. This settlement was reported as Tapkhamikkhuagmyut
by Zagoskin, but he placed it north of Cape Denbigh instead
of south (Zagoskin, 1967, p. 125).

13. Zagoskin, 1967, p. 103.

14. Beechey, 1831, Vol. II, p. 541.

15. The Esquimaux (1867), Vol. I, p. 29. This small
newspaper, edited by John L. Harrington, was published in
1866 and 1867 at "Port Clarence, R. A. [Russian America] and
Plover Bay, E. S. [Eastern Siberia]" by members of the
Western Union Telegraph Expedition stationed at Port
Clarence at Nook, across the water from present-day Teller.

16. Khromchenko, 1824, part 11, p. 244.

17. The map name Sineak River is in the Malemiut
language. The camp name is still known by its Unaluk
counterpart, chingyak.

18. Zagoskin, 1967, map; Giddings, 1964, pp. 11, 116,
118.

19. Hobson, 1854-55. Other references to Hobson in
this paper are from this publication.

20. Zagoskin, 1967, p. 89.

21. Ayak has often been recorded erroneously as aziak. The normal Sledge Island pronunciation for the y in this word is the voiced alveopalatal semivowel with weak friction. In other dialects and languages, including the one around St. Michael where many northern words were first recorded, this semivowel is produced so that it appears to be the voiced alveopalatal spirant. Even Kauwerak speakers (Sledge Island speech was closely related to Kauwerak) sometimes pronounce the y with friction, but their lexicon also includes words with a voiced alveopalatal spirant (as in azure). The name for the island ayak is often written aziak meaning mossberry, but they are two separate words.

22. Map, "Territory of Alaska, Northwest Section" (Treasury Department, U. S. Coast and Geodetic Survey, April, 1898). Kigluaik was spelled Kiglowaic; Brooks, et al., 1901, pp. 27, 28.

23. Grand Central Pass (kigmiu) in the Kigluaik Mountains had a similar pile of rocks built up by people going between Kauwerak village and Salmon Lake.

24. Khromchenko, 1824, Part 11, p. 178.

25. Zagoskin, 1967, p. 92. This village is called Kiktaguk on U. S. Geological Survey map E of Alaska, 1954.

26. The name of Eider Duck Island, first placed on a modern map in 1952 (Orth, 1967, p. 304), was reported as Mkhat in the 1840s by Zagoskin. It was, he said, one of the "ruins of native summer camps: Mkhat, Chyuplyugpak, Kygali, and Kebyakhlyuk [which] have been abandoned since the dispersion or death of the natives at the time of a smallpox epidemic in 1838" (Zagoskin, 1967, p. 92.). In 1968 I hoped to find out where these places were located and whether the names were still in use. I knew only that they were somewhere between St. Michael and Unalakleet. Benjamin Atchak, who died in 1969, was considerably surprised to find that four simple Eskimo names could generate so much interest as we labored over maps in one corner of his huge St. Michael house that had once been a gold rush bakery, but he had just provided me with Zagoskin's abandoned camp names in the same geographical sequence as listed by Zagoskin: mit-thak (Mkhat); chingikpigat (Chyuplyugpak), or Wood Point; kugalik (Kygali) or Five-mile Point; and kepathluk (Kebyakhlyuk), or Eightmile Cove.

27. The English name of Beulah Island came from a woman who took care of army dogs on the island during gold rush days.

28. Khromchenko 1824, Part 11, p. 247. Khromchenko also named Golovnin Bay. According to Vasilii Berkh, Khromchenko first named it Muravev Bay "in honor of the Chief Manager of the American region [but] Muravev, out of respect to Captain-Commander V. M. Golovnin, under whom he

made a trip around the world, asked Khromchenko to change
it to 'Golovnin,' under whose name this bay is presently
marked on maps" (Berkh 1823b, Vol. 2, p. 55).

29. Bourchier, 1852.

30. Zagoskin, 1967, p. 125.

31. The Esquimaux (1867), Vol. I, No. 8, p. 33;
"Northwestern America Showing the Territory Ceded by Russia
to the United States," U. S. Coast Survey, 1867 (map in the
U. S. National Archives, Record Group 59); "Map of the
Yukon or Kwich-pak River" in Whymper, 1869, frontispiece;
W. H. Dall, "Map Showing the Distribution of the Native
Tribes of Alaska and Adjoining Territory," U. S. Coast
Survey, 1875.
    In all of the published and unpublished material pro-
duced by members of the telegraph expedition, only George R.
Adams, who celebrated his twenty-first birthday in Alaska,
used a spelling close to the present Koyuk. In his diary for
July 4, 1867, Adams said that he and a companion, after some
navigational difficulties "found we were at Koyok [possibly
spelled Kuyok since his handwriting falters at this point]--
the very place we wanted to go" (Diary, October 1, 1866 to
October 8, 1867). Portions of this diary were published in
the California Historical Society Quarterly, edited by Harold
F. Taggart, but this information was omitted (1956).

32. In 1902, Arthur J. Collier said, "From the head of
Imuruk Basin to Marys Igloo, a distance of about twenty miles,
the Kuzitrin River has no well-defined channel, but flows
through a succession of small lakes or sloughs with many low
islands between. This part of the river is called Kaviruk by
the natives, and is, in fact, the delta portion of the
Kuzitrin and Kruzgamepa rivers. Small steamers ascend the
river to Marys Igloo, where is the first rapid and the limit
of tidal influence" (Collier, 1902, p. 60).

33. Goodhope is now used as an Eskimo surname by a
family from this area.

34. Zagoskin, 1967, p. 125.

35. Bourchier, 1852.

36. Beechey, 1831, Vol. II, p. 291.

37. Porter, 1893, p. 154.

38. Zagoskin, 1967, p. 100.

39. Beechey, 1831, Vol. I, p. 291.

40. The Esquimaux (1867), Vol. I, No. 7, p. 29.

41. Zagoskin, 1967, p. 125.

42. Khromchenko, 1824, Part 11, p. 180. The strongly stressed initial vowel is sometimes elided by speakers, and even when the a is clearly pronounced, the t is a voiceless alveolar stop with an unusually plosive sound occasioned, in part, by fronting of an ordinarily back vowel, the u sliding quickly into the following i, which causes a palatization of the t.

43. Hobson, 1854-55.

44. The Eskimo Bulletin, 1902, p. 3.

45. Jackson, 1895, p. 97.

46. The Esquimaux (1867), Vol. I, No. 7, p. 29.

47. Beechey, 1831, Vol. II, p. 568. For a brief history of this village see Ray, 1964a.

48. Dall, 1870, p. 234. This name could not, as Nils Holmer says "be interpreted as meaning either 'the uppermost' or 'the outermost'" (1969, p. 147). The Dictionary of Alaska Place Names gives "breeches" as the meaning of Kotlik River (Orth, 1967, p. 542).

49. Holmer, 1969, p. 140.

50. Beechey, 1831, Vol. I, p. 291; Zagoskin, 1967, p. 126.

51. Orth, 1967, p. 694.

52. Zagoskin, 1968, pp. 93, 130.

53. Ibid., p. 281.

54. Jackson, 1903, p. 106.

55. Beechey, 1831, Vol. II, p. 543.

56. Khromchenko, 1824, Part 11, p. 300; Beechey, 1831, Vol. I, p. 291.

57. Bogojavlensky, 1969, p. 9; and personal communication.

58. Zagoskin, 1967, p. 95.

59. Rasmussen, 1941, p. 8.

60. The Esquimaux (1867), Vol. I, No. 8, pp. 34, 35.

APPENDIX

Eskimo names for places with English names

Settlements

Bluff, eksukuchik (or, inukachuk?)
Bonanza (old mining camp), unguktulik
Brevig Mission, singak (sometimes spelled Sinramiut)
Deering, ipmachiuk
Eaton Reindeer Station (in the early 1900s), aplasthlasit
Elephant Point, singyak (abandoned)
Golovin, chinik
Golsovia (nineteenth century post), nuviungnuk
Haycock, kuarak (not an old name)
Mission (early twentieth century, on Golovnin Bay), tuklaktoik
Moses Point, kuinihak or paimiut
Nome, sitnasuak
Safety, chingyak
St. Michael, tachek
Serpentine Hot Springs, iyet
Shishmaref, kikiktuk
Solomon, angutak
Stebbins, atuik in the nineteenth century; tapkak, today
Teller, salinuk, often called nuk
Wales, kingigan; but the two separate parts of it are called
    agianamiut (meaning "opposite" the south village) and
    kiatanamiut, (meaning "front"). A third part, north of
    kiatanamiut is singuarangmiut, with only one inhabited
    house today.
White Mountain, nutsvik or nutchvik

Land Features

Bald Head, uluksak
Black Point (St. Michael area), nuwak
Blueberry Point (Unalakleet), igvayahak
Cape Darby, kikiktaualik
Cape Douglas, kalulik
Cape Nome, ayasayuk
Cape Mountain (at Wales), kingigan
Cape Woolley, singiyak
Cape York, kingauguk
Christmas Mountain (Shaktoolik area), uluksruk
Coffee Point, ikpakpuk
Corwin's Cove (near Golovin), iglu
Eightmile Cove, kepathluk
Elephant Point, singyak
First Portage (on Unalakleet River), nuthluk
Fivemile Point, kugalik
Harris Dome (upper Kuzitrin), palituk
Hunting Point (St. Michael area), nuk
Island Point on Stuart Island, igangnak
Little Rocky Point (Golovin area), uiaalik
McDonald Mountains, ingikpait
Marys Mountain (Kuzitrin River), aviunak
North Point (on Stuart Island), punut
Point Dexter, egrak
Point Romanof, azyateyuk
Point Spencer, amilrak

Ptarmigan Point (on Imuruk Basin), ingikut
Rock Point (St. Michael area), nakinguk
St. Michael Mountain, tachek
The Sisters (St. Michael), nuthlunak
South Spit (Golovnin Bay), chinikchauk
Stephens Hill (St. Michael), chinikthlik
Stuart Mountain, ingektuk
Tolstoi Point, nuwak
Tomcod Hill (Fish River), irathluit
Traeger Hill &Unalakleet), iguikpuk
White Mountain, nutsvik or nutchvik
Wood Point, chingikpigat

Islands

Besboro Island, kikiktuk
Beulah Island, o-ovignak
Eider Duck Island, mit-thak
King Island, ukivuk (or ukiuvuk)
Little Diomede, ingalik
St. Michael Island, tachek
Sarichev Island, kikiktuk
Sledge Island, ayak
Stuart Island, kikiktapuk
Whale Island, kikiktuk

Water features, including rivers

Beeson Creek, kuiyahak (a Nelson Island name)
Beeson Slough, kuyuksak
Bluestone River, klupaluakluzet
Candle Creek, musutoak
Casadepaga River, kuksuktopaga
Chiroskey River, kuikuvloak
Coal Mine Creek, kipiukiovik
Coral Lake (Unalakleet area), narvukluk
Cripple River, kayalashuak
East Fork of the Koyuk River, iluanivit
Espenberg River, enuiknik (I question this)
Fish River, irathluik or ikathluik
Glacier Creek, koluktuk
Goodhope River, pitak
Hastings Creek (Nome), uvgun
Kuzitrin Lake, narvasiuk
Liebes Cove (St. Michael area), mahak
Lost River, amaktulik
Nome River, uinaktauik
North River (Unalakleet), nigakmuthluk
Norton Bay, kungikuchuk
Offield Creek (Teller), kasilinuk
Pilgrim River or Kruzgemapa, kuzgemapa
Poker Creek (Unalakleet), kiku
Powers Creek (Unalakleet), kuihuk
St. Michael Bay, tachek
Snake River, sitnasuak
South River (Unalakleet), angmanik
Spruce Creek, okpiktulik
Telephone Creek, ikyulpak (Fish River area)
Wales River, singluraruk

BIBLIOGRAPHY

Adams, George R. Diary, dated October 1, 1866 to October 8, 1867. E.S.
1866-67   Hubbell Collection, University of Washington Library.
1982   Life on the Yukon, 1865-1867. Edited by Richard A. Pierce,
        The Limestone Press, Kingston, Ontario.
The American Missionary, Vol. 46, December issue. The American
1892   Missionary Association.
Anderson, H. Dewey and Walter C. Eells. Alaska Natives. Stanford
1935   University Press. Stanford University, California.
Andrews, Clarence L. The Story of Sitka. Lowman and Hanford Co.,
1922   Seattle, Washington.
1938   The Story of Alaska. Caxton Printers, Caldwell, Idaho.
n.d.   Notebooks (manuscript, unnumbered). Andrews Collection,
        Sheldon Jackson College, Sitka.
Baker, Marcus. Geographic Dictionary of Alaska. U.S.G.S. Bulletin
1906   No. 299, Washington.
Bancroft, Hubert H. History of California. Vol. 1 (1542-1800). San
1884   Francisco.
1885   History of California. Vol. 2 (1801-1824). San Francisco.
1886   History of Alaska, 1730-1885. Antiquarian Press Ltd., New
        York, 1959 (reprint of 1886 edition).
Bannister, Henry M. The Journal of Henry Martyn Bannister, March 21,
1942   1865-January 20, 1867. In James 1942, pp. 137-264.
Beechey, Frederick W. Narrative of a Voyage to the Pacific and Beering's
1831   Strait. London (two volumes).
Belov, M. I. Arkticheskoe moreplavanie s drevneishikh vremen do serediny
1956   XIX veka (Arctic voyages from the earliest times to the middle
        of the twentieth century), Vol. 1 of the series, Istoriia
        otkrytiia i osvoeniia severnogo morskogo puti. Moscow.
Berkh, Vasilii N. Khronologicheskaia istoriia otkrytiia Aleutskikh
1823a   ostrovov. Saint Petersburg. (Translated as The Chronological
        History of the Discovery of the Aleutian Islands, by Dmitri
        Krenov, Seattle, 1938; reprinted and edited by Richard A.
        Pierce, The Limestone Press, Kingston, Ontario, 1974.)
1823b   Khronologicheskaia istoriia vsekh puteshestvii v severnyia
        poliarnyia strany (Chronological History of all Voyages to the
        Arctic), Saint Petersburg, Vol. 2, pp. 1-20.
Bertholf, E.P. Report of Lieut. E. P. Bertholf, September 1, 1898. In
1899   Report of the Cruise of the...Bear, pp. 103-14.
Bingham, Hiram. A Residence of Twenty-one Years in the Sandwich Islands.
1847   New York.
Birket-Smith, Kaj.
1959   The Eskimos. Methuen, London.
Blake, H. L. History of the Discovery of Gold at Cape Nome. 56 Congress:
1900   1st session, Sen. Doc. 441 (serial 3878).
Bockstoce, John R. Aspects of the Archaeology of Cape Nome, Alaska.
1973   Ph.D. dissertation, Oxford University, England.
Bogojavlensky, Sergei. Imaangmiut Eskimo Careers: Skinboats in Bering
1969   Strait. Ph.D. dissertation, Harvard University.
Bogoras, V. G. The Chukchee. Part 1. Memoirs of the American Museum of
1904   Natural History, New York.
Bourchier, Thomas. Journal of a Journey from Gariska, Russian Fishing
1852   Station Norton Sound to...Grantley Harbour. In Great Britain

Parliament. House of Commons. Sessional Papers. 1852, Vol. 50, #1449, enclosure 15.

Bradley, Harold W. The American Frontier in Hawaii: the Pioneers,
1968   1789-1842. Reprint by Peter Smith, Gloucester, Mass. from the original, Stanford University Press, 1942.

Brevig, T. L. Apaurak in Alaska. Edited by Walter Johnshoy. Dorrance
1944   and Co., Philadelphia.

Brooks, Alfred H., and others. Reconnaissances in the Cape Nome and
1901   Norton Bay Regions, Alaska, in 1900. U. S. Geological Survey, Washington.

Brower, Helen. See Masterson, James R. and Helen Brower.

Bruce, Miner. Report of Miner Bruce, Teller Reindeer Station, June 30,
1894   1893. In Report on Introduction of Domesticated Reindeer into Alaska (Third Report). U.S. Bureau of Education. Whole number 215, pp. 25-121. Washington.

Burns, Flora Hamilton. H.M.S. Herald in Search of Franklin. The Beaver,
1963   autumn, 1963, pp. 3-13, Winnipeg.

Bush, Richard J. Reindeer, Dogs, and Snow-shoes. Sampson Low, Son, and
1872   Marston, London.

Carlson, Leland H. The Discovery of Gold at Nome, Alaska. The Pacific
1946   Historical Review, Vol. 15, No. 3, pp. 259-78.

Castle, N. H. A Short History of Council and Cheenik. The Alaska
1912   Pioneer, Nome, Alaska, Vol. 1, No. 1, pp. 8-14.

Chang, Kwang-Chih. A Typology of Settlement and Community Patterns in
1962   Some Circumpolar Societies. Arctic Anthropology, Vol. 1, No. 1, pp. 28-41, Madison.

Chernenko, M. B. Puteshestviia po chukotskoi zemle i plavanie na aliasku
1957   kazachego sotnika Ivana Kobeleva v 1779 i 1789-1791 gg. (Travels to the land of the Chukchi and voyage to Alaska by the cossack sotnik [leader of a hundred] Ivan Kobelev in 1779 and 1789-1791), Letopis Severa, Vol. 2, pp. 121-41.

[Chimmo, William] (published anonymously) Euryalus; Tales of the Sea, a
1860   Few Leaves from the Diary of a Midshipman. J. D. Potter, London.

Clark, M. Roadhouse Tales; or Nome in 1900. Appeal Publishing Co.,
1902   Girard, Kansas.

Collier, Arthur J. A Reconnaissance of the Northwestern Portion of Seward
1902   Peninsula, Alaska. U.S. Geological Survey Professional Paper No. 2, Washington.

Collier, Arthur J., and others. The Gold Placers of Parts of Seward
1908   Peninsula, Alaska. U.S. Geological Survey Bulletin No. 328, Washington.

Collins, Henry B. Prehistoric Eskimo Culture in Alaska. In Exploration
1930   and Field Work of the Smithsonian Institution in 1929, pp. 147-56, Washington.

1937   Archeology of St. Lawrence Island, Alaska. Smithsonian Miscellaneous Collections, Vol. 96, No. 1. Washington.

1954   Arctic Area. Instituto Panamericano de Geografia e Historia. Mexico.

Collinson, Richard. Journal of H.M.S. Enterprise on the Expedition in
1889   Search of Sir John Franklin's Ships by Behring Strait, 1850-55. Ed. by Major-General T. B. Collinson. Sampson Low, Marston, Searle, and Rivington, London.

Cook, James. A Voyage to the Pacific Ocean. W. and A. Strahan, London.
1784   (Vol. 2).

1794   Chart of the Northwest Coast of America and the Northeast Coast of Asia. Northwest Collection, University of Washington Library, Seattle.

Curtis, Edward S.   The North American Indian.   Vol. 20.   The University
    1930   Press, Cambridge, Mass.
Dall, William H.
    1870   Alaska and Its Resources.   Lee and Shepard, Boston.
Disselhoff, H. D.   Bemerkungen zu einigen Eskimo-masken der Sammlung
    1935   Jacobsen des Berliner Museums für Völkerkunde, Baessler-
              Archiv, Vol. 18, pp. 130-37.
    1936   Bemerkungen zu Fingermasken der Beringmeer-Eskimo, Baessler-
              Archiv, Vol. 19, pp. 181-87.
Dobell, Peter.
    1830   Travels in Kamchatka and Siberia.   Two volumes.   London.
Eakin, H. S.   See Smith, Philip S., and H. M. Eakin.
Education Reports (usually submitted under the name of Sheldon Jackson)
    1893   "Education in Alaska."   In Report of the Commissioner of
              Education [hereafter cited as RCE] for 1889-90, Vol. 2
              (whole no. 199), pp. 1245-1300.   Government Printing Office,
              Washington, D.C.
    1894   "Report on Education in Alaska."   In RCE for 1890-91, Vol. 2
              (whole no. 208), pp. 923-60, Washington.
    1898   "Report on Education in Alaska."   In RCE for 1896-97, Vol. 2
              (whole no. 239), pp. 16-1-46, Washington.
    1901   "Report on Education in Alaska."   In RCE for 1899-1900, Vol. 2,
              pp. 1733-62; tenth reindeer report section, pp. 1763-1785,
              Washington.
    1902   "Report on Education in Alaska."   In RCE for 1900-1901, Vol. 2
              (whole no. 288), pp. 1459-80, Washington.
Eells, Walter C.   See Anderson, H. Dewey and Walter C. Eells.
Efimov, Aleksei V.   Iz istorii russkikh ekspeditsii na Tikhim Okeane.
    1948   Pervaia polovina XVIII veka.   (From the history of Russian
              expeditions to the Pacific Ocean.   First half of the 18th
              century).   Moscow.
    1949   Iz istorii velikikh russkikh geograficheskikh otkrytii...
              (From the history of great Russian discoveries...), Moscow.
    1971   Same title as 1949 volume, but substantially revised and
              enlarged.   Moscow.
Efimov, Aleksei V., editor.   Atlas geograficheskikh otkrytii v Sibiri i
    1964   v severo-zapadnoi Amerike XVII-XVIII vv.   (Atlas of geogra-
              phical discoveries in Siberia and northwestern American in the
              seventeenth and eighteenth centuries.)   Akademiia Nauk SSSR,
              Moscow.
Erman, A.   Expedition der Sloop Blagonamjerenny zur Untersuchung der
    1851   Küsten von Asien und Amerika jenseits der Berings-Strasse, in
              den Jahren 1819 bis 1822, in Archiv fur Wissenschaftliche Kunde
              von Russland, Vol. 9, pp. 272-94.
The Eskimo Bulletin
    1897   Volume 3, published at Cape Prince of Wales, Alaska.
    1902   Volume 5, published at Cape Prince of Wales, Alaska.
The Esquimaux (Newspaper published at Port Clarence, Russian American, and
    1867   Plover Bay, Siberia.   Editor, John J. Harrington.   Turnbull and
              Smith Printers, San Francisco.)
Farrelly, Theodore S.   A Lost Colony of Novgorod in Alaska.   Slavonic
    1944   and East European Review, American Series, III, No. 3, Vol. 22
              No. 60.
Federal Field Committee for Development Planning in Alaska.   Villages in
    1967   Alaska and other Places Having a Native Population of 25 or
              More.   Anchorage.

Fedorova, Svetlana G.   K voprosu o rannikh russkikh poseleniiakh na
    1964   Aliaske (Concerning the question of early Russian settlements
               in Alaska). Letopis severa, Vol. 4, pages 97-113.
    1971   Russkoe naselenie Aliaski i Kalifornii. Konets XVII veka -
               1867 g. Moscow. (Translated as The Russian Population of
               Alaska and California, late 18th Century to 1867, by R. A.
               Pierce and A. S. Donnelly, The Limestone Press, Kingston,
               Ontario, 1973.)
Fisher, Raymond H. Dezhnev's voyage of 1648 in the light of Soviet
    1973   scholarship. Terrae Incognitae, Vol. 5, Amsterdam.
    1981   The Voyage of Semen Dezhnev in 1648: Bering's Precursor.
               Second Series, No. 159, The Hakluyt Society, London.
Foote, Don Charles. American Whalemen in Northwestern Arctic Alaska,
    1964   Arctic Anthropology, Vol. 2, No. 2, pages 16-20.
    1965   Exploration and Resource Utilization in Northwestern Arctic
               Alaska before 1855. Ph.D. dissertation, McGill University.
Fortes, M. and E. E. Evans-Pritchard. African Political Systems.
    1962   Oxford University Press, Oxford, England (reprint).
Gelb, I. J.
    1963   A Study of Writing. University of Chicago Press, Chicago.
Gibson, Arthur
    1908   Map of Seward Peninsula, Alaska. Baltimore.
Giddings, James Louis. The Denbigh Flint Complex. American Antiquity,
    1951   Vol. 16, No. 3, pp. 193-203. Menasha.
    1964   The Archeology of Cape Denbigh. Brown University Press,
               Providence, R.I.
Giddings, J. L., and others. The Archeology of Bering Strait, Current
    1960   Anthropology, Vol. 1, No. 2, pp. 121-38. Chicago.
Golder, Frank A. Guide to Materials for American History in Russian
    1917   Archives. Carnegie Institute of Washington, Publication 239,
               Vol. 1, Washington.
Great Britain. Parliament. House of Commons, Sessional Papers:
               Accounts and Papers.
    1856   (Vol. 41, No. 2124).
Grekov, Vadim L. Ocherki iz istorii russkikh geograficheskikh
    1960   issledovanii v 1725-1765 gg. (Essays from the history of
               Russian geographical explorations, 1725-1765), Moscow.
Grinnell, Joseph. Gold Hunting in Alaska. David C. Cook Publishing
    1901   Co., Chicago.
Harrison, Edward S. Nome and Seward Peninsula. The Metropolitan Press,
    1905   Seattle.
Hawkes, E. W. The Cliff-Dwellers of the Arctic. Wide World Magazine,
    1913   Vol. 30, pp. 377-82, 454-61, 582-88.
Healy, Michael A., and others. Report of the Cruise of the Revenue
    1887   Marine Steamer Corwin in the Arctic Ocean in the year 1885.
               49th Congress; 1st session, H. Ex. Doc. 153 (serial 2400).
    1889   Report of the Cruise of the Revenue Steamer Corwin in the
               Arctic Ocean in the year 1884. 50th Congress; 1st session,
               H. Miscel. Doc. 602 (serial 2583).
Hegarty, Reginald B. Returns of Whaling Vessels Sailing from American
    1959   Ports...1876-1928. New Bedford, Mass.
Heinrich, Albert C. Eskimo Type Kinship and Eskimo Kinship: An Evaluation
    1963a   and a Provisional Model for Presenting Data Pertaining to
               Inupiaq Kinship Systems. Ph.D. dissertation, University of
               Washington, Seattle.
    1963b   Personal Names, Social Structure, and Functional Integration.
               Anthropology and Sociology Papers, No. 27, Montana State
               University, Missoula.

Hillsen, Karl K. Puteshestvie na shliupe "Blagonamerennyi" dlia
     1849   izsledovaniia beregov Azii i Ameriki za Beringovymn prolivom
              s 1819 po 1822 god (Voyage of the sloop Good Intent to explore
              the Asiatic and American shores of Bering Strait, 1819-1822),
              Otechestvennyia zapiski (series 3), Vol. 66, part 8, pp. 213-
              38; Vol. 67, part 8, pp. 1-24, 215-36.
Hinz, John Grammar and Vocabulary of the Eskimo Language. The Society
     1944   for Propagating the Gospel, the Moravian Church, Bethlehem, Pa.
Hobson, W. R. Orders to and Proceedings of Mr. W. R. Hobson...between
     1854-55 February 9 and March 27, 1854. Great Britain Parliament.
              House of Commons. Sessional Papers. 1854-1855, Vol. 35,
              No. 1898.
Hoebel, E. Adamson.
     1949   Man in the Primitive World. McGraw Hill, New York.
     1954   The Law of Primitive Man. Harvard University Press, Cambridge,
              Mass.
Holmberg, H. J. Ethnographische Skizzen über die völker des Russischen
     1855   America, Vol. L. Helsingfors.
Holmer, Nils. The Native Place Names of Arctic America. Names, Vol. 17,
     1969   No. 2.
Hooper, C. L. Report of the Cruise of the U.S. Revenue-Steamer Corwin in
     1881   the Arctic Ocean. Treasury Department Document 118. Washington
     1884   Report of the Second Cruise of the Steamer Corwin in the
              Arctic Ocean, 1881. Washington.
Howay, Frederic W. A List of Trading Vessels in the Maritime Fur Trade,
     1932   1805-1814, Transactions, The Royal Society of Canada, Third
              Series, Vol. 26, Section 2, pp. 43-86.
     1933   A List of Trading Vessels in the Maritime Fur Trade, 1815-1819,
              ibid., Vol. 27, Section 2, pp. 119-47.
     1934   A List of Trading Vessels in the Maritime Fur Trade, 1820-1825,
              ibid., Vol. 28, Section 2, pp. 11-49.
     1973   A List of Trading Vessles in the Maritime Fur Trade, 1785-1825.
              Edited by Richard A. Pierce, The Limestone Press, Kingston,
              Ontario.
Hrdlička, Ales. Anthropological Survey in Alaska. Forty-Sixty Annual
     1930   Report of the Bureau of American Ethnology. Washington.
     1943   Alaska Diary, 1926-1931. The Jaques Cattel Press, Lancaster, Pa
Hulley, Clarence C.
     1953   Alaska 1741-1953. Binfords and Mort, Portland, Oregon.
Hydrographic Map 1890-1892 (See U.S. North Pacific Survey).
Ivashintsov, G.   Kap. Vasil'ev i Shishmarev (Shliupy Otkrytie i
     1849   Blagonamerennyi), 1819-1822, in an article entitled, "Russkiia
              krugosvetnyia puteshestviia" (Russian round-the-world journeys),
              Zapiski Gidrograficheskago Departamenta, Vol. 7, pp. 106-16.
              (Translated by Glynn R. Barrett and published as Russian Round-
              the-World Voyages, 1803-1849..., The Limestone Press, Kingston,
              Ontario, 1980.)
Jackson, Sheldon. Education in Alaska. In Report of the Commissioner
     1893   of Education for the year 1889-1890, Vol. 2, pp. 1245-99.
              Washington.
     1894   Report on Introduction of Domesticated Reindeer Into Alaska.
              (Third Report). U.S. Bureau of Education, Whole Number 215.
              Washington.
     1895   Report on Introduction of Domestic Reindeer into Alaska.
              Fourth Report for 1894. 53 Congress; 3rd session, Sen. Ex.
              Doc. 92 (serial 3280).

1903   Twelfth Annual Report on Introduction of Domestic Reindeer
         into Alaska, 1902. Washington.
1897   Letter to W. T. Harris, Commissioner of Education, dated
         13 September 1897, Bear, St. Michael. U.S. National Archives,
         Record Group 75, Education Division, Alaska Records, Letters
         Sent, pp. 357-58.
Jacobi, A. Carl Heinrich Mercks Ethnographische Beobachtungen über die
1937   Völker des Beringsmeers 1789-91, Baessler-Archiv, Band 20,
         Part 3-4, pp. 113-37. (Translation of the original manuscript
         by Fritz Jaensch, publ. as Siberia and Northwestern America,
         1788-1792, by The Limestone Press, Kingston, Ont., 1980.)
Jacobsen, Johan Adrian. Capitain Jacobsen's Reise an der Nordwestküste
1884   Amerikas, 1881-1883. Edited by A. Woldt. Leipzig.
         (Translation by Erna Gunther, published as Alaskan Voyage,
         1881-1883..., University of Chicago Press. Chicago and London.
James, James Alton. The First Scientific Exploration of Russian America
1942   and the Purchase of Alaska. Northwestern University Studies
         in the Social Sciences, No. 4. Evanston and Chicago. Includes
         Bannister, Henry M. (1942).
Jarvis, D. H. Report of First Lieut. D. H. Jarvis. In Report of the
1899   Cruise of the U.S. Revenue Cutter Bear and the Overland
         Expedition, pp. 28-103. Washington.
Jenness, D. Archaeological Investigations in Bering Strait, 1926. In
1928   National Museum of Canada, Annual Report for 1926, pp. 71-80.
         Ottawa.
Keithahn, Edward L.
1963   Eskimo Adventure. Superior Publishing Co., Seattle.
Kellett, Henry. Narrative of Proceedings of Captain Kellett, dated
1850   November 22, 1849. Great Britain Parliament. House of
         Commons. Sessional Papers. 1850, Volume 35, No. 107.
1851   Letter, dated 14 October 1850, at sea. Great Britain Parlia-
         ment. House of Commons. Sessional Papers. 1851, Volume 33,
         No. 97.
Khromchenko, Vasilii S. Otryvki iz zhurnala plavaniia g. Khromchenki, v
1824   1822 godu (Excerpts from the journal of the 1822 voyage of
         Khromchenko). Severnyi arkhiv, Part 10, pp. 254-76, 303-14;
         Part 11, pp. 38-64, 119-31, 177-86, 235-48, 297-312.
Knapp, Lyman A. Report of the Governor of Alaska for the Fiscal Year
1892   1892. Washington.
Kotzebue, Otto von. A Voyage of Discovery, into the South Sea and
1821   Beering's Straits...in the years 1815-1818. Three volumes.
         Longman, Hurst, Rees, Orme, and Brown, London. Reprinted,
         Da Capo Press, New York, 1967.
Krause, Aurel. The Tlingit Indians. Translated by Erna Gunther from the
1956   original, Die Tlinkit-Indianer, 1885. The American Ethnolo-
         gical Society. The University of Washington Press, Seattle.
Lantis, Margaret. Edward William Nelson. Anthropological Papers of the
1954   University of Alaska. Vol. 3, No. 1, pp. 5-16.
Larsen, Helge. Did Early Alaskans Live in Caves? In Farthest North
1950   Collegian, Vol. 30, No. 2, pp. 13-15, 34-36. College.
1951   De dansk amerikanske Alaska ekspeditioner 1949-50. Geografisk
         Tidsskrift, Vol. 51, Copenhagen.
Lazarev, Aleksei P. Zapiski o plavanii voennogo shliupa Blagonamerennogo
1950   v Beringov proliv i vokrug sveta dlia otkrytii v 1819, 1820,
         1821 i 1822 godakh... (Notes on the Voyage of the Naval Sloop
         Blagonamerennyi into Bering Strait and around the world for
         discoveries in 1819, 1820, 1821, and 1822...)Moscow.

Leighly, John. [Letter about H. M. W. Edmonds] Anthropological Papers
1969   of the University of Alaska, Vol. 14, No. 2, pp. 85-89.
Lopp, William T. A Year Alone in Alaska. In The American Missionary,
1892   Vol. 46, pp. 386-91.
1893,1894 Diary (manuscript). University of Oregon Library. Eugene.
1898   Log of the 1898 Reindeer Drive (manuscript). University of
        Oregon Library. Eugene.
1935   Letter, Lopp to Mrs. Neda Thornton, 13 March 1935. Eugene.
Lopp, W. T. and H. R. Thornton. Our Mission at Cape Prince of Wales.
1891   In The American Missionary, Vol. 45, pp. 357-68.
Lucier, Charles. Buckland Eskimo Myths. Anthropological Papers of the
1954   University of Alaska, Vol. 2, No. 2, pp. 215-33.
McCracken, Harold. God's Frozen Children. Doubleday, Doran and Co.,
1930   Garden City, New York.
McDaniel, W. A. The Skull. The Alaska Sportsman, Vol. 12, No. 9,
1946   pp. 14-15, 34-38.
Mair, Lucy
1962   Primitive Government. Penguin Books.
Masterson, James R., and Helen Brower. Bering's Successors, 1745-1780.
1948   University of Washington Press, Seattle.
Mayokok, Robert.
1959   True Eskimo Stories. Sitka Printing Co., Sitka.
Mehnert, Klaus. The Russians in Hawaii, 1804-1819. University of Hawaii
1939   Occasional Papers, No. 38, Honolulu.
Mendenhall, W. C. A Reconnaissance in the Norton Bay Region, Alaska, in
1901   1900. In Brooks, and others, 1901, pp. 187-218.
Moore, T. E. L. Narrative of the Proceedings of Commander T. E. L. Moore
1851   of Her Majesty's Ship 'Plover," from September 1849 to
        September 1850. Great Britain, Parliament, House of Commons,
        Sessional Papers, accounts and papers, Arctic Expeditions,
        Vol. 33, no. 97: No. 4 (B), pp. 28-34.
Muir, John. The Cruise of the Corwin. Houghton Mifflin Co., Boston and
1917   New York.
Müller, Gerhard.
1758   Sammlung Russischer Geschichte, Vol. 3, Saint Petersburg.
1761   Voyages from Asia to America. London.
Nelson, Edward W. The Eskimo about Bering Strait. Bureau of American
1899   Ethnology, Annual Report, Vol. 18, Part 1, Washington.
Nome News Various issues.
Nome Nugget Various issues.
[Oliver, Esther] Story of Sinrock Mary. Handwritten manuscript, Lopp
1937   Papers, University of Oregon Library, Eugene.
Oquilluk, William A. People of Kauwerak: Legends of the Northern Eskimo.
1973   Alaska Methodist University Book Publication, no. 17
        Alaska Review.
Orth, Donald J. Dictionary of Alaska Place Names. Geological Survey
1967   Professional Paper 567. Washington.
Oswalt, Wendell H. Mission of Change in Alaska. The Huntington Library,
1963a   San Marino, California.
1963b   Napaskiak, an Alaskan Eskimo Community. University of Arizona
        Press, Tucson.
1967   Alaskan Eskimos. Chandler Publishing Co., San Francisco, Cal.
Pallas, Peter S. Neue nordische Beyträge physikalischen und geographischer
1781,1783 Erd- und Völkerbeschreibung, Naturgeschichte, und Oekonomie.
        Vols. 1 and 4. Saint Petersburg and Leipzig.
Petermann, A. Mittheilungen aus Justus Perthes' Geographischer Anstalt
1869   über wichtige Neue Erforschungen auf dem Gesammtgebeite der

Geographie von Dr. A. Petermann. Vol. 15. Justus Perthes, Gotha.

Petroff, Ivan. Report on the Population, Industries, and Resources of
1884   Alaska. In U.S. Tenth Census, Department of the Interior,
        Census Office, Washington.

Pierce, Richard A. Russia's Hawaiian Adventure, 1815-1817. University
1965   of California Press, Berkeley. (Reprint, The Limestone Press,
        Kingston, Ontario, 1976.)

Porter, Kenneth W. John Jacob Astor and the Sandalwood Trade of the
1930   Hawaiian Islands, 1816-1828. Journal of Economic and Business
        History, Vol. 2, No. 3, pp. 495-519.
1931   John Jacob Astor, Business Man. Harvard University Press,
        Cambridge. Two volumes.
1932   More about the Brig Pedler, 1813-1816. Oregon Historical
        Quarterly, Vol. 33, No. 4, pp. 311-12.

Porter, Robert B. Report on Population and Resources of Alaska.
1893   Eleventh Census, 1890. Washington.

Pospisil, Leopold. Law and Societal Structure among the Nunamiut Eskimos.
1964   In W. H. Goodenough (editor), Explorations in Cultural
        Anthropology, McGraw Hill, New York, pp. 395-431.

Pratt, John Francis. Papers of John Francis Pratt, U.S. Coast and
n.d.   Geodetic Survey. Manuscripts Collection, University of
        Washington Library, Seattle.

Rasmussen, Knud. Alaskan Eskimo Words. Edited by H. Ostermann. Report
1941   of the Fifth Thule Expedition, 1921-24, Vol. 3, No. 4,
        Copenhagen.

Ray, Dorothy Jean. Kauwerak, Lost Village of Alaska. The Beaver, Outfit
1964a   295, Autumn, pp. 4-13.
1964b   Nineteenth Century Settlement and Subsistence Patterns in
        Bering Strait. Arctic Anthropology, Vol. 2, No. 2, pp. 61-94.
1967   Eskimo Masks: Art and Ceremony. University of Washington
        Press, Seattle and London.
1971   Eskimo Place-Names in Bering Strait and Vicinity. Names,
        Vol. 19, No. 1, pp. 1-33.
1975a   Early Maritime Trade with the Eskimo of Bering Strait and
        the Introduction of Firearms. Arctic Anthropology, Vol. 12,
        No. 1, pp. 1-9.
1975b   The Eskimos of Bering Strait, 1650-1898. University of
        Washington Press, Seattle and London.
1976   The Kheuveren Legend. The Alaska Journal, Vol. 6, No. 3,
        pp. 146-53.

Ray, Dorothy Jean, ed. The Eskimo of St. Michael and Vicinity as Related
1966   by H. M. W. Edmonds. Anthropological Papers of the University
        of Alaska, Vol. 13, No. 2.

Ray, Verne F. The Columbia Indian Confederacy: A League of Central
1960   Plateau Tribes. In Stanley Diamond (ed.), Culture in History:
        Essays in Honor of Paul Radin. Columbia University Press,
        New York, pp. 771-89.

Reindeer Reports (usually prepared by Sheldon Jackson)
1894   "Report on Introduction of Domesticated Reindeer into Alaska"
        (third report, 1894). 53C:2s, Sen. Ex. Doc. 70 (serial 3160).
1895   "Report on Introduction of Domestic Reindeer into Alaska"
        (fourth report, 1894). 53C:3s, Sen. Ex. Doc. 92 (serial 3280).
1896   "Report on Introduction of Domestic Reindeer into Alaska"
        (fifth report, 1895). 54C:1s, Sen. Doc. no. 111 (serial 3350).
1898a   "Report on Introduction of Domestic Reindeer into Alaska"
        (seventh report, 1897). 55C:2s, Sen. Doc. no. 30 (serial 3590).

272

1898b   "Report on Introduction of Domestic Reindeer into Alaska"
         (eighth report, 1898). 55C:3s, Sen. Doc. no. 34 (serial 3728).
1900   "Ninth Annual Report on Introduction of Domestic Reindeer into
         Alaska" (report for 1899). 56C:1s, Sen. Doc. no. 245 (serial
         3867).
1903   "Twelfth Annual Report on Introduction of Domestic Reindeer
         into Alaska" (report for 1902). 57C:2s, Sen. Doc. no. 70
         (serial 4422).
Report of the Cruise of the U.S. Revenue Cutter Bear and the Overland
         Expedition. 1899. Washington.
Ricks, Melvin B. Directory of Alaska Postoffices and Postmasters,
1965   1867-1965. Tongass Publishing Co., Ketchikan.
Ross, Helen. Jack Underwood and his Book on Alaska. The Town Crier, issue
1913   of 10 May. Seattle.
Sarychev, Gavriil A. Account of a Voyage of Discovery to the Northeast
1806-7   of Siberia, the Frozen Ocean, and the Northeast Sea. Two
         vols. London. Reprint, Da Capo Press, New York, 1969.
Sauer, Martin. An Account of a Geographical and Astronomical Expedition
1802   to the Northern Parts of Russia...in the Years 1785 etc.
         to 1794. T. Cadell, London.
Schapera, I. Government and Politics in Tribal Societies. C. A. Watts
1956   and Co., London.
Schmitt, Alfred. Die Alaska Schrift und ihre Schriftgeschichtliche
1951   Bedeutung. Simons, Verlag, Marburg.
Seemann, Berthold. Narrative of the Voyage of HMS Herald; During the
1853   Years 1845-51, under the Command of Captain Henry Kellett.
         Vol. 2, London.
Shishmarev, Gleb S. Svedeniia o chukchakh Kapitana Shishmareva 1821 goda
1852   (Captain Shishmarev's Observations of the Chukchi in 1821),
         Zapiski Gidrograficheskago Departamenta, Vol. 10, pp. 178-200.
Simpson, John. Observations on the Western Esquimaux and the Country
1854-55 They Inhabit. Great Britain Parliament. House of Commons.
         Sessional Papers. 1854-55, Vol. 35, No. 1898.
Smith, Philip S., and H. M. Eakin. Mineral Resources of the Nulato-
1910   Council Region, in Mineral Resources of Alaska in 1909. U.S.
         Geological Survey Bulletin No. 449, Washington.
Spencer, Robert F. The North Alaskan Eskimo: A Study in Ecology and
1959   Society. Bureau of American Ethnology, Bulletin 171, Washington
Spurr, J. E. From the Yukon Mouth to Point Barrow, in Maps and
1899   Descriptions of Routes of Exploration in Alaska in 1898, U.S.
         Geological Survey, Washington, pp. 124-26.
Steenhoven, Geert van den. Legal Concepts Among the Netsilik Eskimos of
1959   Pelly Bay, N.W.T. Northern Coordination and Research Centre,
         Department of Northern Affairs and National Resources, Ottawa.
Stoney, George M. Naval Explorations in Alaska. The United States Naval
1900   Institute, Annapolis.
Taggart, Harold F. Journal of Wm. H. Ennis, California Historical Society
1954   Quarterly, Vol. 33, No. 1, pp. 1-11, and No. 2, pp. 147-68.
1956   Journal of George Russell Adams, California Historical Society
         Quarterly, Vol. 35, No. 4, pp. 291-307 (abridged version of
         original diary). See Adams, George R.
Thornton, H. R.
1891   See Wm. H. Lopp, and H. R. Thornton.
1931   Among the Eskimos of Wales, Alaska. The Johns Hopkins Press,
         Baltimore.
Tikhmenev, Petr. A. Istoricheskoe obozrenie obrazovaniia Rossiisko-
1861-63 Amerikanskoi kompanii. Saint Petersburg.

1939-40   A Historical Review of the Formation of the Russian-American
           Company and Its Activity up to the Present Time. Translated
           by Dimitri Krenov. Two parts, typewritten copy in the
           University of Washington library.
1978-9   A History of the Russian-American Company. Translated and
           edited by Richard A. Pierce and Alton S. Donnelly. Volume 1,
           The University of Washington Press, Seattle, 1978. Volume 2,
           The Limestone Press, Kingston, Ontario, 1979.
Trollope, Henry. Proccedings of her Majesty's Discovery Ship
    1854-55 "Rattlesnake." Great Britain Parliament. House of Commons.
           Sessional Papers. 1854-55, Vol. 35, No. 1898.
Underwood, John J. Alaska, An Empire in the Making. Dodd, Mead and
    1913   Company, New York.
U.S. Bureau of Education. Report on the Work of the Bureau of Education
    1917   for the Natives of Alaska, 1914-15. Bulletin 1916, No. 47.
           Washington.
U.S. Coast and Geodetic Survey
    1891   Report of the Superintendent of the Coast and Geodetic Survey,
           1889-90.
    1900   Report of the Superintendent of the Coast and Geodetic Survey,
           1898-1899.
    1901a Coast Pilot Notes. Bulletin 40. Washington.
    1901b Report of the Superintendent of the Coast and Geodetic Survey,
           1899-1900.
    1902   Report of the Superintendent of the Coast and Geodetic Survey,
           1900-01.
    1903   Report of the Superintendent of the Coast and Geodetic Survey,
           1901-02.
    1909   Report of the Superintendent of the Coast and Geodetic Survey,
           1908-09.
U.S. Geological Survey
    1950   Alaska topographic series maps.
U.S. North Pacific Survey Expedition in 1855
    1890-1892 Behring's Sea and Arctic Ocean (Hydrographic Map 68).
VanStone, James W., ed. A. F. Kashevarov's Coastal Explorations in
    1977   Northwest Alaska, 1838. Translated by David H. Krause.
           Fieldiana: Anthropology, Vol. 69. Field Museum of Natural
           History, Chicago.
Van Valin, William B.
    1941   Eskimoland Speaks. Caxton Printers, Caldwell, Idaho.
Wallace, F. C. Political Organization and Land Tenure among the North-
    1957   eastern Indians, 1600-1830. Southwestern Journal of
           Anthropology, Vol. 13, pp. 301-21.
Wells, Roger, Jr., and John W. Kelly. Eskimo Vocabularies. In Bureau
    1898   of Education Report, 1896-97. Vol. 2, pp. 1241-1275.
West, Ellsworth L. Skipper of the Corwin. Alaska Sportsman, Vol. 15,
    1949   No. 8, pp. 10-13, 28-32. Ketchikan.
Weyer, Edward M., Jr.
    1932   The Eskimos (1962 edition, Hamden, Connecticut).
Whymper, Frederick.
    1869   Travel and Adventure in the Territory of Alaska. Harper and
           Brothers, New York.
Wickersham, James.
    1927   A Bibliography of Alaskan Literature, 1724-1924.
           Miscellaneous Publications of the Alaska Agricultural
           College and School of Mines, Cordova, Vol. 1.

274

Woolfe, Henry D.   Names of the Native Tribes of Northwest Alaska, Their
   1894   Villages, and Approximate Geographical Positions. In Report
             on Introduction of Domesticated Reindeer into Alaska (Third
             Report), U.S. Bureau of Education. Whole Number 215, pp. 181-83.
Wrangell, Ferdinand von.   Narrative of an Expedition to the Polar Sea in
   1840   the years 1820, 1821, 1822 & 1823.   London.
Youth
   1965?   Unidentified church publication, No. 24.
Zagoskin, L. A.   Puteshestviia i issledovaniia leitenanta Lavrentiia
   1847   Zagoskin v russkoi Amerike 1842. Moscow (1956 edition).
   1967   Lieutenant Zagoskin's Travels in Russian American 1842-1844:
             The First Ethnographic and Geographic Investigations in the
             Yukon and Kuskokwim Valleys of Alaska. Edited by Henry N.
             Michael. Translated by Penelope Rainey. Arctic Institute
             of North America. Anthropology of the North: Translations
             from Russian Sources, No. 7. University of Toronto Press,
             Toronto (Translation of 1956 edition).

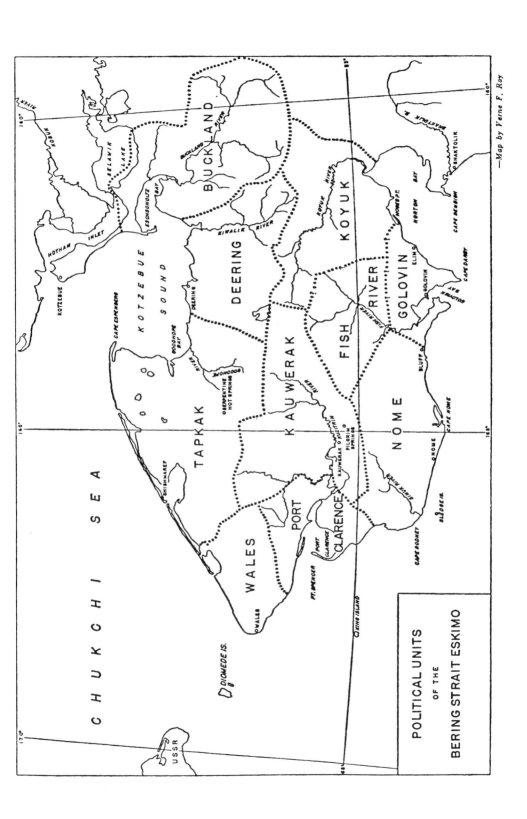

POLITICAL UNITS
OF THE
BERING STRAIT ESKIMO

—Map by Verne F. Roy

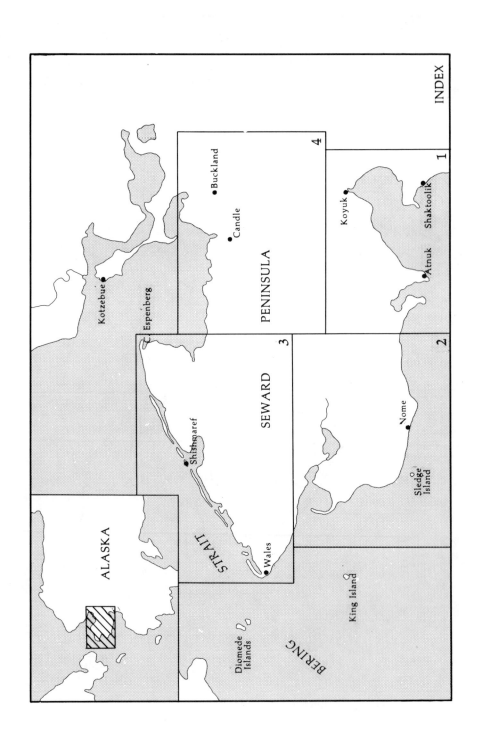

INDEX

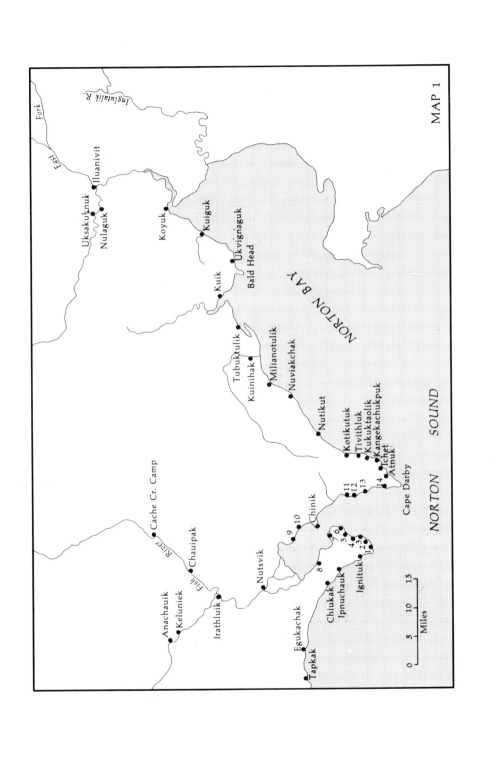

MAP 1

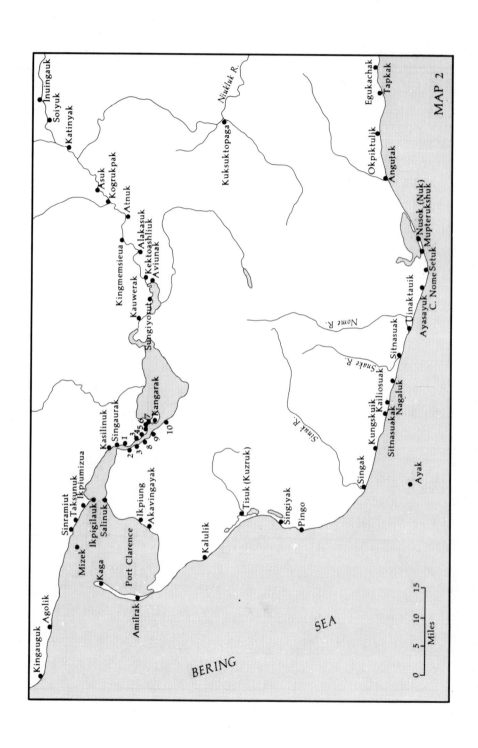

MAP 2

Inuingauk
Soiyuk
Katinyak

Asuk
Kogrukpak
Atnuk
Kingmemsieua
Alakasuk
Kauwerak
Kektoashliuk
Aviunak
Sungiyoyut

Kangarak

Kasilinuk
Singaurak
1
2 3 4 5 6 7
3 8 9
10

Sinramiut
Taksunuk
Kpiumizua
Mizek
Ikpigilauk
Kaga
Salinuk
Ikpiung
Port Clearance
Akavingayak

Amilrak

Kingauguk
Agolik

Kalulik

Tisuk (Kuzruk)

Singiyak
Pingo

Kuksuktopaga

Niuklik R.

Nome R.

Snake R.

Sinuk R.

Egukachak
Tapkak
Okpiktuljk
Angutak
Nusok (Nuk)
Mupterukshuk
Uinaktauik
C. Nome Setuk
Ayasayuk
Sithasuak

Kungskuik
Kailiosuak
Sithnasuakak
Nagaluk

Singak

Ayak

SEA

BERING

0   5   10   15
Miles

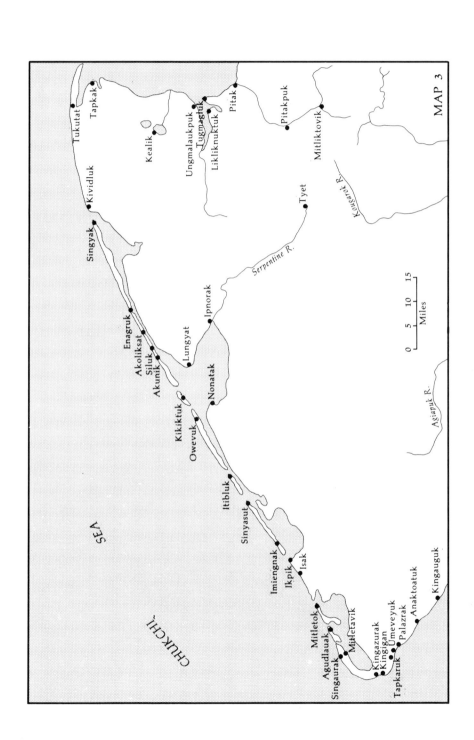

CHUKCHI

SEA

Tukutat
Tapkak
Kividluk
Kealik
Singyak
Ungmalaukpuk
Tugmaghuk
Likliknuktuk
Pitak
Pitakpuk
Mitliktovik
Kongirok R.
Tyet
Serpentine R.
Enagruk
Akoliksat
Siluk
Akunik
Lungyat
Ipnorak
Kikiktuk
Owevuk
Nonatak
Itibluk
Sinyasut
Imiengnak
Ikpik
Isak
Mitletok
Agudlauak
Singaurak
Mitletavik
Kingazurak
Kingigan
Umeveyuk
Tapkaruk
Palazrak
Anaktoatuk
Kingauguk
Asiaruk R.

0   5   10   15
Miles

MAP 3

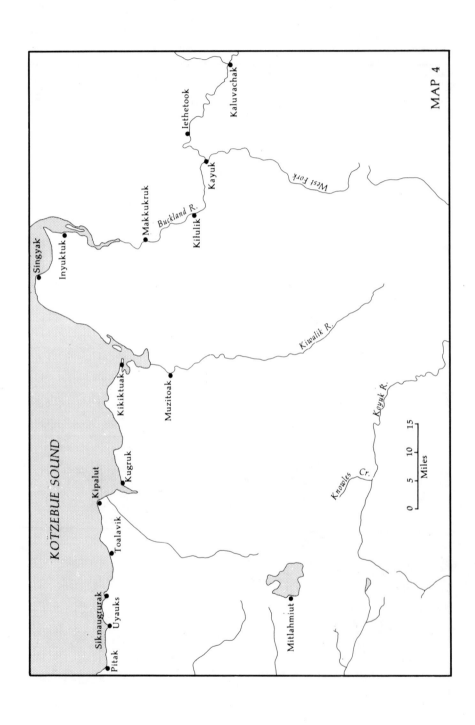

KOTZEBUE SOUND

Singyak
Inyuktuk
Makkukruk
Buckland R.
Kilulik
Kayuk
Iethetook
Kaluvachak
West Fork
Kiwalik R.
Kikiktuak
Muzitoak
Kugruk
Kipalut
Toalavik
Siknaugrurak
Uyauks
Pitak
Koyuk R.
Knowles Cr.
Mitlahmiut

0   5   10   15
Miles

MAP 4

ALASKA HISTORY

(Nos. 1-17: Materials for the Study of Alaska History.)

1. R.A. Pierce. ALASKAN SHIPPING, 1867-1878. ARRIVALS AND DEPARTURES AT THE PORT OF SITKA. 1972. 72 p.

2. F.W. Howay. A LIST OF TRADING VESSELS IN THE MARITIME FUR TRADE, 1785-1825. 1973. 209 p., bibliog., index.

3. K.T. Khlebnikov. BARANOV, CHIEF MANAGER OF THE RUSSIAN COLONIES IN AMERICA. 1973. 140 p. Transl. from the Russian edition (St. Petersburg, 1835) by Colin Bearne. (OUT OF PRINT)

4. S.G. Fedorova. THE RUSSIAN POPULATION IN ALASKA AND CALIFORNIA (LATE 18TH CENTURY TO 1867). 1973. 367 p. Transl. from the Russian ed. (Moscow, 1971) by R.A. Pierce and A.S. Donnelly. (OUT OF PRINT)

5. V.N. Berkh. A CHRONOLOGICAL HISTORY OF THE DISCOVERY OF THE ALEUTIAN ISLANDS. 1974. 121 p. Transl. from the Russian edition (St. P., 1823) by Dmitri Krenov.

6. R.V. Makarova. RUSSIANS ON THE PACIFIC, 1743-1799. 1975. 301 p. Transl. from the Russian edition (M., 1968) by R.A. Pierce and A.S. Donnelly.

7. DOCUMENTS ON THE HISTORY OF THE RUSSIAN-AMERICAN COMPANY. 1976. 220 p. Transl. from the Russian edition (Krasnoiarsk, 1957) by Marina Ramsay. Trade practices, life, and leading figures.

8. R.A. Pierce. RUSSIA'S HAWAIIAN ADVENTURE, 1815-1817. 1976. 245 p. Documents concerning the Alaska-based attempt to take over the (Sandwich) Hawaiian Islands for Russia. Reprint of the 1965 ed., with added maps and illustrations.

9. H.W. Elliott. THE SEAL ISLANDS OF ALASKA. 1976. 176 p., with many illustrations by the author. Reprint of the 1881 edition, prepared for the Tenth Census of the United States. A fundamental work on the Pribilof Islands and the sealing industry soon after the Alaska purchase.

10. G.I. Davydov. TWO VOYAGES TO RUSSIAN AMERICA, 1802-1807. 1977. 257 p. Transl. from the Russian edition (St.P., 1810-1812) by Colin Bearne.

11. THE RUSSIAN ORTHODOX RELIGIOUS MISSION IN AMERICA, 1794-1837. 1978. 186 p. Transl. from the Russian edition (St. P. 1894). The life and works of the monk German (St. Herman). Ethnographic notes by the hieromonk Gedeon.

12. H.M.S. SULPHUR ON THE NORTHWEST AND CALIFORNIA COASTS, 1837 AND 1839. THE ACCOUNTS OF CAPTAIN EDWARD BELCHER AND MIDSHIPMAN FRANCIS GUILLEMARD SIMPKINSON. 1979. 144 p.

13. P.A. Tikhmenev. A HISTORY OF THE RUSSIAN-AMERICAN COMPANY. Vol. 2: DOCUMENTS. 1979. 257 p. Transl. from the Russian edition (St. P., 1861-1863) by Dmitri Krenov. Period 1783-1807.

14. N.A. Ivashintsov. RUSSIAN-ROUND-THE-WORLD VOYAGES, 1803-1849, WITH A SUMMARY OF LATER VOYAGES TO 1867. 1980. 156 p. Transl. from the Russian edition (St. P., 1872) by Glynn R. Barratt.

15. F.P. Wrangell. RUSSIAN AMERICA. STATISTICAL AND ETHNOGRAPHIC INFORMATION. 1980. 204 p. Transl. from the German ed. (St. P., 1839) by Mary Sadouski.

16. THE JOURNALS OF IAKOV NETSVETOV: THE ATKHA YEARS, 1828–1844. 1980. 340 p. Transl. from the Russian manuscript, with introduction and supplementary historical and ethnographic material, by Lydia Black.

17. SIBERIA AND NORTHWESTERN AMERICA, 1785–1795. THE JOURNAL OF CARL HEINRICH MERCK, NATURALIST WITH THE RUSSIAN SCIENTIFIC EXPEDITION LED BY CAPTAIN JOSEPH BILLINGS. 1980. Transl. from the German manuscript, by Fritz Jaensch.

18. D.H. Miller. THE ALASKA TREATY. 1981. 221 p. Definitive account, based largely on original documents, prepared for U.S. Treaty Series in 1944, but never published.

19. G.I. Shelikhov. A VOYAGE TO AMERICA, 1783–1786. 1981. 162 p. Transl. from the Russian edition of 1812, by Marina Ramsay. With supplementary material.

20. E.L. Huggins, et al. KODIAK AND AFOGNAK LIFE, 1868–1870. 1981. 163 p. Diaries, a little known series of articles, and other material on first years after the Alaska purchase.

21. M.D. Teben'kov. ATLAS OF THE NORTHWEST COASTS OF AMERICA. 1981. Reprint of the original ATLAS (39 maps) (St. Petersburg, 1852), with the rare HYDROGRAPHIC NOTES, 109 p., transl. from the Russian.

22. G.R. Adams. LIFE ON THE YUKON, 1865–1867. 1982. Previously unpublished autobiographical sketch and diary of a member of the Western Union Telegraph Expedition.

23. D.J. Ray. ETHNOHISTORY IN THE ARCTIC: THE BERING STRAIT ESKIMO. 1983. 280 p. Early contact with Europeans, picture writing, land tenure and polity, settlement and subsistence patterns, and place names.

OTHER VOLUMES IN PREPARATION

SIBIRIEN

Bujen Notschan

Kamen Sertze od. der Hertzberg

Ichgtschan

Gebirge Nuwugui

Berg Nunemgun

Ts

Kaiser U

Inf. Metschin

Cimelan

Teralo

Gebumra

Urus La

Kurze

Ichgtschin

Chasun

Anadyr Fl.

Fl. Onemen

THEIL DES KAM

Leyamano Tschitelin mithin Quten

Puje

B. Chatyrka

B. Opuka

22. *Matmai oder Atkys*

20 *Kunaschiri*

Buse At.

Bucht Notkama

a. Anadcha

21 *Schigodon*

Bucht tscheriti

Landekke S. Thaddaei

Vorstellung a